W9-BSB-565

THE HYMNAL OF THE UNITED CHURCH OF CHRIST

United Church Press, Philadelphia •

A list of acknowledgments appears at 452 in the back of the hymnal.

The Statement of Faith of the United Church of Christ (p. 11) was approved by the General Synod at Oberlin, Ohio, July 5-9, 1959.

A New Creed (p. 23) is used by permission of the General Council of The United Church of Canada.

Library of Congress Catalog Card No. 74—12571.

ISBN 0-8298-0300-9

United Church Press, 1505 Race Street, Philadelphia, Pa. 19102

Contents

Preface

This is the first hymnal of the United Church of Christ. Commissioned by the Fourth General Synod, the Hymnal Committee was appointed by the Commission on Worship in consultation with the Division of Publication of the United Church Board for Homeland Ministries. The committee's task was to produce a new hymnal for the United Church of Christ as "an instrument for the edifying of Christ's people."

From the beginning, the Hymnal Committee, composed of ministers, church musicians, and seminary professors from a wide cross section of the United Church, has been concerned not to produce just another denominational hymnal but a hymnal consonant with the ecumenical spirit of the United Church. Early in the work a Consultation on Ecumenical Hymnody was called, bringing together representatives from all the major communions to explore the possibilities of cooperation in the area of hymnody. This Consultation has made significant contributions to ecumenical hymnody over the past six years. A list of common texts and tunes for one hundred fifty hymns in use among the churches was agreed upon after much study. Over ninety of these hymns are in this hymnal, and their presence is indicated by an asterisk on the hymn page, and in the indexes where noted. The input of the Consultation is especially significant since the communions represented included Episcopal, Roman Catholic, United Methodist, United Presbyterian, three major Lutheran bodies, Moravian, Covenant, Disciples of Christ, and United Church of Canada. Not only did members of this group seek to bring together significant elements of their own traditions, but they joined efforts in the search for new hymns which speak freshly to this day. Some of the new hymns in this hymnal have come out of the common search. The Hymnal Committee is deeply indebted to colleagues in these other communions who have worked together in the Consultation.

The Hymnal Committee has also been concerned to produce a hymnal that will uniquely serve the congregations of the United Church of Christ, enabling them to draw strength from the richness of their varied roots, and to celebrate their common life. The arrangement of the hymns under the major categories of the Statement of Faith of the United Church of Christ is a symbol of a concern to provide the churches with a hymnbook that will serve both as a resource for worship and as an indispensable instrument for teaching the faith. As a contemporary affirmation, the Statement of Faith sets forth "the faith that unites us," thus providing the means of identity and nurture that are requisite for the community of faith without demanding subscription to a particular interpretation of the Christian tradition.

One of the concerns of contemporary liturgical renewal has been a fresh emphasis on the role of the people in worship. The word liturgy means "the work of the people," in worship and in the world. The committee worked with the goal of making this hymnbook one which the people could use as an instrument of their "work" of worship. Another concern has been the reunion of the service of the word and the service of the sacrament. This will become apparent in the Services of Word and Sacrament as they appear in the hymnal and in the other supplementary worship materials which were made available.

The use of contemporary language in worship and the discovery of new hymns which use metaphors out of the contemporary world have been of major concern to the committee. Where possible, inclusive language has been employed in response to the action of the Ninth General Synod requesting the same. Using the model of the Sacrament of Faith of the United Church, the committee was encouraged to find hymns which express the mission of Christian faith in the world of this time. New hymns that speak to these times, that transpose the ancient harmonies into the new key of this present life, that project with fresh vigor into this day the faith once delivered, are characteristic of the new hymnal.

The Hymnal Committee has worked within a limitation of a total of three hundred hymns. Roughly two-thirds will be found in either the *Pilgrim Hymnal* or *The Hymnal* of the Evangelical and Reformed Church, or in both. The remaining third are either new hymns written in the past decade or are hymns from an earlier time which seem particularly useful for worship in the church today. No one will find here all the hymns loved the best; neither does this book contain all the greatest hymns from all the major classical traditions of hymnody. This is, in the minds of the Hymnal Committee, a "workbook," a book for the people to use in their "work" of worship. It is the committee's hope that those who use it will not be primarily concerned for the hymns which are *not* in it, but for the hymns which *are* in it. It is a book to be studied by both musicians and ministers who lead worship, to seek out and find treasures new and old for their people to use in their worship.

The Hymnal Committee has worked diligently for six years and has found great joy in that work. Coming from different branches of the United Church, members of the committee have grown in their appreciation of the traditions of worship in hymnody which make up the fabric of the church's common life. As they learned from one another, committee members sought to be sensitive to the leading of the Spirit in this time of rapid change in the church and in the world. It is their hope that the work will be useful in enabling more meaningful worship and in strengthening the church for mission in the world.

The committee is indebted to the editors, William Nelson and John Ferguson, who took the committee's work and shaped it into its final form. Appreciation is also due to Marion Meyer, senior editor of the United Church Press; and to Mary Louise VanDyke, who worked at great length on the preparation of the list of scripture references and the indexes.

Lawrence L. Durgin, Charles Hickman, William A. Huenemann, and Oliver G. Powell were unable to complete their work as members of the Hymnal Committee. The committee is, however, deeply appreciative of the rich contributions which they made when they were members of the committee.

Benjamin R. Andrews, Jr., Chairperson, Alfred C. Bartholomew, Ford L. Battles, Charles A. Butts, John Ferguson, Thomas D. Garner, Louis H. Gunnemann, James H. Hargett, Frank Harrison, Marjie H. Hawthorne, Walter H. Krebs, William Nelson, Floyd E. Schlegel, David L. Thorburn

Introduction

Singing the "faith" is characteristic of the Christian church. In the Hebrew-Christian tradition, singing is a means of proclamation and an expression of joy. "I will sing unto the Lord as long as I live. I will praise my God while I have my being." The apostle Paul urged the members of the churches he founded, surrounded as they were by an unfriendly, pagan society, to "encourage one another with psalms and hymns and spiritual songs." This exhortation of Paul remains valid for Christians today. The great hymns of all generations prove their worth by the very fact that they remain relevant for this age. Yet as times change, new hymns need to be added to the great hymns of the past to speak to God's relationship with his people and their relationship with one another.

The core of this hymnal is the great hymns of preceding generations. Yet the Hymnal Committee felt strongly that the hymnal should include a good cross section of newer hymnody. While the *Pilgrim Hymnal* (1958), and *The Hymnal* of the Evangelical and Reformed Church (1941), provided the basic departure point for the selection of the "traditional" hymns, some forty other hymnals and booklets of religious songs were consulted, both for newer hymns and for older hymns which seemed especially appropriate for inclusion in a hymnal for today. In addition, members of the committee provided some original texts and tunes. All manuscripts, solicited and unsolicited, were given careful consideration.

As its work progressed, the Hymnal Committee made certain important decisions which have strongly influenced the character of this book. Long hymns were shortened by omitting stanzas when this could be done without abusing the intent of the author or destroying the continuity of the hymn. "Amens" were omitted unless they were an integral part of the concluding stanza.

The melodic tessiture of all hymns was examined, and tunes were transposed as necessary to assure a comfortable but not too low singing range. Attempts were made to provide for a variety of keys and harmonizations for tunes used more than once; alternate tunes were not printed if they appeared elsewhere in the book, but they were cited in footnotes. Guitar chords were provided for hymns of a folk nature. Optional keyboard accompaniments were provided for some folk tunes with the understanding that the more complete accompaniment need not be limited by the harmonic vocabulary of the guitar accompaniment. Thus certain folk hymns should be accompanied by guitar or organ or piano as one or the other is appropriate and available.

In addition to the scriptural references on hymn pages, which indicate the actual sources of a number of hymns, there is a list of scripture passages related to the hymns. This gives the hymnal increased flexibility as an educational instrument. To encourage the creative use of the hymnal, indexes are provided.

The hymnal provides a comprehensive section of service music, including two complete settings of the portions of Service of Word and Sacrament I that can be sung—one setting in an accompanied style; one in folk style. An attempt was made to provide fresh service music that will encourage innovation and experimentation in worship.

Most hymnals, including the *Pilgrim Hymnal* and the Evangelical and Reformed *Hymnal,* are arranged in the order of the church year, by categories reflecting the content of the texts, or alphabetically. The Hymnal Committee decided early that this hymnal should follow the theological order of the Statement of Faith of the United Church of Christ. For this reason, the user of this hymnal may not find certain hymns where he expects to find them, except, of course, in the alphabetical index. The Statement of Faith has a natural progression which can be stated as follows:

Affirmation of the character of God and his actions.
Proclamation of what God has done and does for his people.
Our responsibility for what we are called to be and do as a result of what God has done.
Our assurance, as set forth in the promises of the gospel.
Doxology, the climactic affirmation of the Faith.

In light of this progression of the Statement of Faith the editors, with the help of the chairman of the Commission on Worship, have arranged the hymns into six divisions, each introduced on a separate page listing subdivisions and including hymn numbers, arranged according to the actual wording of the Statement of Faith.

John Ferguson and William Nelson, Editors

The Ordering of Corporate Worship

These services are for the assistance of the church in its corporate worship. When the church is at worship the people of God give public expression to the faith that shapes their lives. By their common actions and words they symbolize the oneness of their life in Christ.

The Service of Word and Sacrament is at the very heart of the corporate life of the people of God. While this service may be used at any time, it is the chief service of the church for weekly worship. Other services are provided for use on those occasions of a congregation's life that also call for the celebration of God's presence and his work on behalf of his people. The Service of Baptism marks the entrance of the individual into the corporate life of the Christian community, while others mark the transition points of life where worship of God expresses the singular meaning of our personal and corporate existence.

Throughout the preparation of these services and the other materials for worship that follow, an effort was made to utilize the results of ecumenical studies. New versions of the Lord's Prayer, the Apostles' Creed, the Nicene Creed, the Sanctus, and the Gloria in Excelsis were prepared by the International Consultation on English in the Liturgy, composed of Roman Catholic and Protestant churches in countries where English is spoken. The same consultative procedures yielded the new lectionary which combines the rich traditions of the churches in the Consultation on Church Union with those of the Roman Catholic and Lutheran churches.

The Commission on Worship has been greatly assisted in the preparation of the services by pastors and congregations who responded to early drafts of the material. The members of the Commission on Worship who prepared these materials are listed below. In addition, credit is due to many who served as members of the commission in the early stages of the work but whose terms have expired: Chalmers Coe, William K. Laurie, Arnold M. Kenseth, Walter H. Krebs, D. Bard Thompson, Harland G. Lewis, Marvin P. Halverson, David L. Beebe, Horton M. Davies, Thomas C. Dick, Jr., Frederick D. Hayes, Roger P. Horton, William A. Huenemann, Olga Klepper, Donald L. Powers, Friedrich O. Rest, John C. Shetler, Leonard A. Stark, and Arthur G. Swartz.

The Commission membership now includes: Benjamin R. Andrews, Jr., John B. Forsyth, Louis H. Gunnemann, R. Howard Paine, Morris D. Slifer, Eugene S. Wehrli, William R. Booth, Betty Jackson King, Elwood W. Paske, Albert C. Ronander, Waldo Savage, John R. Washington, Vernon D. Bader, Kenneth E. Claus, Jr., Jean Cleland, Robert A. Kinsey, Morris D. Pike, Catherine E. Thiedt.

Statement of Faith

We believe in God, the Eternal Spirit, Father of our Lord Jesus Christ and our Father, and to his deeds we testify:

He calls the worlds into being,
creates man in his own image,
and sets before him the ways of life and death.

He seeks in holy love to save all people from aimlessness and sin.

He judges men and nations by his righteous will declared through prophets and apostles.

In Jesus Christ, the man of Nazareth, our crucified and risen Lord,
he has come to us
and shared our common lot,
conquering sin and death
and reconciling the world to himself.

He bestows upon us his Holy Spirit,
creating and renewing the church of Jesus Christ,
binding in covenant faithful people of all ages, tongues, and races.

He calls us into his church
to accept the cost and joy of discipleship,
to be his servants in the service of men,
to proclaim the gospel to all the world and resist the powers of evil,
to share in Christ's baptism and eat at his table,
to join him in his passion and victory.

He promises to all who trust him
forgiveness of sins and fullness of grace,
courage in the struggle for justice and peace,
his presence in trial and rejoicing,
and eternal life in his kingdom which has no end.

Blessing and honor, glory and power be unto him. Amen.

Service of Word and Sacrament I

The people shall stand. The service shall open with suitable words of adoration through a hymn and any of the following sentences of scripture.

The minister, standing at the Lord's table, shall say:

In the name of the Father, and of the Son, and of the Holy Spirit. **Amen.**

ADORATION

The Lord is in his holy temple, let all the earth keep silence before him.

O come, let us worship and bow down, let us kneel before the Lord, our Maker! For he is our God, and we are the people of his pasture, and the sheep of his hand.

God is spirit, and those who worship him must worship in spirit and truth.

Make a joyful noise to the Lord, all the lands! Serve the Lord with gladness!

The heavens are telling the glory of God; and the firmament proclaims his handiwork.

Our help is in the name of the Lord, who made heaven and earth.

In this the love of God was made manifest among us, that God sent his only Son into the world, so that we might live through him.

Draw near to God and he will draw near to you. Humble yourselves before the Lord and he will exalt you.

Other suitable sentences of scripture may be used; the introit of the day may be used in place of the sentences.

CONFESSION OF SIN

If we confess our sins, he is faithful and just, and will forgive our sins and cleanse us from all unrighteousness. Let us confess our sins to almighty God.

The people may kneel.

Gracious God, Father of our Lord Jesus Christ, you have promised to receive us when we come to you. We confess that we have sinned against

you in thought, word, and deed. We have disobeyed your law. We have not loved you or our neighbors as we should. Forgive us, O God, and grant that we may live and serve you in newness of life; through Jesus Christ our Lord. Amen.

Here may be sung or said the Kyrie Eleison.

Lord, have mercy on us.

Lord, have mercy on us.

Christ, have mercy on us.

Christ, have mercy on us.

Lord, have mercy on us.

Lord, have mercy on us.

ASSURANCE OF PARDON

Then shall the minister say:

Beloved, God has promised us mercy and has given us his Son, Jesus Christ, to die for our sins that we may live in newness of life, obedient to his will. Therefore, I announce, in the name of Christ, that your sins are forgiven according to his promises in the gospel. **Amen.**

or

God shows his love for us in that while we were yet sinners Christ died for us.

God so loved the world that he gave his only Son, that whoever believes in him should not perish but have eternal life.

There is therefore now no condemnation for those who are in Christ Jesus. **Amen.**

PRAISE

O Lord, open our lips,

And our mouths shall show forth your praise.

Here may be sung the Gloria in Excelsis, a psalm, the Gloria Patri, or a hymn of praise.

Glory to God in heaven,
peace and grace to his people on earth.

We praise you for your great glory,
we worship you, we give you thanks,
Lord God, heavenly King,
almighty God and Father.
Lord Jesus Christ, Lamb of God,
only Son of the Father,
you take away the sin of the world,
have mercy on us.
You sit at the right hand of the Father,
hear our prayer.
You alone are the Holy One,
you alone are the Lord,
you alone are the Most High,
Jesus Christ,
with the Holy Spirit,
in the glory of the Father. Amen.

THE HOLY SCRIPTURES

Before the reading of scripture, the collect for the day may be said; or a prayer for illumination.

A lesson from the Old Testament and a lesson, or lessons, from the New Testament shall be read. Before each lesson, the reader shall say:

Hear the word of God in the . . . . .

After each lesson, the reader shall say:

Here ends the lesson (*or* Epistle *or* Gospel).

When a Gospel lesson is announced, the people may say:

Glory be to you, O Lord.

After the Gospel has been read, the people may respond:

Praise be to you, O Christ.

When the scripture has been read, it shall be expounded in

THE PREACHING OF THE SERMON

AFFIRMATION OF FAITH

The people shall stand to confess their faith using the Statement of Faith, the Apostles' Creed, or the Nicene Creed:

We believe in God, the Eternal Spirit, Father of our Lord Jesus Christ and our Father, and to his deeds we testify:

He calls the worlds into being,
creates man in his own image,
and sets before him the ways of life and death.

He seeks in holy love to save all people from aimlessness and sin.

He judges men and nations by his righteous will declared through prophets and apostles.

In Jesus Christ, the man of Nazareth, our crucified and risen Lord,
he has come to us
and shared our common lot,
conquering sin and death
and reconciling the world to himself.

He bestows upon us his Holy Spirit,
creating and renewing the church of Jesus Christ,
binding in covenant faithful people of all ages, tongues, and races.

He calls us into his church
to accept the cost and joy of discipleship,
to be his servants in the service of men,
to proclaim the gospel to all the world and resist the powers of evil,
to share in Christ's baptism and eat at his table,
to join him in his passion and victory.

He promises to all who trust him
forgiveness of sins and fullness of grace,
courage in the struggle for justice and peace,
his presence in trial and rejoicing,
and eternal life in his kingdom which has no end.

Blessing and honor, glory and power be unto him. Amen.

or

I believe in God, the Father, the Almighty,
creator of heaven and earth.

I believe in Jesus Christ, his only Son, our Lord.

He was conceived by the power of the Holy Spirit and born of the virgin Mary.
He suffered under Pontius Pilate;
he was crucified, died, and was buried.
He went to the dead.
On the third day he rose again,
entered into heaven,
and is seated at the right hand of the Father.
He will come again to judge the living and the dead.

I believe in the Holy Spirit,
the holy catholic church,
the communion of saints,
the forgiveness of sins,
the resurrection of the body,
and the life eternal. Amen.

or

We believe in one God, almighty Father,
maker of heaven and earth,
and of all things visible and invisible.

We believe in the one Lord, Jesus Christ,
the only Son of God,
begotten of the Father from all eternity:
God from God, Light from Light, true God from true God:
begotten, not made, one in being with the Father.
Through him all things were made.
For us men and for our salvation he came down from heaven.
By the power of the Holy Spirit
he was born of the virgin Mary and became Man.
He was crucified for us under Pontius Pilate; he suffered, died, and was buried.
He arose on the third day in accordance with the scriptures.
He entered into heaven and is seated at the right hand of the Father.
He will come again in glory to judge the living and the dead,
and his kingdom will never end.

We believe in the Holy Spirit, the Lord, the giver of life,
who proceeds from the Father (and the Son).
Together with the Father and the Son he is adored and glorified.
He has spoken through the prophets.

We believe in one, holy, catholic, and apostolic church.
We acknowledge one baptism for the forgiveness of sins.
We look for the resurrection of the dead and the life of the world to come.
Amen.

Here a hymn or anthem may be sung.

PRAYERS

The minister, or the congregation in unison, may offer thanksgiving and petitions and any or all of the following intercessions; or other prayers or litanies as may be desired.

The Lord be with you,

And with you also.

Let us pray.

Almighty God, you have taught us to pray for all people, and promised in Christ Jesus that whatever we ask in his name will be granted to us. Hear us as we bring to you the needs of the world, and answer our prayers according to your will; through Jesus Christ our Lord. **Amen.**

If biddings are used, silent prayer shall follow each of them.

Let us pray for the church:

Silent prayer

Most gracious God, you have set one table before us and called us into fellowship with you; we pray that the church, gathered by your word and Spirit, may be a faithful witness to you in the world; through Jesus Christ our Lord. **Amen.**

Let us pray for peace:

Silent prayer

Eternal God, our Father, grant peace and goodwill on earth, that your people everywhere may live together in harmony; through Jesus Christ our Lord. **Amen.**

Let us pray for those who rule:

Silent prayer

Mighty God, Lord of the nations, govern those who govern us, your servant ...., the President of the United States, and those who share the public trust in every land, that they may be led by your wisdom to govern righteously; through Jesus Christ our Lord. **Amen.**

Let us pray for those who work:

Silent prayer

Everlasting Father, who looking at all your creation called it good, bless the work of our hands and our minds and grant that all we do may be well done and approved by you; through Jesus Christ our Lord. **Amen.**

Let us pray for the sick and the sorrowing:

Silent prayer

Holy God, bearer of the world's pain, look with compassion upon those who are sick and sorrowing (and especially upon . . .) that they may know your love and, by your grace, be delivered from distress; through Jesus Christ our Lord. **Amen.**

Let us pray for the troubled:

Silent prayer

O God, our strength, be with those who are anxious or tempted or doubting; guard them in their trials that they may be upheld and patiently await your deliverance; through Jesus Christ our Lord. **Amen.**

Let us pray for our families and friends:

Silent prayer

Almighty God, since you have set us in families and among friends, we commend to your never-failing care all those who are dear to us, that they may remain forever in your keeping; through Jesus Christ our Lord. **Amen.**

Let us pray for our enemies:

Silent prayer

O Lord our God, whom we cannot love unless we love our neighbor, remember in mercy our enemies, and grant that they and we may be reconciled in Jesus Christ, to whom be glory forever. **Amen.**

Here special intercessions may be said.

O Lord God, our present help and promised hope, we thank you for all your servants who having witnessed to you in this life now dwell with you in life eternal. Grant us grace so to walk in your way that we may share with them the joy of your presence; through Jesus Christ our Lord. **Amen.**

O God, the Father of our Lord Jesus Christ, of whom the whole family in heaven and earth is named, we rejoice before you in the blessed communion of all your saints, wherein you give us also to have part. We praise you for the holy fellowship of patriarchs and prophets, apostles and martyrs, and the whole glorious company of the redeemed of all ages, who have died in the Lord, and now live with him forevermore. We give thanks to you for your great grace and many gifts bestowed on those who have gone before us in the way of salvation, and by whom we are now compassed about in our Christian course, as a cloud of witnesses looking down upon us from the heavenly world. Enable us to follow their faith that we may enter at death into their joy, and so abide with them in rest and peace, till both they and we shall reach our common consummation of redemption and bliss in the glorious resurrection of the last day. **Amen.**

Almighty God, you have given us grace at this time with one accord to make our common supplications to you and have promised through your beloved Son that where two or three agree, you will grant their requests. Fulfill now, O Lord, the desires and petitions of your servants, as may be most suitable for them; granting us in this world knowledge of your truth, and in the world to come life everlasting. **Amen.**

OFFERING

The offerings of the people shall be received and may be brought to the table with the bread and wine. A doxology may be sung. As the offerings of the people are gathered, there may be an anthem or appropriate music.

If the Lord's Supper is not to be celebrated, the service following the offering shall be concluded with a prayer of thanksgiving, the Lord's Prayer, a hymn, the commission, and the blessing.

INVITATION

The people standing, the minister shall say:

Luke the Evangelist records that on the evening of the first day of the week, the same day on which our Lord rose from the dead, when he was at table with two of the disciples, he took bread and blessed and broke it, and gave it to them, and their eyes were opened, and they knew him.

Beloved, this is the joyful feast of the people of God. Come from the East and the West, and from the North and the South, and gather about the table of the Lord.

Behold how good and pleasant it is when brothers dwell in unity.

The peace of our Lord Jesus Christ be with you all. **Amen.**

THE GREAT THANKSGIVING

Lift up your hearts.

We lift them to the Lord.

Let us give thanks to the Lord our God.

It is meet and right so to do.

We give thanks to you, O holy Lord, almighty and everlasting God, for the universe which you have created, for the heavens and the earth, and for every living thing. We thank you that you have formed us in your own image and made us for yourself. We bless you that when we rebelled against you, you did not forsake us, but delivered us from bondage, and revealed your righteous will and steadfast love by the law and the prophets.

Above all, we thank you for the gift of your Son, the Redeemer of all people, who was born of Mary, lived on earth in obedience to you, died on the cross for our sins, and rose from the dead in victory; who rules over us, Lord above all, prays for us continually, and will come again in triumph.

We thank you for your Holy Spirit and for your holy church, for the means of grace and for the promise of eternal life. With patriarchs and prophets, apostles and martyrs, with your church on earth and with all the company of heaven, we magnify and praise you, we worship and adore you, O Lord Most Holy:

Holy, holy, holy, Lord God almighty,
your glory fills all heaven and earth.
Hosanna in the highest.
Blessed is he who comes in the name of the Lord.
Hosanna in the highest.

or

Holy, holy, holy,
Lord God of Sabaoth,

Heaven and earth are full
Of the majesty of your glory.
Hosanna in the highest!
Blessed is he who comes
In the name of the Lord.
Hosanna in the highest!

We thank you that the Lord Jesus on the night when he was betrayed took bread, and, when he had given thanks, broke it and said, "Take, eat, this is my body which is for you"; and that he also took the cup, saying, "Drink of it, all of you; this is the new covenant in my blood. Do this in remembrance of me."

Obeying the commandment of our Lord Jesus Christ, we, your people, offer you this bread and this cup, recalling his incarnate life, his atoning death, his resurrection and ascension until he come.

Bless and sanctify by your Holy Spirit both us and these your gifts of bread and wine, that in this holy communion of the body and blood of Christ we may be made one with him and he with us, and that we may remain faithful members of his body until we feast with him in your heavenly kingdom.

Here we offer ourselves in obedience to you, through the perfect offering of your Son Jesus Christ, giving you thanks that you have called us to be a royal priesthood, a holy nation, your own people; and to you, O Father, as to the Son and the Holy Spirit, be ascribed blessing and honor and glory and power forever and ever. Amen.

OUR LORD'S PRAYER

Our Father in heaven:
Hallowed be your name,
Your kingdom come,
Your will be done,
on earth as in heaven.
Give us today our daily bread.
Forgive us our sins,
as we forgive those who sin against us.
Save us from the time of trial,
and deliver us from evil.
For yours is the kingdom, the power, and the glory, forever. Amen.

or

Our Father, who art in heaven, hallowed be thy name. Thy kingdom come. Thy will be done on earth as it is in heaven. Give us this day our

daily bread. And forgive us our debts, as we forgive our debtors. And lead us not into temptation, but deliver us from evil. For thine is the kingdom, and the power, and the glory, forever. Amen.

THE BREAKING OF THE BREAD

The minister shall take the bread and break it, saying:

The bread which we break is the communion of the body of Christ.

THE POURING OF THE WINE

The minister shall pour the wine, saying:

The cup of blessing which we bless is the communion of the blood of Christ.

Then shall the minister say:

Come, for all things are now ready.

THE COMMUNION

In giving the bread, the minister shall say:

Take and eat; this is the body of Christ, which is broken for you.

And, in giving the cup:

This cup is the new covenant in the blood of Christ. Drink of it, all of you.

When table communion is used the following words of dismissal may be said:

The Lord Jesus Christ keep and preserve you to everlasting life. **Amen.**

Depart in peace.

Then shall the minister say:

Let us give thanks.

Almighty and eternal God, you have fed us with the Holy Communion of the body and blood of your Son, our Savior Jesus Christ; we thank you for this gift, by which you assure us that we are members of the mystical body of your Son and heirs through hope of your everlasting kingdom. So assist us by your Holy Spirit that we may grow daily in knowledge of your truth, and in faithfulness to your will, abiding in that fellowship in which all your saints have part; through Jesus Christ our Lord, to whom with you and the Holy Spirit be all honor and glory, world without end. **Amen.**

After the singing of a hymn or the Nunc Dimittis, the minister shall say:

COMMISSION

Go forth into the world in peace; be of good courage; hold fast to that which is good; render to no one evil for evil; strengthen the fainthearted; support the weak; help the afflicted; honor all people; love and serve the Lord, rejoicing in the power of the Holy Spirit.

BLESSING

The grace of the Lord Jesus Christ, and the love of God, and the communion of the Holy Spirit, be with you all. **Amen.**

or

The peace of God which passes all understanding, keep your hearts and minds in the knowledge and love of God, and of his Son Jesus Christ our Lord; and the blessing of God Almighty, the Father, the Son, and the Holy Spirit, remain with you always. **Amen.**

A New Creed

We believe in God:
who has created and is creating,
who has come in the true Man, Jesus,
to reconcile and make new,
who works in us and others by his Spirit.
We trust him.

He calls us to be his church:
to celebrate his presence,
to love and serve others,
to seek justice and resist evil,
to proclaim Jesus, crucified and risen, our judge and our hope.

In life, in death, in life beyond death,
God is with us.
We are not alone.

Thanks be to God.

(The United Church of Canada)

Service of Word and Sacrament II

The minister shall say:

Cry out with joy to the Lord, all the earth; serve the Lord with gladness.

Come before him, singing for joy.

A hymn of adoration shall be sung, the people standing.

The minister shall say:

Christ is with us!

He is with us indeed!

In joy and contrition we come before God.

Let us confess our sins.

Gracious God, Creator and Father, we come before you a rebellious people. We have denied your intentions for us; we have preferred our way to Christ's way; we have disobeyed your commandments; and we have worshiped ourselves and the things we have made. Forgive us, restore in us the knowledge of who we are, and make us alive to serve you in faith, obedience, and joy; through Jesus Christ our Lord. Amen.

The minister shall say:

Hear the promises of God: "Ask, and it will be given you; seek, and you will find; knock, and it will be opened to you." "If we confess our sins, he is faithful and just, and will forgive our sins."

The minister may say:

I announce, therefore, in the name of Jesus Christ, that we are forgiven. **Amen.**

The minister shall say:

Praise the Lord.

The Lord be praised.

The Gloria Patri or a hymn of praise shall be sung.

The people shall be seated and a lesson from the Old Testament and a lesson, or lessons, from the New Testament shall be read. Before each lesson, the reader may say:

Hear the word of God in the . . . . .

After each lesson, the reader may say:

Here ends the reading (*or* Epistle *or* Gospel).

The sermon shall be preached.

After the sermon, the minister shall say:

Let us say what we believe.

or

Let us say again what we have promised God and one another.

The Statement of Faith, a historic creed, or a church covenant shall be said, the people standing.

A hymn or anthem may be sung.

INTERCESSIONS

The minister shall say:

The Lord be with you,

And with you also.

Let us pray.

O God, whose Son, Jesus Christ, taught us to pray for all people, let our prayers for others be honest, asking for them those things which they need and which you desire for them. Amen.

The minister, or the congregation in unison, may offer any or all of the following prayers, or other prayers:

Let us pray for the world:

Silent prayer

Lord of all worlds and lover of us all, we pray for the peoples and nations, the orders and societies of this world. Convert all destructive forces, crush every tyranny, condemn each injustice, and reconcile to your will all conflicting interests, that in freedom everyone may enjoy the good world you have made, and know fully what it is to be human; through Jesus Christ our Lord. **Amen.**

Let us pray for our nation and those who govern it:

Silent prayer

Mighty God, whose governing hand is upon all the world, we ask your mercy upon this nation, that your ruling power may be recognized and obeyed. Grant to the President of the United States, and the Governor of the state, and to all in public authority, the humility to see themselves as your servants, that they may act responsibly toward their own people and the world's peoples, and that we may follow their leadership with confidence; through Jesus Christ our Lord. **Amen.**

Let us pray for the church:

Silent prayer

O God, who called a people to serve others in their need, and to show your love, recall your church from serving itself, and compel it to take the risks by which people are reconciled to you and to one another; through Jesus Christ our Lord. **Amen.**

Let us pray for those in need:

Silent prayer

Holy God, bearer of the world's pain, compassionate to those who suffer, whether at their own hand or at the hands of others, we commit to you all persons in need and offer ourselves to serve them, that they may know an end to all needless pain and new meaning for the suffering that must be borne; through Jesus Christ our Lord. **Amen.**

Prayer of Thanksgiving (used when the Lord's Supper is not to be celebrated)

Let us give thanks.

O God, we are made glad by the good news of your love for us and all people. We thank you for creating us and giving us all that is necessary for life. We thank you for your action in Christ by which our lives are measured, found wanting, and renewed. Help us to remember your gifts, that we may praise you with lives of joy and service; through Jesus Christ our Lord. **Amen.**

Our Father in heaven:
Hallowed be your name,
Your kingdom come,
Your will be done,
on earth as in heaven.
Give us today our daily bread.
Forgive us our sins,

as we forgive those who sin against us.
Save us from the time of trial,
and deliver us from evil.
For yours is the kingdom, the power, and the glory, forever. Amen.

The offerings of the people shall be received and may be brought to the Lord's table with the bread and wine.

A doxology may be sung.

If the Lord's Supper is not celebrated, the service will conclude with a prayer of dedication, a hymn, and the blessing.

When the Lord's Supper is celebrated, the minister, after the Lord's Prayer and before the offering, may say:

We shall bring to the Lord's table with our offerings the bread and wine for the Lord's Supper. We invite to this table all who are members of a Christian church, who desire peace with their neighbor, and who seek the mercy of God.

The people standing, the minister shall say:

Luke the Evangelist wrote of our risen Lord, that when he was at table with two of the disciples, he took bread and blessed and broke it, and gave it to them, and their eyes were opened, and they recognized him.

In company with all believers in every time and beyond time, we come to this table to know him in the breaking of the bread.

For the Lord Jesus, on the night he was betrayed, took bread, and, when he had given thanks, he broke it, and said, "This is my body which is broken for you. Do this in remembrance of me." In the same way also he took the cup, after supper, saying, "This cup is the new covenant in my blood. Do this as often as you drink it, in remembrance of me."

Lift up your hearts.

We lift them to the Lord.

Let us give thanks to the Lord God.

It is good that we do.

We give you thanks, Lord God, our Creator, for bringing the worlds into being, for forming us in your likeness, for recalling us when we rebel against you, and for keeping the world in your steadfast love. We praise you especially for Jesus Christ; who was born of Mary and lived as one of us; who knew exactly the life we know, and yet was obedient to your purposes, even to his death on a cross. We thank you that you stamped his death with victory by raising him in power and by making him head over all things. We rejoice in the continuing presence of the Holy Spirit, in the church you have gathered, in its task of obedience, and in the promise of eternal life. With the faithful in every place and time, we praise with joy your holy name.

Holy, holy, holy,
God of love and majesty,
The whole universe speaks of your glory,
O God, Most High.

Therefore bless now, by your Word and Spirit, both us and these gifts of bread and wine, that in receiving them at this table, and in offering here our faith and praise, we may be united with Christ and one another, and remain faithful to the tasks he sets before us.

In the strength Christ gives we offer ourselves to you, giving thanks that you have called us to serve you. Amen.

Then the minister shall take the bread and say:

Through the broken bread

(*here the minister shall break the bread*)

we participate in the body of Christ.

Then the minister shall take the cup and say:

Through the cup of blessing we participate in the new life Christ gives.

Then the minister shall say:

Come, for all things are ready.

The people shall be seated.

In giving the bread, the minister shall say:

Eat this, for it is the body of Christ, broken for you.

And, in giving the cup:

Drink this, for it is the blood of Christ, shed for you.

Then the minister shall say:

Let us give thanks.

The people shall stand and give thanks.

We give thanks, almighty God, that you have refreshed us at your table by granting us the presence of your Son, Jesus Christ. Strengthen our faith, increase our love for one another, and send us forth into the world in courage and peace, rejoicing in the power of the Holy Spirit, through Jesus Christ our Lord. Amen.

A hymn shall be sung.

The minister shall say:

The grace of the Lord Jesus Christ and the love of God and the communion of the Holy Spirit, be with you all. **Amen.**

The Sacrament for the Baptism of Infants

The sacrament should be celebrated in the presence of the congregation during a regular service of worship after the reading of the lessons and the preaching of the sermon. (When circumstances make baptism necessary apart from the presence of the congregation, suitable office bearers of the church should be present to represent it.) At least one of the parents presenting a child for baptism shall be a member of a Christian congregation in full communion; otherwise sponsors, who are members of a Christian congregation in full communion, shall join in answering the baptismal questions. Parents bringing a child for baptism shall stand before the minister. They may be accompanied by brothers and sisters of the child and sponsors, if any.

The minister shall say:

Grace and peace to you from God the Father and the Lord Jesus Christ.

Our Lord gave this commandment: "You are to go and make disciples of all the nations and baptize them in the name of the Father and of the Son and of the Holy Spirit. Teach them to observe all that I have commanded you." We receive these words from Matthew in the belief that our children are included in the benefits and joy of this discipleship. As we read in Luke's Gospel, "People even brought little children to him, for him to touch them; but when the disciples saw this they turned them away. But Jesus called the children to him and said, 'Let the little children come to me, and do not stop them; for it is to such as these that the kingdom of God belongs. I tell you solemnly, anyone who does not welcome the kingdom of God like a little child will never enter it.' "

In the sacrament of baptism we celebrate the grace and forgiveness of

God that we know in Jesus Christ. Here we proclaim that all life is God's gift and the gift is good. We thank God for this child. We praise God for the ever new possibilities which lie open to (him-her) as a child of God. We receive (him-her) into the love and care of the Christian church, so that as (he-she) grows and matures (he-she) may come to know God and offer (him-her)self in God's service in the world.

The minister shall say to the congregation:

Into what faith are we baptizing this child?

The congregation shall respond by repeating the Apostles' Creed or some other statement of faith.

The minister shall say to the parents or sponsors:

Do you desire to have (this child) baptized into this faith and do you promise, with God's help, by your life and teaching to lead (him-her) toward an understanding of this faith and into the service of Jesus Christ?

Parents or sponsors answer:

I do.

The congregation shall say:

We receive this child as a new person in Christ. We offer our understanding and support as (he-she) explores life. We enfold this child in our love, seeking together to grow in wisdom and stature and in favor with God and all people. We join with these parents in telling the gospel in our midst so that this child may live with us for Christ, showing forth his love for all people.

The minister shall offer the following prayer:

O Lord, giver of life and power, you have promised not only to be our God but also the God and Father of our children. Sanctify with your spirit (this child) whom we baptize according to your word, and bless this water, that it may be a sign and seal of new life in Christ our Lord. **Amen.**

The minister shall say:

What is the name of this child?

The parents or sponsors shall give the name and the minister shall repeat it. The minister shall then baptize the child with water saying:

..........................., you are baptized in the name of the Father and of the Son and of the Holy Spirit. **Amen.**

The minister shall say:

We praise God for calling this child into the company of Christ's people. We accept (him-her) with joy. Thanks be to God. **Amen.**

A suitable hymn or doxology may be sung.

The minister shall conclude with the following or another blessing:

The peace of the Lord Jesus Christ be with you all. **Amen.**

The Order for Confirmation

Before confirmation the elders or diaconate shall be satisfied that the confirmands have been properly instructed in the Christian faith and desire to receive the rite. Confirmation shall be administered in the presence of the worshiping congregation, except in cases of extremity when it may be administered privately in the presence of elders or diaconate.

After the sermon has been preached an elected representative of the church shall announce the names of the confirmands and invite them to stand before the congregation, saying:

Dear friends in Christ: The church bestows on those who have been received into the fellowship of Christ through baptism the rite of confirmation. These persons have studied the word of God and have been instructed in the practice of the Christian faith. They are here to profess their faith and to be confirmed by God for service in his world.

The minister shall say to the confirmands:

You have come that God may claim you publicly for his service, confirm you in his covenant, and invoke upon you the Holy Spirit by whose help alone you are able to fulfill your vows.

Hear the word of our Lord concerning the gift of the Spirit.

The minister shall read one or more of the following passages of scripture:

If you love me, you will keep my commandments. And I will pray the Father, and he will give you another Counselor, to be with you forever, even the Spirit of truth, whom the world cannot receive, because it neither sees him nor knows him; you know him, for he dwells with you, and will be with you.

You shall receive power when the Holy Spirit has come upon you; and you shall be my witnesses in Jerusalem and in all Judea and Samaria and to the end of the earth.

Ask, and it will be given you; seek, and you will find; knock, and it will be opened to you. For every one who asks receives, and he who seeks finds, and to him who knocks it will be opened.

The minister shall ask the questions and the confirmands shall answer:

Do you confess your faith in Christ as Lord and Savior?

I confess my faith.

Do you promise, according to the grace given you, always to remain a faithful member of the church of our Lord Jesus Christ, to come to the Lord's table, to love and serve God in the world, bearing witness to the risen Lord?

I promise.

The confirmands with the congregation may confess their faith through the Statement of Faith or the Apostles' Creed, or may affirm with the congregation the following or another covenant:

We covenant with the Lord and with one another, and bind ourselves in the presence of God to live together in all his ways, as he reveals them to us through his word of truth.

If there be any confirmand who is not baptized, the minister shall offer the following prayer:

Almighty and everlasting God, in infinite mercy and goodness you have promised not only to be our God, but also the God and Father of our children. As you have called us to be partakers of your great mercy, sanctify with your Spirit this your (servant), whom we baptize according to your word, and bless this water, that it may be the sign and seal of cleansing to new life in Christ our Lord. **Amen.**

The minister shall baptize each of these confirmands, saying:

...................................., I baptize you in the name of the Father and of the Son and of the Holy Spirit. **Amen.**

The minister shall say:

Let us pray.

Almighty God, who in baptism received these your servants into the church, forgave their sins, and promised them eternal life, increase in them the gifts of your Holy Spirit; love for others, joy in serving you, peace in dissension, patience in suffering, kindness toward all people, goodness in evil times, faithfulness in temptation, gentleness in the face of opposition, self-control in all things; and so strengthen them for their ministry in the world; through Christ our Lord. **Amen.**

Here the Lord's Prayer shall be offered.

The confirmands may kneel and the minister, laying a hand on the head of each one by one, shall say:

The God of peace sanctify you wholly; and I pray that you be preserved blameless to the coming of our Lord Jesus Christ. **Amen.**

or

The Father of mercies multiply in you his grace and peace, enable you truly and faithfully to keep your vows, defend you in every time of danger, preserve you to the end, and finally bring you to rest with all the saints in glory everlasting. **Amen.**

or

Strengthen, O Lord, this your servant with your heavenly grace, that (he-she) may continue yours forever; and daily increase in (him-her) your Holy Spirit, until (he-she) comes into your everlasting kingdom. **Amen.**

or

O God, our Father, in the grace of Jesus Christ you have accepted this your servant through the water of baptism. Nourish in (him-her) eternal life and increase in (him-her) the power of your Holy Spirit that (he-she) may serve you in the world. **Amen.**

Let us pray.

We give you thanks, most merciful God, for the goodness you have shown toward (these persons) by moving them to affirm their baptism. Help them to live not for themselves but for Christ and for those whom Christ loves. Keep them steady and abounding in hope, never giving up, pressing toward the goal of life with God, in Jesus Christ. **Amen.**

The minister and a representative of the congregation shall extend the hand of fellowship, and the representative shall say:

In the name of Jesus Christ and on behalf of .... we extend to you the hand of Christian love.

All standing, a representative of the congregation shall say:

We greet you with joy.

Another representative shall say:

We pledge to you our friendship in the Lord, and will give you our support in prayer and service that you may continue to grow in the knowledge and love of God and be witnesses to Jesus Christ, our risen Lord.

The newly confirmed members shall take their places in the worshiping congregation. A hymn may be sung. The service shall continue in the usual manner and may conclude with these words:

Go forth into the world in peace; be of good courage; hold fast to that which is good; render to no one evil for evil; strengthen the faint-hearted; support the weak; help the afflicted; honor all people; love and serve the Lord, rejoicing in the power of the Holy Spirit.

The peace of God which passes all understanding keep your hearts and minds in the knowledge and love of God and of his Son Jesus Christ, our Lord; and the blessing of God Almighty, the Father, the Son, and the Holy Spirit, be among you and remain with you always. **Amen.**

The Order for Receiving Communicants by Reaffirmation of Faith or by Letter of Transfer

Following the affirmation of faith the minister shall say:

The following baptized persons have indicated their desire to unite with us in this household of faith. They are here to profess their faith, and to join us in serving Jesus Christ.

The minister shall announce the names of those being received, and they shall present themselves before the congregation.

The minister shall say:

Hear the words of our Lord:

"You did not choose me, but I chose you and appointed you that you should go and bear fruit and that your fruit should abide."

"Everyone who acknowledges me before men, I also will acknowledge before my Father who is in heaven."

Jesus Christ has chosen you, and, in baptism, has joined you to himself. He has called you, together with us, into the church, which is his body. Now, he has brought you to this time and place to unite with us in the ministries and blessings of this congregation. As you come into our midst, we invite you to reaffirm your faith as members of the church of Jesus Christ.

Do you reaffirm your faith in God as your Father, in Christ as your Lord, and in the Holy Spirit as your Strength?

I do.

Do you promise to participate in the life and mission of this family of God's people, sharing regularly in the worship of God, and enlisting in the work of this congregation as it serves the community and the world?

I do.

Let us, the members of ...., express our welcome and affirm our mutual ministry.

The congregation shall stand, and, together with the minister, shall say:

We welcome you with joy as partners in the common life of this church. We promise you our friendship and prayers as we share the hopes and labors of the church of Jesus Christ. God grant that together we may continue to grow in his knowledge and love and be witnesses of our risen Lord.

The minister and a representative of the congregation shall extend the hand of fellowship, and the representative shall say:

In the name of Jesus Christ and on behalf of .... we extend to you the hand of Christian love, welcoming you into the company of this congregation.

The minister or the representative shall offer this prayer:

Let us pray.

Eternal God our Father, we praise you for calling us to be your servant people, and for gathering us into the body of Christ. We thank you for sending to us these fellow believers that we may work together in serving the needs of others. Confirm in us the power of your covenant that we may live in your Spirit and so love each other that we may have among us the same mind which was in Christ Jesus our Lord, to whom be all honor and glory. **Amen.**

The minister shall dismiss the new members, saying:

Go; serve the Lord.

The peace of God which passes all understanding keep your hearts and minds in Christ Jesus our Lord. **Amen.**

The newly received members shall take their places in the worshiping congregation, and the service shall continue.

We Believe in God, the Eternal Spirit, Father of Our Lord Jesus Christ and Our Father, and to His Deeds We Testify

He Calls the Worlds into Being, Creates Man in His Own Image, and Sets Before Him the Ways of Life and Death

He Seeks in Holy Love to Save All People from Aimlessness and Sin

He Judges Men and Nations by His Righteous Will Declared Through Prophets and Apostles

From All That Dwell Below the Skies

Ps. 117
Isaac Watts, 1719

LASST UNS ERFREUEN L.M. *with Alleluias*
Geistliche Kirchengesäng, *Cologne, 1623*
Harm. by R. Vaughan Williams, 1906

Unison
1. From all that dwell be-low the skies Let the Cre - a -tor's praise a -
2. E - ter- nal are thy mer-cies, Lord; E - ter -nal truth at-tends thy
rise; Al- le - lu - ia! Al-le - lu - ia! Let the Re-deem-er's name be
word: Al- le - lu - ia! Al-le - lu - ia! Thy praise shall sound from shore to
sung Through ev - 'ry land, by ev - 'ry tongue.
shore Till suns shall rise and set no more.
Al- le - lu - ia,
Al-le - lu - ia, Al-le - lu - ia, Al-le - lu - ia, Al-le- lu - ia!

A higher setting may be found at No. 30.

2

*All People That on Earth Do Dwell

OLD HUNDREDTH L.M.

Ps. 100
William Kethe, 1561, alt.

Attr. to Louis Bourgeois, c.1510-c.1561
Genevan Psalter, *1551*

1. All peo-ple that on earth do dwell, Sing to the Lord with cheer-ful voice;
2. Know that the Lord is God in - deed; With - out our aid he did us make;
3. O en - ter then his gates with praise, Ap-proach with joy his courts un - to;
4. For why? the Lord our God is good, His mer-cy is for - ev - er sure;
5. To Fa-ther, Son, and Ho - ly Ghost, The God whom heav'n and earth a - dore,

Him serve with mirth, his praise forth tell, Come ye be-fore him and re - joice.
We are his folk, he doth us feed, And for his sheep he doth us take.
Praise, laud, and bless his name al - ways, For it is seem-ly so to do.
His truth at all times firm - ly stood, And shall from age to age en - dure.
From men and from the an - gel host Be praise and glo - ry ev - er - more.

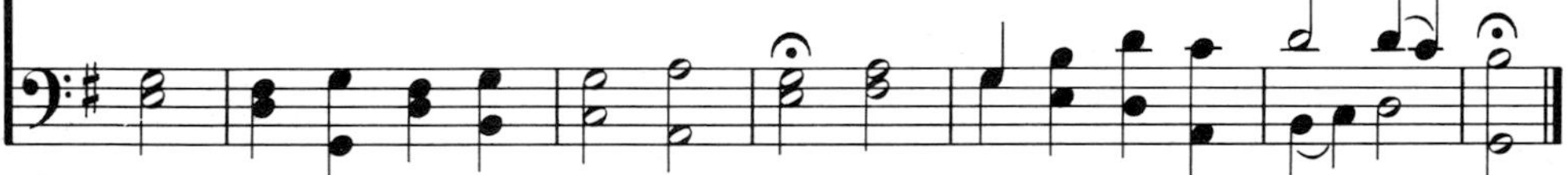

3

*We Praise Thee, O God

KREMSER 12.11.12.11.
Netherlands Folk Song, 1626

Julia Bulkley Cady Cory, 1902

Arr. by Edward Kremser, 1877

1. We praise thee, O God, our Re - deem - er, Cre - a - tor, In grate-ful de -
2. We wor-ship thee, God of our fa-thers, we bless thee; Through trou-ble and
3. With voic- es u - nit - ed our prais - es we of - fer, To thee, great Je -

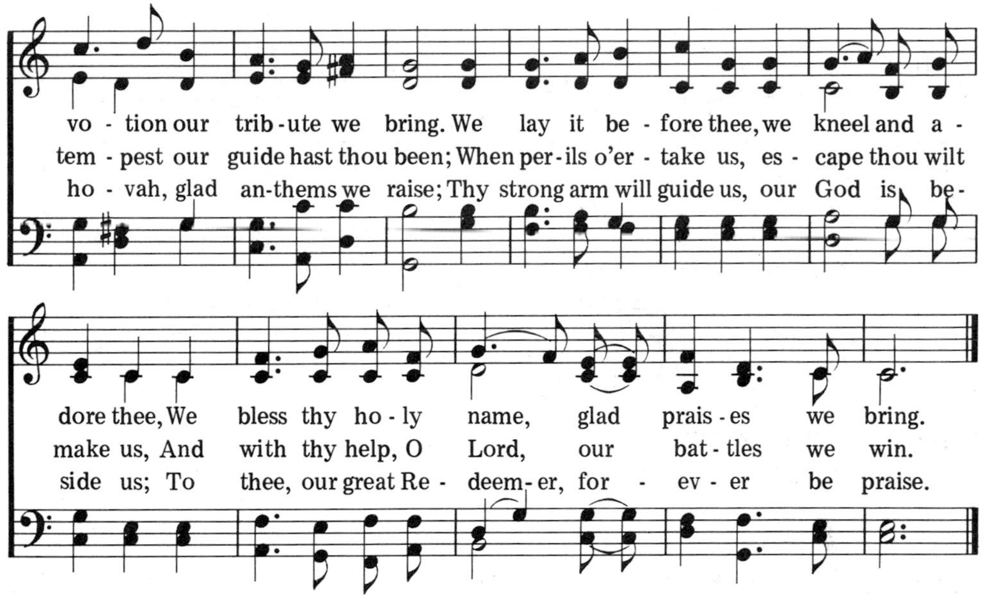

vo - tion our trib-ute we bring. We lay it be - fore thee, we kneel and a -
tem - pest our guide hast thou been; When per-ils o'er - take us, es - cape thou wilt
ho - vah, glad an-thems we raise; Thy strong arm will guide us, our God is be -
dore thee, We bless thy ho - ly name, glad prais - es we bring.
make us, And with thy help, O Lord, our bat - tles we win.
side us; To thee, our great Re - deem - er, for - ev - er be praise.

4

We Gather Together

KREMSER 12.11.12.11.

Netherlands Folk Song, 1626
Tr. Theodore Baker, 1917

Netherlands Folk Song, 1626
Arr. by Edward Kremser, 1877

1. We gather together to ask the Lord's blessing,
   He chastens and hastens his will to make known;
   The wicked oppressing now cease from distressing.
   Sing praises to his name; he forgets not his own.

2. Beside us to guide us, our God with us joining,
   Ordaining, maintaining his kingdom divine,
   So from the beginning the fight we were winning;
   Thou, Lord, wast at our side, all glory be thine.

3. We all do extol thee, thou leader triumphant,
   And pray that thou still our defender wilt be.
   Let thy congregation escape tribulation.
   Thy name be ever praised! O Lord, make us free!

We Believe in One True God

Tobias Clausnitzer, 1668
Tr. Catherine Winkworth, 1863

RATISBON 7.7.7.7.7.7.
Arr. from J. G. Werner's Choralbuch, 1815

1. We be-lieve in one true God, Fa-ther, Son, and Ho-ly Ghost,
2. We be-lieve in Je-sus Christ, Son of God and Mar-y's son,
3. We con-fess the Ho-ly Ghost, Who from both for-e'er pro-ceeds;
Ev-er-pres-ent help in need, Praised by all the heav'n-ly host;
Who de-scend-ed from his throne And for us sal-va-tion won;
Who up-holds and com-forts us In all tri-als, fears, and needs.
By whose might-y power a-lone All is made and wrought and done.
By whose cross and death are we Res-cued from sin's mis-e-ry.
Blest and Ho-ly Trin-i-ty, Praise for-ev-er be to thee!

*The God of Abraham Praise

Revised Version of the Yigdal
Daniel ben Judah, c.1400
Tr. Newton Mann and Max Landsberg

LEONI 6.6.8.4.D.
Traditional Hebrew Melody
Adapted by Meyer Lyon, 1770

1. The God of A - bra'm praise, All prais - ed be his name,
Who was and is and is to be, For aye the same!
The one e - ter - nal God, Ere aught that now ap - pears;
The First, the Last: be - yond all thought His time - less years!

2. His spir - it flow - eth free, High surg - ing where it will;
In proph-et's word he spoke of old; He speak - eth still.
Es - tab-lished is his law, And change-less it shall stand,
Deep writ up - on the hu - man heart, On sea or land.

3. He hath e - ter - nal life Im - plant - ed in the soul;
His love shall be our strength and stay, While a - ges roll.
Praise to the liv - ing God! All prais - ed be his name
Who was and is and is to be, For aye the same!

7

O My Soul, Bless God, the Father

Ps. 103
Anon.
United Presbyterian
Book of Psalms U. S. A., *1871*

STUTTGART 8.7.8.7.
Melody attr. to Christian F. Witt, 1660-1716
Psalmodia Sacra, *Gotha, 1715*

1. O my soul, bless God, the Fa - ther; All with - in me bless his name;
2. Who for - giv - eth thy trans-gres - sions, Thy dis - eas - es all who heals,
3. Far as east from west is dis - tant, He hath put a - way our sin;
4. As it was with - out be - gin - ning, So it lasts with - out an end;
5. Un - to such as keep his cove-nant And are stead-fast in his way,
6. Bless the Fa - ther, all his crea-tures, Ev - er un - der his con-trol;
Bless the Fa - ther, and for - get not All his mer - cies to pro-claim.
Who re-deems thee from de - struc-tion, Who with thee so kind - ly deals,
Like the pit - y of a fa - ther Hath the Lord's com - pas - sion been.
To their chil-dren's chil - dren ev - er Shall his righ - teous - ness ex - tend:
Un - to those who still re - mem-ber His com-mand-ments and o - bey.
All through-out his vast do - min - ion Bless the Fa - ther, O my soul.
8
Praise the Lord
Ps. 148
Richard D. Wetzel, 1971
RANSHAW 7.5.7.4.
Richard D. Wetzel, 1971
Unison
1. Praise the Lord from high - est heav'n; Praise him all his hosts.
2. Sun and moon and stars of light, Fire and hail and snow;
3. Beasts and cat - tle, creep - ing things, Drag - ons and all deeps;
4. Kings and princ - es, praise his name, Judg - es of the earth;
5. Praise the Lord from high - est heav'n; Praise him from the earth.

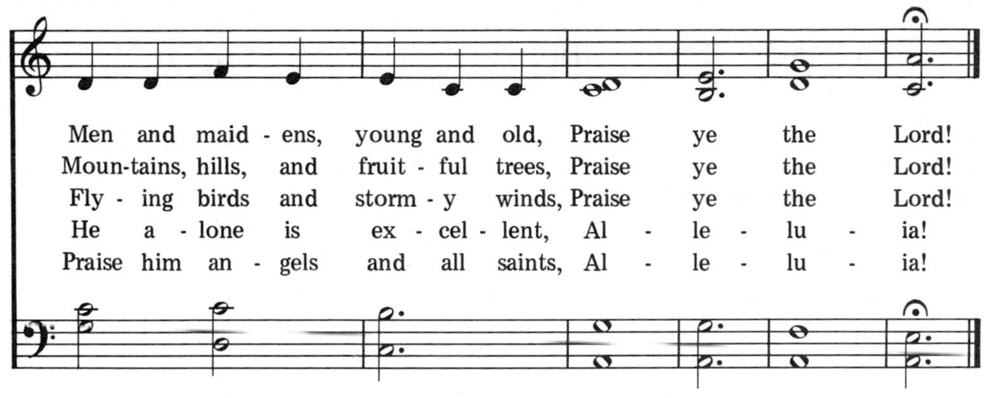
Men and maid - ens, young and old, Praise ye the Lord!
Moun-tains, hills, and fruit - ful trees, Praise ye the Lord!
Fly - ing birds and storm - y winds, Praise ye the Lord!
He a - lone is ex - cel - lent, Al - le - lu - ia!
Praise him an - gels and all saints, Al - le - lu - ia!

9

*Our God, Our Help in Ages Past

Ps. 90
Isaac Watts, 1719

ST. ANNE C.M.
Attr. to William Croft, 1708

1. Our God, our help in a - ges past, Our hope for years to come,
2. Un - der the shad - ow of thy throne Thy saints have dwelt se - cure;
3. Be - fore the hills in or - der stood, Or earth re - ceived her frame,
4. A thou - sand a - ges in thy sight Are like an eve - ning gone,
5. Time, like an ev - er - roll-ing stream, Bears all its sons a - way;
6. Our God, our help in a - ges past, Our hope for years to come,

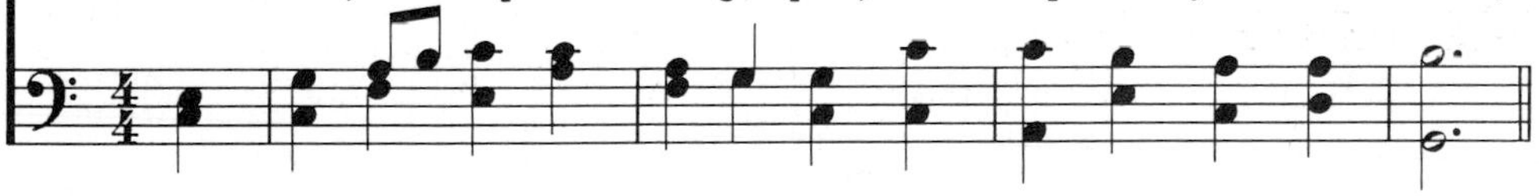

Our shel - ter from the storm - y blast, And our e - ter - nal home,
Suf - fi - cient is thine arm a - lone, And our de - fense is sure.
From ev - er - last - ing thou art God, To end - less years the same.
Short as the watch that ends the night Be - fore the ris - ing sun.
They fly, for - got - ten, as a dream Dies at the op - 'ning day.
Be thou our guard while trou - bles last, And our e - ter - nal home.

10

O God, Beneath Thy Guiding Hand

DUKE STREET L.M.

Leonard Bacon, 1833 *John Hatton, 1793*

1. O God, be - neath thy guid - ing hand Our ex - iled
2. Laws, free - dom, truth, and faith in God Came with those
3. And here thy name, O God of love, Their chil - dren's
fa - thers crossed the sea, And when they trod the
ex - iles o'er the waves, And where their pil - grim
chil - dren shall a - dore, Till these e - ter - nal
win - try strand, With prayer and psalm they wor-shiped thee.
feet have trod, The God they trust - ed guards their graves.
hills re - move, And spring a - dorns the earth no more.

Men and Children Everywhere

John J. Moment, 1930

ROCK OF AGES Irregular
Traditional Hebrew Melody

1. Men and chil-dren ev-'ry-where, With sweet mu-sic fill the air!
2. Morn-ing, eve-ning, bless his name, Skies with crim-son clouds a-flame,
3. Storm and flood and o-cean's roar, Break-ers crash-ing on the shore,
Na-tions, come, your voic-es raise To the Lord in hymns of praise!
Rain-bow arch, his cov-'nant sign, Count-less stars by night that shine!
Wa-ter-falls that nev-er sleep, Tow-'ring moun-tain, can-yon deep,
Join the an-gel song, All the worlds to him be-long!
Through his far do-main, Love is king where he doth reign!
Tell ye forth his might, Lord of life and truth and right!
Ho-ly, ho-ly, To our God all glo-ry be.

O Be Joyful in the Lord

Ps. 100
Curtis Beach, 1958

ROCK OF AGES *Irregular*
Traditional Hebrew Melody

1. O be joy - ful in the Lord! Sing be - fore him, all the earth!
2. Know ye that the Lord is king! All his works his wis-dom prove!
3. En - ter now his ho - ly gate; Let our bur-dened hearts be still;
4. For the Lord our God is kind, And his love shall con-stant be;
Praise him with a glad ac - cord And with lives of no - blest worth.
By his might the heav - ens ring; In his love we live and move.
In the sa - cred si - lence wait, As we seek to know his will.
In his will our peace we find; In his ser - vice, lib - er - ty.
Sons of ev - ery land, Hum - bly now be - fore him stand!
By him we are made, So we trust him un - a - fraid.
Let our lives ex - press Our a - bun - dant thank - ful - ness;
Yea, his law is sure; In his light we walk se - cure;
Raise your voice and re - joice In the boun - ty of his hand.
Stand - ing fast to the last, By his hand our lives are stayed.
All our days, all our ways, Shall our Fa - ther's love con - fess.
Ev - er - more, as of yore, Shall his change-less truth en - dure.

*Joyful, Joyful, We Adore Thee

HYMN TO JOY 8.7.8.7.D.
Arr. from Ludwig van Beethoven, 1824
Edward Hodges, 1846

Henry van Dyke, 1907

1. Joy - ful, joy - ful, we a - dore thee, God of glo - ry, Lord of love;
2. All thy works with joy sur-round thee, Earth and heav'n re - flect thy rays,
3. Thou art giv - ing and for - giv - ing, Ev - er bless - ing, ev - er blest,
4. Mor - tals, join the might - y cho - rus Which the morn - ing stars be - gan;

Hearts un - fold like flowers be - fore thee, Open - ing to the sun a - bove.
Stars and an - gels sing a - round thee, Cen - ter of un - bro - ken praise.
Well-spring of the joy of liv - ing, O - cean depth of hap - py rest!
Fa - ther love is reign - ing o'er us, Broth - er love binds man to man.

Melt the clouds of sin and sad - ness, Drive the dark of doubt a - way;
Field and for - est, vale and moun - tain, Flow - ery mead - ow, flash - ing sea,
Thou our Fa - ther, Christ our broth - er, All who live in love are thine;
Ev - er sing - ing, march we on - ward, Vic - tors in the midst of strife,

Giv - er of im - mor - tal glad - ness, Fill us with the light of day.
Chant - ing bird and flow - ing foun - tain, Call us to re - joice in thee.
Teach us how to love each oth - er, Lift us to the joy di - vine.
Joy - ful mu - sic leads us sun - ward In the tri - umph song of life.

14

*O Splendor of God's Glory Bright

John 8:12
Latin: Splendor paternae gloriae
Ambrose of Milan, 340-397
Tr. Robert S. Bridges, 1899

PUER NOBIS NASCITUR L.M.
Adapted by Michael Praetorius, 1609

1. O Splen - dor of God's glo - ry bright, O thou that bring - est light from light, O Light of light, light's liv - ing spring, O Day, all days il - lu - min - ing,

2. O thou true Sun, on us thy glance Let fall in roy - al ra - di - ance; The Spir - it's sanc - ti - fy - ing beam Up - on our earth - ly sen - ses stream.

3. The Fa - ther, too, our prayers im - plore, Fa - ther of glo - ry ev - er - more, The Fa - ther of all grace and might, To ban - ish sin from our de - light:

4. To guide what - e'er we no - bly do, With love all en - vy to sub - due; To make ill for - tune turn to fair, And give us grace our wrongs to bear.

An alternate setting may be found at No. 133.

*Come, Thou Almighty King

Ps. 45:3-4
Anon., c.1757
Whitfield's Collection

ITALIAN HYMN 6.6.4.6.6.6.4.
Felice de Giardini, 1769

1. Come, thou al - might - y King, Help us thy
2. Come, thou in - car - nate Word, Gird on thy
3. Come, ho - ly Com - fort - er, Thy sa - cred
4. To the great One in Three E - ter - nal
name to sing; Help us to praise: Fa - ther, all
might - y sword; Our prayer at - tend: Come, and thy
wit - ness bear In this glad hour! Thou who al -
prais - es be Hence ev - er - more! His sov - ereign
glo - ri - ous, O'er all vic - to - ri - ous,
peo - ple bless, And give thy word suc - cess;
might - y art, Now rule in ev - ery heart,
maj - es - ty May we in glo - ry see,
Come, and reign o - ver us, An - cient of Days.
'Stab - lish thy righ - teous-ness, Sav - ior and friend.
And ne'er from us de - part, Spir - it of power.
And to e - ter - ni - ty Love and a - dore.

16

*Strong Son of God, Immortal Love

2 Cor. 5:7
Alfred Tennyson, 1850

ANGEL'S SONG (SONG 34) L.M.
Orlando Gibbons, 1623

1. Strong Son of God, im - mor - tal Love, Whom we, that have not seen thy face, By faith, and faith a - lone, em - brace, Be - liev - ing where we can - not prove.
2. Thou wilt not leave us in the dust; Thou mad - est man, he knows not why; He thinks he was not made to die; And thou hast made him: thou art just.
3. Thou seem - est hu - man and di - vine, The high - est, ho - liest man - hood, thou: Our wills are ours, we know not how; Our wills are ours, to make them thine.
4. Our lit - tle sys - tems have their day; They have their day and cease to be; They are but bro - ken lights of thee; And thou, O Lord, art more than they.
5. Let knowl - edge grow from more to more, But more of rev - 'rence in us dwell, That mind and soul, ac - cord - ing well, May make one mu - sic as be - fore.

17

*O Worship the King, All Glorious Above

Ps. 104
HANOVER 10.10.11.11.
Robert Grant, 1833
William Croft, 1708
1. O wor - ship the King, all glo - rious a - bove,
2. O tell of his might, O sing of his grace,
3. Thy boun - ti - ful care what tongue can re - cite?
4. Frail chil - dren of dust, and fee - ble as frail;
O grate - ful - ly sing his won - der - ful love;
Whose robe is the light, whose can - o - py space;
It breathes in the air, it shines in the light;
In thee do we trust, nor find thee to fail;
Our Shield and De - fend - er, the An - cient of Days,
His char - iots of wrath the deep thun - der - clouds form,
It streams from the hills, it de - scends to the plain,
Thy mer - cies how ten - der, how firm to the end,
Pa - vil - ioned in splen - dor and gird - ed with praise.
And dark is his path on the wings of the storm.
And sweet - ly dis - tills in the dew and the rain.
Our Mak - er, De - fend - er, Re - deem - er, and Friend!

Alternate tune, Lyons, No. 196

18

Holy, Holy, Holy Lord, God of Hosts

SPANISH HYMN 7.7.7.7.D.

James Montgomery, 1832 — *Arr. by Benjamin Carr, 1824*

1. Ho - ly, Ho - ly, Ho - ly Lord, God of hosts, when heav'n and earth
2. Ho - ly, Ho - ly, Ho - ly! thee, One Je - ho - vah ev - er - more,
3. Ho - ly, Ho - ly, Ho - ly! All heav'n's tri - um-phant choir shall sing,

Out of dark - ness, at thy word, Is - sued in - to glo - rious birth,
Fa - ther, Son, and Spir - it, we, Dust and ash - es, would a - dore:
While the ran - somed na - tions fall At the foot - stool of their King:

All thy works be - fore thee stood, And thine eyes be - held them good,
Light - ly by the world es - teemed, From that world by thee re - deemed,
Then shall saints and ser - a - phim, Harps and voic - es swell one hymn,

While they sang with sweet ac - cord, Ho - ly, Ho - ly, Ho - ly Lord!
Sing we here with glad ac - cord, Ho - ly, Ho - ly, Ho - ly Lord!
Blend - ing in sub - lime ac - cord, Ho - ly, Ho - ly, Ho - ly Lord!

*Holy, Holy, Holy! Lord God Almighty

Rev. 4:8-11 | NICAEA 11.12.12.10.
Reginald Heber, 1826 | *John B. Dykes, 1861*

1. Ho - ly, ho - ly, ho - ly! Lord God Al - might - y!
2. Ho - ly, ho - ly, ho - ly! all the saints a - dore thee,
3. Ho - ly, ho - ly, ho - ly! though the dark - ness hide thee,
4. Ho - ly, ho - ly, ho - ly! Lord God Al - might - y!
Ear - ly in the morn - ing our song shall rise to thee;
Cast - ing down their gold - en crowns a - round the glass - y sea;
Though the eye of sin - ful man thy glo - ry may not see;
All thy works shall praise thy name in earth and sky and sea;
Ho - ly, ho - ly, ho - ly! mer - ci - ful and might - y;
Cher - u - bim and ser - a - phim fall - ing down be - fore thee,
On - ly thou art ho - ly; there is none be - side thee,
Ho - ly, ho - ly, ho - ly! mer - ci - ful and might - y;
God in three per - sons, bless - ed Trin - i - ty!
Which wert and art and ev - er - more shalt be.
Per - fect in power, in love, and pur - i - ty.
God in three per - sons, bless - ed Trin - i - ty!

Great God, We Sing That Mighty Hand

Acts 26:22
Philip Doddridge, 1755

TRURO L.M.
Thomas Williams' Psalmodia Evangelica, *1789*

1. Great God, we sing that might - y hand By which sup -
2. By day, by night, at home, a - broad, Still are we
3. With grate - ful hearts the past we own; The fu - ture,
4. In scenes ex - alt - ed or de - pressed, Thou art our
port - ed still we stand; The open - ing year thy
guard - ed by our God: By his in - ces - sant
all to us un - known, We to thy guard - ian
joy, and thou our rest; Thy good - ness all our
mer - cy shows; That mer - cy crowns it till it close.
boun - ty fed, By his un - err - ing coun - sel led.
care com - mit, And, peace - ful, leave be - fore thy feet.
hopes shall raise, A - dored through all our chang-ing days.

A lower setting may be found at No. 76.

*Immortal, Invisible, God Only Wise

1 Tim. 1:17
Walter C. Smith, 1867, alt.

ST. DENIO 11.11.11.11.
Welsh Hymn Melody, 1839

1. Im - mor - tal, in - vis - i - ble, God on - ly wise,
2. Un - rest - ing, un - hast - ing, and si - lent as light,
3. To all, life thou giv - est to both great and small;
4. Great Fa - ther of glo - ry, pure Fa - ther of light,
In light in - ac - ces - si - ble hid from our eyes,
Nor want - ing, nor wast - ing, thou rul - est in might;
In all life thou liv - est, the true life of all;
Thine an - gels a - dore thee, all veil - ing their sight;
Most bless - ed, most glo - rious, the An - cient of Days,
Thy jus - tice like moun - tains high soar - ing a - bove
We blos - som and flour - ish as leaves on the tree,
All praise we would ren - der; O help us to see
Al - might - y, vic - to - rious, thy great name we praise.
Thy clouds which are foun - tains of good - ness and love.
And with - er and per - ish, but naught chang - eth thee.
'Tis on - ly the splen - dor of light hid - eth thee.

22

*Praise the Lord! Ye Heavens Adore Him

Ps. 148
The Foundling Hospital Collection, *1796*

AUSTRIAN HYMN 8.7.8.7.D.
Franz Joseph Haydn, 1797

1. Praise the Lord! ye heav'ns a-dore him; Praise him, an-gels, in the height;
2. Praise the Lord! for he is glo-rious; Nev-er shall his prom-ise fail;
Sun and moon, re-joice be-fore him; Praise him, all ye stars of light.
God hath made his saints vic-to-rious; Sin and death shall not pre-vail.
Praise the Lord! for he hath spo-ken; Worlds his might-y voice o-beyed;
Praise the God of our sal-va-tion! Hosts on high, his power pro-claim;
Laws which nev-er shall be bro-ken For their guid-ance hath he made.
Heav'n and earth and all cre-a-tion Laud and mag-ni-fy his name.

Alternate tune, Hyfrydol, No. 274

*Praise, My Soul, the King of Heaven

Ps. 103
Henry F. Lyte, 1834

PRAISE MY SOUL 8.7.8.7.8.7.
John Goss, 1869

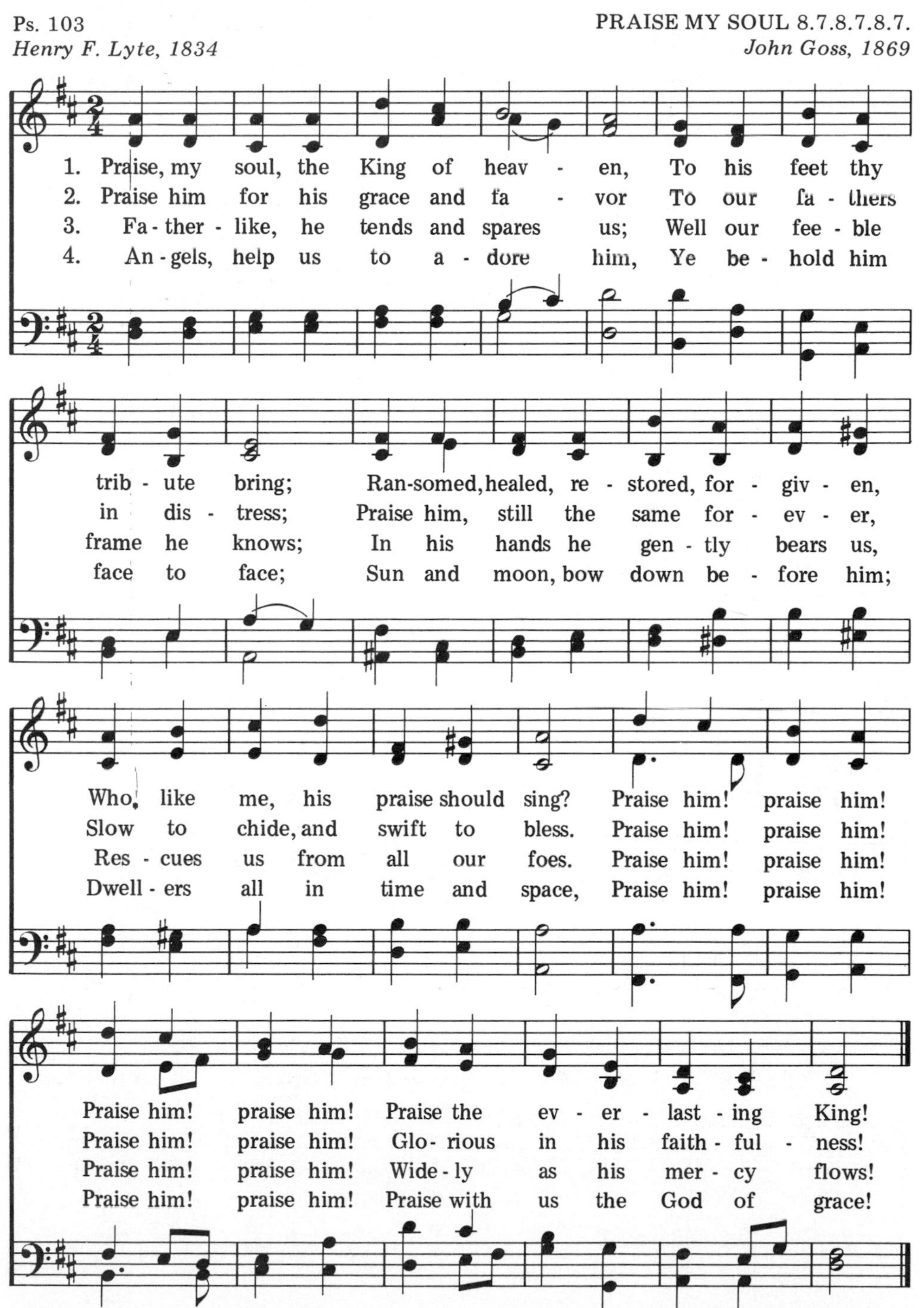
1. Praise, my soul, the King of heav - en, To his feet thy
2. Praise him for his grace and fa - vor To our fa - thers
3. Fa - ther - like, he tends and spares us; Well our fee - ble
4. An - gels, help us to a - dore him, Ye be - hold him
trib - ute bring; Ran-somed, healed, re - stored, for - giv - en,
in dis - tress; Praise him, still the same for - ev - er,
frame he knows; In his hands he gen - tly bears us,
face to face; Sun and moon, bow down be - fore him;
Who, like me, his praise should sing? Praise him! praise him!
Slow to chide, and swift to bless. Praise him! praise him!
Res - cues us from all our foes. Praise him! praise him!
Dwell - ers all in time and space, Praise him! praise him!
Praise him! praise him! Praise the ev - er - last - ing King!
Praise him! praise him! Glo - rious in his faith - ful - ness!
Praise him! praise him! Wide - ly as his mer - cy flows!
Praise him! praise him! Praise with us the God of grace!

24

Sing Praise to God Who Reigns Above

Johann J. Schütz, 1675
Tr. Frances E. Cox, 1864

MIT FREUDEN ZART 8.7.8.7.8.8.7.
Bohemian Brethren's Kirchengesänge, *1566*

1. Sing praise to God who reigns a - bove, The God of all cre - a - tion,
2. What God's al-might - y power hath made, His gra-cious mer- cy keep-eth;
3. Then all my glad-some way a - long, I sing a - loud thy prais - es,
4. O ye who name Christ's ho - ly name, Give God all praise and glo - ry;
The God of power, the God of love, The God of our sal - va - tion;
By morn-ing glow or eve -ning shade His watch-ful eye ne'er sleep-eth;
That men may hear the grate - ful song My voice un - wea - ried rais - es;
All ye who own his power, pro-claim A - loud the won- drous sto - ry!
With heal - ing balm my soul he fills, And ev - ery faith - less
With - in the king - dom of his might, Lo! all is just and
Be joy - ful in the Lord, my heart, Both soul and bod - y
Cast each false i - dol from his throne, The Lord is God, and
mur - mur stills: To God all praise and glo - ry.
all is right: To God all praise and glo - ry.
bear your part: To God all praise and glo - ry.
he a - lone: To God all praise and glo - ry.

*Praise to the Lord, the Almighty

Ps. 103
Joachim Neander, 1680
Tr. Catherine Winkworth and others

LOBE DEN HERREN 14.14.4.7.8.
Stralsund Gesangbuch, *1665*

1. Praise to the Lord, the Al - might - y, the King of cre -
2. Praise to the Lord, who o'er all things so won - drous - ly
3. Praise to the Lord, who doth pros - per thy work and de -
4. Praise to the Lord! O let all that is in me a -
a - tion! O my soul, praise him, for he is thy health and sal -
reign - eth, Shel - ters thee un - der his wings, yea, so gent - ly sus -
fend thee; Sure - ly his good - ness and mer - cy here dai - ly at -
dore him! All that hath life and breath, come now with prais - es be -
va - tion! Come, ye who hear, Broth - ers and
tain - eth! Hast thou not seen All that is
tend thee. Pon - der a - new All the Al -
fore him. Let the A - men Sound from his
sis - ters draw near; Praise him in glad ad - o - ra - tion!
need - ful hath been Grant - ed in what he or - dain - eth?
might - y can do, He who with love doth be - friend thee.
peo - ple a - gain: Glad - ly for aye we a - dore him.

26

Praise the Lord, His Glories Show

Ps. 150
Henry F. Lyte, 1834

LLANFAIR 7.7.7.7. *with Alleluias*
Melody by Robert Williams, 1817

27

Praise We the Lord

FRAGRANCE 9.8.9.8.9.8.
French Carol Melody
Arr. by Martin Shaw, 1928

Steuart Wilson, 1928

1. Praise we the Lord, who made all beau - ty For all our sen - ses
2. Praise him who makes our life a plea - sure, Send-ing us things which
3. Praise him who by a sim - ple flow - er Lifts up our hearts to
4. Praise we the Lord, who made all beau - ty For all our sen - ses
to en - joy; Give we our hum - ble thanks and du - ty
glad our eyes; Thank him who gives us wel - come lei - sure,
things a - bove; Thank him who gives to each one pow - er
to en - joy; Give we our hum - ble thanks and du - ty
That sim - ple plea-sures nev - er cloy; Praise we the Lord, who
That in our heart sweet thoughts may rise; Praise him who makes our
To find a friend to know and love; Praise him who by a
That sim - ple plea-sures nev - er cloy; Praise we the Lord, who
made all beau - ty For all our sen - ses to en - joy.
life a plea - sure Send-ing us things which glad our eyes.
sim - ple flow - er Lifts up our hearts to things a - bove.
made all beau - ty For all our sen - ses to en - joy.

28

I Sing the Mighty Power of God

James 1:17
Isaac Watts, 1709, alt.

BETHLEHEM C.M.D.
Gottfried W. Fink, 1842

1. I sing the might-y pow'r of God, That made the moun-tains rise,
2. I sing the good-ness of the Lord, That filled the earth with food;
3. There's not a plant or flow'r be-low, But makes thy glo - ries known;
That spread the flow - ing seas a-broad, And built the loft - y skies.
He formed the crea - tures with his word, And then pro-nounced them good.
And clouds a - rise and tem-pests blow By or - der from thy throne,
I sing the wis-dom that or-dained The sun to rule the day;
Lord, how thy won-ders are dis-played, Wher-e'er I turn my eye:
While all that bor-rows life from thee Is ev - er in thy care,
The moon shines full at his com-mand, And all the stars o - bey.
If I sur - vey the ground I tread Or gaze up - on the sky!
And ev - 'ry - where that man can be, Thou, God, art pres-ent there.

Alternate tune, Ellacombe, No. 88

29

Morning Has Broken

BUNESSAN 5.5.5.4.D.
Gaelic Melody
Harm. by David Evans, 1927

Eleanor Farjeon, 1931

Unison

1. Morn - ing has bro - ken Like the first morn - ing, Black-bird has
2. Sweet the rain's new fall Sun - lit from heav - en, Like the first
3. Mine is the sun - light! Mine is the morn - ing Born of the

spo - ken Like the first bird. Praise for the sing - ing!
dew - fall On the first grass. Praise for the sweet - ness
one light E - den saw play! Praise with e - la - tion,

Praise for the morn - ing! Praise for them, spring - ing Fresh from the Word!
Of the wet gar - den, Sprung in com - plete - ness Where his feet pass.
Praise ev - ery morn - ing, God's re - cre - a - tion Of the new day!

*All Creatures of Our God and King

Ps. 148
Francis of Assisi, 1225
Tr. William H. Draper, 1926

LASST UNS ERFREUEN L.M. *with Alleluias*
Melody from Geistliche Kirchengesäng, *Cologne, 1623*
Harm. by R. Vaughan Williams, 1906

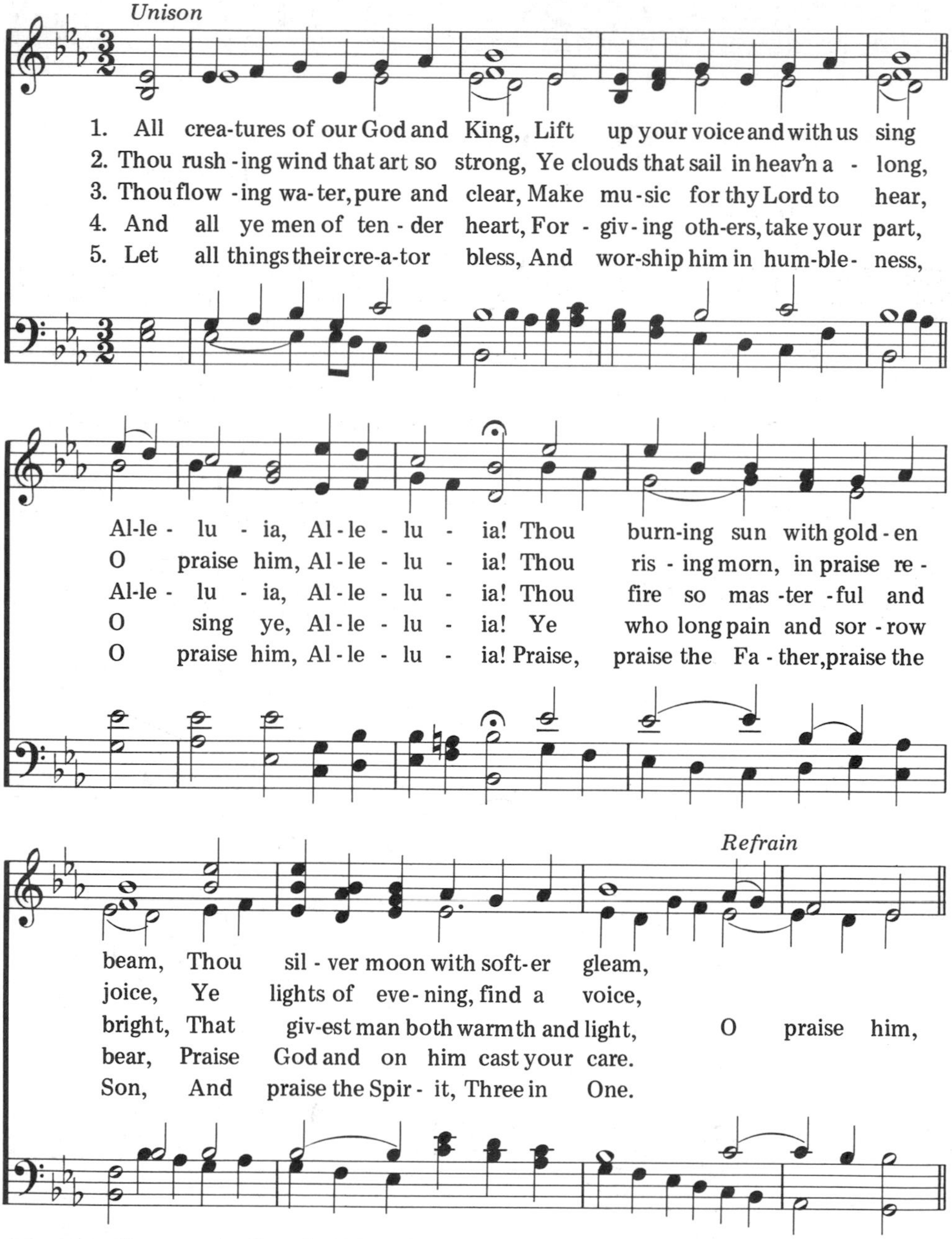

Unison

1. All crea-tures of our God and King, Lift up your voice and with us sing
2. Thou rush - ing wind that art so strong, Ye clouds that sail in heav'n a - long,
3. Thou flow - ing wa- ter, pure and clear, Make mu - sic for thy Lord to hear,
4. And all ye men of ten - der heart, For - giv - ing oth-ers, take your part,
5. Let all things their cre-a-tor bless, And wor-ship him in hum-ble - ness,

Al-le - lu - ia, Al - le - lu - ia! Thou burn-ing sun with gold - en
O praise him, Al - le - lu - ia! Thou ris - ing morn, in praise re -
Al-le - lu - ia, Al - le - lu - ia! Thou fire so mas -ter -ful and
O sing ye, Al - le - lu - ia! Ye who long pain and sor - row
O praise him, Al - le - lu - ia! Praise, praise the Fa - ther, praise the

Refrain

beam, Thou sil - ver moon with soft - er gleam,
joice, Ye lights of eve - ning, find a voice,
bright, That giv-est man both warmth and light, O praise him,
bear, Praise God and on him cast your care.
Son, And praise the Spir - it, Three in One.

A lower setting may be found at No. 1.

O praise him, Al-le - lu - ia, Al-le - lu - ia, Al-le - lu - ia!
God of Concrete
31
Ps. 24:1
MINTERNE 7.7.7.7.7.7.
Richard G. Jones, 1926-
Cyril Taylor, 1969
Unison
1. God of con-crete, God of steel, God of pis - ton and of wheel,
2. Lord of sci - ence, Lord of art, God of map and graph and chart,
3. God whose glo - ry fills the earth, Gave the u - ni - verse its birth,
God of py - lon, God of steam, God of gird-er and of beam,
Lord of phys-ics and re - search, Word of Bi - ble, faith of church,
Loosed the Christ with Eas-ter's might, Saves the world from e-vil's blight,
God of at - om, God of mine, All the world of pow'r is thine.
Lord of se - quence and de - sign, All the world of truth is thine.
Claims man - kind by grace di - vine, All the world of love is thine.

32

*This Is My Father's World

* First Tune

KENTUCKY 93rd S.M.
Ps. 50:10-12
Missouri Harmony
Maltbie D. Babcock, 1901
Harm. by John Ferguson, 1973
1. This is my Fa - ther's world, And to my lis - t'ning ears All na - ture sings, and round me rings The mu - sic of the spheres.
2. This is my Fa - ther's world, I rest me in the thought Of rocks and trees, of skies and seas, His hand the won - ders wrought.
3. This is my Fa - ther's world, The birds their car - ols raise; The morn - ing light, the lil - y white, De - clare their Mak - er's praise.
4. This is my Fa - ther's world; Why should my heart be sad? The Lord is King, let the heav - ens ring; God reigns, let the earth be glad!

This Is My Father's World

Second Tune

TERRA BEATA S.M.D.
Traditional English Melody
Adapted by Franklin L. Sheppard, 1915

Ps. 50:10-12
Maltbie D. Babcock, 1901

1. This is my Fa-ther's world, And to my lis-t'ning ears All
2. This is my Fa-ther's world, The birds their car-ols raise; The
na-ture sings, and round me rings The mu-sic of the spheres.
morn-ing light, the lil-y white, De-clare their Mak-er's praise.
This is my Fa-ther's world; I rest me in the thought Of
This is my Fa-ther's world; Why should my heart be sad? The
rocks and trees, of skies and seas, His hand the won-ders wrought.
Lord is King, let the heav-ens ring; God reigns, let the earth be glad!

34

*For the Beauty of the Earth

DIX 7.7.7.7.7.7.
Abridged from a chorale by Conrad Kocher, 1838

Folliott S. Pierpoint, 1864, alt.

1. For the beau - ty of the earth, For the beau - ty of the skies,
2. For the beau - ty of each hour Of the day and of the night,
3. For the joy of ear and eye, For the heart and mind's de - light,
4. For the joy of hu - man love, Broth-er, sis - ter, par - ent, child,
For the love which from our birth O - ver and a - round us lies,
Hill and vale and tree and flower, Sun and moon and stars of light,
For the mys - tic har - mo - ny Link - ing sense to sound and sight,
Friends on earth, and friends a - bove, For all gen - tle thoughts and mild,
Lord of all, to thee we raise This our hymn of grate-ful praise.

A higher setting may be found at No. 118.

O How Glorious, Full of Wonder

IN BABILONE 8.7.8.7.D.

Ps. 8 | *Traditional Dutch Melody*

Curtis Beach, 1958 | *Arr. by Julius Röntgen, c.1906*

1. O how glo-rious, full of won-der Is thy name o'er all the earth;
2. When we see thy lights of heav-en, Moon and stars, thy power dis-played,
3. Thou hast giv - en man do-min-ion O'er the won-ders of thy hand,
4. O how won-drous, O how glo-rious Is thy name in ev - ery land!

Thou who wrought cre - a - tion's splen-dor, Bring-ing suns and stars to birth!
What is man that thou shouldst love him, Crea-ture that thy hand hath made?
Made him fly with ea - gle pin - ion, Mas-ter o - ver sea and land.
Thou whose pur-pose moves be - fore us Toward the goal that thou hast planned

Rapt in rev-erence we a - dore thee, Mar-veling at thy mys- tic ways.
Child of earth, yet full of yearn-ing, Mix-ture strange of good and ill,
Soar-ing spire and ru - ined cit - y, These our hopes and fail - ures show.
'Tis thy will our hearts are seek -ing, Con-scious of our hu - man need.

Hum-bly now we bow be - fore thee, Lift - ing up our hearts in praise.
From thy ways so of - ten turn-ing, Yet thy love doth seek him still.
Teach us more of hu - man pit - y, That we in thine im - age grow.
Spir - it in our spir- it speak-ing, Make us sons of God in - deed!

An alternate setting may be found at No. 203.

All Beautiful the March of Days

FOREST GREEN C.M.D.
Traditional English Melody
Arr. by R. Vaughan Williams, 1906

Frances W. Wile, 1910

1. All beau - ti - ful the march of days, As sea - sons come and go;
2. O'er white ex - pan - ses spar - kling pure The ra - diant morns un - fold;
3. O thou from whose un - fath - omed law The year in beau - ty flows,

The hand that shaped the rose hath wrought The crys - tal of the snow,
The sol - emn splen - dor of the night Burn bright - er through the cold.
Thy - self the vi - sion pass - ing by In crys - tal and in rose,

Hath sent the hoar - y frost of heav'n, The flow - ing wa - ters sealed,
Life mounts in ev - ery throb - bing vein, Love deep - ens round the hearth,
Day un - to day doth ut - ter speech, And night to night pro - claim,

And laid a si - lent love - li - ness On hill and wood and field.
And clear - er sounds the an - gel hymn, "Good will to men on earth."
In ev - er - chang - ing words of light, The won - der of thy name.

*Before Jehovah's Aweful Throne

First Version

Ps. 100
Isaac Watts, 1719, alt.
Alt. by John Wesley, 1737
WINCHESTER NEW L.M.
Adapted from Musikalisches Handbuch, Hamburg, 1690
1. Be - fore Je - ho - vah's awe - ful throne, Ye nations, bow with sa - cred joy; Know that the Lord is God a - lone; He can cre - ate, and he de - stroy.
2. His sov - ereign power with - out our aid, Made us of clay, and formed us men; And when, like wan - d'ring sheep, we strayed, He brought us to his fold a - gain.
3. We are his peo - ple, we his care, Our souls, and all our mor - tal frame; What last - ing hon - ors shall we rear, Al - might - y Mak - er, to thy name?
4. We'll crowd thy gates with thank - ful songs, High as the heav'ns our voic - es raise; And earth, with her ten thou - sand tongues, Shall fill thy courts with sound - ing praise.
5. Wide as the world is thy com - mand, Vast as e - ter - ni - ty thy love; Firm as a rock thy truth must stand, When roll - ing years shall cease to move.

Before the Lord Jehovah's Throne

Second Version

Ps. 100
Isaac Watts, 1719
Alt. by John Wesley, 1737

DE TAR L.M.
Calvin Hampton, 1973

The melody line should be played as part of the accompaniment. The descant is optional.

Sts. 1, 2, 3, 4
St. 5
stroy.
gain.
name?
praise.
move.
A - - men.

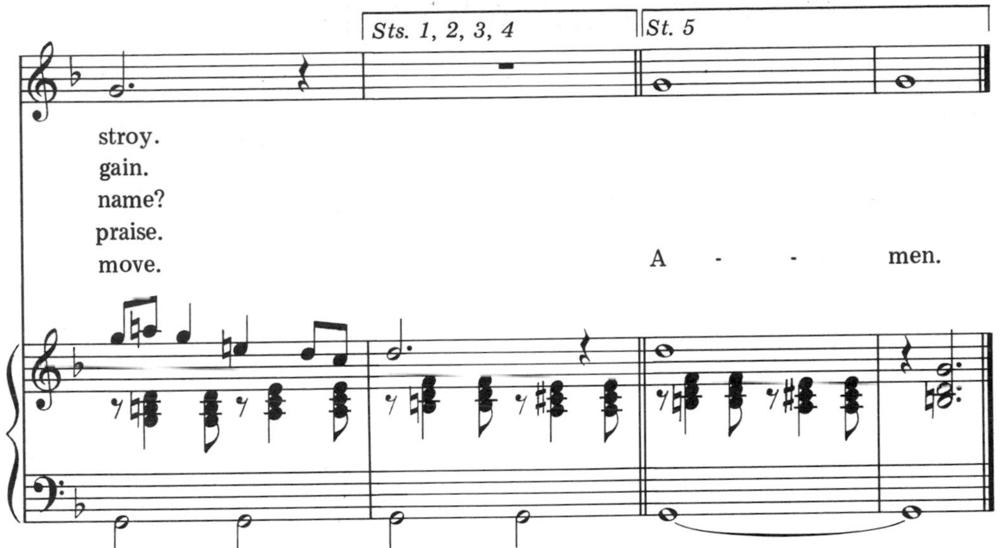

*God Moves in a Mysterious Way 39

John 13:7
William Cowper, 1744

DUNDEE C.M.
Scottish Psalter, *1615*

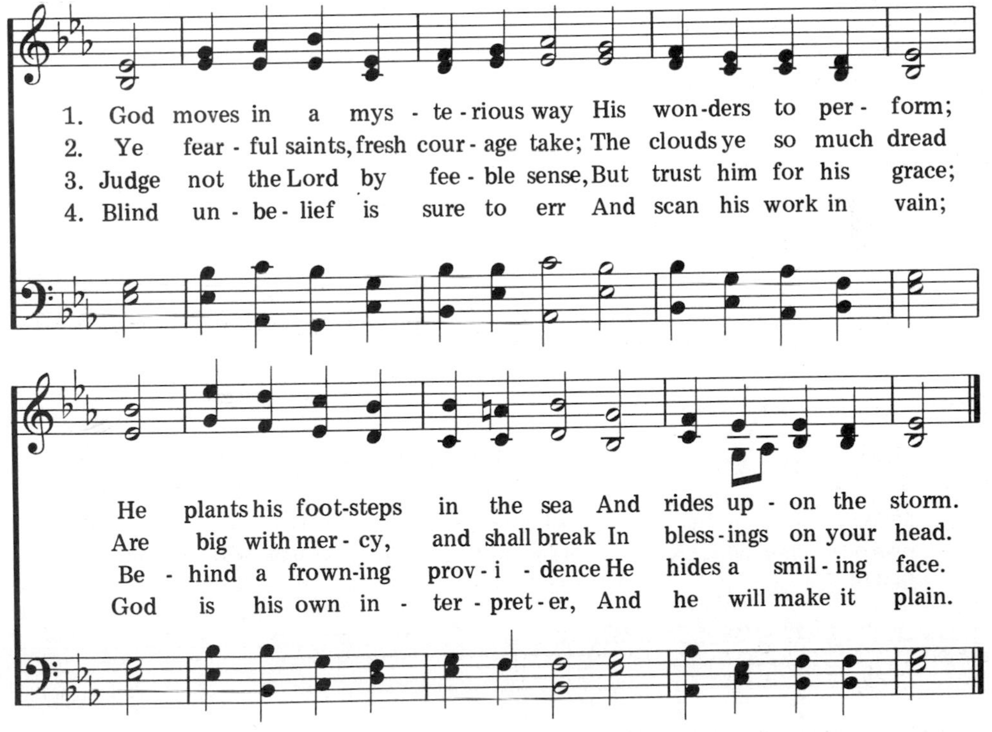

1. God moves in a mys - te - rious way His won-ders to per - form;
2. Ye fear - ful saints, fresh cour - age take; The clouds ye so much dread
3. Judge not the Lord by fee - ble sense, But trust him for his grace;
4. Blind un - be - lief is sure to err And scan his work in vain;
He plants his foot-steps in the sea And rides up - on the storm.
Are big with mer - cy, and shall break In bless - ings on your head.
Be - hind a frown-ing prov - i - dence He hides a smil - ing face.
God is his own in - ter - pret - er, And he will make it plain.

When I, O Lord

O STORE GUD *Irregular with Refrain*

Carl Boberg, 1886 *Swedish Folk Melody*

Tr. Avis B. Christiansen *Arr. by R. J. Hughes, 1956*

1. When I, O Lord, be-hold thy vast cre - a - tion, The won-drous
2. When thou dost speak with might-y roar-ing thun-der, Or through the
3. When thou shalt come, O Lord, in clouds de - scend-ing, To sum-mon

works which thy great hands have wrought, And when I view in
whis - per of the sum - mer breeze, And when I see thee
to thy - self thy wait - ing bride, When I shall dwell with

awe and ad - mi - ra - tion The might-y worlds which thou hast formed from
in the light-ning yon-der, Or in the rain - bow gleam-ing o'er the
thee in bliss un - end-ing, Then, Lord, shall I be ful - ly sat - is -

Refrain

naught.
seas. Then all my heart cries out, my God, to thee, Great is thy
fied!

love, Great is thy love. Then all my heart cries out, my God, to
thee, Great is thy love, Great is thy love!

41

*Let Us with a Gladsome Mind

MONKLAND 7.7.7.7.

Ps. 136
John Milton, 1624

Hymn Tunes of the United Brethren, *1824*
Arr. by John B. Wilkes, 1861

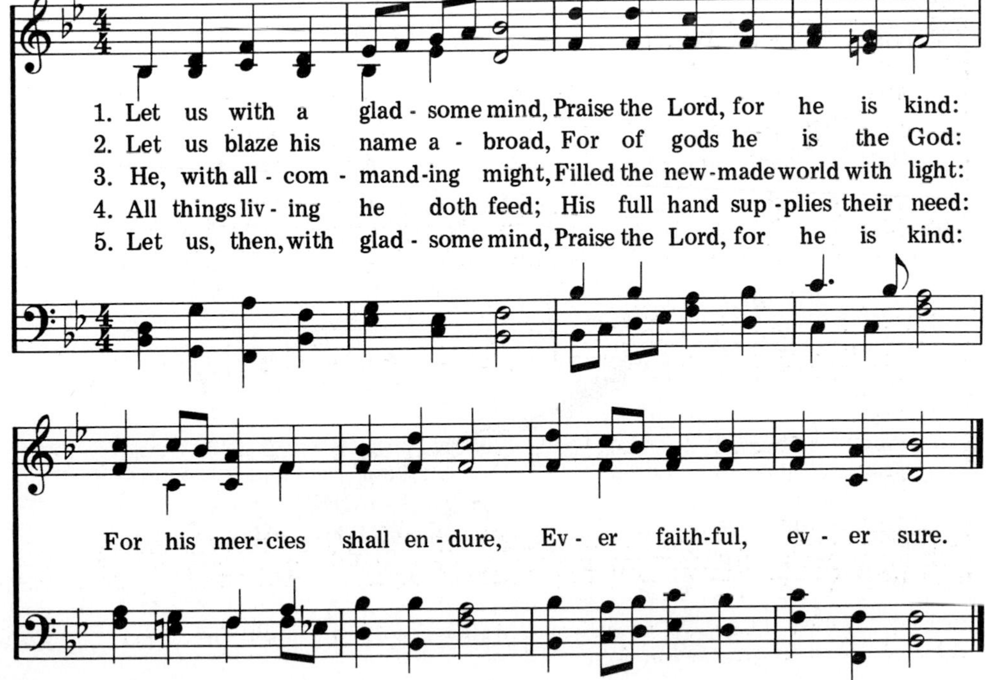
1. Let us with a glad - some mind, Praise the Lord, for he is kind:
2. Let us blaze his name a - broad, For of gods he is the God:
3. He, with all - com - mand-ing might, Filled the new-made world with light:
4. All things liv - ing he doth feed; His full hand sup -plies their need:
5. Let us, then, with glad - some mind, Praise the Lord, for he is kind:
For his mer-cies shall en - dure, Ev - er faith-ful, ev - er sure.

*Come, Ye Thankful People, Come

Matt. 13:29-30 — ST. GEORGE'S WINDSOR 7.7.7.7.D.

Henry Alford, 1844 — *George J. Elvey, 1858*

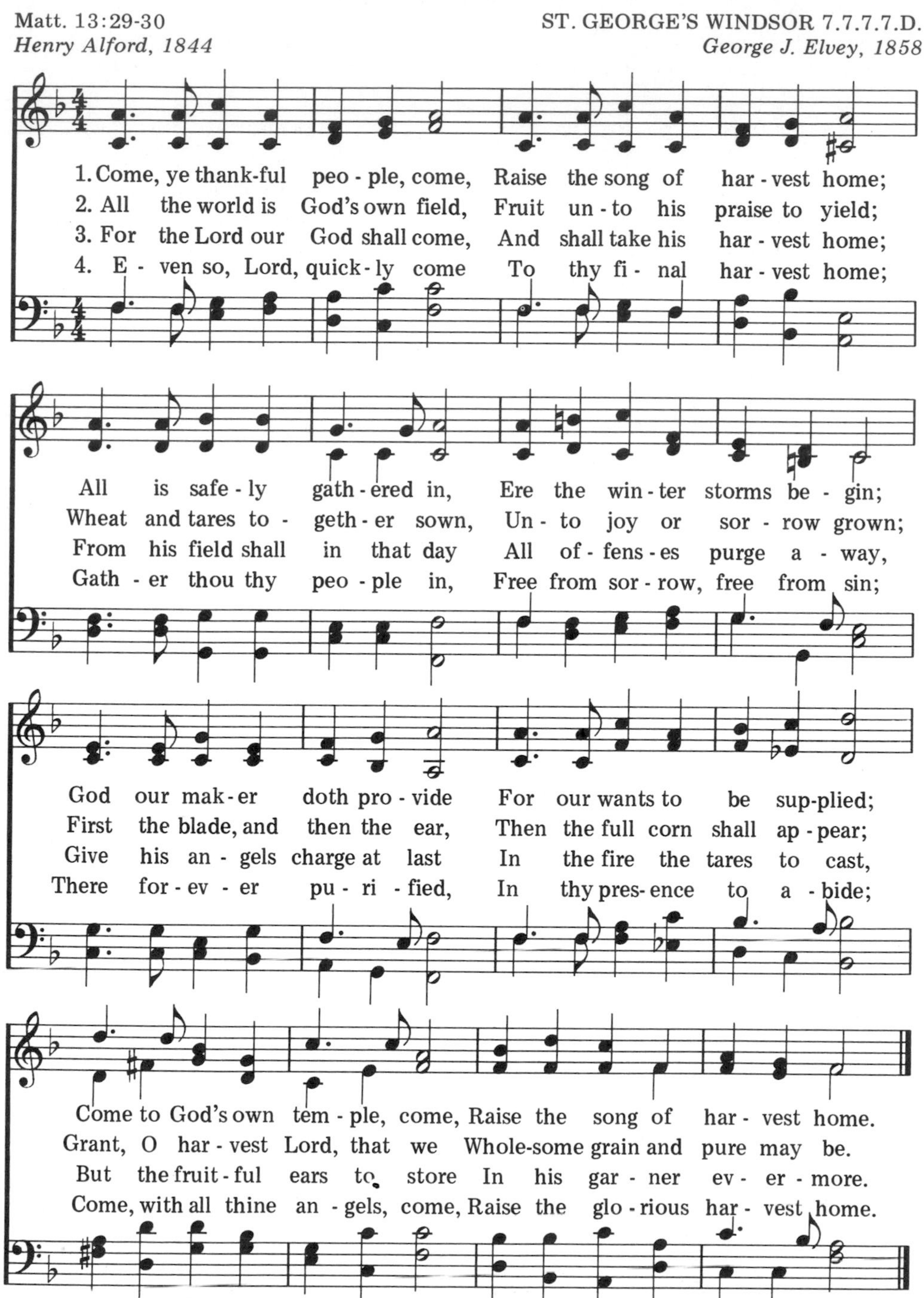
1. Come, ye thank-ful peo - ple, come, Raise the song of har - vest home;
All is safe - ly gath - ered in, Ere the win - ter storms be - gin;
God our mak - er doth pro - vide For our wants to be sup-plied;
Come to God's own tem - ple, come, Raise the song of har - vest home.
2. All the world is God's own field, Fruit un - to his praise to yield;
Wheat and tares to - geth - er sown, Un - to joy or sor - row grown;
First the blade, and then the ear, Then the full corn shall ap - pear;
Grant, O har - vest Lord, that we Whole-some grain and pure may be.
3. For the Lord our God shall come, And shall take his har - vest home;
From his field shall in that day All of - fens - es purge a - way,
Give his an - gels charge at last In the fire the tares to cast,
But the fruit - ful ears to store In his gar - ner ev - er - more.
4. E - ven so, Lord, quick - ly come To thy fi - nal har - vest home;
Gath - er thou thy peo - ple in, Free from sor - row, free from sin;
There for - ev - er pu - ri - fied, In thy pres - ence to a - bide;
Come, with all thine an - gels, come, Raise the glo - rious har - vest home.

43

Come, Ye Thankful People, Come

Thanksgiving Version

Henry Alford, 1844
Anna L. Barbauld, 1743-1825, and others

ST. GEORGE'S WINDSOR 7.7.7.7.D.
George J. Elvey, 1858

1. Come, ye thankful people, come,
Raise the song of harvest home;
All is safely gathered in
Ere the winter storms begin;
God our maker doth provide
For our wants to be supplied;
Come to God's own temple, come,
Raise the song of harvest home.

2. All the blessings of the field,
All the stores the gardens yield,
All the fruits in full supply,
Ripened 'neath the summer sky,
All that spring with bounteous hand
Scatters o'er the smiling land,
All that liberal autumn pours
From her rich o'erflowing stores,

3. These to thee, our God, we owe,
Source whence all our blessings flow;
And for these our souls shall raise
Grateful vows and solemn praise.
Come, then, thankful people, come,
Raise the song of harvest home;
Come to God's own temple, come,
Raise the song of harvest home.

44

The Mountains Rise in Ranges

EARL AVENUE 10.10.10.10.

William Nelson, 1967

Richard Warner, 1968

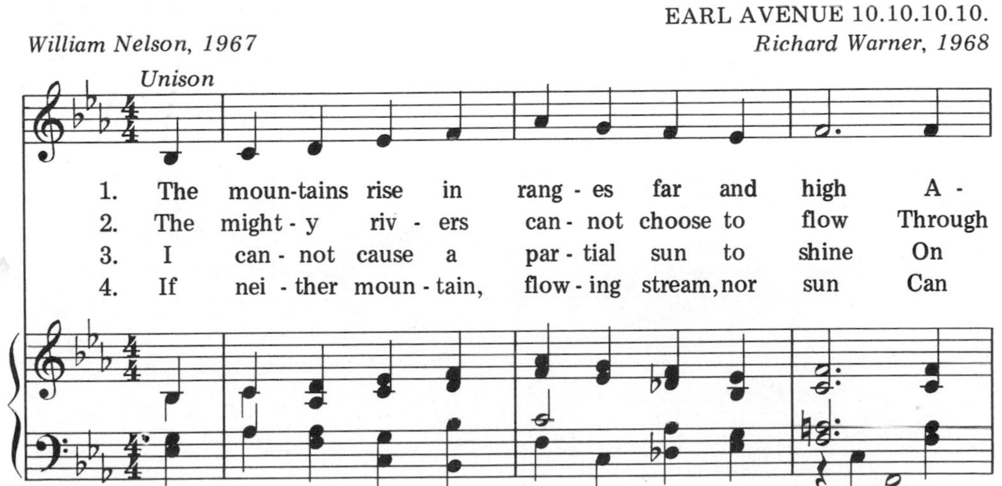
Unison
1. The moun-tains rise in rang - es far and high A -
2. The might - y riv - ers can - not choose to flow Through
3. I can - not cause a par - tial sun to shine On
4. If nei - ther moun - tain, flow - ing stream, nor sun Can

bove the walls men throw a - gainst the sky; I
this land, and through that re - fuse to go; They
those whose col - or is the same as mine, And
choose one peo - ple and an - oth - er shun, Then
can - not bid them stay on bor - der lines, Em -
take the wa - ter from one neigh - bor's rain, And
keep in dark - ness those who should be free To
I, O Lord, must let no bar - rier stand Be -
boss - ing earth the way my will de - fines.
make an - oth - er's de - sert green with grain.
build a bet - ter world a - long with me.
tween me and my broth - er's out - stretched hand.

O Lord of Every Shining Constellation

LOMBARD STREET 11.10.11.10.

Albert F. Bayly, 1950, alt., 1968 *Frederick George Russell, 1925*

Unison
1. O Lord of every shining constellation
2. You, Lord, have made the atom's hidden forces,
3. You, Lord, have stamped your image on your creatures,
4. Great Lord of nature, shaping and renewing,
That wheels in splendor through the midnight sky;
Your laws its mighty energies fulfill;
And, though they mar that image, love them still;
You made us more than nature's sons to be;
Grant us your Spirit's true illumination
Teach us, to whom you give such rich resources,
Lift up our eyes to Christ, that in his features
You help us tread, with grace our souls enduing,
To read the secrets of your work on high.
In all we use, to serve your holy will.
We may discern the beauty of your will.
The road to life and immortality.

46

Creation's Lord, We Give Thee Thanks

RAMWOLD L.M.
William DeWitt Hyde, 1903, alt.
Richard Warner, 1958
1. Cre - a - tion's Lord, we give thee thanks That this thy world is in - com - plete, That bat - tle calls our mar - shaled ranks, That work a - waits our hands and feet.
2. Be - yond the pres - ent sin and shame, Wrong's bit - ter, cru - el, scorch - ing blight, We see the beck - oning vi - sion flame, The bless - ed king - dom of the right.
3. What though the king-dom long de - lay, And still with haugh - ty foes must cope? It gives us that for which to pray, A field for toil and faith and hope.
Unison

47

Praise to the Living God

DIADEMATA S.M.D.

Curtis Beach, 1966 *George J. Elvey, 1868*

1. Praise to the liv - ing God, The Lord of love and light,
2. Praise to the liv - ing God, From whom all things de - rive,
3. Praise to the liv - ing God, Who knows our joy and pain,
4. Praise to the liv - ing God, A - round, with - in, a - bove,
Whose word brought forth the myr - i - ad suns And set the worlds in flight;
Whose Spir - it formed up - on this sphere The first faint seeds of life;
Who shares with us our com-mon life, The sa - cred and pro - fane.
Be - yond the grasp of hu - man mind, But whom we know as love.
Whose in - fi - nite de - sign, Which we but dim - ly see,
Who caused them to e - volve, Un - wit - ting, toward his goal
He toils wher-e'er men toil, In street and mart and mill;
In these tu - mul - tuous days, So full of hope and strife,
Per - vades all na - ture, mak-ing all A cos-mic un - i - ty.
Till man stood up-right on the earth, A liv - ing, think-ing soul.
And deep with-in the heart of man, He leads us for - ward still.
May we bear wit - ness to the Way, O Source and Goal of life.

A lower setting may be found at No. 309.

O Grant Us Light

HESPERUS L.M.

Lawrence Tuttiett, 1864 *Henry Baker, 1854*

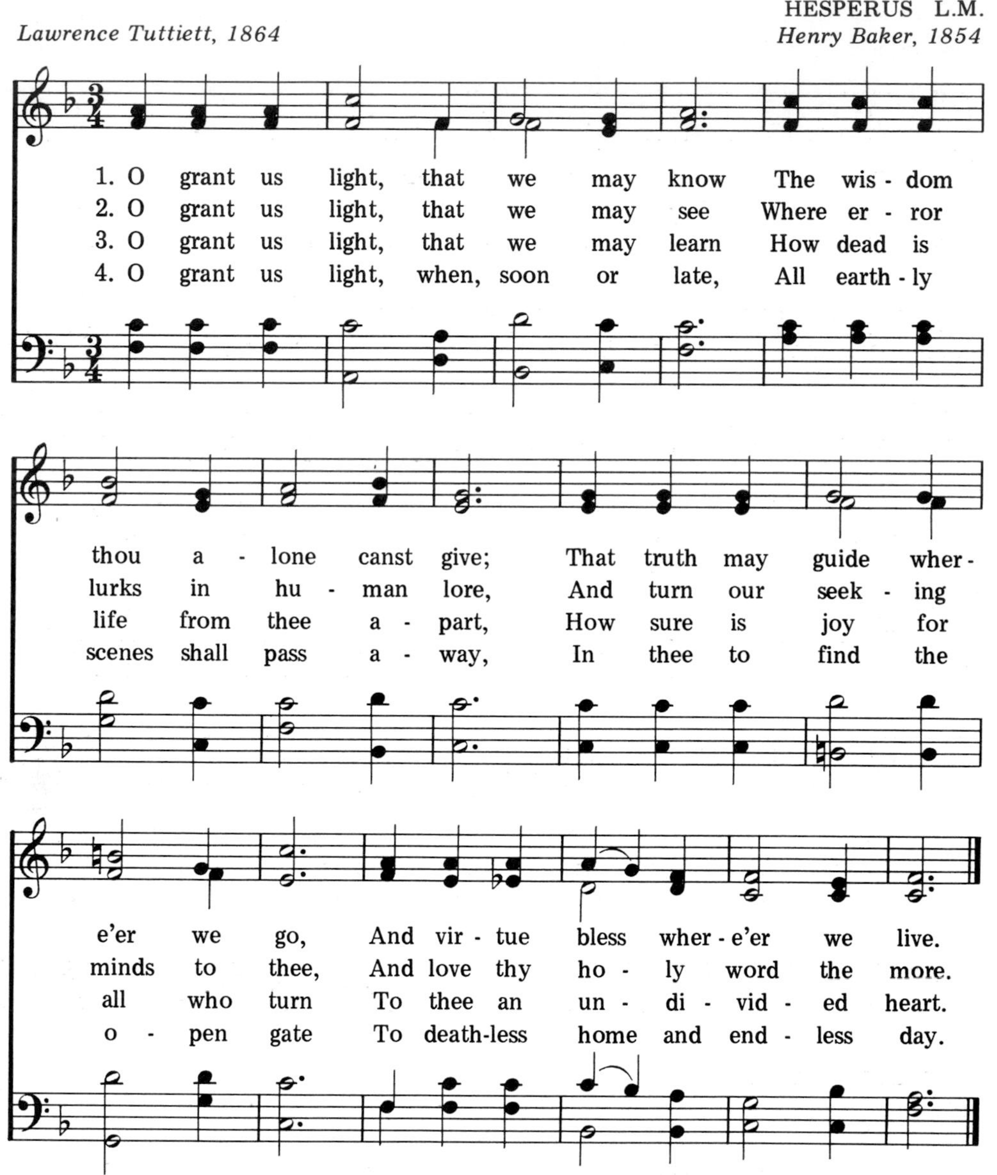
1. O grant us light, that we may know The wis - dom thou a - lone canst give; That truth may guide wher - e'er we go, And vir - tue bless wher - e'er we live.
2. O grant us light, that we may see Where er - ror lurks in hu - man lore, And turn our seek - ing minds to thee, And love thy ho - ly word the more.
3. O grant us light, that we may learn How dead is life from thee a - part, How sure is joy for all who turn To thee an un - di - vid - ed heart.
4. O grant us light, when, soon or late, All earth - ly scenes shall pass a - way, In thee to find the o - pen gate To death-less home and end - less day.

An alternate setting may be found at No. 262.

*The Day Thou Gavest, Lord, Is Ended

COMMANDMENTS 9.8.9.8.

John Ellerton, 1870

Louis Bourgeois, 1543

1. The day thou gav - est, Lord, is end - ed,
2. We thank thee that thy church, un - sleep - ing
3. So be it, Lord; thy throne shall nev - er,
The dark - ness falls at thy be - hest;
While earth rolls on - ward in - to light,
Like earth's proud em - pires, pass a - way;
To thee our morn - ing hymns as - cend - ed,
Through all the world her watch is keep - ing,
Thy king - dom stands and grows for - ev - er,
Thy praise shall sanc - ti - fy our rest.
And rests not now by day or night.
Till all thy crea - tures own thy way.

*The Duteous Day Now Closeth

INNSBRUCK 7.7.6.7.7.8.

Paul Gerhardt, 1647
Para. by Robert S. Bridges, 1899

Attr. to Heinrich Isaak, c.1450-1527
Harm. by Johann Sebastian Bach, 1729

1. The du - teous day now clos - eth, Each flower and tree re - pos - eth, Shade creeps o'er wild and wood. Let us, as night is fall - ing, On God, our Mak - er, call - ing, Give thanks to him, the Giv - er good.
2. Now all the heav'n-ly splen - dor Breaks forth in star - light ten - der From myr - iad worlds un - known, And man, the mar - vel see - ing, For - gets his self - ish be - ing, For joy of beau - ty not his own.
3. A - while his mor - tal blind - ness May miss God's lov - ing - kind - ness, And grope in faith - less strife, But when life's day is o - ver Shall death's fair night dis - cov - er The fields of ev - er - last - ing life.

I Will Sing of the Mercies

Ps. 89:1
Para. by Willard Budnick, 1971

COMMUNE *Irregular*
Willard Budnick, 1971

The feeling of spontaneous joy in this hymn encourages the improvisation of additional words for the lower voices to heighten the musical drive.

sing of the mer-cies of the Lord; For-ev-er I will sing of the mer-cies of the

1.

Lord. I will

2.

sing of the mer-cies of the Lord, Sing of the mer-cies of the Lord.

52

From the Slave Pens of the Delta

OMNI DIE 8.7.8.7.D.

T. Herbert O'Driscoll, 1965, alt. *German Proper Melody, 1625*

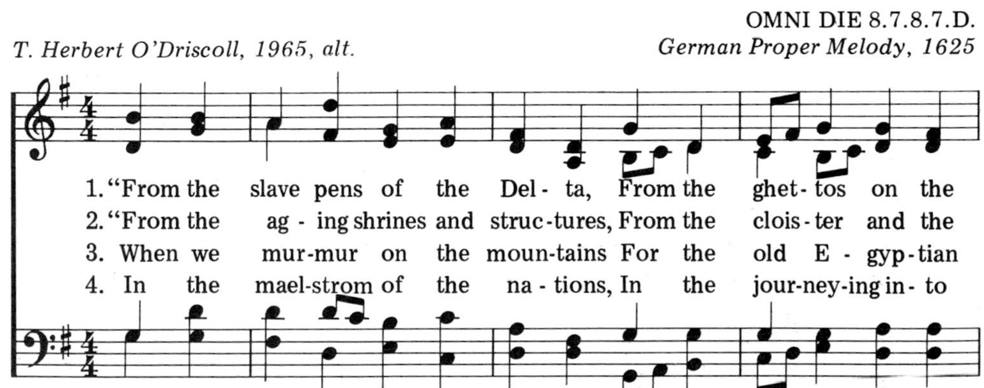
1. "From the slave pens of the Del - ta, From the ghet - tos on the
2. "From the ag - ing shrines and struc - tures, From the clois - ter and the
3. When we mur - mur on the moun - tains For the old E - gyp - tian
4. In the mael - strom of the na - tions, In the jour - ney - ing in - to

Nile, Let my peo - ple seek their free - dom In the
aisle, Let my peo - ple seek their free - dom In the
plains, When we miss our an - cient bond - age And the
space, In the clash of gen - er - a - tions, In the
wil - der - ness a - while": So God spake from out of
wil - der - ness a - while": So the Son of God has
hope, the prom - ise, wanes, Then the rock shall yield its
hun - ger - ing for grace, In man's ag - o - ny and
Si - nai, So he spake and it was done, And his peo - ple
spo - ken, And the storm-clouds are un - furled, For his peo - ple
wa - ter And the man - na fall by night, And with vi - sions
glo - ry, We are called to new - er ways By the Lord of
crossed the wa - ters T'ward the ri - sing of the sun.
must be scat - tered To be ser - vants in the world.
of a fu - ture Shall we march on t'ward the light.
our to - mor - rows And the God of earth's to - days.

53

God Is Love: Let Heaven Adore Him

WEISSE FLAGGEN 8.7.8.7.D.

Timothy Rees, 1874-1939 — Tochter Sion, *Cologne, 1741*

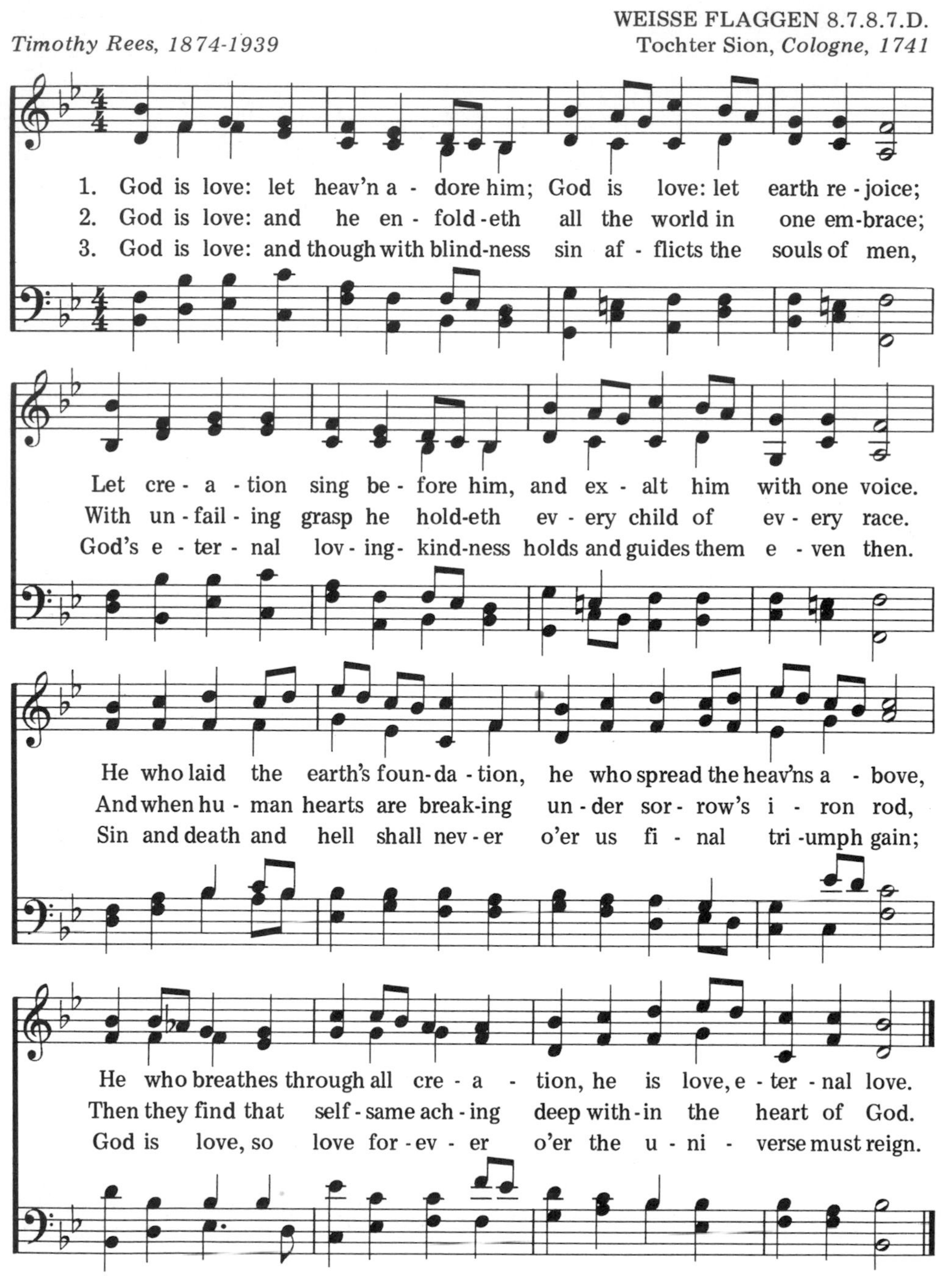
1. God is love: let heav'n a - dore him; God is love: let earth re - joice;
2. God is love: and he en - fold - eth all the world in one em - brace;
3. God is love: and though with blind - ness sin af - flicts the souls of men,
Let cre - a - tion sing be - fore him, and ex - alt him with one voice.
With un - fail - ing grasp he hold - eth ev - ery child of ev - ery race.
God's e - ter - nal lov - ing - kind - ness holds and guides them e - ven then.
He who laid the earth's foun - da - tion, he who spread the heav'ns a - bove,
And when hu - man hearts are break - ing un - der sor - row's i - ron rod,
Sin and death and hell shall nev - er o'er us fi - nal tri - umph gain;
He who breathes through all cre - a - tion, he is love, e - ter - nal love.
Then they find that self - same ach - ing deep with - in the heart of God.
God is love, so love for - ev - er o'er the u - ni - verse must reign.

54

I Sing the Praise of Love Unbounded

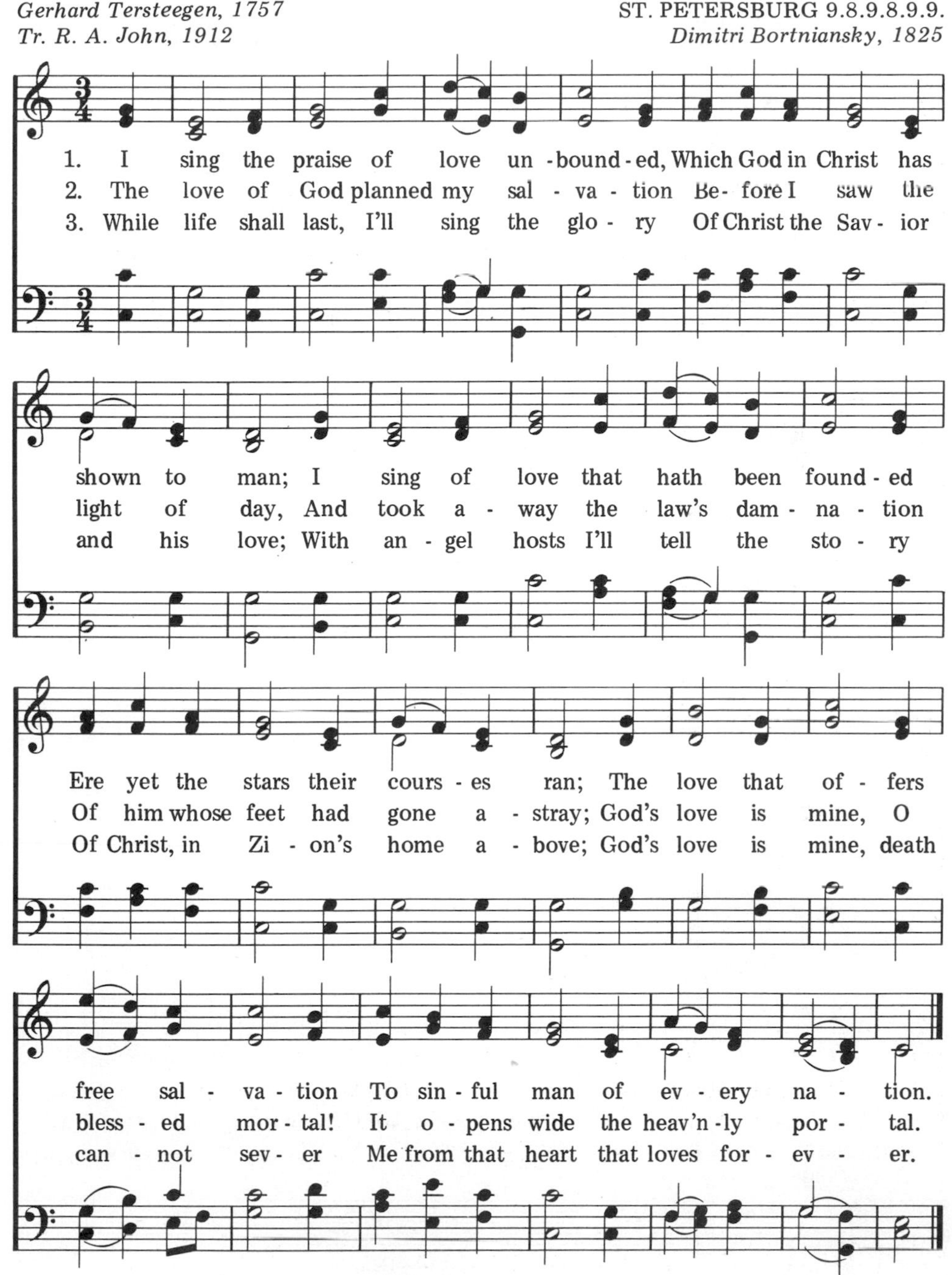

Gerhard Tersteegen, 1757
Tr. R. A. John, 1912
ST. PETERSBURG 9.8.9.8.9.9.
Dimitri Bortniansky, 1825
1. I sing the praise of love un - bound - ed, Which God in Christ has
2. The love of God planned my sal - va - tion Be - fore I saw the
3. While life shall last, I'll sing the glo - ry Of Christ the Sav - ior
shown to man; I sing of love that hath been found - ed
light of day, And took a - way the law's dam - na - tion
and his love; With an - gel hosts I'll tell the sto - ry
Ere yet the stars their cours - es ran; The love that of - fers
Of him whose feet had gone a - stray; God's love is mine, O
Of Christ, in Zi - on's home a - bove; God's love is mine, death
free sal - va - tion To sin - ful man of ev - ery na - tion.
bless - ed mor - tal! It o - pens wide the heav'n - ly por - tal.
can - not sev - er Me from that heart that loves for - ev - er.

55

Comfort, Comfort Ye My People

First Tune

Isa. 40:1-8
Johann Olearius, 1671
Tr. Catherine Winkworth, 1862

PSALM 42 8.7.8.7.7.7.8.8.
Genevan Psalter, *1551*

Comfort, Comfort Ye My People

Second Tune

57

God Is Working His Purpose Out

Hab. 2:14
Arthur C. Ainger, 1894
PURPOSE Irregular
Martin Shaw, 1931
Unison
1. God is work - ing his pur - pose out As year suc -
2. From ut - most east to ut - most west, Wher - e'er man's
3. March we forth in the strength of God With the ban-ner of
4. All we can do is noth - ing worth Un - less God
Octaves to the end
ceeds to year; God is work - ing his
foot hath trod, By the mouth of man - y
Christ un - furled, That the light of the glo - rious
bless-es the deed; Vain - ly we hope for the
pur- pose out, And the time is draw - ing near; Near- er and
mes- sen - gers Goes forth the voice of God; Give ear to
gos- pel of truth May shine through-out the world; Fight we the
har - vest - tide Till God gives life to the seed; Yet near- er and

near - er draws the time, The time that shall sure - ly be,
me, ye con - ti - nents, Ye isles, give ear to me,
fight with sorrow and sin To set their cap - tives free,
near - er draws the time, The time that shall sure - ly be,
When the earth shall be filled with the glo - ry of God
That the earth may be filled with the glo - ry of God
That the earth may be filled with the glo - ry of God
When the earth shall be filled with the glo - ry of God
St. 1, 2, 3
St. 4
As the wa - ters cov - er the sea.
As the wa - ters cov - er the sea.
As the wa - ters cov - er the sea.
As the wa - ters cov - er the sea.

*Judge Eternal, Throned in Splendor

RHUDDLAN 8.7.8.7.8.7.
Traditional Welsh Melody
Henry S. Holland, 1902, alt. *Adapted in* The English Hymnal, *1906*

1. Judge E - ter - nal, throned in splen - dor, Lord of lords and
2. Still the wea - ry folk are pin - ing For the hour that
3. Crown, O God, thine own en - deav - or; Cleave our dark - ness

King of kings, With thy liv - ing fire of judg - ment
brings re - lease; And the cit - y's crowd - ed clan - gor
with thy sword; Feed the faint and hun - gry peo - ples

Purge this land of bit - ter things; So - lace all its
Cries a - loud for sin to cease; And the home-steads
With the rich - ness of thy Word; Cleanse the bod - y

wide do - min - ion With the heal - ing of thy wings.
and the wood - lands Plead in si - lence for their peace.
of this na - tion Through the glo - ry of the Lord.

Thou Judge by Whom Each Empire Fell

NUN FREUT EUCH 8.7.8.7.8.8.7.
Melody by Martin Luther in Klug's Geistliche Lieder, *Wittenberg, 1535*

Percy Dearmer, 1925

1. Thou Judge by whom each em - pire fell, When pride of power o'er - came it,
2. Search, Lord, our spir - its in thy sight, In best and worst re - veal us;
3. Lo, fear - ing nought we come to thee, Though by our fault con - found-ed;

Con - vict us now, if we re - bel, Our na - tion judge, and shame it.
Shed on our souls a blaze of light, And judge, that thou may'st heal us.
Though self - ish, mean, and base we be, Thy jus - tice is un - bound - ed:

In each sharp cri - sis, Lord, ap - pear, For - give, and show our
The pres - ent be our judg - ment day, When all our lack thou
So large, it nought but love re - quires, And, judg - ing, par - dons,

du - ty clear: To serve thee by re - pen - tance.
dost sur - vey: Show us our - selves and save us.
frees, in - spires. De - liv - er us from e - vil!

What Does the Lord Require

Mic. 6:6-8
Albert F. Bayly, 1969

SHARPTHORNE 6.6.6.6.3.3.6.
Erik Routley, 1969

Unison
1. What does the Lord re - quire for praise and of - fer - ing?
2. Rul - ers of men, give ear! should you not jus - tice know?
3. Mas - ters of wealth and trade, all you for whom men toil,
4. Still down the a - ges ring the proph - et's stern com-mands:
5. How shall our life ful - fill God's law so hard and high?
What sac - ri - fice, de - sire, or trib - ute bid you
Will God your plead - ing hear, while crime and cruel - ty
Think not to win God's aid, if lies your com - merce
To mer-chant, work - er, king, he brings God's high de -
Let Christ en - due our will with grace to for - ti -
bring? Do just - ly, Love mer - cy; Walk
grow? Do just - ly, Love mer - cy; Walk
soil. Do just - ly, Love mer - cy; Walk
mands: Do just - ly, Love mer - cy; Walk
fy. Then just - ly, In mer - cy, We'll

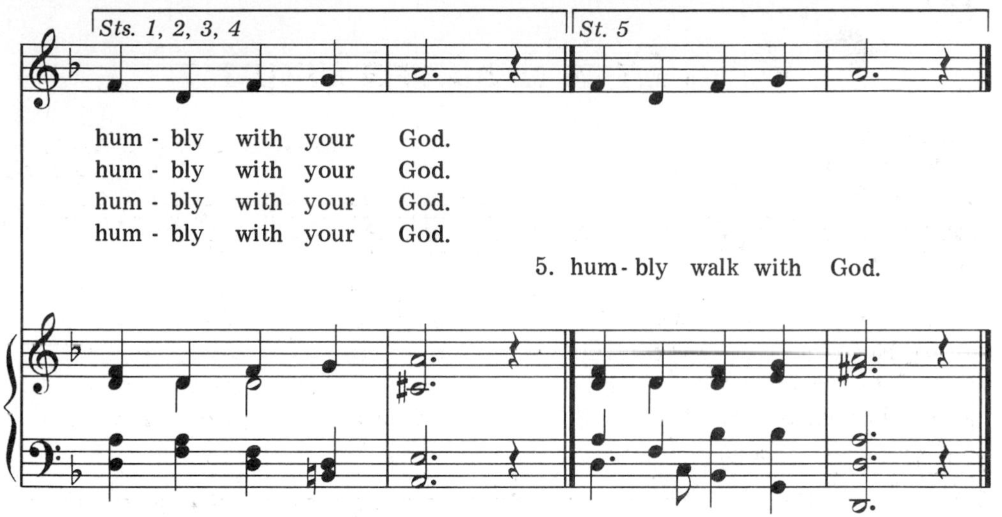
Sts. 1, 2, 3, 4
St. 5
hum - bly with your God.
hum - bly with your God.
hum - bly with your God.
hum - bly with your God.
5. hum- bly walk with God.

61

Mine Eyes Have Seen the Glory

BATTLE HYMN OF THE REPUBLIC *Irregular*

American Camp Meeting Song

Julia Ward Howe, 1861, alt. *Attr. to William Steffe, c.1852*

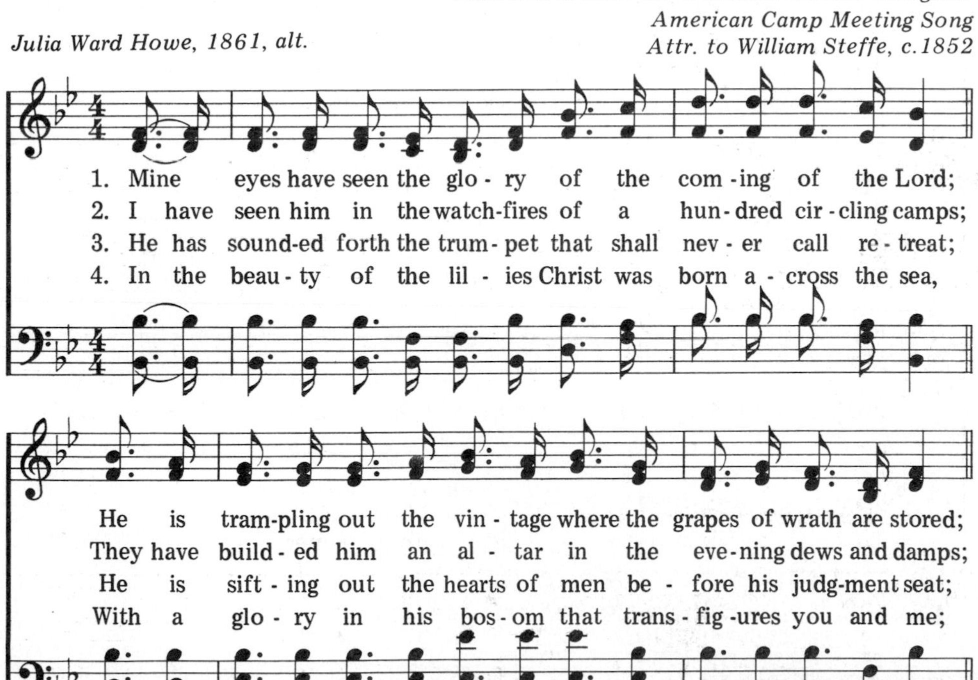
1. Mine eyes have seen the glo - ry of the com - ing of the Lord;
2. I have seen him in the watch-fires of a hun - dred cir - cling camps;
3. He has sound-ed forth the trum - pet that shall nev - er call re - treat;
4. In the beau - ty of the lil - ies Christ was born a - cross the sea,
He is tram-pling out the vin - tage where the grapes of wrath are stored;
They have build - ed him an al - tar in the eve - ning dews and damps;
He is sift - ing out the hearts of men be - fore his judg-ment seat;
With a glo - ry in his bos - om that trans - fig -ures you and me;

He has loosed the fate - ful light - ning of his ter - ri - ble swift sword;
I can read his righ - teous sen - tence by the dim and flar - ing lamps,
O be swift, my soul, to an - swer him; be ju - bi - lant, my feet!
As he died to make men ho - ly, let us die to make men free!
His truth is march - ing on.
His day is march - ing on.
Our God is march - ing on.
While God is march - ing on.
Refrain
Glo - ry! glo - ry! Hal - le - lu - jah! Glo - ry! glo - ry! Hal - le - lu - jah!
Glo - ry! glo - ry! Hal - le - lu - jah! His truth is march - ing on.

God of the Prophets

TOULON 10.10.10.10.

Denis Wortman, 1884 — *Abridged from* Genevan Psalter, *1551*

1. God of the proph - ets, bless the proph-ets' sons:
2. A - noint them proph - ets! Make their ears at - tent
3. A - noint them priests! Strong in - ter - ces - sors they
4. Make them a - pos - tles! Her - alds of thy cross,
E - li - jah's man - tle o'er E - li - sha cast.
To thy di - vin - est speech: their hearts a - wake
For par - don and for char - i - ty and peace!
Forth may they go to tell all realms thy grace;
Each age its sol - emn task may claim but once:
To hu - man need; their lips make el - o - quent
Ah, if with them the world might pass a - stray,
In - spired of thee, may they count all but loss,
Make each one no - bler, strong - er than the last!
To as - sure the right and ev - ery e - vil break.
In - to the dear Christ's life of sac - ri - fice.
And stand at last with joy be - fore thy face.

Turn Back, O Man

OLD 124th 10.10.10.10.10.

Clifford Bax, 1916

Genevan Psalter, *1551*

1. Turn back, O man, for - swear thy fool - ish ways. Old now is
2. Earth might be fair and all men glad and wise. Age aft - er
3. Earth shall be fair, and all her peo - ple one; Nor till that
earth, and none may count her days; Yet thou, her child, whose
age their trag - ic em - pires rise, Built while they dream, and
hour shall God's whole will be done. Now, e - ven now, once
head is crowned with flame, Still wilt not hear thine in - ner God pro-
in that dream-ing weep; Would man but wake from out his haunt - ed
more from earth to sky, Peals forth in joy man's old un - daunt - ed
claim: "Turn back, O man, for - swear thy fool - ish ways!"
sleep, Earth might be fair and all men glad and wise.
cry: "Earth shall be fair, and all her folk be one!"

My Lord, What a Mourning

MOURNING *Irregular*

Negro Spiritual *Negro Melody*

Refrain
My Lord, what a mourn-ing, My Lord, what a mourn-ing,
Fine
My Lord, what a mourn-ing, When the stars be-gin to fall.
1. You'll hear the trum-pet sound,
2. You'll hear the sin-ner mourn, To wake the na-tions un-der-ground,
3. You'll hear the Chris-tian shout,
D.C.
Look-ing to my God's right hand, When the stars be-gin to fall.

This spiritual has its inspiration in the book of Revelation, and the spirit of the text is such that it should be sung mournfully.

65

My Country, 'Tis of Thee

AMERICA 6.6.4.6.6.6.4.

Samuel F. Smith, 1832

Anon. in Thesaurus Musicus, *1740*

1. My coun- try, 'tis of thee, Sweet land of lib - er - ty,
2. My na - tive coun - try, thee, Land of the no - ble free,
3. Let mu - sic swell the breeze, And ring from all the trees
4. Our fa - thers' God, to thee, Au - thor of lib - er - ty,

Of thee I sing; Land where my fa - thers died, Land of the
Thy name I love; I love thy rocks and rills, Thy woods and
Sweet free-dom's song; Let mor - tal tongues a - wake; Let all that
To thee we sing; Long may our land be bright With free - dom's

pil - grims' pride, From ev - ery moun - tain - side Let free - dom ring.
tem - pled hills; My heart with rap - ture thrills Like that a - bove.
breathe par - take; Let rocks their si - lence break; The sound pro - long.
ho - ly light; Pro - tect us by thy might, Great God, our King.

66

God Bless Our Native Land

Sts. 1 and 2, Siegfried A. Mahlmann, 1815
St. 3, William E. Hickson, 1836

AMERICA 6.6.4.6.6.6.4.
Anon. in Thesaurus Musicus, *1740*

1. God bless our na - tive land; Firm may she
2. For her our prayers shall rise To God a -
3. Not for this land a - lone, But be God's
ev - er stand Through storm and night: When the wild
bove the skies; On him we wait; Thou who art
mer - cies shown From shore to shore; And may the
tem - pests rave, Rul - er of wind and wave,
ev - er nigh, Guard - ing with watch - ful eye,
na - tions see That men should broth - ers be,
Do thou our coun - try save By thy great might.
To thee a - loud we cry, "God save the State!"
And form one fam - i - ly The wide world o'er.

*Not Alone for Mighty Empire

GENEVA 8.7.8.7.D.

William Pierson Merrill, 1911 *George Henry Day, 1940*

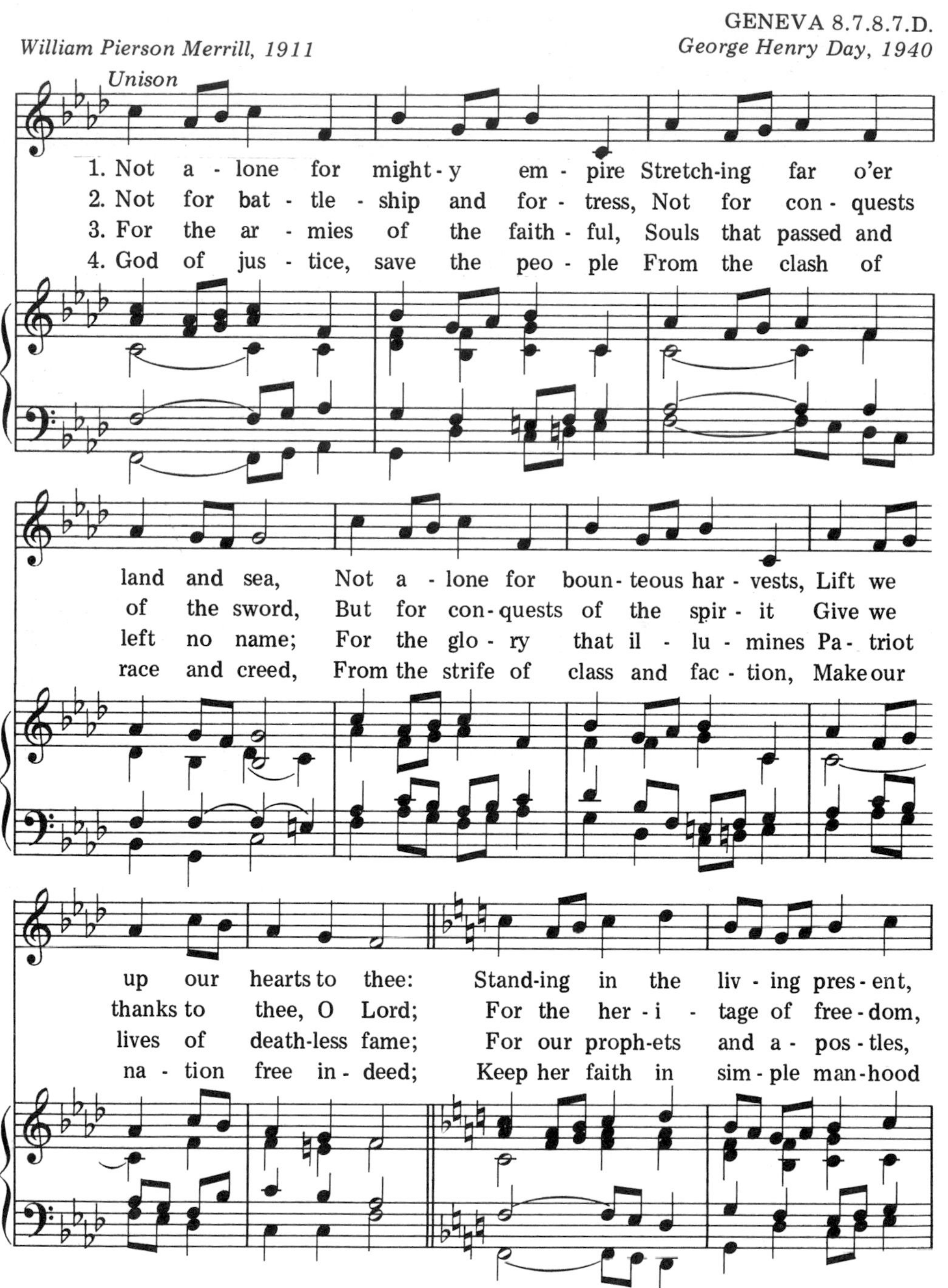

Alternate tune, Hyfrydol, No. 274

Mem - o - ry and hope be - tween, Lord, we would with
For the home, the church, the school, For the o - pen
Loy - al to the liv - ing word, For all he - roes
Strong as when her life be - gan, Till it find its
deep thanks-giv - ing Praise thee most for things un - seen.
door to man - hood In a land the peo - ple rule.
of the spir - it, Give we thanks to thee, O Lord.
full fru - i - tion In the broth - er - hood of man.

O Beautiful for Spacious Skies

MATERNA C.M.D.

Katharine Lee Bates, 1895 *Samuel A. Ward, 1882*

1. O beau - ti - ful for spa-cious skies, For am - ber waves of grain,
2. O beau - ti - ful for pil - grim feet, Whose stern, im - pas-sioned stress
3. O beau - ti - ful for he - roes proved In lib - er - at - ing strife,
4. O beau - ti - ful for pa-triot dream That sees be - yond the years

For pur - ple moun-tain maj - es - ties A - bove the fruit-ed plain!
A thor - ough-fare for free - dom beat A - cross the wil - der - ness!
Who more than self their coun - try loved, And mer - cy more than life!
Thine al - a - bas - ter cit - ies gleam, Un-dimmed by hu - man tears!

A - mer - i - ca! A - mer - i - ca! God shed his grace on thee,
A - mer - i - ca! A - mer - i - ca! God mend thine ev - ery flaw,
A - mer - i - ca! A - mer - i - ca! May God thy gold re - fine,
A - mer - i - ca! A - mer - i - ca! God shed his grace on thee,

And crown thy good with broth - er - hood From sea to shin - ing sea.
Con - firm thy soul in self - con - trol, Thy lib - er - ty in law.
Till all suc - cess be no - ble - ness, And ev - ery gain di - vine.
And crown thy good with broth - er - hood From sea to shin - ing sea.

In Jesus Christ,
the Man of Nazareth,
Our Crucified and Risen Lord,
He Has Come to Us
and Shared Our Common Lot,
Conquering Sin and Death
and Reconciling the World
to Himself

*At the Name of Jesus

Phil. 2:5-11
Caroline M. Noel, 1861

KING'S WESTON 6.5.6.5.D.
R. Vaughan Williams, 1925

Unison
1. At the name of Je - sus Ev - ery knee shall bow,
2. Hum-bled for a sea - son, To re - ceive a name
3. Bore it up tri - um - phant, With its hu - man light,
4. In your hearts en - throne him; There let him sub - due
Ev - ery tongue con - fess him King of glo - ry now;
From the lips of sin - ners, Un - to whom he came.
Through all ranks of crea - tures, To the cen - tral height,
All that is not ho - ly, All that is not true.
'Tis the Fa - ther's plea - sure We should call him Lord,
Faith-ful - ly he bore it, Spot-less to the last,
To the throne of God - head, To the Fa - ther's breast;
Crown him as your cap - tain In temp- ta - tion's hour;
Who from the be - gin - ning Was the might - y Word.
Brought it back vic - to - rious, When from death he passed;
Filled it with the glo - ry Of that per - fect rest.
Let his will en - fold you In its light and power.

All Praise to Thee

ENGELBERG 10.10.10. *with Alleluias*

F. Bland Tucker, 1938 *Charles V. Stanford, 1904*

1. All praise to thee, for thou, O King di - vine, Didst yield the
2. Thou cam'st to us in low - li - ness of thought; By thee the
3. Let this mind be in us which was in thee, Who wast a
4. Let ev - ery tongue con-fess with one ac - cord In heav'n and
glo - ry that of right was thine, That in our dark - ened hearts thy
out - cast and the poor were sought, And by thy death was God's sal -
ser - vant that we might be free, Hum-bling thy - self to death on
earth that Je - sus Christ is Lord; And God the Fa - ther be by
grace might shine.
va - tion wrought.
Cal - va - ry.
all a - dored.
Al - le - lu - ia! Al - le - lu - ia!
Sts. 1, 2, 3
St. 4

Two Adams Walked upon the Earth

Adapted from Irenaeus of Lyon, 2d century
by F. L. Battles, 1969

WILLCOX 8.8.8.10.
Joseph Willcox Jenkins, 1970

Unison
1. Two Ad - ams walked up - on the earth:
2. Two Ad - ams bridg - ing man and God:
3. Two Ad - ams plunged in death's dark sea:
4. Two Ad - ams weighed in Fa - ther's scale:
For woe, for woe,
for joy, for joy.
Two Eves came to fill a dearth: For woe,
Two Eves brought to man a rod: For woe,
Two Eves wept be - side the tree: For woe,
To Eve, fare-well! To Mar - y, hail! Go woe,
for woe; for joy, for joy, for joy!
for woe; for joy, for joy, for joy!
for woe; for joy, for joy, for joy!
go woe; come joy, come joy, come joy!

*Of the Father's Love Begotten

Col. 1:15-17
Aurelius Clemens Prudentius, 348-c.410
Tr. John M. Neale, 1854, St. 1, alt.
Tr. Henry W. Baker, 1859, Sts. 2, 3

DIVINUM MYSTERIUM 8.7.8.7.8.7.7.
13th century Plainsong
Harm. by C. Winfred Douglas, 1940

Unison
1. Of the Fa - ther's love be - got - ten, Ere the worlds be - gan to be,
2. O ye heights of heav'n, a - dore him; An - gel hosts, his prais - es sing;
3. Christ, to thee with God the Fa - ther, And, O Ho - ly Ghost, to thee,
He is Al - pha and O - me - ga, He the source, the end - ing he;
Powers, do-min - ions, bow be - fore him, And ex - tol our God and King;
Hymn and chant and high thanks-giv - ing, And un - wea - ried prais - es be:
Of the things that are, that have been, And that
Let no tongue on earth be si - lent, Ev - ery
Hon - or, glo - ry, and do - min - ion, And e -

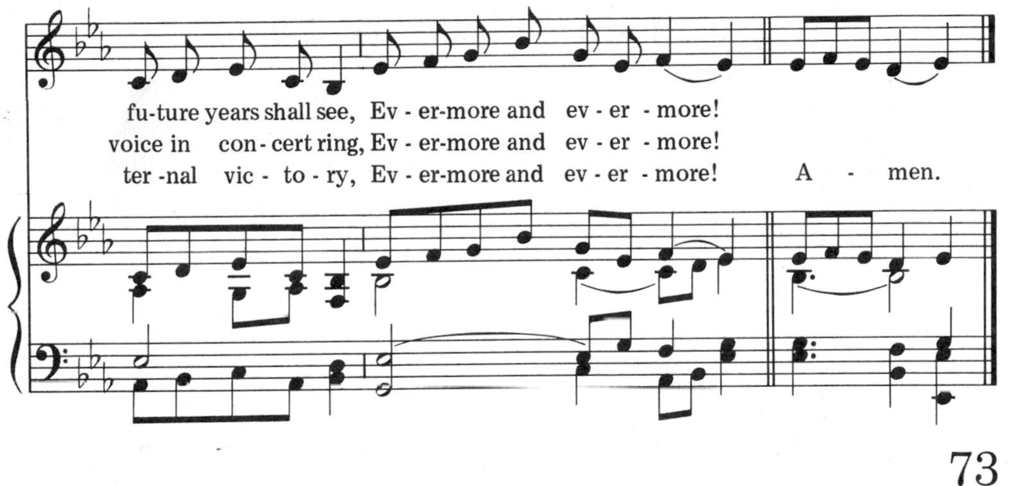

fu-ture years shall see, Ev - er-more and ev - er - more!
voice in con-cert ring, Ev - er-more and ev - er - more!
ter -nal vic - to - ry, Ev - er-more and ev - er - more! A - men.

73

*While Shepherds Watched Their Flocks

Luke 2:8-14
Nahum Tate, 1700

WINCHESTER OLD C.M.
Thomas Este's Whole Book of Psalms, *1592*

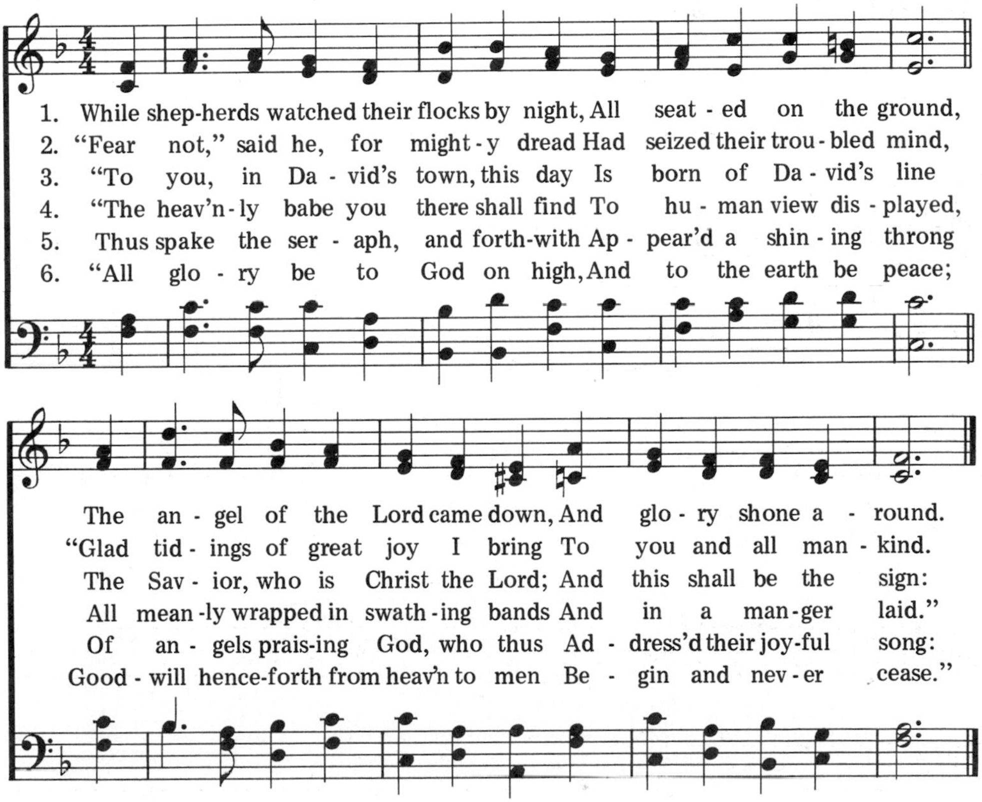

1. While shep-herds watched their flocks by night, All seat - ed on the ground,
2. "Fear not," said he, for might - y dread Had seized their trou - bled mind,
3. "To you, in Da - vid's town, this day Is born of Da - vid's line
4. "The heav'n - ly babe you there shall find To hu - man view dis - played,
5. Thus spake the ser - aph, and forth-with Ap - pear'd a shin - ing throng
6. "All glo - ry be to God on high, And to the earth be peace;

The an - gel of the Lord came down, And glo - ry shone a - round.
"Glad tid - ings of great joy I bring To you and all man - kind.
The Sav - ior, who is Christ the Lord; And this shall be the sign:
All mean -ly wrapped in swath - ing bands And in a man - ger laid."
Of an - gels prais-ing God, who thus Ad - dress'd their joy-ful song:
Good - will hence-forth from heav'n to men Be - gin and nev - er cease."

74

My Song Is Love Unknown

LOVE UNKNOWN 6.6.6.6.4.4.8.

Samuel Crossman, 1664

John Ireland, 1925

1. My song is love un - known, My Sav - ior's love to
2. He came from his blest throne, Sal - va - tion to be -
3. Some - times they strew his way, And his sweet prais - es
4. Why, what hath my Lord done? What makes this rage and
5. Here might I stay and sing, No sto - ry so di -
me, Love to the love - less shown, That they might love - ly
stow; But men made strange, and none The longed-for Christ would
sing; Re - sound - ing all the day Ho - san - nas to their
spite? He made the lame to run, He gave the blind their
vine; Nev - er was love, dear King, Nev - er was grief like
be. O who am I, That for my sake
know. But O, my friend, My friend in - deed,
king. Then "Cru - ci - fy!" Is all their breath,
sight. Sweet in - jur - ies! Yet they at these
thine. This is my friend, In whose sweet praise
My Lord should take Frail flesh and die.
Who at my need His life did spend.
And for his death They thirst and cry.
Them - selves dis - please, And 'gainst him rise.
I all my days Could gai - ly spend.

The King of Glory

PROMISED ONE 12.12.12.12.
Israeli Folk Song
Arr. by John Ferguson, 1973

W. F. Jabusch, 1967

Unison
Refrain
Em
B7
Em
The King of glo - ry comes, the na - tion re - joic - es.
Em
B7
Em
O - pen the gates be - fore him, lift up your voic - es.
G
D7
G
1. Who is the King of glo - ry; how shall we call him?
2. In all of Gal - i - lee, in cit - y or vil - lage,
3. Sing then of Da - vid's Son, our sav - ior and broth - er;
4. He gave his life for us, the pledge of sal - va - tion;
5. He con - quered sin and death; he tru - ly has ris - en.
Repeat refrain after each stanza
G
Em
G
D7
G
He is Em - man - u - el, the prom-ised of a - ges.
He goes a - mong his peo - ple, cur - ing their ill - ness.
In all of Gal - i - lee was nev - er an - oth - er.
He took up - on him - self the sins of the na - tion.
And he will share with us his heav - en - ly vi - sion.

Gradually increasing tempo and changing to higher key(s) can heighten the sense of joy and power in this hymn.

76

*Lift Up Your Heads, Ye Mighty Gates

Ps. 24
Georg Weissel, 1641
Tr. Catherine Winkworth, 1855

TRURO L.M.
Thomas Williams' Psalmodia Evangelica, *1789*

1. Lift up your heads, ye might - y gates; Be - hold the King of glo - ry waits! The King of kings is draw - ing near; The Sav - ior of the world is here.
2. Fling wide the por - tals of your heart; Make it a tem - ple, set a - part From earth - ly use for heav - en's em-ploy, A - dorned with prayer and love and joy.
3. Re - deem - er, come, with us a - bide; Our hearts to thee we o - pen wide; Let us thy in - ner pres - ence feel, Thy grace and love in us re - veal.

A higher setting may be found at No. 20.

Hark! A Thrilling Voice Is Sounding

Latin: 5th century
Tr. Edward Caswall, 1849

MERTON 8.7.8.7.
William Henry Monk, 1850

1. Hark! a thrill - ing voice is sound - ing; "Christ is
2. Wak - ened by the sol - emn warn - ing, Let the
3. Lo, the Lamb, so long ex - pect - ed, Comes with
4. So when next he comes in glo - ry, And the
5. Hon - or, glo - ry, might, and bless - ing Be to
nigh," it seems to say. "Cast a - way the
earth - bound soul a - rise; Christ, her sun, all
par - don down from heav'n; Let us haste, with
world is wrapped in fear, With his mer - cy
God: the Fa - ther, Son, And the ev - er -
works of dark - ness, O ye chil - dren of the day."
ill dis - pel - ling, Shines up - on the morn - ing skies.
tears of sor - row, One and all to be for - given;
may he shield us, And with words of love draw near.
last - ing Spir - it, While e - ter - nal a - ges run.

*Come, Thou Long-expected Jesus

*First Tune

JEFFERSON 8.7.8.7.D.
Southern Harmony, *1835*
Harm. by John Ferguson, 1973

Charles Wesley, 1744, alt.

Unison
1. Come, thou long - ex - pect - ed Je - sus, Born to set thy
2. Born thy peo - ple to de - liv - er, Born a child, and
peo - ple free; From our fears and sins re - lease us; Let us find our
yet a king! Born to reign in us for - ev - er, Now thy gra - cious
rest in thee. Is - rael's strength and con - so - la - tion, Hope of all the
king - dom bring. By thine own e - ter - nal Spir - it Rule in all our

earth thou art; Dear de-sire of ev-'ry na-tion, Joy of ev-'ry long-ing heart.
hearts a - lone; By thine all-suf - fi-cient mer-it Raise us to thy glo-rious throne.

79

Come, Thou Long-expected Jesus

Second Tune

STUTTGART 8.7.8.7.
Melody attr. to Christian F. Witt, 1660-1716
Psalmodia Sacra, *1715*

Charles Wesley, 1744, alt.

1. Come, thou long-ex - pect-ed Je - sus, Born to set thy peo-ple free;
2. Is-rael's strength and con - so - la - tion, Hope of all the earth thou art;
3. Born thy peo-ple to de-liv - er, Born a child, and yet a king!
4. By thine own e - ter - nal Spir-it Rule in all our hearts a - lone;

From our fears and sins re-lease us; Let us find our rest in thee.
Dear de-sire of ev-'ry na-tion, Joy of ev-'ry long-ing heart.
Born to reign in us for-ev-er, Now thy gra-cious king-dom bring.
By thine all-suf - fi-cient mer-it Raise us to thy glo-rious throne.

80

There's a Voice in the Wilderness

Isa. 40:3-11
J. Lewis Milligan, 1930
ASCENSION Irregular
Henry Hugh Bancroft, 1938
Unison
1. There's a voice in the wil - der - ness cry - ing, a call from the ways un - trod: Pre - pare in the de - sert a high - way, a high - way for our God! The
2. O Zi - on, that bring - est good tid - ings, get thee up to the heights and sing! Pro - claim to a des - o - late peo - ple the com - ing of their King. Like the
3. But the word of our God en - dur - eth, the arm of the Lord is strong; He stands in the midst of na - tions, and he will right the wrong. He shall

val - leys shall be ex - alt - ed, the loft - y hills brought
flowers of the field they per - ish, the works of men de -
feed his flock like a shep - herd, and fold the lambs to his
low: make straight all the crook - ed pla - ces
cay, the power and pomp of na - tions
breast: in pas - tures of peace he'll lead them,
where the Lord our God may go!
shall pass like a dream a - way.
and give to the wea - ry rest.

81

*Sleepers, Wake

Matt. 25:1-13
Philipp Nicolai, 1597
Tr. Jay Macpherson, 1970

WACHET AUF 8.9.8.8.9.8.6.6.4.8.8.
Melody by Philipp Nicolai, 1597
Harm. by Johann Sebastian Bach, 1731

1. "Sleep-ers, wake!" the watch are call - ing, Their notes from Zi - on's
2. Zi - on hears the watch-men sing - ing, Her heart with - in for
3. Let all crea - tures sound thy prais - es, Now earth her voice with
watch-tower fall - ing: "A - wake, a - wake, Je - ru - sa - lem!
joy is spring - ing, She wakes, she speeds with glad sur - prise.
heav - en rais - es, With harps' and cym - bals' joy - ful tone.
Mid-night comes, no long - er slum - ber, Nor let dull sleep your
For her Lord comes down all glo - rious, In grace most strong, in
Gates of pearl swing wide be - fore us, Thy guests who join that
sens - es cum - ber. Wise vir - gins, haste, or do you dream?
truth vic - to - rious, Her light is come, her star doth rise,
bless - ed cho - rus Of an - gels that sur - round thy throne.

The bride-groom draw-eth near! A - rise, your lamps show clear.
Wel - come! thou wor-thy Crown, Lord Je - sus, God's own Son,
No eye hath seen, nor ear Was yet so blest to hear
Hal - le - lu - jah! Your - selves ar - ray this mar - riage day
Ho - san - na! We join the throng that streams a - long
Such re - joic- ing! Hence - forth may we e - ter - nal - ly
To meet the bride - groom on his way."
And fills the ban - quet hall with song.
Sing hal - le - lu - jahs un - to thee.

Hark, the Glad Sound

Isa. 61:1
Philip Doddridge, 1735
LOBT GOTT IHR CHRISTEN 8.6.8.6.6.
Melody by Nicholaus Hermann, 1554
1. Hark, the glad sound, the Sav - ior comes, The
2. He comes the pris - 'ners to re - lease, In
3. He comes, the bro - ken heart to bind, The
4. Our glad ho - san - nas, Prince of peace, Thy
Sav - ior prom - ised long: Let ev - ery heart pre -
Sa - tan's bond - age held: The gates of brass be -
bleed - ing soul to cure, And would with trea - sures
wel - come shall pro - claim; And heav'n's e - ter - nal
pare a throne, And ev - ery voice a
fore him burst, The i - ron fet - ters
of his grace En - rich the hum - ble
arch - es ring With thy be - lov - ed
song, And ev - ery voice a song.
yield, The i - ron fet - ters yield.
poor, En - rich the hum - ble poor.
name, With thy be - lov - ed name.

83

*Let All Mortal Flesh Keep Silence

Liturgy of St. James of Jerusalem, 5th century
Tr. Gerard Moultrie, 1864

PICARDY 8.7.8.7.8.7.
Traditional French Carol

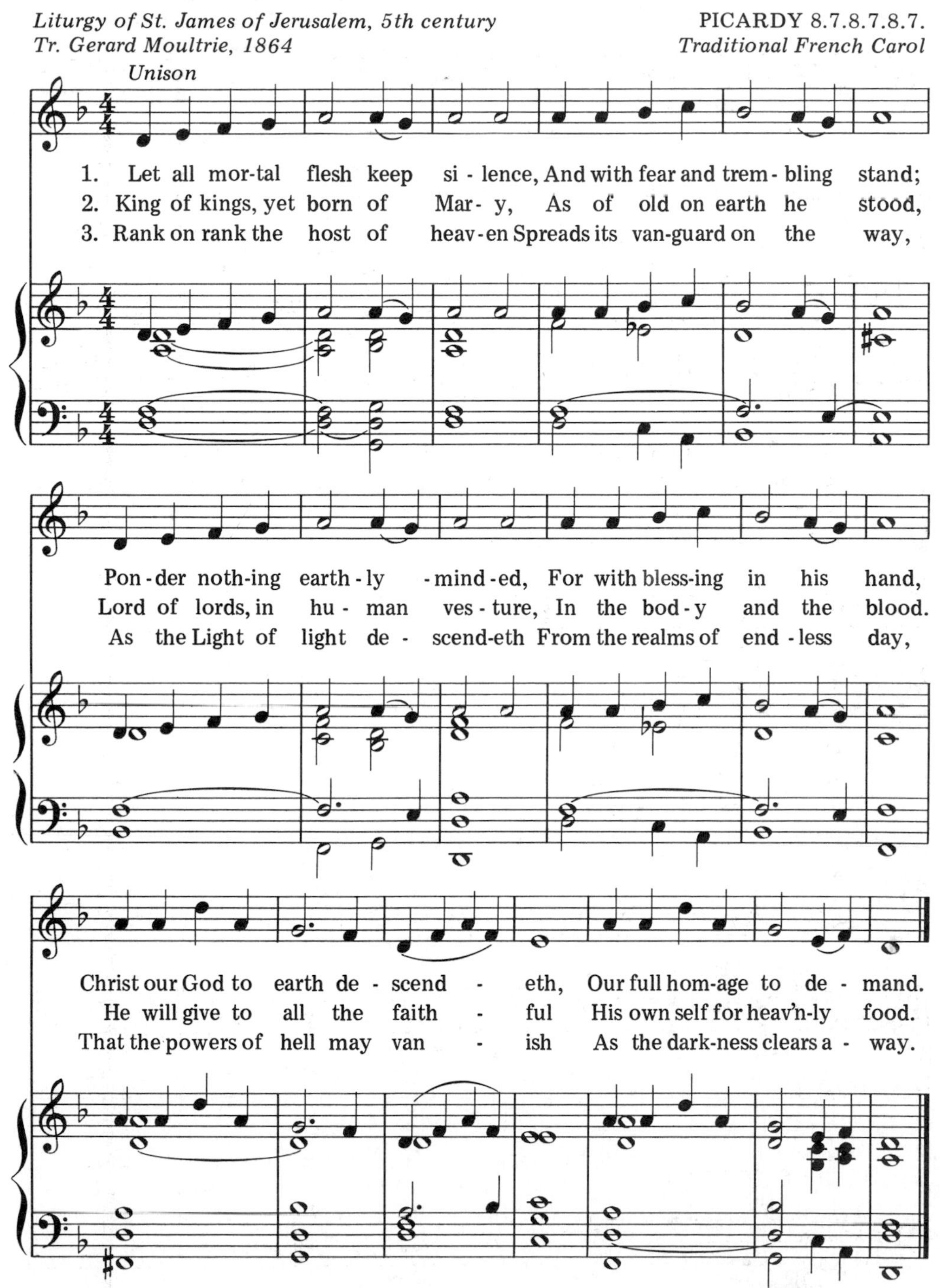
Unison
1. Let all mor-tal flesh keep si - lence, And with fear and trem - bling stand;
2. King of kings, yet born of Mar- y, As of old on earth he stood,
3. Rank on rank the host of heav-en Spreads its van-guard on the way,
Pon - der noth-ing earth - ly - mind - ed, For with bless-ing in his hand,
Lord of lords, in hu - man ves - ture, In the bod - y and the blood.
As the Light of light de - scend-eth From the realms of end - less day,
Christ our God to earth de - scend - eth, Our full hom-age to de - mand.
He will give to all the faith - ful His own self for heav'n-ly food.
That the powers of hell may van - ish As the dark-ness clears a - way.

84

*On Jordan's Bank

Isa. 40:3-5; Luke 2:4
Charles Coffin, 1736
Tr. John Chandler, 1837, alt.

WINCHESTER NEW L.M.
Musikalisches Handbuch, *Hamburg, 1690*

1. On Jor - dan's bank the Bap - tist's cry An -
2. Then cleansed be ev - ery breast from sin; Make
3. For thou art our sal - va - tion, Lord, Our
4. To heal the sick stretch out thine hand, And
5. All praise, e - ter - nal Son, to thee, Whose

nounc-es that the Lord is nigh; A - wake and hear - ken,
straight the way of God with - in, And let each heart pre -
ref - uge, and our great re - ward: With - out thy grace we
bid the fall - en sin - ner stand; Shine forth, and let thy
ad - vent doth thy peo - ple free; Whom with the fa - ther

for he brings Glad tid - ings of the King of kings!
pare a home Where such a might - y guest may come.
waste a - way Like flowers that with - er and de - cay.
light re - store Earth's own true love - li - ness once more.
we a - dore And Ho - ly Spir - it ev - er - more.

*Watchman, Tell Us of the Night

Isa. 21:11-12
John Bowring, 1825

ABERYSTWYTH 7.7.7.7.D.
Joseph Parry, 1879

1. Watch-man, tell us of the night, What its signs of prom-ise are.
2. Watch-man, tell us of the night, High-er yet that star as-cends.
3. Watch-man, tell us of the night, For the morn-ing seems to dawn.
Trav-'ler, o'er yon moun-tain's height, See that glo-ry-beam-ing star.
Trav-'ler, bless-ed-ness and light, Peace and truth its course por-tends.
Trav-'ler, dark-ness takes its flight, Doubt and ter-ror are with-drawn.
Watch-man, does its beau-teous ray Aught of joy or hope fore-tell?
Watch-man, will its beams a-lone Gild the spot that gave them birth?
Watch-man, let thy wan-d'rings cease; Hie thee to thy qui-et home.
Trav-eler, yes; it brings the day, Prom-ised day of Is-ra-el.
Trav-eler, a-ges are its own; See, it bursts o'er all the earth.
Trav-eler, lo, the Prince of peace, Lo, the Son of God is come.

86

*O Come, O Come, Emmanuel

Psalteriolum Cantionum Catholicarum, *1710*
Tr. John M. Neale, 1851, Sts. 1, 2, alt.
Tr. Henry S. Coffin, 1916, Sts. 3, 4

VENI EMMANUEL 8.8.8.8.8.8.
Adapted from Plainsong
Thomas Helmore, 1854

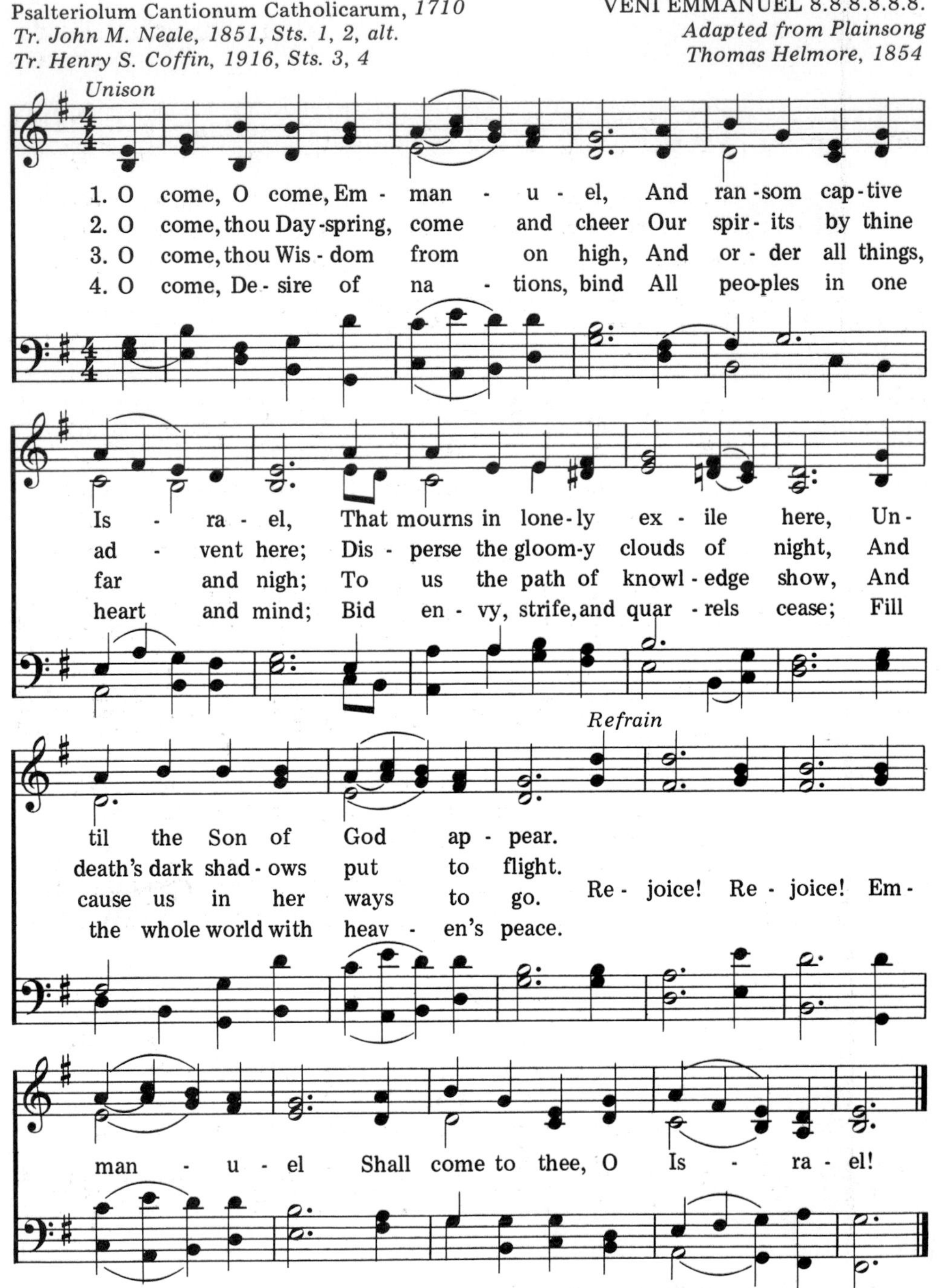
Unison
1. O come, O come, Em - man - u - el, And ran - som cap - tive
2. O come, thou Day - spring, come and cheer Our spir - its by thine
3. O come, thou Wis - dom from on high, And or - der all things,
4. O come, De - sire of na - tions, bind All peo-ples in one
Is - ra - el, That mourns in lone - ly ex - ile here, Un -
ad - vent here; Dis - perse the gloom - y clouds of night, And
far and nigh; To us the path of knowl - edge show, And
heart and mind; Bid en - vy, strife, and quar - rels cease; Fill
Refrain
til the Son of God ap - pear.
death's dark shad - ows put to flight.
cause us in her ways to go.
the whole world with heav - en's peace.
Re - joice! Re - joice! Em -
man - u - el Shall come to thee, O Is - ra - el!

87

Rejoice, Rejoice, Believers

Matt. 25:1-13
Laurentius Laurenti, 1700
Tr. Sarah B. Findlater, 1854
LANCASHIRE 7.6.7.6.D.
Henry Smart, 1836
1. Re - joice, re - joice, be - liev - ers, And let your light ap - pear;
2. See that your lamps are burn - ing; Re - plen - ish them with oil,
3. Our hope and ex - pec - ta - tion, O Je - sus, now ap - pear!
The eve - ning is ad - van - cing, And dark - er night is near:
And wait for your sal - va - tion The end of earth - ly toil.
A - rise, thou Sun so longed for, O'er this be - night - ed sphere!
The Bride - groom is a - ris - ing, And soon he draw - eth nigh;
The watch - ers on the moun - tain Pro - claim the Bride-groom near,
With hearts and hands up - lift - ed, We plead, O Lord, to see
Up, pray and watch and wres - tle: At mid-night comes the cry.
Go meet him as he com - eth, With al - le - lu - ias clear.
The day of earth's re - demp - tion That brings us un - to thee.

A lower setting may be found at No. 231.

*Hail to the Lord's Anointed

Ps. 72
James Montgomery, 1821

ELLACOMBE C.M.D.
Gesangbuch, *Wirtemberg, 1784*

1. Hail to the Lord's a - noint - ed, Great Da - vid's great - er Son!
2. He shall come down like show - ers Up - on the fruit - ful earth,
3. Kings shall bow down be - fore him And gold and in - cense bring;
Hail, in the time ap - point - ed, His reign on earth be - gun!
And joy and hope, like flow - ers, Spring in his path to birth.
All na - tions shall a - dore him, His praise all peo - ples sing;
He comes to break op - pres - sion, To set the cap - tive free,
Be - fore him on the moun - tains Shall peace, the her - ald, go,
To him shall prayer un - ceas - ing And dai - ly vows as - cend,
To take a - way trans - gres - sion, And rule in eq - ui - ty.
And righ - teous-ness, in foun - tains, From hill to val - ley flow.
His king - dom still in - creas - ing, A king - dom with - out end.

*O Come, All Ye Faithful

Latin: John F. Wade, 1751
Tr. Frederick Oakeley, 1841, and others

ADESTE FIDELES *Irregular*
John F. Wade's Cantus Diversi, *1751*

1. O come, all ye faith - ful, joy - ful and tri - um - phant, O come ye, O come ye to Beth - le - hem; Come and be - hold him, born the King of an - gels;
2. Sing, choirs of an - gels, sing in ex - ul - ta - tion, Sing, all ye cit - i - zens of heaven a - bove! Glo - ry to God, all glo - ry in the high - est;
3. Yea, Lord, we greet thee, born this hap - py morn - ing, Je - sus, to thee be all glo - ry given; Word of the Fa - ther, now in flesh ap - pear - ing;

O come, let us a - dore him, O come, let us a - dore him, O come, let us a - dore him, Christ, the Lord!

*Angels We Have Heard on High

GLORIA 7.7.7.7. *with Refrain*
French Carol Melody

Traditional French Carol

1. An - gels we have heard on high Sweet - ly sing - ing o'er the plains,
2. Shep-herds, why this ju - bi - lee? Why your joy - ous strains pro - long?
3. Come to Beth- le - hem and see Him whose birth the an- gels sing;

And the moun-tains in re - ply Ech - o - ing their joy- ous strains.
What the glad - some ti - dings be Which in - spire your heav'n-ly song?
Come, a - dore on bend - ed knee Christ, the Lord, the new-born King.

Glo - - - - - - - - - ri - a

in ex - cel - sis De - o, Glo - - - - - -

*Angels, from the Realms of Glory 91

REGENT SQUARE 8.7.8.7.8.7.

James Montgomery, 1816 *Henry T. Smart, 1867*

1. An- gels, from the realms of glo - ry, Wing your flight o'er all the earth;
2. Shep-herds, in the fields a - bid- ing, Watch-ing o'er your flocks by night,
3. Sa - ges, leave your con - tem - pla - tions, Bright - er vi - sions beam a - far;
4. Though an in - fant now we view him, He shall fill his Fa-ther's throne,
5. All cre - a - tion, join in prais-ing God, the Fa-ther, Spir - it, Son,

Ye who sang cre - a - tion's sto - ry, Now pro - claim Mes - si - ah's birth:
God with man is now re - sid - ing, Yon-der shines the in - fant light:
Seek the great De - sire of na - tions, Ye have seen his na - tal star:
Ga - ther all the na - tions to him; Ev - ery knee shall then bow down:
Ev - er - more your voic - es rais - ing, To the eter - nal Three in One:

Come and wor - ship, come and wor - ship, Wor - ship Christ, the new-born King.

92

*Good Christian Men, Rejoice

German-Latin Carol, 14th century
Para. by John M. Neale, 1853

IN DULCI JUBILO *Irregular*
German Melody, 14th century

1. Good Chris-tian men, re - joice, With heart and soul and voice;
2. Good Chris-tian men, re - joice, With heart and soul and voice;
3. Good Chris-tian men, re - joice, With heart and soul and voice;
Give ye heed to what we say: Je - sus Christ is born to - day;
Now ye hear of end - less bliss; Je - sus Christ was born for this!
Now ye need not fear the grave; Je - sus Christ was born to save!
Ox and ass be - fore him bow, And he is in the man - ger now.
He hath oped the heav'n-ly door, And man is bless - ed ev - er - more.
Calls you one and calls you all, To gain his ev - er - last - ing hall.
Christ is born to - day! Christ is born to - day!
Christ was born for this! Christ was born for this!
Christ was born to save! Christ was born to save!

*Away in a Manger

CRADLE SONG 11.11.11.11.
William J. Kirkpatrick, 1838-1921
Harm. by John Ferguson, 1972

Anon. American Carol, c.1884

Unison

1. A - way in a man-ger, no crib for a bed, The
2. The cat - tle are low - ing, the ba - by a - wakes, But

lit - tle Lord Je - sus laid down his sweet head. The
lit - tle Lord Je - sus no cry - ing he makes. I

stars in the bright sky looked down where he lay, The
love thee, Lord Je - sus! Look down from the sky, And

lit - tle Lord Je - sus, a - sleep on the hay.
stay by my side un - til morn - ing is nigh.

94

*Hark! The Herald Angels Sing

MENDELSSOHN 7.7.7.7.D. *with Refrain*
Felix Mendelssohn, 1840
Charles Wesley, 1739, alt. — *Arr. by William H. Cummings, 1856*

1. Hark! the her - ald an - gels sing, "Glo - ry to the new - born King;
2. Christ, by high - est heav'n a - dored; Christ, the ev - er - last - ing Lord!
3. Hail the heav'n born Prince of peace! Hail the Sun of righ - teous - ness!

Peace on earth, and mer - cy mild, God and sin - ners rec - on - ciled!"
Late in time be - hold him come, Off - spring of the Vir - gin's womb.
Light and life to all he brings, Risen with heal - ing in his wings,

Joy - ful, all ye na - tions, rise, Join the tri - umph of the skies;
Veiled in flesh the God - head see; Hail the in - car - nate De - i - ty,
Mild he lays his glo - ry by, Born that man no more may die,

With the an - gel - ic host pro - claim, "Christ is born in Beth - le - hem!"
Pleased as man with men to dwell, Je - sus, our Em - man - u - el.
Born to raise the sons of earth, Born to give them sec - ond birth.

Hark! the her- ald an - gels sing, "Glo - ry to the new - born King!"

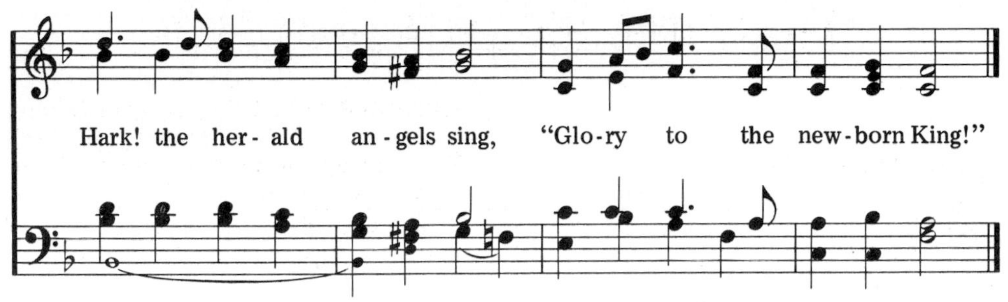

95

*Silent Night, Holy Night

Joseph Mohr, 1818
Tr. John F. Young, c.1863

STILLE NACHT *Irregular*
Franz Gruber, 1818

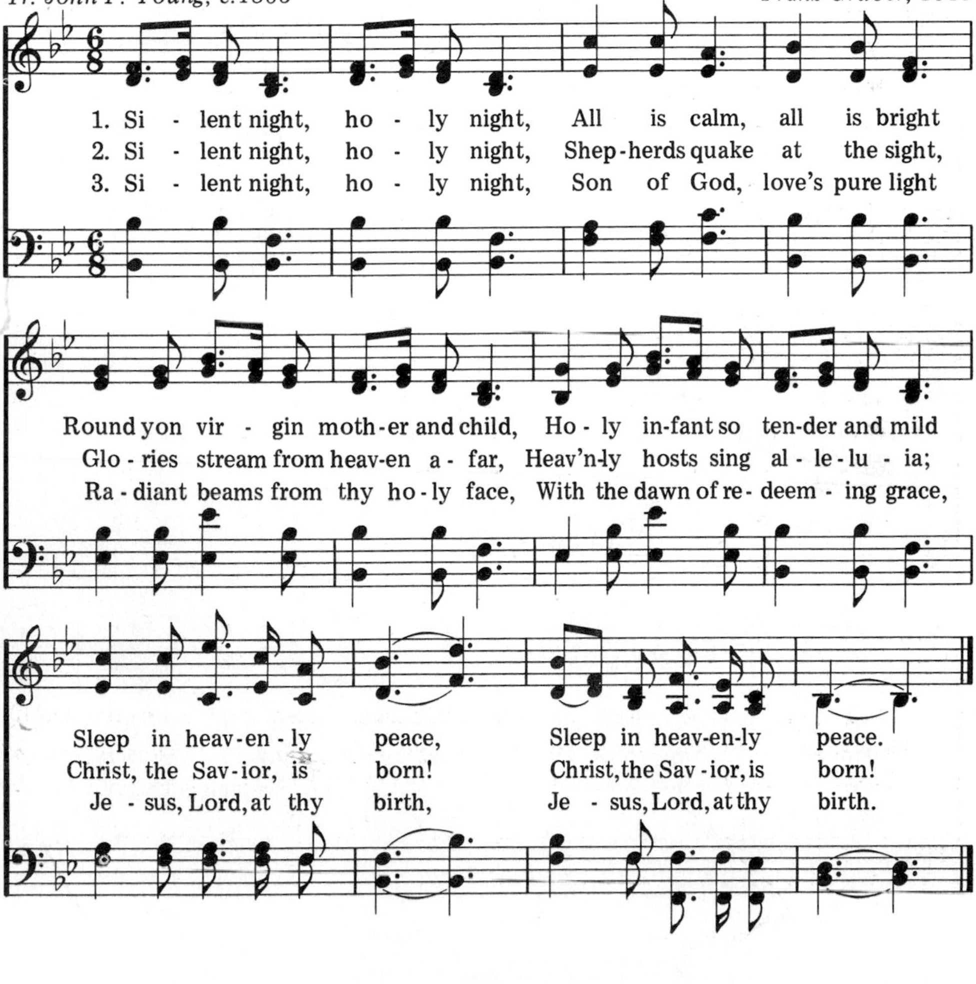

1. Si - lent night, ho - ly night, All is calm, all is bright
2. Si - lent night, ho - ly night, Shep - herds quake at the sight,
3. Si - lent night, ho - ly night, Son of God, love's pure light
Round yon vir - gin moth - er and child, Ho - ly in - fant so ten - der and mild
Glo - ries stream from heav - en a - far, Heav'n - ly hosts sing al - le - lu - ia;
Ra - diant beams from thy ho - ly face, With the dawn of re - deem - ing grace,
Sleep in heav - en - ly peace, Sleep in heav - en - ly peace.
Christ, the Sav - ior, is born! Christ, the Sav - ior, is born!
Je - sus, Lord, at thy birth, Je - sus, Lord, at thy birth.

96

Stille Nacht, Heilige Nacht

STILLE NACHT *Irregular*

Joseph Mohr, 1818 — *Franz Gruber, 1818*

1. Stille Nacht, heilige Nacht!
Alles schläft, einsam wacht
Nur das traute, hochheilige Paar
Holder Knabe im lockigen Haar,
Schlaf in himmlischer Ruh,
Schlaf in himmlischer Ruh!

2. Stille Nacht, heilige Nacht!
Hirten erst kundgemacht
Durch der Engel Alleluja,
Tönt es laut von fern und nah':
Christ der Retter ist da,
Christ der Retter ist da!

3. Stille Nacht, heilige Nacht!
Gottes Sohn, o wie lacht
Lieb' aus deinem göttlichen Mund,
Da uns schlägt die rettende Stund':
Christ, in deiner Geburt,
Christ, in deiner Geburt!

97 My Master Was So Very Poor

HERRNHUT L.M.

Harry Lee, 1927 — *Bartholomaeus Gesius, c.1555-c.1613*

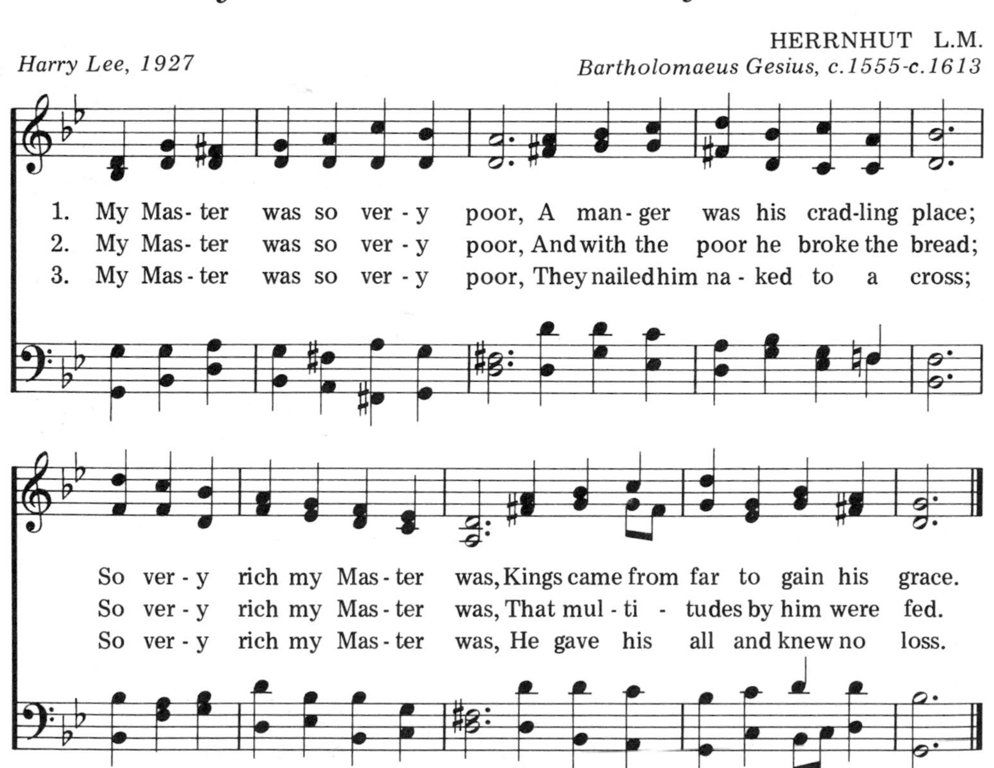

1. My Mas- ter was so ver - y poor, A man- ger was his crad-ling place;
2. My Mas- ter was so ver - y poor, And with the poor he broke the bread;
3. My Mas - ter was so ver - y poor, They nailed him na - ked to a cross;
So ver - y rich my Mas - ter was, Kings came from far to gain his grace.
So ver - y rich my Mas - ter was, That mul - ti - tudes by him were fed.
So ver - y rich my Mas - ter was, He gave his all and knew no loss.

A Stable Lamp Is Lighted

Luke 19:39-40
Richard Wilbur, 1961
FAIRVIEW 7.6.7.6.6.7.6.
Walter Watson, 1972
1. A sta - ble lamp is light - ed Whose glow shall wake the sky;
child through Da - vid's cit - y Shall ride in tri - umph by;
he shall be for - sak - en, And yield - ed up to die;
now, as at the end - ing, The low is lift - ed high;
The stars shall bend their voic - es, And ev - 'ry stone shall cry,
The palm shall strew its branch-es, And ev - 'ry stone shall cry,
The sky shall groan and dark - en, And ev - 'ry stone shall cry,
The stars shall bend their voic - es, And ev - 'ry stone shall cry,
And straw like gold shall shine; A barn shall har - bor heav - en, A
Though heav - y, dull, and dumb, And lie with-in the road - way To
For ston - y hearts of men: God's blood up - on the spear - head, God's
In prais - es of the child By whose de-scent a - mong us The
Sts. 1, 2, 3
St. 4
stall be - come a shrine. 2. This
pave his king - dom come. 3. Yet
love re - fused a - gain. 4. But
worlds are re - con - ciled.

*O Little Town of Bethlehem

ST. LOUIS 8.6.8.6.7.6.8.6.

Phillips Brooks, 1868 *Lewis H. Redner, 1868*

1. O lit - tle town of Beth- le - hem, How still we see thee lie!
2. For Christ is born of Mar - y, And gath - ered all a - bove,
3. How si - lent - ly, how si - lent - ly, The won - drous gift is given!
4. O ho - ly Child of Beth- le - hem! De - scend to us, we pray;

A - bove thy deep and dream-less sleep The si - lent stars go by;
While mor - tals sleep, the an - gels keep Their watch of won-dering love.
So God im -parts to hu - man hearts The bless - ings of his heav'n.
Cast out our sin and en - ter in; Be born in us to - day.

Yet in thy dark streets shin - eth The ev - er - last - ing Light;
O morn - ing stars, to - geth - er Pro - claim the ho - ly birth!
No ear may hear his com - ing, But in this world of sin,
We hear the Christ-mas an - gels The great glad tid - ings tell;

The hopes and fears of all the years Are met in thee to - night.
And prais - es sing to God the King, And peace to men on earth.
Where meek souls will re - ceive him, still The dear Christ en - ters in.
O come to us, a - bide with us, Our Lord Em - man - u - el!

*The First Nowell

THE FIRST NOWELL *Irregular with Refrain*
Traditional English Melody
Traditional English Carol — *Harm. by John Stainer, 1871*

1. The first Now - ell, the an - gel did say, Was to
2. They look - ed up and saw a star Shin-ing
3. And by the light of that same star Three
4. This star drew nigh to the north - west, O'er
5. Then let us all with one ac - cord Sing

cer - tain poor shep-herds in fields as they lay; In fields where
in the east, be - yond them far, And to the
wise men came from coun - try far; To seek for a
Beth - le - hem it took its rest, And there it
prais - es to our heav'n - ly Lord, That hath made

they lay keep - ing their sheep, On a cold win - ter's
earth it gave great light, And so it con -
king was their in - tent, And to fol - low the
did both stop and stay, Right o - ver the
heav'n and earth of naught, And with his

night that was so deep.
tin - ued both day and night.
star wher - ev - er it went.
place where Je - sus lay.
blood man - kind hath bought.

Refrain

Now - ell, Now - ell, Nowell, Now - ell, Born is the King of Is - ra - el.

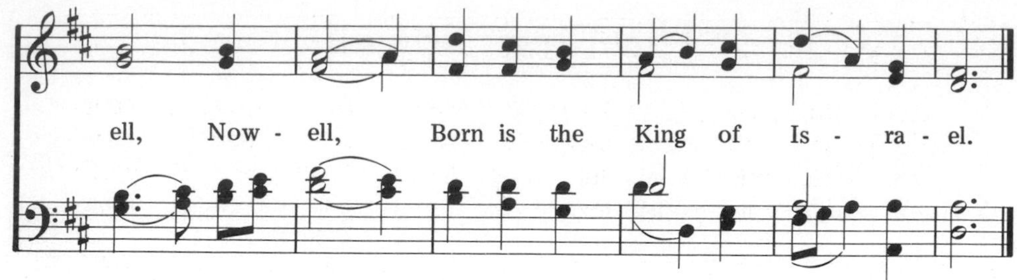

101

On Christmas Night

SUSSEX CAROL 8.8.8.8.8.8.

English Traditional
Collected by R. Vaughan Williams, 1919

Arr. by R. Vaughan Williams, 1919
Adapted by E. Harold Geer, 1956

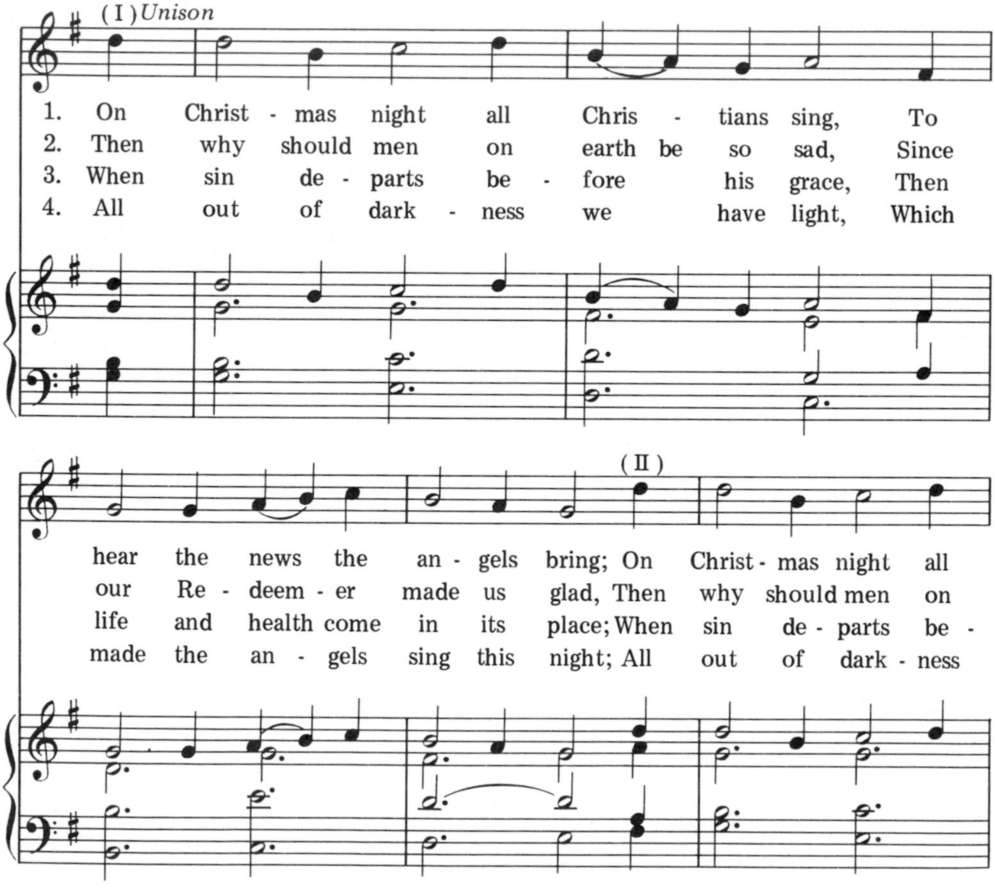

(I) Unison
1. On Christ - mas night all Chris - tians sing, To
2. Then why should men on earth be so sad, Since
3. When sin de - parts be - fore his grace, Then
4. All out of dark - ness we have light, Which
(II)
hear the news the an - gels bring; On Christ - mas night all
our Re - deem - er made us glad, Then why should men on
life and health come in its place; When sin de - parts be -
made the an - gels sing this night; All out of dark - ness

This hymn may be sung antiphonally, the choir leading (I), the congregation responding (II), choir and congregation (III).

Chris - tians sing, To hear the news the an - gels bring—
earth be so sad, Since our Re - deem - er made us glad,
fore his grace, Then life and health come in its place;
we have light, Which made the an - gels sing this night;
News of great joy, news of great mirth,
When from our sin he set us free,
An - gels and men with joy may sing,
"Glo - ry to God and peace to men,
(III)
News of our mer - ci - ful King's birth.
All for to gain our li - ber - ty.
All for to see the new - born King.
Now and for - ev - er - more. A - men."

*In the Bleak Midwinter

CRANHAM *Irregular*

Christina G. Rossetti, 1872, alt.

Gustav T. Holst, 1906

1. In the bleak mid - win - ter, Frost-y wind made moan,
2. Our God, heav'n can-not hold him, Nor earth sus - tain;
3. What can I give him, Poor as I am?
Earth stood hard as i - ron, Wa - ter like a stone;
Heav'n and earth shall flee a - way When he comes to reign;
If I were a shep - herd, I would bring a lamb;
Snow had fall - en, snow on snow, Snow on snow,
In the bleak mid - win - ter A sta - ble place suf - ficed The
If I were a wise man, I would do my part; Yet
In the bleak mid - win - ter, Long a - go.
Lord God al - might - y, Je - sus Christ.
what I can I give him - Give my heart.

On a Day When Men Were Counted

KOREA 8.7.8.7.D.
Korean Carol
As in The Hymnbook *(Canadian, 1971)*

Daniel T. Niles, 1963

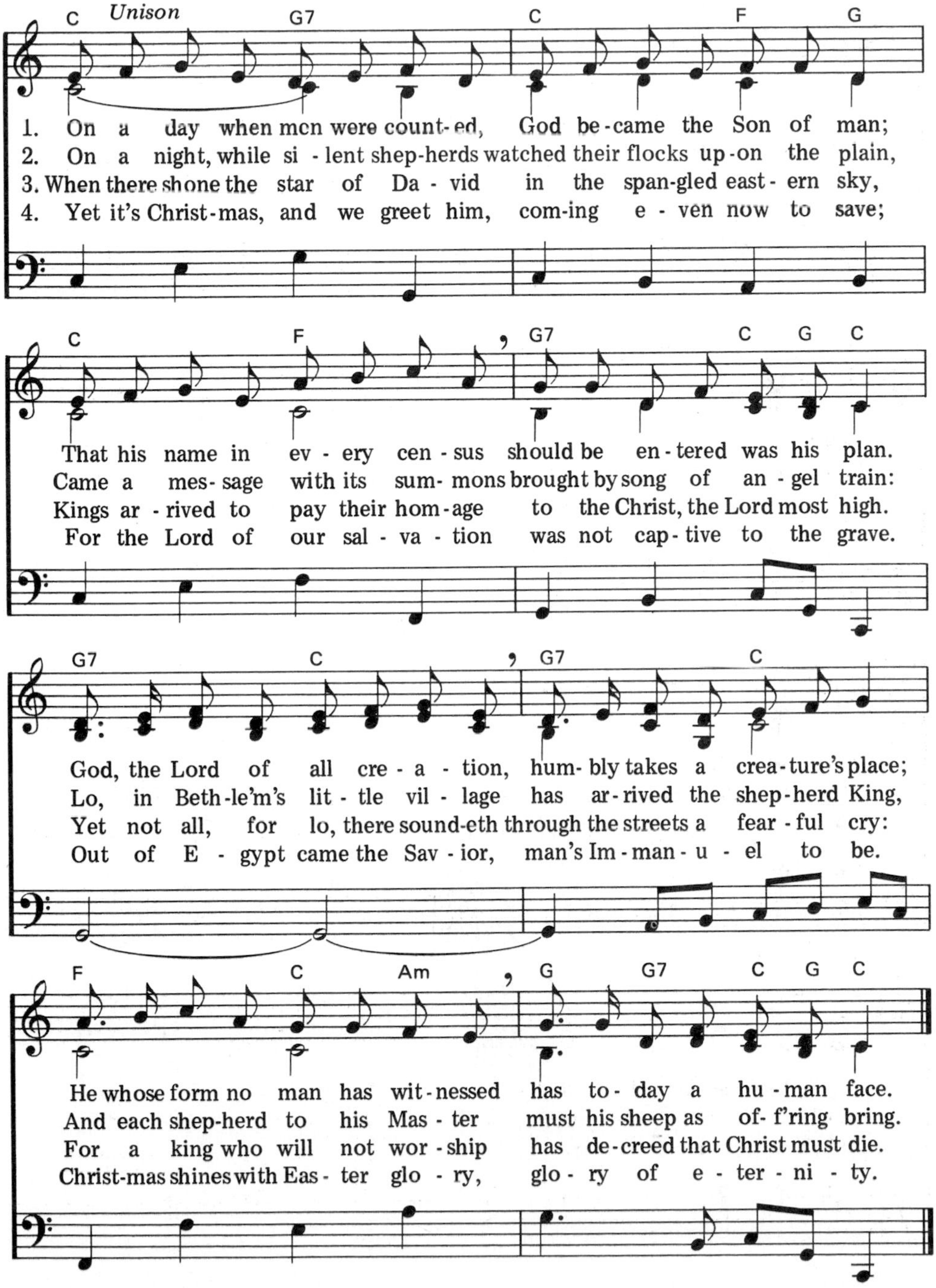
Unison
C G7 C F G
1. On a day when men were count-ed, God be-came the Son of man;
2. On a night, while si-lent shep-herds watched their flocks up-on the plain,
3. When there shone the star of Da-vid in the span-gled east-ern sky,
4. Yet it's Christ-mas, and we greet him, com-ing e-ven now to save;
C F G7 C G C
That his name in ev-ery cen-sus should be en-tered was his plan.
Came a mes-sage with its sum-mons brought by song of an-gel train:
Kings ar-rived to pay their hom-age to the Christ, the Lord most high.
For the Lord of our sal-va-tion was not cap-tive to the grave.
G7 C G7 C
God, the Lord of all cre-a-tion, hum-bly takes a crea-ture's place;
Lo, in Beth-le'm's lit-tle vil-lage has ar-rived the shep-herd King,
Yet not all, for lo, there sound-eth through the streets a fear-ful cry:
Out of E-gypt came the Sav-ior, man's Im-man-u-el to be.
F C Am G G7 C G C
He whose form no man has wit-nessed has to-day a hu-man face.
And each shep-herd to his Mas-ter must his sheep as of-f'ring bring.
For a king who will not wor-ship has de-creed that Christ must die.
Christ-mas shines with Eas-ter glo-ry, glo-ry of e-ter-ni-ty.

Once in Royal David's City

IRBY 8.7.8.7.7.7.
Henry J. Gauntlett, 1849
Cecil Frances Alexander, 1848 *Harm. by A. H. Mann, 1919*

1. Once in roy - al Da - vid's cit - y Stood a low - ly cat - tle shed,
2. He came down to earth from heav - en, Who is God and Lord of all,
3. And our eyes at last shall see him, Through his own re - deem - ing love;
Where a moth - er laid her ba - by In a man - ger for his bed:
And his shel - ter was a sta - ble, And his cra - dle was a stall;
For that child so dear and gen - tle Is our Lord in heav - en a - bove;
Mar - y was that moth - er mild, Je - sus Christ her lit - tle child.
With the poor and mean and low - ly, Lived on earth our Sa - vior ho - ly.
And he leads his chil - dren on To the place where he has gone.

Go, Tell It on the Mountain

Negro Spiritual
Adapted by John W. Work, 1901-1967

GO TELL IT ON THE MOUNTAIN Irregular
Negro Melody

Refrain
Go, tell it on the moun - tain, O- ver the hills and ev - ery-where;
Go, tell it on the moun - tain That Je - sus Christ is born!
Fine
1. While shep-herds kept their watch-ing O'er si - lent flocks by night, Be - held through-out the heav - ens There shone a ho - ly light.
2. The shep-herds feared and trem - bled When lo! a - bove the earth Rang out the an - gel cho - rus That hailed our Sav - ior's birth.
3. Down in a low - ly man - ger The hum - ble Christ was born, And God sent us sal - va - tion That bless - ed Christ - mas morn.
D.C.

*From Heaven Above to Earth I Come

Martin Luther, 1535
Tr. Catherine Winkworth, 1855
VOM HIMMEL HOCH L.M.
Geistliche Lieder, Leipzig, 1539
1. From heav'n a - bove to earth I come To bear good news to
2. To you, this night, is born a child Of Mar- y, cho - sen
3. Ah, dear - est Je - sus, ho - ly child, Make thee a bed, soft,
4. Glo - ry to God in high- est heav'n, Who un - to man his
ev - ery home; Glad tid - ings of great joy I bring,
moth - er mild; This lit - tle child, of low - ly birth,
un - de - filed With - in my heart, that it may be
son hath given, While an - gels sing with pi - ous mirth,
Where - of I now will say and sing.
Shall be the joy of all your earth.
A qui - et cham - ber kept for thee.
A glad new year to all the earth.

107

*Break Forth, O Beauteous Heavenly Light

St. 1, Johann Rist, 1641
Tr. attr. to John Troutbeck, 1873
St. 2, Dalton E. McDonald, 1972
ERMUNTRE DICH 8.7.8.7.8.8.7.7.
Melody by Johann Schop?, c. 1641
Harm. by Johann Sebastian Bach, 1734
1. Break forth, O beau-teous heav'n-ly light, And ush - er in the morn - ing; Ye shep-herds, shrink not with af - fright, But hear the an - gel's warn - ing. This child, now born in in - fan-cy, Our con - fi - dence and joy shall be, The power of Sa - tan break - ing, Our peace e - ter - nal mak - ing.
2. He comes to rec - on - cile all men, And men to God for - ev - er; He comes to mend the cords of love Wher - ev - er sin does sev - er. He is the light up - on our way To bring us to the prom-ised day—This child, God's in - car - na - tion, Our hope and our sal - va - tion!

108

On This Day Earth Shall Ring

Piae Cantiones, *1582*
Tr. Jane M. Joseph, 1924

PERSONENT HODIE 6.6.6.6.6. *with Refrain*
Piae Cantiones, *1582*
Arr. by Gustav T. Holst, 1925

Unison
1. On this day earth shall ring With the song
2. His the doom, ours the mirth; When he came
3. God's bright star, o'er his head, Wise men three
4. On this day an- gels sing; With their song
chil- dren sing To the Lord, Christ our King, Born on earth to
down to earth, Beth - le - hem saw his birth; Ox and ass be -
to him led, Kneel- ing low by his bed, Lay their gifts be -
earth shall ring, Prais - ing Christ, heav - en's King, Born on earth to
Refrain
save us; Him the Fa - ther gave us.
side him From the cold would hide him. Id - e - o - o - o,
fore him, Praise him and a - dore him.
save us. Peace and love he gave us.
R.H.
R.H. L.H.

Id-e-o - o - o, Id-e-o glo-ri-a in ex-cel-sis De-o!

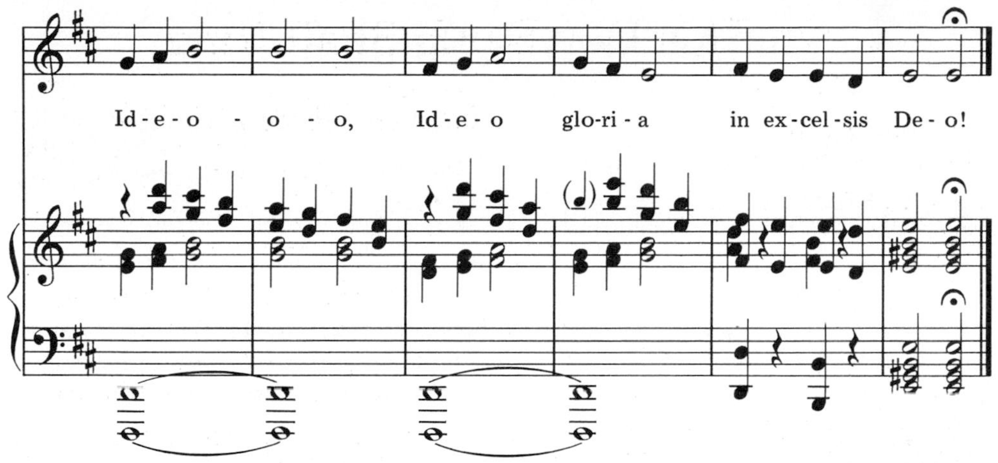

109

Thou Art the Way

John 14:6
George Washington Doane, 1824

NUN DANKET ALL' C.M.
Melody by Johann Crüger, 1647

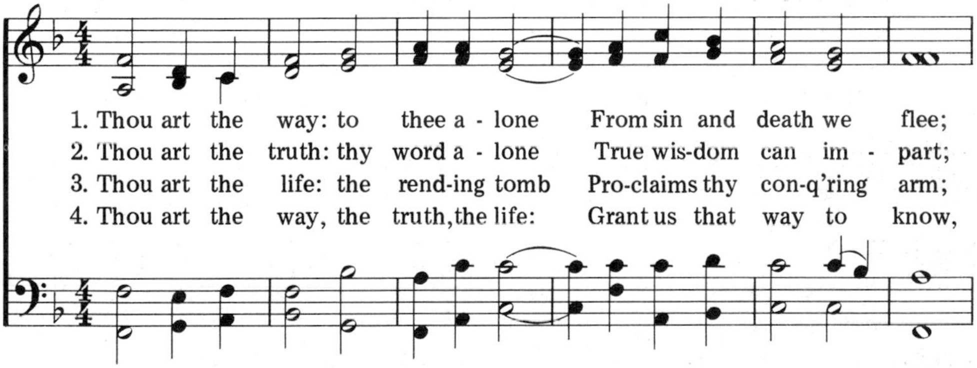

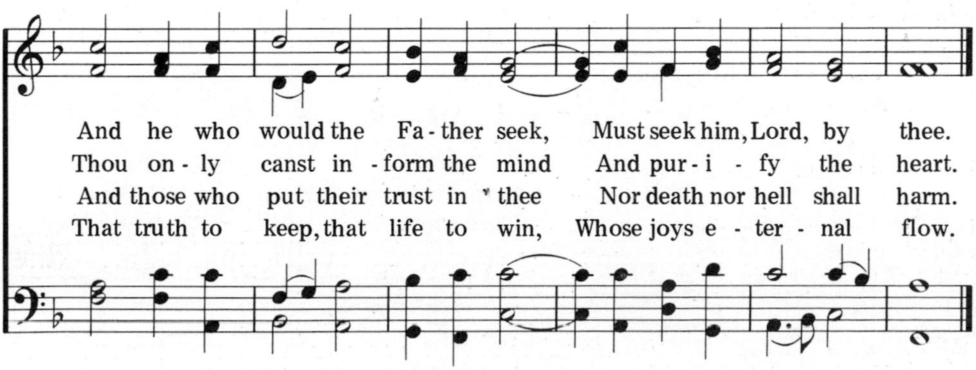

1. Thou art the way: to thee a - lone From sin and death we flee;
2. Thou art the truth: thy word a - lone True wis-dom can im - part;
3. Thou art the life: the rend-ing tomb Pro-claims thy con-q'ring arm;
4. Thou art the way, the truth, the life: Grant us that way to know,

And he who would the Fa-ther seek, Must seek him, Lord, by thee.
Thou on - ly canst in - form the mind And pur - i - fy the heart.
And those who put their trust in thee Nor death nor hell shall harm.
That truth to keep, that life to win, Whose joys e - ter - nal flow.

As Ancient Sunlight

CHHATTISGAHR 8.7.8.7.D.

Luke 2:8-20
William Nelson, 1969

Indian Melody
Adapted by Mary Louise VanDyke, 1973

Unison

1. As an-cient sun-light reach-es now The earth in all its glo-ry,
So God from end-less a-ges past Re-peats his sav-ing sto-ry
Of peace on earth, good will to men, Of low-ly shep-herds' won-der,
When Christ was born on Christ-mas

2. "Fear not," they sang and as a-gain We hear their voic-es ring-ing,
Then in the crowd-ed streets of life Our hearts re-new their sing-ing,
For broth-er-hood is more than dream, And hope no id-le yearn-ing,
Since Christ was born on Christ-mas

3. Re-joice, good friend, and when de-spair Would threat-en to un-do you,
Re-mem-ber then his bound-less love, And how he brought it to you;
En-shrined with-in man's mor-tal flesh, The ho-ly gift was giv-en,
When Christ was born on Christ-mas

morn, And an - gels sang in splen - dor.
morn, And all God's lamps are burn - ing.
morn, And earth was joined to heav - en.

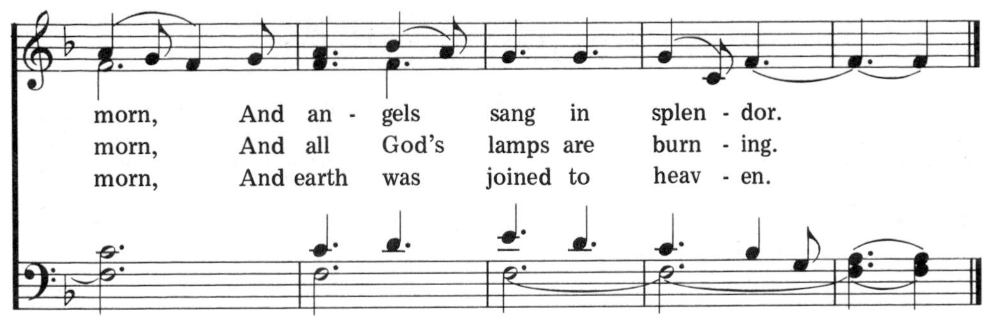

111

*All My Heart This Night Rejoices

Paul Gerhardt, 1653
Tr. Catherine Winkworth, 1858, alt.

WARUM SOLLT ICH 8.3.3.6.D.
Melody by Johann G. Ebeling, 1666

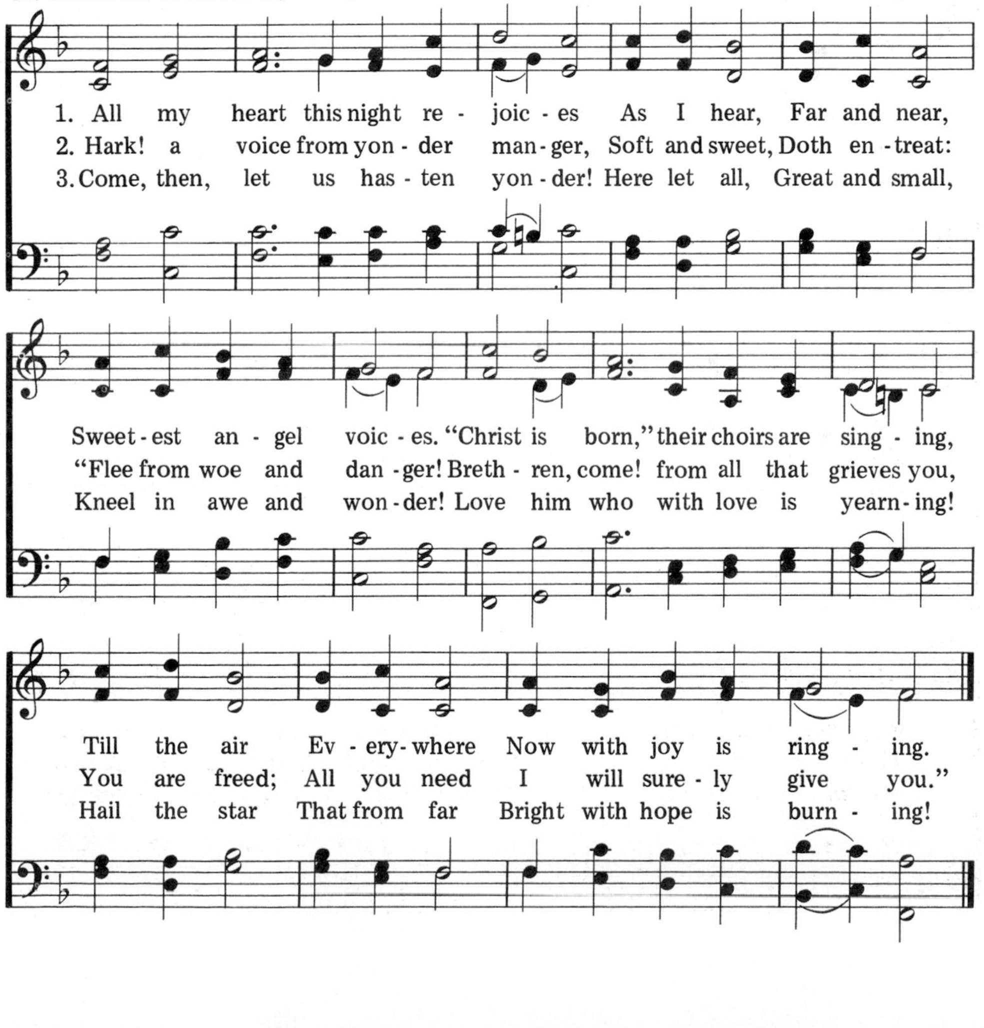

1. All my heart this night re - joic - es As I hear, Far and near,
2. Hark! a voice from yon - der man - ger, Soft and sweet, Doth en - treat:
3. Come, then, let us has - ten yon - der! Here let all, Great and small,
Sweet - est an - gel voic - es. "Christ is born," their choirs are sing - ing,
"Flee from woe and dan - ger! Breth - ren, come! from all that grieves you,
Kneel in awe and won - der! Love him who with love is yearn - ing!
Till the air Ev - ery - where Now with joy is ring - ing.
You are freed; All you need I will sure - ly give you."
Hail the star That from far Bright with hope is burn - ing!

112

O Morning Star, How Fair and Bright

2 Peter 1:19
Philipp Nicolai, 1599
Tr. Catherine Winkworth, 1863, alt.

WIE SCHÖN LEUCHTET 8.8.7.8.8.7.4.8.4.8.
Melody by Philipp Nicolai, 1599
Harm. by Johann Sebastian Bach, 1740

1. O Morn-ing Star, how fair and bright Thou beam-est forth in
2. Thou heav'n-ly Bright-ness! Light di-vine! O deep with-in my
truth and light! O Sov-ereign meek and low-ly! Thou Root of Jes-se,
heart now shine, And make thee there an al-tar! Fill me with joy and
Da-vid's Son, My Lord and Mas-ter, thou hast won My heart to serve thee
strength to be Thy mem-ber, ev-er joined to thee In love that can-not
sole-ly! Thou art ho-ly, Fair and glo-rious, all-vic-to-rious,
fal-ter; Toward thee long-ing Doth pos-sess me; turn and bless me;

Rich in bless - ing, Rule and might o'er all pos - ses - sing.
Here in sad - ness Eye and heart long for thy glad - ness!

113

O Thou Joyful

German: St. 1, J. Falk; sts. 2, 3, anon.
Tr. H. Katterjohn, 1919

SICILIAN MARINERS' HYMN 9.7.6.6.10.
Sicilian Melody, 1794

1. O thou joy - ful, O thou won - der - ful Grace re - veal - ing Christ - mas - tide! Je - sus came to win us From all sin with-in us: Glo - ri - fy, glo - ri - fy the ho - ly child.

2. O thou joy - ful, O thou won - der - ful Love re - veal - ing Christ - mas - tide! Loud ho - san - nas sing - ing And all prais-es bring - ing, May thy love, may thy love with us a - bide.

3. O thou joy - ful, O thou won - der - ful Peace re - veal - ing Christ - mas - tide! Dark-ness dis - ap - pear - eth, God's own light now near-eth, Peace and joy, peace and joy to all be - tide.

O Thou Who by a Star Didst Guide

KINGSFOLD C.M.D.
Traditional English Melody
Collected by Lucy Broadwood, 1858-1929
Arr. by R. Vaughan Williams, 1906

John Mason Neale, 1842

1. O thou who by a star didst guide The wise men on their way,
Un - til it came and stood be - side The place where Je - sus lay;
Al - though by stars thou dost not lead Thy ser - vants now be - low,
Thy Ho - ly Spir - it, when they need, Will show them how to go.

2. As yet we know thee but in part, But still we trust thy word
That bless - ed are the pure in heart, For they shall see the Lord.
O Sav - ior, give us then thy grace To make us pure in heart,
That we may see thee, face to face, Here - af - ter as thou art.

What Star Is This

PUER NOBIS NASCITUR L.M.
Charles Coffin, 1736
Tr. John Chandler, 1837, alt.
Adapted by Michael Praetorius, 1609
Harm. by George R. Woodward, 1904
Unison
1. What star is this, with beams so bright, More love - ly than the noon - day light? 'Tis sent to an - nounce a new - born king, Glad tid - ings of our God to bring.
2. 'Tis now ful - filled what God de - creed, "From Ja - cob shall a star pro - ceed"; And lo! the east - ern sa - ges stand, To read in heav'n the Lord's com - mand.
3. O Je - sus, while the star of grace Im - pels us on to seek thy face, Let not our sloth - ful hearts re - fuse The guid - ance of thy light to use.
4. To God the Fa - ther, heav'n - ly Light, To Christ, re - vealed in earth - ly night, To God the Ho - ly Ghost we raise An end - less song of thank - ful praise!

An alternate setting may be found at No. 14.

Every Star Shall Sing a Carol

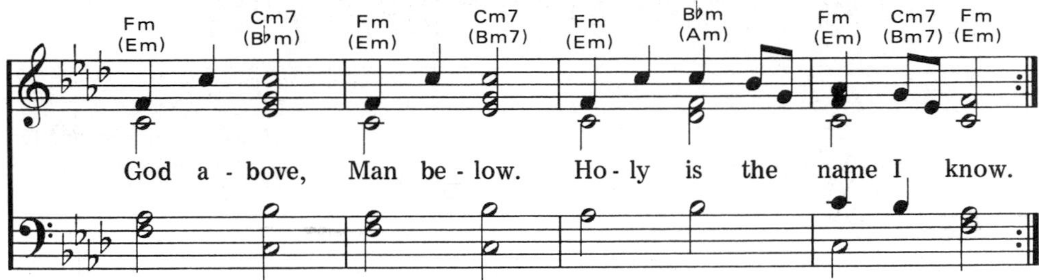

117

Behold the Lamb of God

John 1:36
Matthew Bridges, 1848

ECCE AGNUS 6.6.6.4.8.8.4.
George William Warren, 1894

1. Be - hold the Lamb of God! O thou for sin - ners slain,
2. Be - hold the Lamb of God! All hail, In - car - nate Word!
3. Be - hold the Lamb of God! Wor - thy is he a - lone

Let it not be in vain That thou hast died. Thee for my Sav - ior
Thou ev - er - last - ing Lord, Sav - ior most blest! Fill us with love that
To sit up - on the throne Of God a - bove, One with the An - cient

let me take, My on - ly ref - uge let me make thy pier - ced side!
nev - er faints, Grant us, with all thy bless - ed saints, E - ter - nal rest.
of all days, One with the Com - fort - er in praise, All Light, all Love!

118

*As with Gladness Men of Old

DIX 7.7.7.7.7.7.
Matt. 2:1-2
William C. Dix, 1861, alt.
Adapted from a chorale
by Conrad Kocher, 1838
1. As with glad-ness men of old Did the guid - ing star be - hold;
2. As with joy - ful steps they sped To that low - ly man-ger bed,
3. As they of - fered gifts most rare At the man-ger rude and bare,
4. Ho - ly Je - sus, ev - ery day Keep us in the nar - row way;
As with joy they hailed its light, Lead - ing on - ward, beam - ing bright;
There to bend the knee be - fore Him whom heav'n and earth a - dore;
So may we with ho - ly joy, Pure and free from sin's al - loy,
And, when earth - ly things are past, Bring our ran - somed souls at last
So, most gra-cious God, may we Ev - er - more be led to thee.
So may we with will - ing feet Ev - er seek thy mer - cy seat.
All our cost - liest trea - sures bring, Christ, to thee, our heav'n - ly King.
Where they need no star to guide, Where no clouds thy glo - ry hide.

A lower setting may be found at No. 34.

I Wonder as I Wander

Anointed of God

DUQUESNE 9.9.10.10.

F. L. Battles, 1970 — Joseph Willcox Jenkins, 1970

(I)
(II)
1. A - noint-ed of God, how can we see you, A-noint - ed of God, how
2. First-born of God, how can we greet you, First-born of God, how
3. Cho - sen of God, how can we hear you, Cho - sen of God, how
4. Sav - ior from God, how can we grasp you, Sav - ior from God, how
(I)
(II)
can we see you, O Word un- fleshed in proph - e - cy fore - told, O
can we greet you, O Word en - fleshed to whom a star now leads, O
can we hear you, O Word en - voiced to whom the dove now points, O
can we grasp you, O Word pro-claimed whose death is life for us, O

This hymn may be sung antiphonally, the choir leading (I), the congregation responding (II).

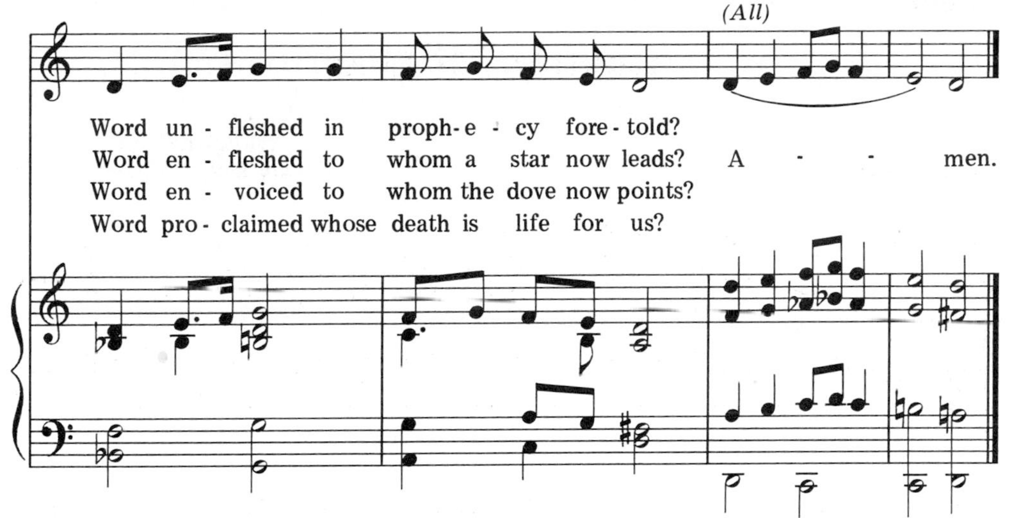
(All)
Word un - fleshed in proph- e - cy fore - told?
Word en - fleshed to whom a star now leads? A - - men.
Word en - voiced to whom the dove now points?
Word pro - claimed whose death is life for us?

121

Alone Thou Goest Forth, O Lord

Peter Abelard, c.1129
Tr. F. Bland Tucker, 1940

BANGOR C.M.
William Tans'ur, 1735

1. A - lone thou go - est forth, O Lord, In sac - ri - fice to die;
Is this thy sor - row naught to us Who pass un - heed-ing by?

2. Our sins, not thine, thou bear - est, Lord, Make us thy sor - row feel,
Till through our pit - y and our shame Love an - swers love's ap - peal.

3. This is earth's dark - est hour, but thou Dost light and life re - store;
Then let all praise be giv - en thee Who liv - est ev - er - more.

4. Give us com - pas - sion for thee, Lord, That as we share this hour,
Thy cross may bring us to thy joy And res - ur - rec - tion power.

122

Each Winter as the Year Grows Older

CAROL OF HOPE 9.6.9.6.6.
William Gay, 1969
Annabeth Gay, 1969
Unison
Em Am
1. Each win - ter as the year grows old - er, A man grows old - er
2. When race and class cry out for trea - son, When si - rens call for
3. But I be - lieve be - yond be - liev - ing, That life can spring from
4. So e - ven as the sun is turn - ing, To jour - ney to the
5. O Child of ec - sta - sy and sor - rows, O Prince of peace and
Em Em A Em
too. The chill sets in a lit - tle cold - er; The
war, They o - ver - shout the voice of rea - son, And
death; That growth can flow - er from our griev - ing; That
north, The liv - ing flame, in se - cret burn - ing, Can
pain, Bright - en to - day's world by to - mor - row's, Re -
C D Bm Em
ver - i - ties I knew Seem shak - en and un - true.
scream till we ig - nore All we held dear be - fore.
man can catch his breath And turn trans - fixed by faith.
kin - dle on the earth, And bring God's love to birth.
new our lives a - gain; Lord Je - sus, come and reign!

*All Glory, Laud, and Honor

Theodulph of Orleans, 820
Tr. John M. Neale, 1854, alt.

ST. THEODULPH 7.6.7.6.D.
Melody by Melchior Teschner, 1615

Refrain
All glo - ry, laud, and hon - or To thee, Re - deem - er, King,
To whom the lips of chil - dren Made sweet ho - san - nas ring!
1. Thou art the king of Is - ra - el, Thou Da - vid's roy - al son,
2. The com - pa - ny of an - gels Are prais - ing thee on high,
3. The peo - ple of the He - brews With palms be - fore thee went;
4. To thee, be - fore thy pas - sion, They sang their hymns of praise;
5. Thou didst ac - cept their prais - es; Ac - cept the prayers we bring,
Repeat refrain after each stanza
Who in the Lord's name com - est, The King and bless - ed one.
And mor - tal men and all things Cre - a - ted make re - ply.
Our praise and prayer and an - thems Be - fore thee we pre - sent.
To thee, now high ex - alt - ed Our mel - o - dy we raise.
Who in all good de - light - est, Thou good and gra - cious king!

This hymn may be treated antiphonally, the congregation singing the refrain, the choir the stanzas.

124

*Ride On, Ride On in Majesty

Zech. 9:9
Henry H. Milman, 1827, alt.
THE KING'S MAJESTY L.M.
Graham George, 1939
Unison
1. Ride on, ride on in ma - - jes - ty! Hark! all the tribes ho - san - na cry; O Sav - ior meek, pur - sue thy road With palms and scat - tered gar - ments strowed.
2. Ride on, ride on in ma - - jes - ty! In low - ly pomp ride on to die; O Christ, thy tri - umphs now be - gin O'er cap - tive death and con - quered sin.
3. Ride on, ride on in ma - - jes - ty! Thy last and fierc - est strife is nigh: Bow thy meek head to mor - tal pain, Then take, O God, thy pow'r and reign.

Draw Nigh to Thy Jerusalem

WOODLANDS 10.10.10.10.
Jeremy Taylor, 1655, alt.
Walter Greatorex, 1916
Unison
1. Draw nigh to thy Je - ru - sa - lem, O Lord,
2. Thy road is read - y; and thy paths made straight,
3. Ho - san - na! wel - come to our hearts! for here
Thy faith - ful peo - ple cry with one ac - cord;
With long - ing ex - pec - ta - tion seem to wait
Thou hast a tem - ple, too, as Zi - on dear;
Ride on in tri - umph; Lord, be - hold we lay
The con - se - cra - tion of thy beau - teous feet,
O en - ter in, dear Lord, un - bar the door;
Our pas - sions, lusts, and proud wills in thy way!
And si - lent - ly thy prom - ised ad - vent greet!
And in that tem - ple dwell for - ev - er - more.

An alternate setting may be found at No. 306.

*Go to Dark Gethsemane

REDHEAD NO. 76 7.7.7.7.7.7.
James Montgomery, 1820, alt.
Richard Redhead, 1853
1. Go to dark Geth-sem-a-ne, Ye that feel the temp-ter's pow'r;
2. See him at the judg-ment hall, Beat-en, bound, re-viled, ar-raigned;
3. Cal-vary's mourn-ful moun-tain view; There the Lord of glo-ry see,
Your Re-deem-er's con-flict see; Watch with him one bit-ter hour;
See him meek-ly bear-ing all! Love to man his soul sus-tained.
Made a sac-ri-fice for you, Dy-ing on the ac-cur-sed tree.
Turn not from his griefs a-way; Learn from him to watch and pray.
Shun not suf-fering, shame, or loss; Learn of Christ to bear the cross.
"It is fin-ished!" hear his cry: Trust in Christ and learn to die.

127

*O Sacred Head, Now Wounded

Latin: 12th century
German: Paul Gerhardt, 1656
Tr. James W. Alexander, 1830, alt.

PASSION CHORALE 7.6.7.6.D.
Melody by Hans Leo Hassler, 1601
Harm. by Johann Sebastian Bach, 1729

1. O sacred head, now wounded,
With grief and shame weighed down,
Now scornfully surrounded
With thorns, thine only crown;
O sacred head, what glory,
What bliss till now was thine!
Yet, though despised and gory,
I joy to call thee mine.

2. How art thou pale with anguish,
With sore abuse and scorn;
How does that visage languish
Which once was bright as morn!
Thy grief and bitter passion
Were all for sinners' gain;
Mine, mine was the transgression,
But thine the deadly pain.

3. What language shall I borrow
To thank thee, dearest Friend,
For this thy dying sorrow,
Thy pity without end?
O make me thine forever,
And should I fainting be,
Lord, let me never, never
Outlive my love to thee.

4. Be near when I am dying,
O show thy cross to me!
And, for my succor flying,
Come, Lord, to set me free.
These eyes, new faith receiving,
From thee shall never move;
For he who dies believing
Dies safely in thy love.

*A higher setting may be found at No. 228.

128

*Ah, Holy Jesus, How Hast Thou Offended

Johann Heermann, 1630
Tr. Robert S. Bridges, 1899

HERZLIEBSTER JESU 11.11.11.5.
Johann Crüger, 1640

1. Ah, ho - ly Je - sus, how hast thou of - fend - ed,
2. Who was the guilt - y? Who brought this up - on thee?
3. For me, kind Je - sus, was thy in - car - na - tion,
4. There - fore, kind Je - sus, since I can - not pay thee,

That man to judge thee hath in hate pre - tend - ed? By foes de -
A - las, my trea - son, Je - sus, hath un - done thee! 'Twas I, Lord
Thy mor - tal sor - row, and thy life's ob - la - tion; Thy death of
I do a - dore thee, and will ev - er pray thee, Think on thy

rid - ed, by thine own re - ject - ed, O most af - flict - ed!
Je - sus, I it was de - nied thee; I cru - ci - fied thee.
an - guish and thy bit - ter pas - sion, For my sal - va - tion.
pit - y and thy love un - swerv - ing, Not my de - serv - ing.

129

*When I Survey the Wondrous Cross

Phil. 3:7-8 HAMBURG L.M.

Isaac Watts, 1707 *Arr. by Lowell Mason, 1825*

1. When I survey the wondrous cross
On which the Prince of glory died,
My richest gain I count but loss,
And pour contempt on all my pride.

2. Forbid it, Lord, that I should boast,
Save in the death of Christ, my God;
All the vain things that charm me most
I sacrifice them to his blood.

3. See, from his head, his hands, his feet,
Sorrow and love flow mingled down!
Did e'er such love and sorrow meet,
Or thorns compose so rich a crown?

4. Were the whole realm of nature mine,
That were a tribute far too small;
Love so amazing, so divine,
Demands my soul, my life, my all.

130

Christ the Lord Is Risen Today

EASTER HYMN 7.7.7.7. *with Alleluias*

Charles Wesley, 1739, alt. — *Arr. from* Lyra Davidica, *1708*

1. Christ the Lord is risen to - day,
2. Lives a - gain our glo - rious King,
3. Love's re - deem - ing work is done,
4. Hail, the Lord of earth and heaven!

Al - - le - lu - ia!

Sons of men and an - gels say:
Where, O death, is now thy sting?
Fought the fight, the bat - tle won,
Praise to thee by both be given,

Al - - le - lu - ia!

Raise your joys and tri - umphs high,
Dy - ing once, he all doth save,
Death in vain for - bids him rise,
Thee we greet tri - um - phant now,

Al - - le - lu - ia!

Sing ye heav'ns, and earth re - ply:
Where thy vic - to - ry, O grave?
Christ has o - pened par - a - dise,
Hail, the Res - ur - rec - tion thou!

Al - - le - lu - ia!

131

*Alleluia! The Strife Is O'er

VICTORY 8.8.8. with Alleluias
Latin: 17th century
Tr. Francis Pott, 1859
Arr. from G. P. Sante da Palestrina, 1591
William H. Monk, 1861
Al - le - lu - ia! Al - le - lu - ia! Al - le - lu - ia!
1. The strife is o'er, the bat - tle done; Now is the vic - tor's tri - umph won; Now be the song of praise be - gun:
2. Death's might-iest pow'rs have done their worst, And Je - sus has his foes dis - persed; Let shouts of praise and joy out - burst:
3. On the third morn, he rose a - gain Glo - rious in maj - es - ty to reign; O let us swell the joy - ful strain:
4. Lord, by the stripes that wound - ed thee From death's dread sting thy ser - vants free, That we may live and sing to thee:
Al - le - lu - ia!
D.S.

132

Sunset to Sunrise

Clement of Alexandria, c.170-220
Para. by Howard C. Robbins, 1938

WAREHAM L.M.
William Knapp, 1738

1. Sun - set to sun - rise chang - es now,
2. E'en though the sun with - holds its light,
3. Here in o'er - whelm - ing fi - nal strife
For God doth make his world a - new;
Lo! a more heav'n - ly lamp shines here,
The Lord of life hath vic - to - ry;
On the Re - deem - er's thorn - crowned brow
And from the cross on Cal - v'ry's height
And sin is slain, and death brings life,
The won - ders of that dawn we view.
Gleams of e - ter - ni - ty ap - pear.
And sons of earth hold heav'n in fee.

Joy Dawned Again on Easter Day

PUER NOBIS NASCITUR L.M.
Adapted by Michael Praetorius, 1609
Harm. by George R. Woodward, 1904

Latin: 5th century?
Tr. John M. Neale, 1852, alt.

Unison
1. Joy dawned a - gain on Eas - ter Day, The sun shone out with fair ar - ray, When to their long - ing eyes re - stored, The a - pos - tles saw their ris - en Lord.
2. O Je - sus, King of gen - tle - ness, Do thou thy - self our hearts pos - sess That we may give thee all our days The will - ing trib - ute of our praise.
3. O Lord of all, with us a - bide In this our joy - ful Eas - ter - tide; From ev - ery weap - on death can wield Thine own re - deemed for - ev - er shield.

An alternate setting may be found at No. 14.

Alleluia! Hearts to Heaven

HYFRYDOL 8.7.8.7.D.

Christopher Wordsworth, 1862 *Melody by Rowland H. Prichard, 1855*

1. Al - le - lu - ia! Al - le - lu - ia! Hearts to heav'n and voic - es raise;
2. Now the i - ron bars are bro - ken, Christ from death to life is born;
3. Al - le - lu - ia! Al - le - lu - ia! Glo - ry be to God on high;

Sing to God a hymn of glad - ness, Sing to God a hymn of praise.
Glo - rious life, and life im - mor - tal, On this ho - ly Eas - ter morn;
Al - le - lu - ia to the Sav - ior Who has won the vic - to - ry;

He who on the cross as Sav - ior For the world's sal - va - tion bled,
Christ has tri - umphed, and we con - quer By his might - y en - ter - prise,
Al - le - lu - ia to the Spir - it, Fount of love and sanc - ti - ty;

Je - sus Christ, the King of glo - ry, Now is ris - en from the dead.
We with him to life e - ter - nal By his res - ur - rec - tion rise.
Al - le - lu - ia! Al - le - lu - ia! To the tri - une ma - jes - ty.

135

*O Sons and Daughters of the King

Jean Tisserand, d.1494
Tr. John M. Neale, 1851, alt.

O FILII ET FILIAE 8.8.8. *with Alleluias*
French: 15th century

Unison
Al - le - lu - ia! Al - le - lu - ia! Al - le - lu - ia!
1. O sons and daugh - ters of the King, Whom heav'n - ly
2. That Eas - ter morn, at break of day, The faith - ful
3. An an - gel clad in white they see, Who sat and
4. Bless - ed are they that have not seen And yet whose
5. On this most ho - ly day of days, To God your
hosts in glo - ry sing, To - day the grave has
wom - en went their way To seek the tomb where
spoke un - to the three, "Your Lord is gone to
faith has con - stant been; In life e - ter - nal
hearts and voic - es raise In laud and ju - bi -
lost its sting.
Je - sus lay.
Gal - i - lee." Al - le - lu - ia!
they shall reign.
lee and praise.
D.S.

*The Day of Resurrection

HERZLICH TUT MICH ERFREUEN 7.6.7.6.D.

John of Damascus, 8th century
Tr. John Mason Neale, 1862, alt.

German Tune, 16th century
Recast by Johann Walther, 1552

1. The day of res - ur - rec - tion, Earth, tell it out a - broad,
2. Our hearts be pure from e - vil That we may see a - right
3. Now let the heav'ns be joy - ful, Let earth her song be - gin,
4. Then praise we God the Fa - ther, And praise we Christ his Son,
The Pass - o - ver of glad - ness, The Pass - o - ver of God.
The Lord in rays e - ter - nal Of res - ur - rec - tion light
Let all the world keep tri - umph And all that is there - in.
With them the Ho - ly Spir - it, E - ter - nal Three in One,
From death to life e - ter - nal, From this world to the
And, lis - t'ning to his ac - cents, May hear, so calm and
Let all things, seen and un - seen, Their notes of glad - ness
Till all the ran - somed num - ber Fall down be - fore the
sky, Our Christ has brought us o - ver With hymns of vic - to - ry.
plain, His own "All hail!" and, hear - ing, May raise the vic - tor strain.
blend; For Christ the Lord has ris - en, Our joy that has no end.
throne, And hon - or, pow'r, and glo - ry As - cribe to God a - lone.

Good Christian Men, Rejoice and Sing

GELOBT SEI GOTT 8.8.8. *with Alleluias*

Cyril A. Alington, 1925 — *Melody by Melchior Vulpius, 1609*

1. Good Chris - tian men, re - joice and sing! Now is the tri - umph of our King! To all the world glad news we bring:
2. The Lord of life is risen for aye; Bring flowers of song to strew his way; Let all man - kind re - joice and say:
3. Praise we in songs of vic - to - ry That love, that life which can - not die, And sing with hearts up - lift - ed high:
4. Thy name we bless, O ris - en Lord, And sing to - day with one ac - cord The life laid down, the life re - stored:
Refrain
Al - le - lu - ia! Al-le- lu - ia! Al-le-lu - ia!

Rejoice, the Lord Is Risen

LOCUST GROVE 7.6.7.6. *with Refrain*

Robert D. Loggie, 1968

Walter Watson, 1972

Unison

1. Re - joice, the Lord is ris - en, We now need nev - er fear.
For Christ has burst his pris - on; We know his pres - ence here.

2. Give praise and glad thanks - giv - ing, Death's pow - er can - not claim.
Christ Je - sus rules the liv - ing; We tri - umph in his name.

3. His death our one sal - va - tion, His love has quelled our fear.
No threat, nor dread temp - ta - tion Can harm while he is near.

4. Re - make us in your im - age, O Je - sus, Lord, we pray.
To men of faith give cour - age On this glad Eas - ter day.

Al - le - lu - ia! Al - le - lu - ia! Al - le - lu - - ia!

5. Ring in the new cre - a - tion, The old shall nev - er stay.
New life our bright pos - ses - sion In realms of end - less day.
Al - le - lu - ia! Al - le - lu - ia! Al - le - lu - ia! A - men.

Thine Is the Glory

Edmond L. Budry, 1904
Tr. R. Birch Hoyle, 1923

JUDAS MACCABEUS 5.5.6.5.6.5.6.5. *with Refrain*
Georg F. Handel, 1751

1. Thine is the glo - ry, Ris- en, con-quering Son; End-less is the
2. Lo! Je - sus meets thee, Ris- en from the tomb; Lov- ing - ly he
3. No more we doubt thee, Glo-rious Prince of life! Life is nought with-

vic - tory Thou o'er death hast won. An - gels in bright rai - ment
greets thee, Scat - ters fear and gloom; Let his church with glad - ness
out thee; Aid us in our strife; Make us more than con-querors,

Rolled the stone a - way, Kept the fold - ed grave - clothes
Hymns of tri - umph sing, For her Lord now liv - eth;
Through thy death - less love; Bring us safe through Jor - dan

Where thy bod - y lay.
Death hath lost its sting.
To thy home a - bove.

Refrain

Thine is the glo - ry, Ris- en, con-quering

Son; End-less is the vic - tory Thou o'er death hast won.

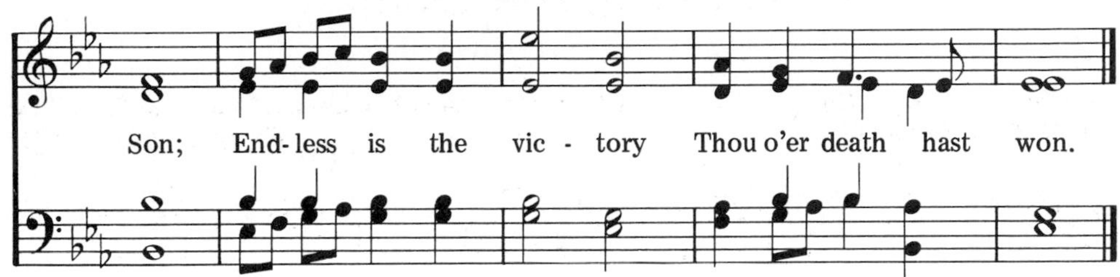

140

*Fairest Lord Jesus

Münster Gesangbuch, *1677*
Schlesische Volkslieder, 1842
Tr. Church Chorals and Choir Studies, *1850*

SCHÖNSTER HERR JESU 5.6.8.5.5.8.
Silesian Melody

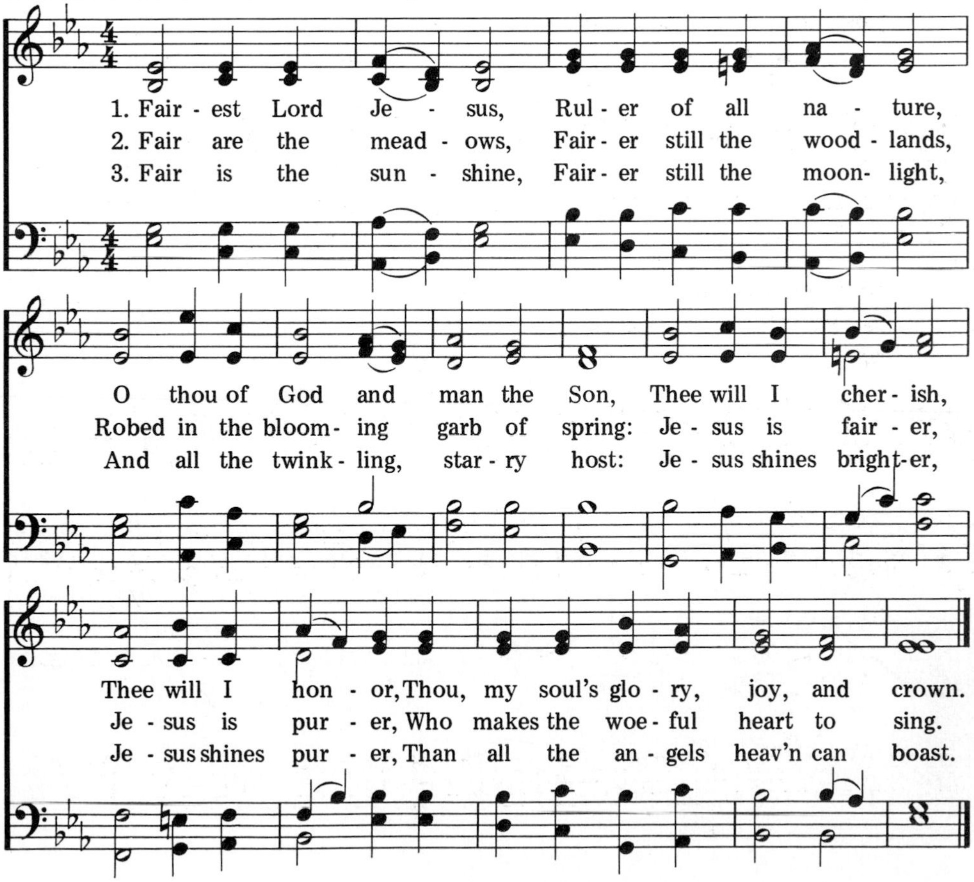

1. Fair - est Lord Je - sus, Rul - er of all na - ture,
2. Fair are the mead - ows, Fair - er still the wood - lands,
3. Fair is the sun - shine, Fair - er still the moon- light,
O thou of God and man the Son, Thee will I cher - ish,
Robed in the bloom - ing garb of spring: Je - sus is fair - er,
And all the twink - ling, star - ry host: Je - sus shines bright - er,
Thee will I hon - or, Thou, my soul's glo - ry, joy, and crown.
Je - sus is pur - er, Who makes the woe - ful heart to sing.
Je - sus shines pur - er, Than all the an - gels heav'n can boast.

141

*Beautiful Savior

Münster Gesangbuch, *1677*
Schlesische Volkslieder, 1842
Tr. Joseph Augustus Seiss, 1823-1904

SCHÖNSTER HERR JESU 5.6.8.5.5.8.
Silesian Melody

1. Beau - ti - ful Sav - ior, King of cre - a - tion,
2. Fair are the mead - ows, Fair are the wood-lands,
3. Fair is the sun - shine, Fair is the moon-light,
4. Beau - ti - ful Sav - ior, Lord of the na - tions,

Son of God and Son of man! Tru - ly I'd love thee,
Robed in flow'rs of bloom - ing spring; Je - sus is fair - er,
Bright the spar - kling stars on high; Je - sus shines bright - er,
Son of God and Son of man! Glo - ry and hon - or,

Tru - ly I'd serve thee, Light of my soul, my joy, my crown.
Je - sus is pur - er, He makes our sor-rowing spir - it sing.
Je - sus shines pur - er, Than all the an - gels in the sky.
Praise, ad - o - ra - tion, Now and for - ev - er - more be thine.

Rejoice, the Lord Is King

DARWALL'S 148th 6.6.6.6.8.8.

Charles Wesley, 1746 — *John Darwall, 1770*

1. Re - joice, the Lord is king! Your Lord and King a -
2. The Lord our sav - ior reigns, The God of truth and
3. His king - dom can - not fail, He rules o'er earth and

dore! Re - joice, give thanks, and sing, And tri - umph
love; When he had purged our stains, He took his
heav'n; The keys of death and hell Are to our

ev - er - more:
seat a - bove:
Je - sus given:

Refrain

Lift up your heart, lift up your voice! Re - joice, a - gain I say, re - joice!

Christ Is the World's True Light

O GOTT, DU FROMMER GOTT 6.7.6.7.6.6.6.6.

John 1:9
George W. Briggs, 1931

Melody by Ahasuerus Fritsch, 1679
Harm. by Johann Sebastian Bach, 1726

1. Christ is the world's true light, Its captain of salvation,
The daystar clear and bright Of every man and nation;
New life, new hope awakes Where-e'er men own his sway;
Freedom her bondage breaks, And night is turned to day.

2. In Christ all races meet, Their ancient feuds forgetting,
The whole round world complete, From sunrise to its setting;
When Christ is throned as Lord, Men shall forsake their fear,
To plough-share beat the sword, To pruning-hook the spear.

3. One Lord, in one great name Unite us all who own thee;
Cast out our pride and shame That hinder to enthrone thee;
The world has waited long, Has travailed long in pain;
To heal its ancient wrong, Come, Prince of peace, and reign.

144

I Greet Thee, Who My Sure Redeemer Art

TOULON 10.10.10.10.

John Calvin, 1545

Genevan Psalter, *1551*

1. I greet thee, who my sure Re - deem - er art,
2. Thou art the life, by which a - lone we live,
3. Our hope is in no oth - er save in thee;
My on - ly Trust and Sav - ior of my heart,
And all our sub - stance and our strength re - ceive;
Our faith is built up - on thy prom - ise free;
Who pain didst un - der - go for my poor sake;
Sus - tain us by thy faith and by thy power,
Lord, give us peace and make us calm and sure,
I pray thee from our hearts all cares to take.
And give us strength in ev - ery try - ing hour.
That in thy strength we ev - er - more en dure.

145

Father Eternal, Ruler of Creation

LANGHAM 11.10.11.10.10.

Laurence Housman, 1919 *Geoffrey Shaw, 1919*

Unison
1. Fa - ther e - ter nal, Rul - er of cre - a - tion, Spir - it of
2. Ra - ces and peo - ples, lo, we stand di - vid - ed, And shar-ing
3. Lust of pos - ses - sion work-eth des - o - la - tions; There is no
4. How shall we love thee, ho - ly, hid - den Be - ing, If we love
life, which moved ere form was made, Through the thick dark - ness
not our griefs, no joy can share; By wars and tu - mults
meek - ness in the sons of earth; Led by no star, the
not the world which thou hast made? O give us broth - er -
cov-ering ev - ery na - tion, Light to man's blind - ness, O be thou our
love is mocked, de - rid - ed, His con-quering cross no king-dom wills to
rul - ers of the na - tions Still fail to bring us to the bliss-ful
love for bet - ter see - ing Thy Word made flesh, and in a man-ger
aid: Thy king - dom come, O Lord, thy will be done.
bear: Thy king - dom come, O Lord, thy will be done.
birth. Thy king - dom come, O Lord, thy will be done.
laid: Thy king - dom come, O Lord, thy will be done.

He Bestows upon Us
His Holy Spirit,
Creating and Renewing
the Church of Jesus Christ,
Binding in Covenant
Faithful People of All Ages,
Tongues, and Races

Come, Holy Ghost, Our Souls Inspire

VENI CREATOR L.M.
Plainsong
Vesperale Romanum *(Mechlin)*

Latin: 9th century
Tr. John Cosin, 1627

Unison

1. Come, Ho - ly Ghost, our souls in - spire And light-en with ce -
2. Thy bless - ed unc - tion from a - bove Is com-fort, life, and
3. A - noint and cheer our soil - ed face With the a - bun - dance
4. Teach us to know the Fa - ther, Son, And thee, of both, to

les - tial fire; Thou the a - noint - ing Spir - it art
fire of love; En - a - ble with per - pet - ual light
of thy grace; Keep far our foes, give peace at home;
be but one; That through the a - ges all a - long

Who dost thy seven - fold gifts im - part.
The dull-ness of our blind - ed sight.
Where thou art guide no ill can come.
This may be our end - less song: Praise to thy e -

After last stanza

ter - nal mer-it, Fa - ther, Son, and Ho - ly Spir-it. A - men.

*Come Down, O Love Divine

Bianco da Siena, c.1367-1434
Tr. Richard F. Littledale, 1867
DOWN AMPNEY 6.6.11.D.
R. Vaughan Williams, 1906
1. Come down, O Love di - vine, Seek thou this soul of
2. O let it free - ly burn, Till earth - ly pas - sions
3. And so the yearn - ing strong With which the soul will
mine, And vis - it it with thine own ar - dor glow - ing;
turn To dust and ash - es in its heat con - sum - ing;
long, Shall far out - pass the power of hu - man tell - ing;
O Com - fort - er, draw near, With - in my heart ap - pear,
And let thy glo - rious light Shine ev - er on my sight,
For none can guess its grace, Till he be - come the place
And kin - dle it, thy ho - ly flame be - stow - ing.
And clothe me round, the while my path il - lum - ing.
Where - in the Ho - ly Spir - it makes his dwell - ing.

Creator Spirit, Come to Us

Latin: 9th century
Tr. F. L. Battles, 1970

GROVE STREET 12.12.12.12.
Joseph Willcox Jenkins, 1970

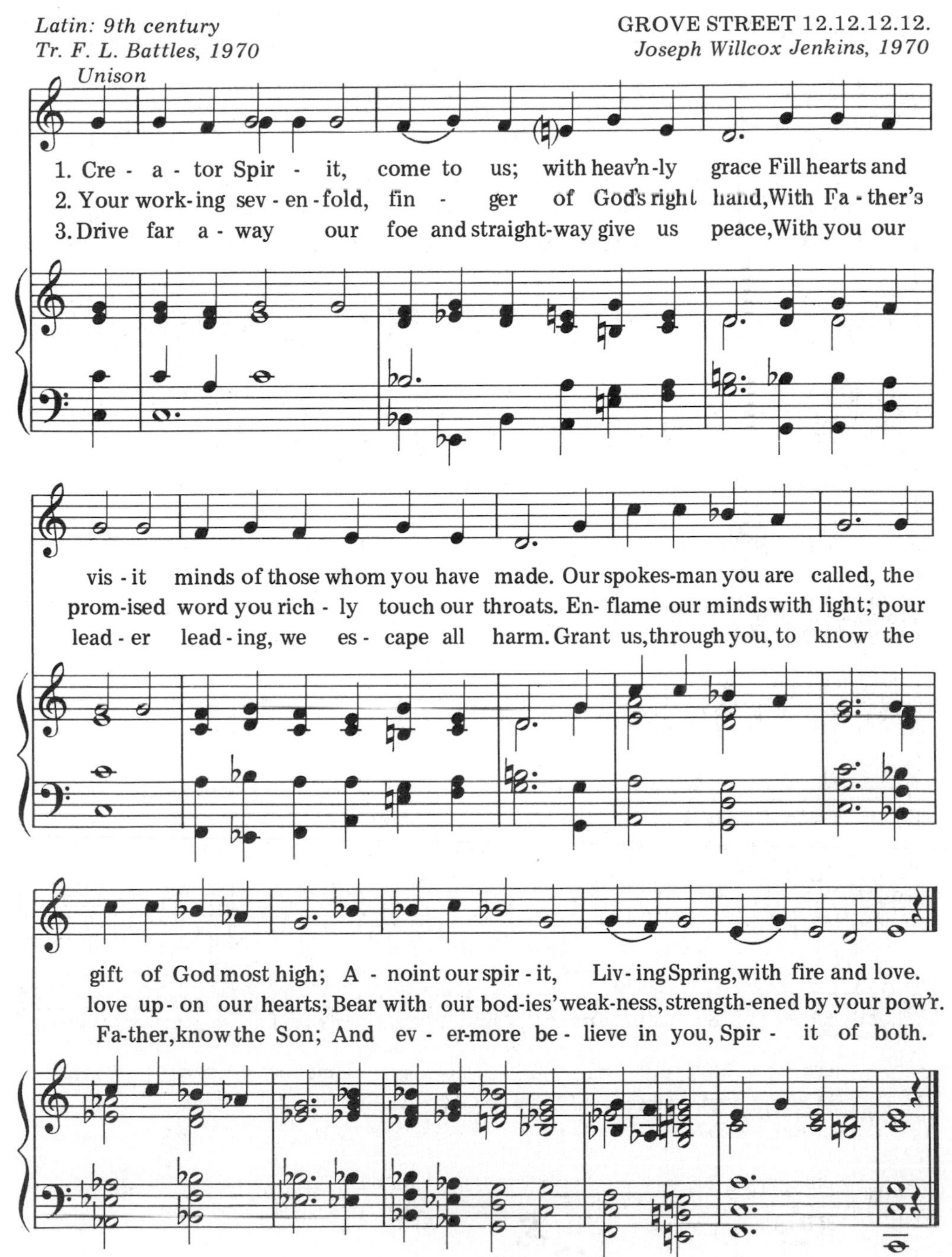
Unison
1. Cre - a - tor Spir - it, come to us; with heav'n-ly grace Fill hearts and
2. Your work-ing sev - en - fold, fin - ger of God's right hand, With Fa - ther's
3. Drive far a - way our foe and straight-way give us peace, With you our
vis - it minds of those whom you have made. Our spokes-man you are called, the
prom-ised word you rich - ly touch our throats. En- flame our minds with light; pour
lead - er lead - ing, we es - cape all harm. Grant us, through you, to know the
gift of God most high; A - noint our spir - it, Liv - ing Spring, with fire and love.
love up- on our hearts; Bear with our bod-ies' weak-ness, strength-ened by your pow'r.
Fa-ther, know the Son; And ev - er-more be - lieve in you, Spir - it of both.

149

On God the Spirit We Rely

Para. of the
United Church of Christ "Statement of Faith"
Mary Louise VanDyke, 1973

TRURO L.M.
Thomas Williams'
Psalmodia Evangelica, *1789*

1. On God the Spir - it we re - ly; To his great
2. His love shall guide, his judg - ments stay, His righ - teous
3. Thus bound in cov - e - nant, we search For ways to
4. His help we seek to face our time; Through trial we
deeds we tes - ti - fy; All worlds are his, all
will di - rect our way. He shares our hum - ble,
serve him through his church; By serv - ing man wher -
trust his grace di - vine; Man's jus - tice, peace, O
man - kind shares Cre - a - tion's pow'r and the choice it bears.
hu - man frame; His res - ur - rec - tion we pro - claim.
e'er is need, Our lives from self and death are freed.
Church, de - fend; Help shape God's king - dom with - out end.

A higher setting may be found at No. 20.

150

O Spirit of the Living God

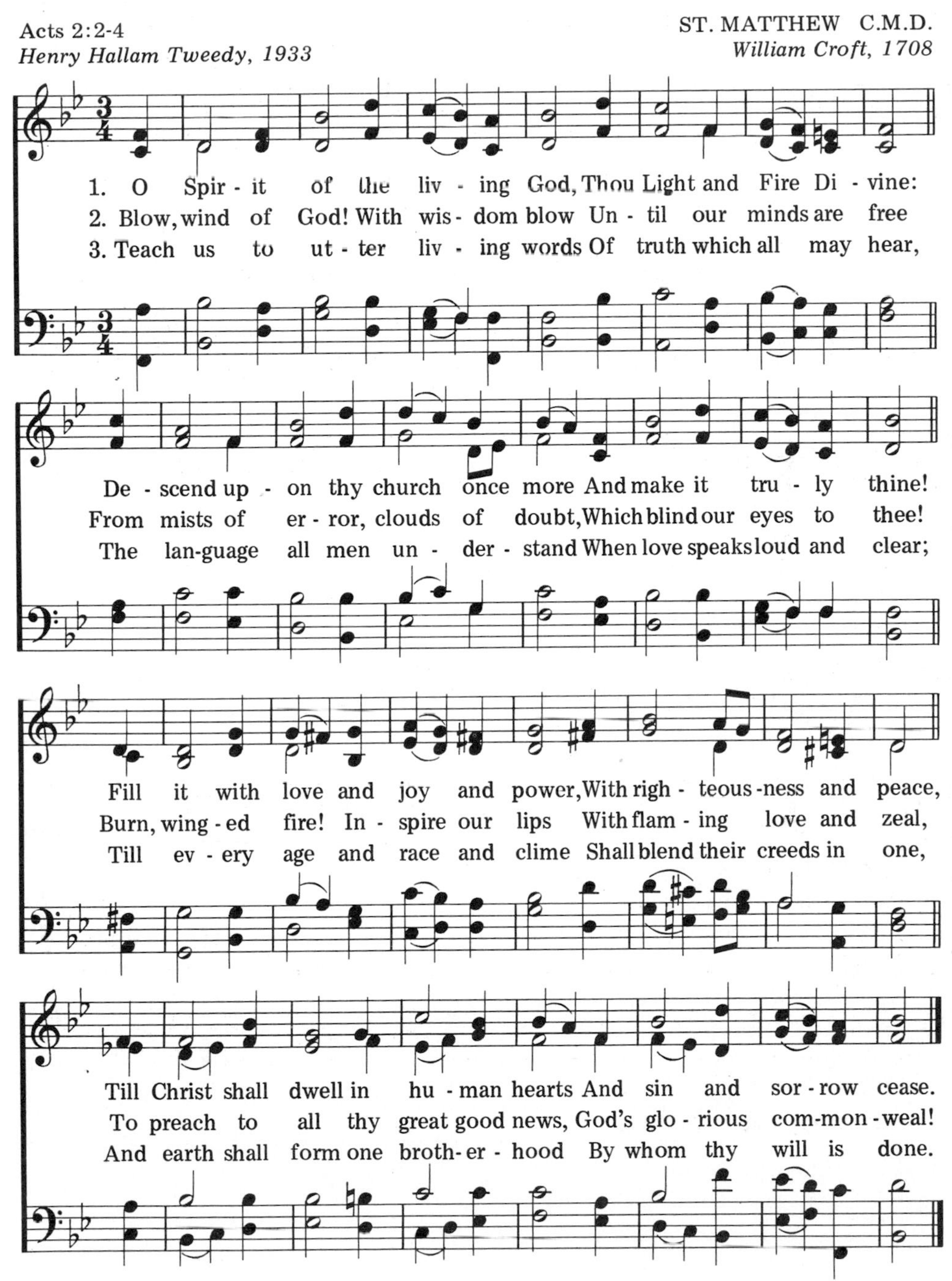

Acts 2:2-4
Henry Hallam Tweedy, 1933
ST. MATTHEW C.M.D.
William Croft, 1708
1. O Spir - it of the liv - ing God, Thou Light and Fire Di - vine:
2. Blow, wind of God! With wis - dom blow Un - til our minds are free
3. Teach us to ut - ter liv - ing words Of truth which all may hear,
De - scend up - on thy church once more And make it tru - ly thine!
From mists of er - ror, clouds of doubt, Which blind our eyes to thee!
The lan-guage all men un - der - stand When love speaks loud and clear;
Fill it with love and joy and power, With righ - teous - ness and peace,
Burn, wing - ed fire! In - spire our lips With flam - ing love and zeal,
Till ev - ery age and race and clime Shall blend their creeds in one,
Till Christ shall dwell in hu - man hearts And sin and sor - row cease.
To preach to all thy great good news, God's glo - rious com-mon - weal!
And earth shall form one broth - er - hood By whom thy will is done.

Come, Gracious Spirit, Heavenly Dove

MENDON L.M.
German Melody
Arr. by Samuel Dyer, 1828

Simon Browne, 1720, alt.

1. Come, gra - cious Spir - it, heav'n - ly Dove, With light and com - fort from a - bove; Be thou our guard - ian, thou our guide, O'er ev - ery thought and step pre - side.
2. The light of truth to us dis - play And make us know and choose thy way; Plant ho - ly fear in ev - ery heart, That we from thee may ne'er de - part.
3. Lead us to Christ, the liv - ing Way, Nor let us from his pre - cepts stray; Lead us to ho - li - ness, the road That we must take to dwell with God.
4. Lead us to heav'n, that we may share Full - ness of joy for - ev - er there; Lead us to God, our fi - nal rest, To be with him for - ev - er blest.

A higher setting may be found at No. 154.

152

*The Church's One Foundation

2 Cor. 5:17
Samuel J. Stone, 1866

AUELIA 7.6.7.6.D.
Samuel S. Wesley, 1864

1. The church's one foun - da - tion Is Je - sus Christ her Lord;
2. E - lect from ev - ery na - tion, Yet one o'er all the earth,
3. 'Mid toil and trib - u - la - tion, And tu - mult of her war,
4. Yet she on earth hath un - ion With God, the Three in One,

She is his new cre - a - tion By wa - ter and the word;
Her char - ter of sal - va - tion, One Lord, one faith, one birth,
She waits the con - sum - ma - tion Of peace for - ev - er - more;
And mys - tic sweet com - mun - ion With those whose rest is won.

From heav'n he came and sought her To be his ho - ly bride;
One ho - ly name she bless - es, Par - takes one ho - ly food,
Till with the vi - sion glo - rious, Her long - ing eyes are blest,
O hap - py ones and ho - ly! Lord, give us grace that we

With his own blood he bought her, And for her life he died.
And to one hope she press - es, With ev - ery grace en - dued.
And the great church vic - to - rious Shall be the church at rest.
Like them, the meek and low - ly, On high may dwell with thee.

The Church of Christ Is One

Rom. 11:17-21
Cyprian of Carthage, 3d century
De Unitate Ecclesiae, V
Tr. F. L. Battles, 1971

OIKOUMENE *Irregular*
Stanley Tagg, 1971

Unison

1. The church of Christ is one: Man- y are the rays of the sun, but
2. The church of Christ is one: Man- y are the bran-ches of a tree, but
3. The church of Christ is one: Man- y are the streams of a spring: the

on - ly one par - ent light. Take a ray from the sun, Un - cleft the
root-ed in the earth one trunk. Break a branch from a tree, The branch will
source un- di - vid - ed stands. Choke a stream at the source, The stream will

sun re -mains; The church of Christ is bathed–suf - fused in the Lord's un-dy-ing
cease to grow; The bran-ches of the church are spread through the earth, and
fail — go dry; The Well-spring of the church out-flows in man-y streams, and

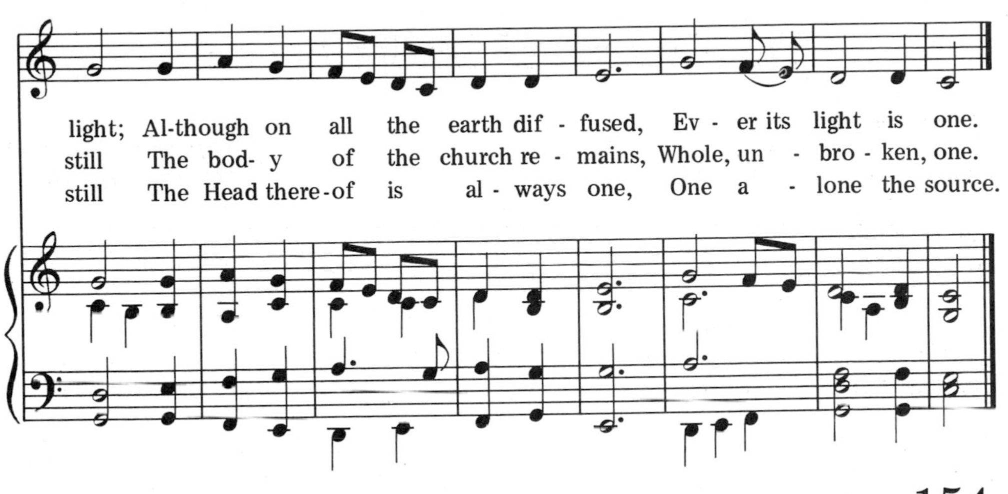
light; Al-though on all the earth dif - fused, Ev - er its light is one.
still The bod- y of the church re - mains, Whole, un - bro - ken, one.
still The Head there-of is al - ways one, One a - lone the source.

154

Founded on Thee, Our Only Lord

MENDON L.M.
German Melody
Arr. by Samuel Dyer, 1828

Matt. 16:18
Samuel F. Smith, 1889

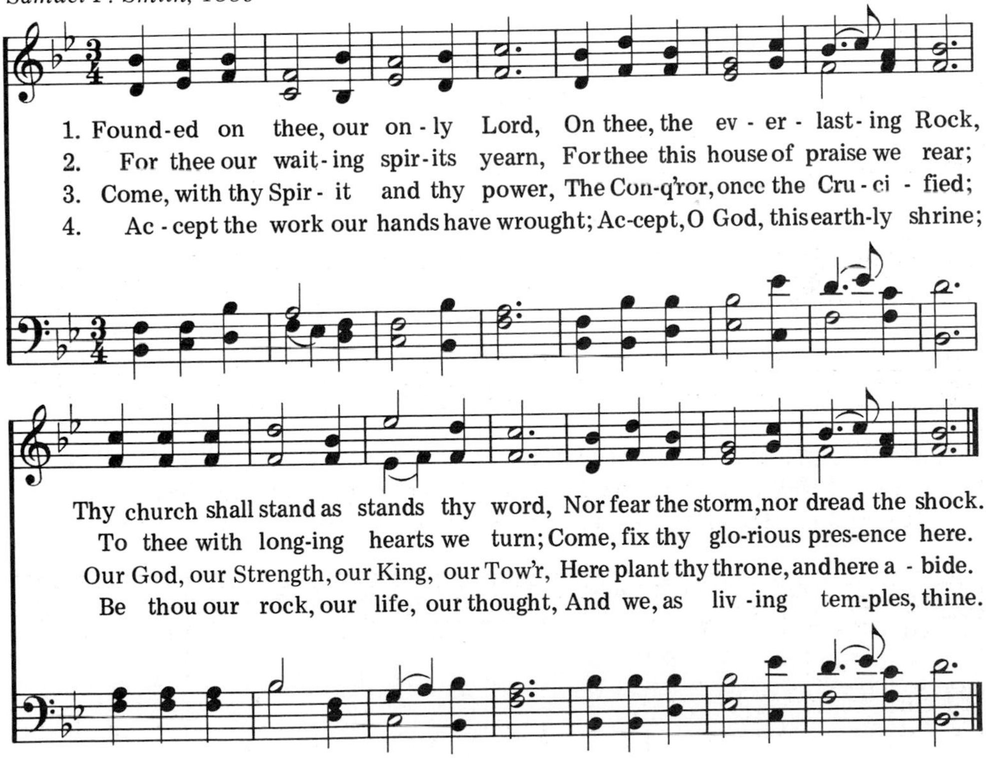

1. Found-ed on thee, our on - ly Lord, On thee, the ev - er - last- ing Rock,
Thy church shall stand as stands thy word, Nor fear the storm, nor dread the shock.

2. For thee our wait- ing spir- its yearn, For thee this house of praise we rear;
To thee with long-ing hearts we turn; Come, fix thy glo-rious pres-ence here.

3. Come, with thy Spir - it and thy power, The Con-q'ror, once the Cru - ci - fied;
Our God, our Strength, our King, our Tow'r, Here plant thy throne, and here a - bide.

4. Ac - cept the work our hands have wrought; Ac-cept, O God, this earth-ly shrine;
Be thou our rock, our life, our thought, And we, as liv -ing tem-ples, thine.

A lower setting may be found at No. 151.

God Is Love

1 John 4:7-8
From the Liturgy of Maundy Thursday
Tr. James Quinn

GOD IS LOVE 13.12.12.12.12.
A. Gregory Murray, 1939

Refrain, Unison

God is love, and where true love is God him - self is there.

Harmony

1. Here in Christ we gath - er, love of Christ our call - ing.
2. When we Chris-tians gath - er, mem-bers of one bod - y,
3. Grant us love's ful - fill - ment, joy with all the bless - ed,

Christ, our love, is with us, glad-ness be his greet - ing.
Let there be in us no dis - cord but one spir - it.
When we see your face, O Sav - ior, in its glo - ry.

Let us fear him, yes, and love him, God e - ter - nal.
Ban-ished now be an - ger, strife, and ev - ery quar - rel.
Shine on us, O pur - est Light of all cre - a - tion,

Rejoice, Ye Pure in Heart 156

MARION S.M. *with Refrain*

Edward H. Plumptre, 1865 — *Arthur H. Messiter, 1883*

1. Re - joice, ye pure in heart; Re - joice, give thanks and sing;
2. Bright youth and snow-crowned age, Strong men and maid-ens meek,
3. Yes, on through life's long path, Still chant-ing as ye go,
4. Praise him who reigns on high, The Lord whom we a - dore,

Your fes-tal ban-ner wave on high, The cross of Christ your king!
Raise high your free, ex - ult - ing song, God's won-drous prais-es speak.
From youth to age, by night and day, In glad-ness and in woe.
The Fa - ther, Son, and Ho - ly Ghost, One God for ev - er - more!

Re - joice, re - joice, Re - joice, give thanks and sing.

Re - joice, re - joice,

157

*Christ, Thou Art the Sure Foundation

1 Peter 2:4-6; Eph. 2:20-22; Rev. 21
Latin: 7th century
Tr. John M. Neale, 1851, alt.
REGENT SQUARE 8.7.8.7.8.7.
Henry T. Smart, 1867
1.Christ, thou art the sure foun-da - tion, Thou the head and cor - ner - stone;
2. To this tem-ple, where we call thee, Come, O Lord of hosts, to - day;
3.Here vouch-safe to all thy ser - vants What they ask of thee to gain,
4.Praise and hon - or to the Fa - ther, Praise and hon - or to the Son,
Cho - sen of the Lord and pre - cious, Bind-ing all the church in one;
With thy wont-ed lov - ing - kind-ness, Hear thy ser - vants as they pray;
What they gain from thee for - ev - er With the bless - ed to re - tain,
Praise and hon - or to the Spir - it, Ev - er three and ev - er one;
Thou thy Zi - on's help for - ev - er And her con - fi - dence a - lone.
And thy full - est ben - e - dic - tion Shed with - in these walls al - way.
And here-af - ter in thy glo - ry Ev - er - more with thee to reign.
One in might and one in glo - ry While un - end - ing a - ges run.

An Ancient Dwelling Is the Church

Nicolai F. S. Grundtvig, 1837
Tr. Edward A. Hansen, 1971

KIRKEN DEN ER ET 8.8.8.8.8.8.8.
Ludvig M. Lindeman, 1840

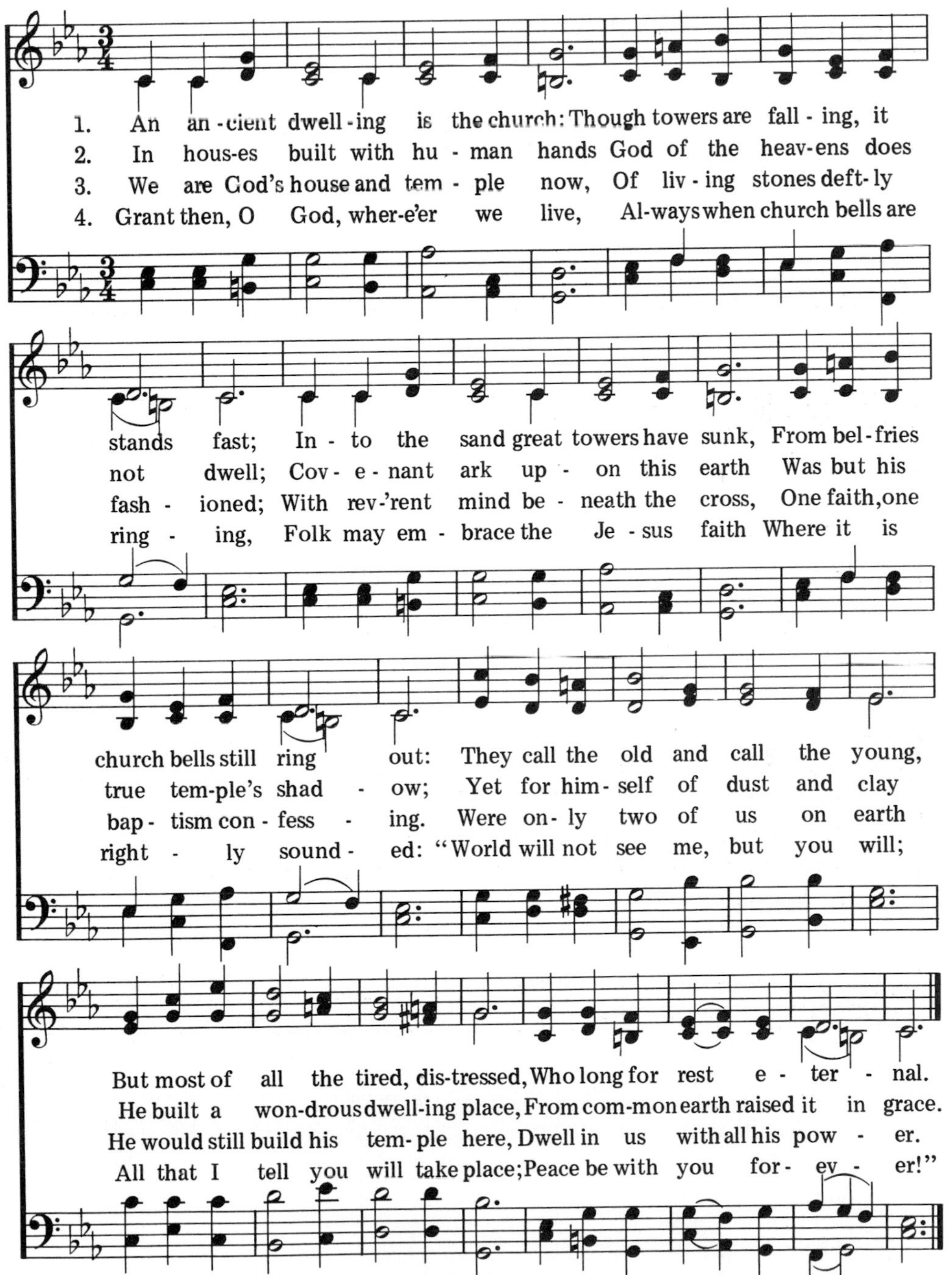
1. An an - cient dwell - ing is the church: Though towers are fall - ing, it
2. In hous-es built with hu - man hands God of the heav-ens does
3. We are God's house and tem - ple now, Of liv - ing stones deft- ly
4. Grant then, O God, wher-e'er we live, Al-ways when church bells are
stands fast; In - to the sand great towers have sunk, From bel - fries
not dwell; Cov - e - nant ark up - on this earth Was but his
fash - ioned; With rev-'rent mind be - neath the cross, One faith, one
ring - ing, Folk may em - brace the Je - sus faith Where it is
church bells still ring out: They call the old and call the young,
true tem-ple's shad - ow; Yet for him - self of dust and clay
bap - tism con - fess - ing. Were on - ly two of us on earth
right - ly sound - ed: "World will not see me, but you will;
But most of all the tired, dis-tressed, Who long for rest e - ter - nal.
He built a won-drous dwell-ing place, From com-mon earth raised it in grace.
He would still build his tem - ple here, Dwell in us with all his pow - er.
All that I tell you will take place; Peace be with you for - ev - er!"

Christ Is the King

George K. A. Bell, 1933

GELOBT SEI GOTT 8.8.8. *with Alleluias*
Melody by Melchior Vulpius, 1609

1. Christ is the king! O friends, re - joice; Broth - ers and sis - ters, with one voice Make all men know he is your choice.
2. O Chris - tian wom - en, Chris - tian men, All the world o - ver, seek a - gain The way dis - ci - ples fol - lowed then.
3. Christ through all a - ges is the same: Place the same hope in his great name, With the same faith his word pro - claim.
4. Let love's un - con - quer - a - ble might Your scat - tered com - pa - nies u - nite In ser - vice to the Lord of light.
5. So shall God's will on earth be done, New lamps be lit, new tasks be - gun, And the whole church at last be one.
Refrain
Al - le - lu - ia! Al - le - lu - ia! Al - le - lu - ia!

Lord, We Thank Thee for Our Brothers

PLEADING SAVIOUR 8.7.8.7.D.
Melody The Christian Lyre, *1831*

Roger Powell, 1948

1. Lord, we thank thee for our broth-ers Keep-ing faith with us and thee,
2. God be praised for con-gre-ga-tions Com-ing side by side to thee;
3. Hal-low-ed be thy name for-ev-er! Heal our dif-fer-en-ces of old:

Join-ing heart to heart with oth-ers, Mak-ing strong our com-pa-ny.
Man-y tongues of man-y na-tions Sing the great-er un-i-ty.
Bless thy church-'s new en-deav-or; For thy king-dom make us bold.

With the cross our on-ly stan-dard Let us sing with one great voice,
Sweet the psalm and sweet the car-ol, When our song is raised as one.
One our Christ and one our gos-pel, Make us one we now im-plore.

Glo-ry, glo-ry, thine the king-dom: Church-es in thy church re-joice.
Glo-ry, glo-ry, thine the pow-er, As in heav'n thy will be done.
Glo-ry, glo-ry, thine the glo-ry Through the a-ges ev-er-more.

161

Rejoice, O People

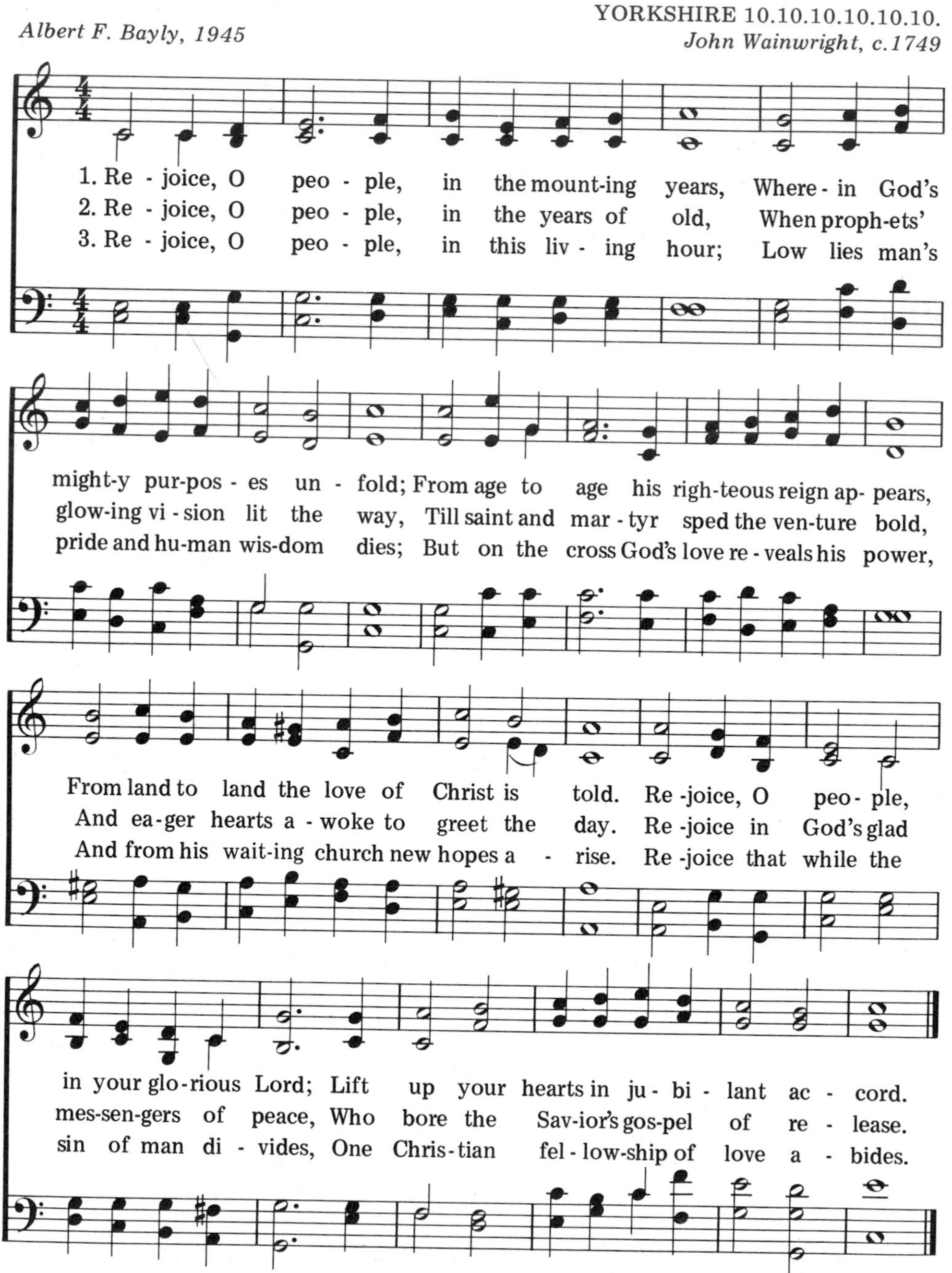
Albert F. Bayly, 1945
YORKSHIRE 10.10.10.10.10.10.
John Wainwright, c.1749
1. Re - joice, O peo - ple, in the mount-ing years, Where - in God's
2. Re - joice, O peo - ple, in the years of old, When proph-ets'
3. Re - joice, O peo - ple, in this liv - ing hour; Low lies man's
might-y pur-pos - es un - fold; From age to age his righ-teous reign ap- pears,
glow-ing vi - sion lit the way, Till saint and mar - tyr sped the ven-ture bold,
pride and hu-man wis-dom dies; But on the cross God's love re - veals his power,
From land to land the love of Christ is told. Re -joice, O peo- ple,
And ea-ger hearts a - woke to greet the day. Re -joice in God's glad
And from his wait-ing church new hopes a - rise. Re -joice that while the
in your glo-rious Lord; Lift up your hearts in ju - bi - lant ac - cord.
mes-sen-gers of peace, Who bore the Sav-ior's gos-pel of re - lease.
sin of man di - vides, One Chris-tian fel - low-ship of love a - bides.

162

When from the Shores

ALL SAINTS NEW C.M.D.
William Nelson, 1956
Henry S. Cutler, 1872
1. When from the shores of oth - er lands, Through per-ils of the sea,
2. We dif - fer, Lord, in man - y ways, With man - y voic- es sing,
3. O heal the rifts of Chris - ten - dom, That oth- er men may see
Came men op-pressed and pil - grim bands In quest of lib - er - ty;
Yet tune our souls to com- mon praise, And one de - vo - tion bring.
One Spir - it in our midst, and come To share our u - ni - ty.
They kept their faith though sore - ly tried; They hum-bly knelt to pray.
O grant us now the zeal that fills With cour-age from a - bove;
Teach us to love be - yond our creed, To care be - yond our kin;
O thou who blessed them, stand be - side And strength-en us to - day.
U - nite our hearts and move our wills To com-mon works of love.
Turn no - ble thought to val - iant deed, The whole wide world to win.

Lord, Bless Our Homes

CHARTERHOUSE 11.10.11.10.

Frank von Christierson, 1957 *David Evans, 1927*

Unison
1. Lord, bless our homes with peace and love and laugh - ter,
2. May ev - ery heart re - ceive his lov - ing spir - it
3. For - give the hurts our self - ish - ness in - flict - ed
4. Fa - ther, in grat - i - tude for homes and loved ones,
With un - der - stand - ing and with loy - al - ty.
And know the truth that makes life tru - ly free;
On those we love and those who love us best.
We o - pen now our hearts to all man - kind.
May we to - geth - er fol - low Christ the Mas - ter
Then, in that spir - it may we live u - nit - ed,
Christ, heal the scars, and draw us all to - geth - er
Grant us your spir - it — love for all our broth - ers —

And know the bless - ing of his sov - 'reign - ty.
And find in God our deep se - cur - i - ty.
In him whose will is peace and joy and rest.
So in your peace may we our con - cord find.

164

*In Christ There Is No East or West

McKEE C.M.
Negro Melody
John Oxenham, 1908 *Adapted by Harry T. Burleigh, 1940*

1. In Christ there is no East or West, In him no South or North; But one great fel - low - ship of love Through-out the whole wide earth.
2. In him shall true hearts ev - ery-where Their high com-mu - nion find; His ser - vice is the gold- en cord Close - bind - ing all man - kind.
3. Join hands, then, broth-ers of the faith, What-e'er your race may be! Who serves my Fa - ther as a son Is sure - ly kin to me.
4. In Christ now meet both East and West, In him meet South and North; All Christ - ly souls are one in him Through-out the whole wide earth.

We Come unto Our Fathers' God

NUN FREUT EUCH 8.7.8.7.8.8.7.
Melody by Martin Luther in Klug's Geistliche Lieder, *Wittenberg, 1535*

Thomas H. Gill, 1868

1. We come un - to our fa - thers' God; Their rock is our sal - va - tion;
2. Their joy un - to the Lord we bring; Their song to us de - scend-eth;
3. Ye saints to come, take up the strain, The same sweet theme en-deav - or;

The e - ter - nal arms, their dear a - bode, We make our hab - i - ta - tion.
The Spir - it who in them did sing To us his mu - sic lend - eth:
Un - bro-ken be the gold - en chain! Keep on the song for - ev - er!

We bring thee, Lord, the praise they brought, We seek thee as thy
His song in them, in us, is one; We raise it high, we
Safe in the same dear dwell - ing place, Rich with the same e -

saints have sought In ev - ery gen - er - a - tion.
send it on, The song that nev - er end - eth.
ter - nal grace, Bless the same bound - less Giv - er.

Our Father, by Whose Name

Eph. 3:14-15
F. Bland Tucker, 1941

RHOSYMEDRE 6.6.6.6.8.8.8.
John D. Edwards, 1840

1. Our Fa - ther, by whose name All fa - ther - hood is known,
2. O Christ, thy - self a child With - in an earth - ly home,
3. O Spir - it, who dost bind Our hearts in u - ni - ty,
Who dost in love pro - claim Each fam - i - ly thine own,
With heart still un - de - filed, Thou didst to man - hood come;
Who teach - est us to find The love from self set free,
Bless thou all par - ents, guard - ing well, With con - stant love as
Our chil - dren bless, in ev - ery place, That they may all be -
In all our hearts such love in - crease, That ev - ery home, by
sen - ti - nel, The homes in which thy peo - ple dwell.
hold thy face, And know - ing thee may grow in grace.
this re - lease, May be the dwell - ing place of peace.

H*e Calls Us into His Church to Accept the Cost and Joy of Discipleship*

To Be His Servants in the Service of Men

To Proclaim the Gospel to All the World and Resist the Powers of Evil

To Share in Christ's Baptism and Eat at His Table

To Join Him in His Passion and Victory

All My Hope on God Is Founded

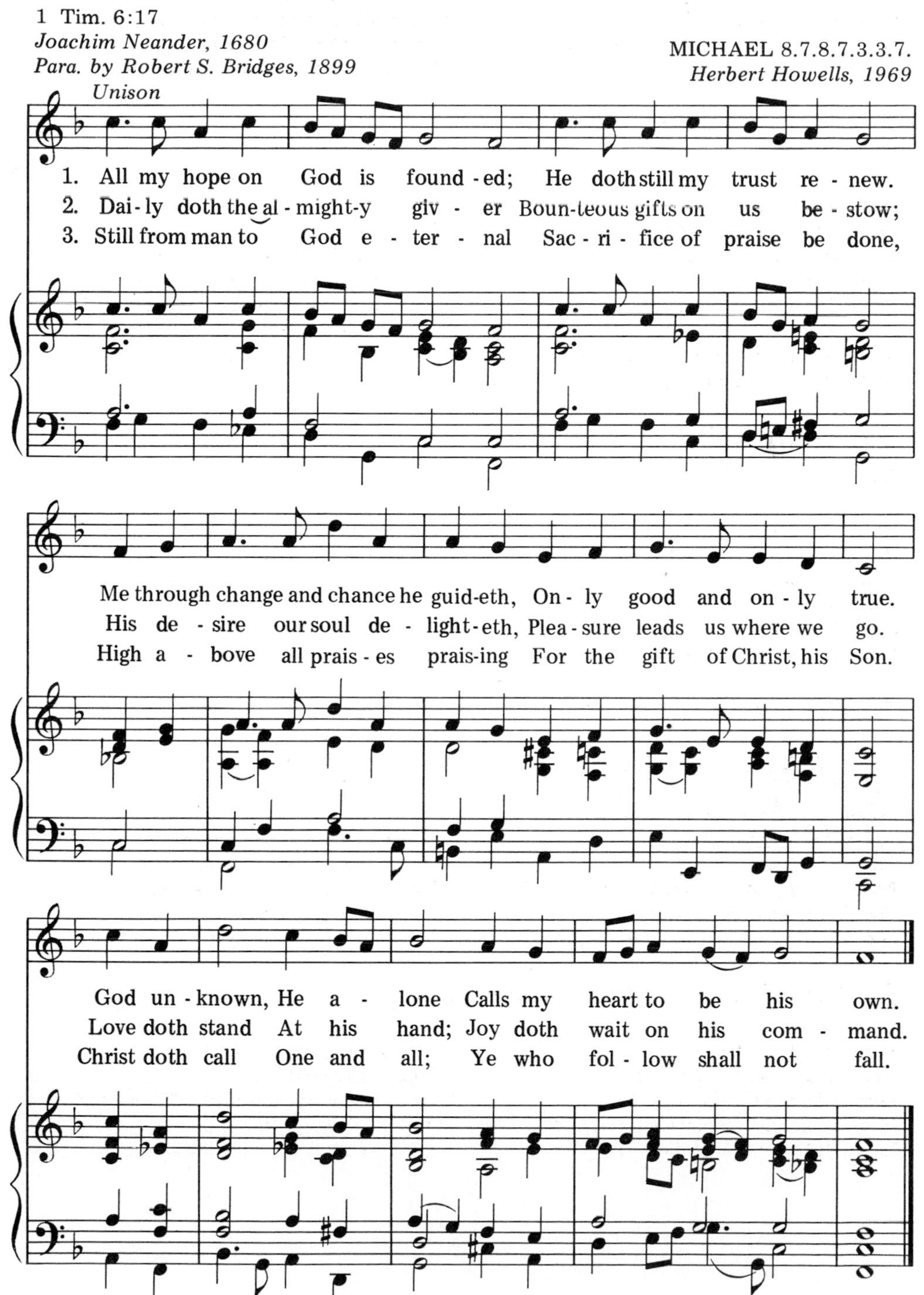
1 Tim. 6:17
Joachim Neander, 1680
Para. by Robert S. Bridges, 1899
MICHAEL 8.7.8.7.3.3.7.
Herbert Howells, 1969
Unison
1. All my hope on God is found-ed; He doth still my trust re-new.
2. Dai-ly doth the al-might-y giv-er Boun-teous gifts on us be-stow;
3. Still from man to God e-ter-nal Sac-ri-fice of praise be done,
Me through change and chance he guid-eth, On-ly good and on-ly true.
His de-sire our soul de-light-eth, Plea-sure leads us where we go.
High a-bove all prais-es prais-ing For the gift of Christ, his Son.
God un-known, He a-lone Calls my heart to be his own.
Love doth stand At his hand; Joy doth wait on his com-mand.
Christ doth call One and all; Ye who fol-low shall not fall.

A Christian Must by Faith Be Filled

HERR JESU CHRIST, DICH ZU L.M.

Martin Luther, 1520
Para. by F. L. and M. D. Battles, 1965

Pensum Sacrum, *Görlitz, 1648*
Harm. from Cantionale Sacrum, *Gotha, 1651*

1. A Chris - tian must by faith be filled, And
2. From faith flow forth both love and joy; From
3. How glo - rious is the Chris - tian life: All
4. The name of Chris - tian that we bear Be -

be made rich, like Christ, his head; By faith, his righ - teous-
love, a joy - ful, will - ing mind, A mind that free - ly
things it has; it noth - ing lacks. Lord ov - er sin and
speaks no ab - sent Christ, but here, With - in he dwells and

ness and life, He is to Christ's great boun - ty led.
serves each man, And to all praise and blame is blind.
death and hell, All men it serves and noth - ing slacks.
we in him: We, Christs, to fel - low - men draw near.

Soldiers of Christ, Arise

Eph. 6:10-18
Charles Wesley, 1749, alt.

DIADEMATA S.M.D.
George J. Elvey, 1868

1. Sol - diers of Christ, a - rise, And put your ar - mor on;
2. Stand, then, in his great might, With all his strength en - dued,
3. Leave no un-guard - ed place, No weak - ness of the soul,
Strong in the strength which God sup - plies Through his e - ter - nal Son,
And take, to arm you for the fight, The pan - o - ply of God,
Take ev - 'ry vir - tue, ev - 'ry grace, And for - ti - fy the whole.
Strong in the Lord of hosts, And in his might - y power,
That, hav - ing all things done, And all your con - flicts past,
From strength to strength go on; Wres - tle and fight and pray;
Who in the strength of Je - sus trusts Is more than con - quer - or.
Ye may o'er-come through Christ a - lone And stand en - tire at last.
Tread all the powers of dark-ness down And win the well-fought day.

A lower setting may be found at No. 309.

Have Thine Own Way, Lord

Isa. 64:8
Adelaide A. Pollard, 1902

ADELAIDE 5.4.5.4.D.
George C. Stebbins, 1907

1. Have thine own way, Lord! Have thine own way! Thou art the Pot - ter; I am the clay. Mold me and make me Aft - er thy will, While I am wait - ing, Yield - ed and still.
2. Have thine own way, Lord! Have thine own way! Search me and try me, Mas - ter, to - day! Whit - er than snow, Lord, Wash me just now, As in thy pres-ence Hum - bly I bow.
3. Have thine own way, Lord! Have thine own way! Wound-ed and wea - ry, Help me, I pray! Pow - er— all pow - er— Sure - ly is thine! Touch me and heal me, Sav - ior di - vine!
4. Have thine own way, Lord! Have thine own way! Hold o'er my be - ing Ab - so - lute sway! Fill with thy spir - it Till all shall see Christ on - ly, al - ways, Liv - ing in me!

As Men of Old Their First Fruits Brought

FOREST GREEN C.M.D.
Traditional English Melody
Arr by R. Vaughan Williams, 1906

Frank von Christierson, 1961

1. As men of old their first fruits brought Of or - chard, flock, and field
2. A world in need now sum-mons us To la - bor, love, and give;
3. In grat - i - tude and hum - ble trust We bring our best to thee
To God the giv - er of all good, The source of boun-teous yield;
To make our life an of - fer - ing To God, that man may live;
To serve thy cause and share thy love With all hu - man - i - ty.
So we to - day first fruits would bring, The wealth of this good land,
The church of Christ is call - ing us To make the dream come true:
O thou who gav - est us thy - self In Je - sus Christ, thy son,
Of farm and mar- ket, shop and home, Of mind and heart and hand.
A world re-deemed by Christ- like love; All life in Christ made new.
Teach us to give our - selves each day Un - til life's work is done.

172

*Make Me a Captive, Lord

First Tune

CORONA S.M.D.
George Matheson, 1890
Charles Hylton Stewart, 1884-1932
1. Make me a cap- tive, Lord, And then I shall be free; Force
2. My heart is weak and poor Un - til it mas - ter find; It
3. My power is faint and low Till I have learned to serve; It
4. My will is not my own Till thou hast made it thine; If
me to ren - der up my sword, And I shall con - q'ror be. I
has no spring of ac - tion sure, It var - ies with the wind. It
wants the need- ed fire to glow, It wants the breeze to nerve; It
it would reach a mon-arch's throne It must its crown re - sign; It
sink in life's a - larms, When by my - self I stand; Im -
can- not free - ly move Till thou hast wrought its chain; En -
can- not drive the world Un - til it - self be driven; Its
on - ly stands un - bent, A - mid the clash - ing strife, When
pris- on me with - in thine arms, And strong shall be my hand.
slave it with thy match-less love, And death-less it shall reign.
flag can on - ly be un- furled When thou shalt breathe from heav'n.
on thy bo - som it has leant, And found in thee its life.

Make Me a Captive, Lord

Second Tune

LEOMINSTER S.M.D.

George William Martin, 1862

George Matheson, 1890 *Harm. by Arthur Sullivan, 1874*

1. Make me a cap - tive, Lord, And then I shall be free;
2. My heart is weak and poor Un - til it mas - ter find;
3. My power is faint and low Till I have learned to serve;
4. My will is not my own Till thou hast made it thine;

Force me to ren - der up my sword, And I shall con-q'ror be.
It has no spring of ac - tion sure, It var - ies with the wind;
It wants the need - ed fire to glow, It wants the breeze to nerve;
If it would reach a mon-arch's throne It must its crown re - sign;

I sink in life's a - larms, When by my - self I stand;
It can - not free - ly move Till thou hast wrought its chain;
It can - not drive the world Un - til it - self be driven;
It on - ly stands un - bent A - mid the clash - ing strife,

Im - pris - on me with - in thine arms, And strong shall be my hand.
En - slave it with thy match-less love, And death - less it shall reign.
Its flag can on - ly be un - furled When thou shalt breathe from heav'n.
When on thy bo - som it has leant, And found in thee its life.

174

We Would Be Building

FINLANDIA 10.10.10.10.10.10.

Matt. 7:24-27 | *Jean Sibelius, 1899*

Purd E. Deitz, 1936 | *Arr. for* The Hymnal *(Presby.), 1933*

1. We would be build - ing; tem-ples still un - done O'er crum-bling
2. Teach us to build; up - on the sol - id rock We set the
3. O keep us build - ing, Mas-ter; may our hands Ne'er fal - ter

walls their cross-es scarce - ly lift, Wait - ing till love can
dream that hard - ens in - to deed, Ribbed with the steel that
when the dream is in our hearts, When to our ears there

raise the bro-ken stone, And hearts cre - a - tive bridge the hu-man rift.
time and change doth mock, The un-fail-ing pur - pose of our no-blest creed.
come di - vine com - mands And all the pride of sin - ful will de - parts.

We would be build - ing; Mas - ter, let thy plan
Teach us to build; O Mas - ter, lend us sight
We build with thee, O grant en - dur - ing worth

Re - veal the life that God would give to man.
To see the tow - ers gleam - ing in the light.
Un - til the heav'n - ly king - dom comes on earth.

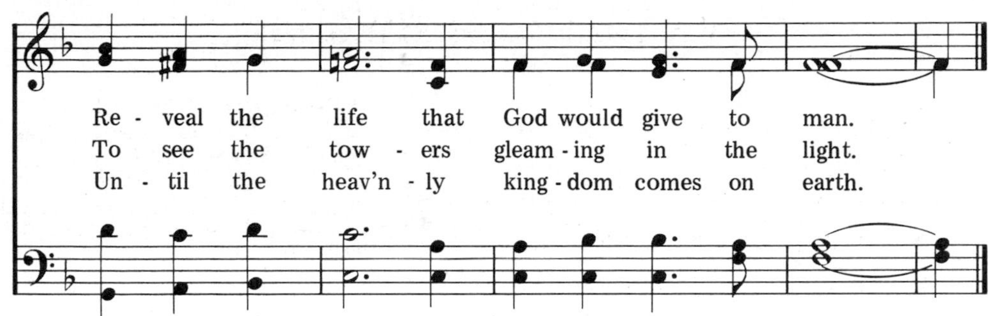

O God of Life 175

ZU MEINEM HERRN 11.10.11.10.

Walter Krebs, 1970 *Johann Gottfried Schicht, 1819*

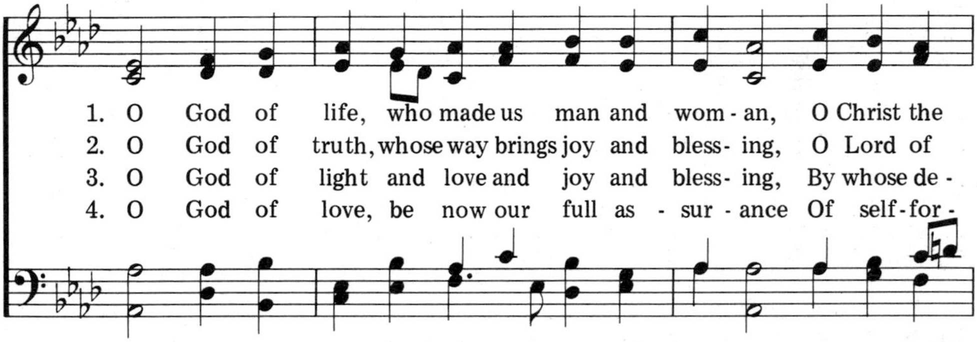

1. O God of life, who made us man and wom - an, O Christ the
2. O God of truth, whose way brings joy and bless- ing, O Lord of
3. O God of light and love and joy and bless- ing, By whose de -
4. O God of love, be now our full as - sur - ance Of self-for -

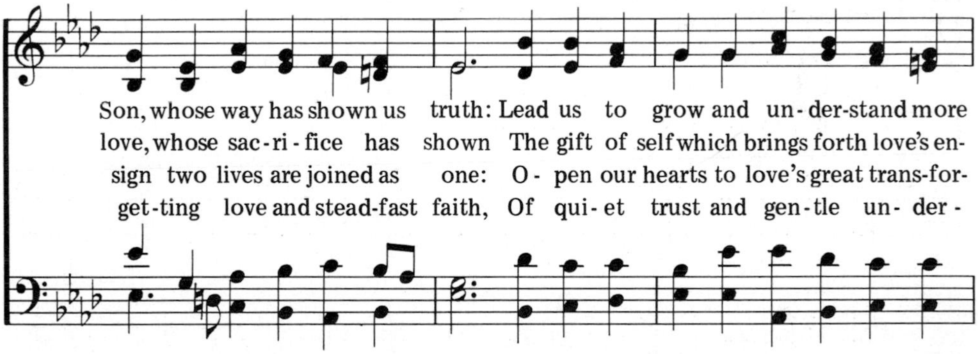

Son, whose way has shown us truth: Lead us to grow and un-der-stand more
love, whose sac-ri-fice has shown The gift of self which brings forth love's en-
sign two lives are joined as one: O - pen our hearts to love's great trans-for-
get-ting love and stead-fast faith, Of qui-et trust and gen-tle un-der -

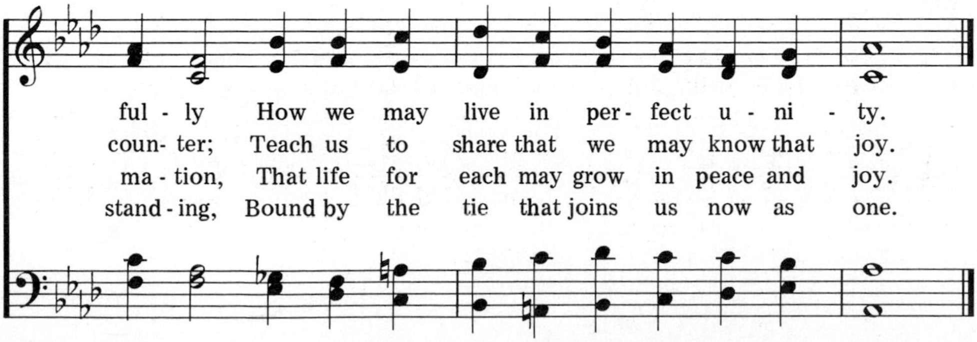

ful - ly How we may live in per- fect u - ni - ty.
coun- ter; Teach us to share that we may know that joy.
ma - tion, That life for each may grow in peace and joy.
stand - ing, Bound by the tie that joins us now as one.

176

O Thou Whose Favor Hallows

OAKWOOD 11.10.11.10.11.10.
Miriam Drury, 1960
John Ferguson, 1971
Unison
1. O thou whose fa - vor hal-lows all oc - ca - sions, Be pres-ent at this cov-e - nant-ing rite; May ev - 'ry pledge of true and last-ing pur-pose Be con-se - crat-ed in thy ho-ly sight; Con-fer on those be - fore thee heav'n-ly aid To
2. Long may they keep the sense of high ad - ven - ture, The gift of joy, the mar-vel of a dream, Nor ev - er lose the vi - sion as they cher-ish Each for the oth-er, hon-or and es - teem; En-rich them with the bless-ing of thy grace, And
3. Al-might-y God, Re-deem-er and De-fend-er, Be thou their stay what-ev-er may be - tide; In - creas-ing - ly may each new year dis - cov - er Their lives ma-tured, their mar-riage sanc-ti - fied, Their hearts firm fixed on this ex - alt - ed goal; The

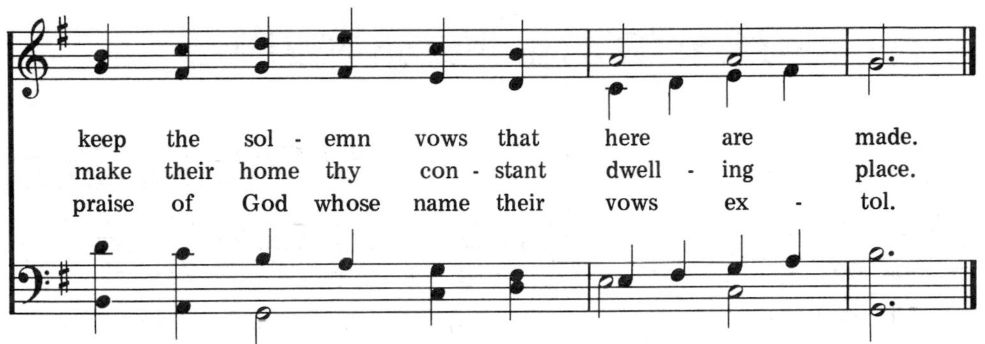
keep the sol - emn vows that here are made.
make their home thy con - stant dwell - ing place.
praise of God whose name their vows ex - tol.

Awake, Awake to Love and Work 177

MORNING SONG 8.6.8.6.8.6.
Melody, Kentucky Harmony, *c.1815*
Harm. by C. Winfred Douglas, 1940

Geoffrey A. Studdert-Kennedy, 1921

1. A - wake, a - wake to love and work! The lark is in the sky;
2. Come, let thy voice be one with theirs, Shout with their shout of praise;
3. To give and give, and give a - gain, What God hath giv - en thee;

The fields are wet with dia-mond dew; The worlds a - wake to cry
See how the gi - ant sun soars up, Great lord of years and days!
To spend thy - self nor count the cost; To serve right glo-rious - ly

Their bless-ings on the Lord of life, As he goes meek-ly by.
So let the love of Je - sus come And set thy soul a - blaze.
The God who gave all worlds that are, And all that are to be.

He Who Would Valiant Be

ST. DUNSTAN'S 6.5.6.5.6.6.6.5.

John Bunyan, 1684, alt. *C. Winfred Douglas, 1917*

1. He who would val - iant be 'Gainst all di - sas - ter,
2. Who so be - set him round With dis - mal sto - ries,
3. Since, Lord, thou dost de - fend Us with thy Spir - it,
Let him in con - stan - cy Fol - low the Mas - ter.
Do but them - selves con - found; His strength the more is.
We know we at the end Shall life in - her - it.
There's no dis - cour - age - ment Shall make him once re - lent
No foes shall stay his might, Though he with gi - ants fight;
Then fan - cies, flee a - way! I'll fear not what men say;
His first a - vowed in - tent To be a pil - grim.
He will make good his right To be a pil - grim.
I'll la - bor night and day To be a pil - grim.

O Brother Man, Fold to Thy Heart

Eph. 4:31-32; 5:1-2
John Greenleaf Whittier, 1848

WELWYN 11.10.11.10.
Alfred Scott-Gatty, 1902

1. O broth - er man, fold to thy heart thy broth - er:
2. Fol - low with rev - 'rent steps the great ex - am - ple
3. Then shall all shack - les fall: the storm - y clan - gor
Where pit - y dwells, the peace of God is there;
Of him whose ho - ly work was do - ing good:
Of wild war mu - sic o'er the earth shall cease;
To wor - ship right - ly is to love each oth - er,
So shall the wide earth seem our Fa - ther's tem - ple,
Love shall tread out the bale - ful fire of an - ger,
Each smile a hymn, each kind - ly deed a prayer.
Each lov - ing life a psalm of grat - i - tude.
And in its ash - es plant the tree of peace.

Am I My Brother's Keeper?

Gen. 4:9; Matt. 27:24
Ian Ferguson, 1967

BROTHER'S KEEPER 7.6.7.6.D.
Reginald Barrett-Ayres, 1967

Unison
1. "Am I my broth-er's keep-er?" The mut-tered cry was drowned; By A - bel's life-blood shout-ing In si - lence from the ground. For no man is an is - land di - vid - ed from the main; The bell that toll'd for A - bel Toll'd
2. The rul - er called for wa - ter And thought his hands were clean. Christ count-ed less than or - der, The man than the ma - chine. The crowd cried, "Cru-ci - fy him," Their mal - ice would-n't budge, So Pi - late call'd for wa - ter And
3. As long as peo - ple hun - ger, As long as peo - ple thirst, And ig - no - rance and ill - ness And war - fare do their worst, As long as there's in - jus - tice In an - y of God's lands, I am my broth-er's keep - er, I

St. 1, 2
St. 3
e - qual - ly for Cain.
his - to - ry's his judge.
dare not wash my hands.

181

How Swift the Wing

DUNDEE C.M.

William Nelson, 1957

Scottish Psalter, *1615*

1. How swift the wing, how keen the eye, How sen - si - tive the ear;
2. Nor time nor space nor earth can keep Me from my broth-er's side,
3. So match our cour - age to the task, And by thy might - y power
4. Then shall the prom - ise of this age, So bless'd with hu - man skill,

No hand lifts now be - yond our grasp, And dis - tant needs draw near.
But on - ly self - ish un - con - cern, And false and fool - ish pride.
Stretch mind and soul that we may grasp The mean-ing of the hour.
Its true di - rec - tion find at last, With - in the Mas - ter's will.

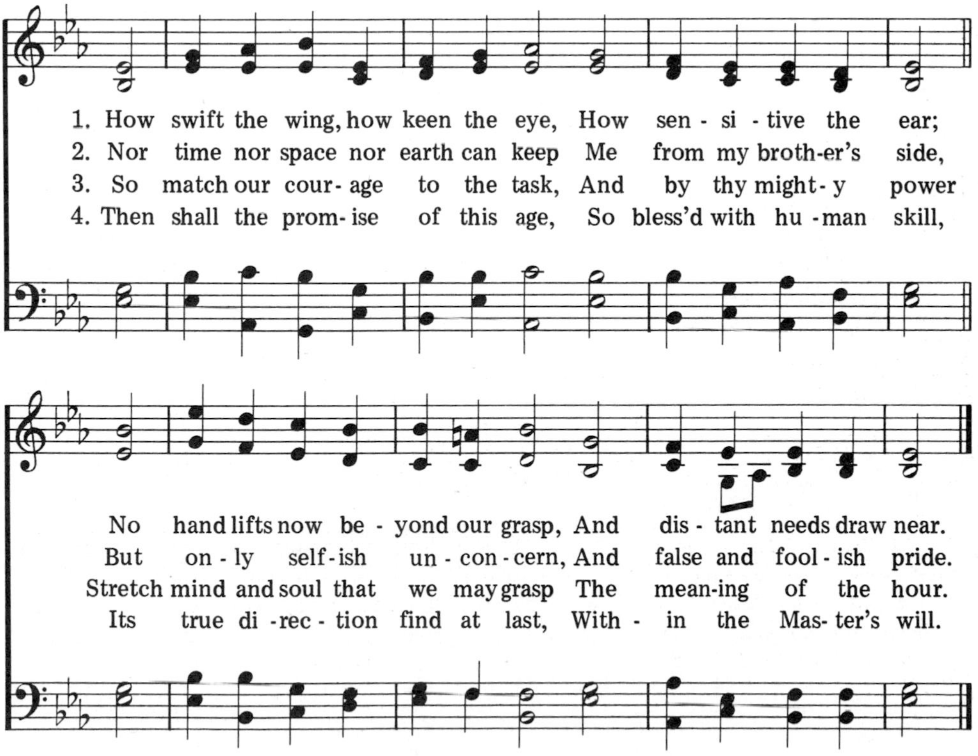

When the Church of Jesus

KING'S WESTON 6.5.6.5.D.

F. Pratt Green, 1903- *R. Vaughan Williams, 1925*

Unison

1. When the church of Jesus Shuts its outer door,
Lest the roar of traffic Drown the voice of prayer:
May our prayers, Lord, make us Ten times more aware
That the world we banish is our Christian care.

2. If our hearts are lifted Where devotion soars
High above this hungry Suff'ring world of ours:
Lest our hymns should drug us To forget its needs,
Forge our Christian worship into Christian deeds.

3. Lest the gifts we offer, Money, talents, time,
Serve to salve our conscience To our secret shame:
Lord, reprove, inspire us By the way you give;
Teach us, dying Savior, how true Christians live.

Renew Thy Church

ALL IS WELL 10.6.10.6.8.8.8.6.

Kenneth L. Cober, 1960 *Old English Melody*

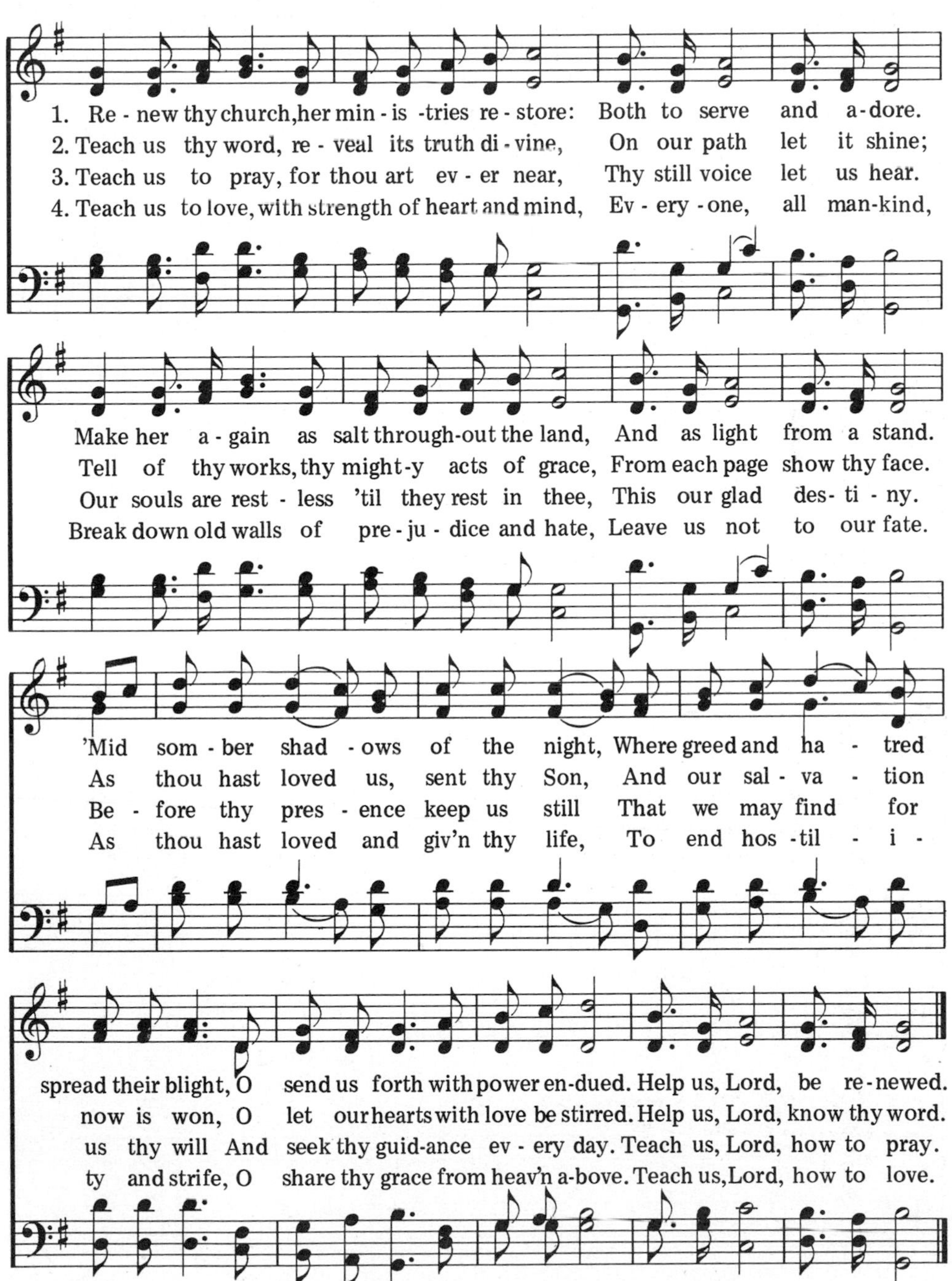
1. Re - new thy church, her min - is -tries re - store: Both to serve and a - dore.
2. Teach us thy word, re - veal its truth di - vine, On our path let it shine;
3. Teach us to pray, for thou art ev - er near, Thy still voice let us hear.
4. Teach us to love, with strength of heart and mind, Ev - ery - one, all man-kind,
Make her a - gain as salt through-out the land, And as light from a stand.
Tell of thy works, thy might - y acts of grace, From each page show thy face.
Our souls are rest - less 'til they rest in thee, This our glad des - ti - ny.
Break down old walls of pre - ju - dice and hate, Leave us not to our fate.
'Mid som - ber shad - ows of the night, Where greed and ha - tred
As thou hast loved us, sent thy Son, And our sal - va - tion
Be - fore thy pres - ence keep us still That we may find for
As thou hast loved and giv'n thy life, To end hos - til - i -
spread their blight, O send us forth with power en-dued. Help us, Lord, be re-newed.
now is won, O let our hearts with love be stirred. Help us, Lord, know thy word.
us thy will And seek thy guid-ance ev - ery day. Teach us, Lord, how to pray.
ty and strife, O share thy grace from heav'n a-bove. Teach us, Lord, how to love.

184

When I Needed a Neighbor

Matt. 25:31-46
Sydney Carter, 1965
NEIGHBOR *Irregular*
Sydney Carter, 1965
Arr. by John Birch, 1969
Unison
Em
Em
B
1. When I need-ed a neigh-bor, were you there, were you there? When I need-ed a neigh-bor, were you there?
hun-gry and thirst-y, were you there, were you there? I was hun-gry and thirst-y, were you there?
cold, I was na-ked, were you there, were you there? I was cold, I was na-ked, were you there?
need-ed a shel-ter, were you there, were you there? When I need-ed a shel-ter, were you there?
need-ed a heal-er, were you there, were you there? When I need-ed a heal-er, were you there?
ev-er you trav-el, I'll be there, I'll be there. Where ev-er you trav-el, I'll be there.
Em
D7
G
And the creed and the col-or and the name won't mat-ter. Were you there?
C
B7
Sts. 1, 2, 3, 4, 5
E
St. 6
E
2. I was
3. I was
4. When I
5. When I
6. Where
6. there?

Come, Labor On

Matt. 9:37-38
Jane L. Borthwick, 1859, alt.
ORA LABORA 4.10.10.10.4.
T. Tertius Noble, 1918
Unison
1. Come, la - bor on. Who dares stand i - dle on the har-vest plain
2. Come, la - bor on. Claim the high call - ing an - gels can - not share;
3. Come, la - bor on. A - way with gloom-y doubts and faith-less fear!
4. Come, la - bor on. No time for rest, till glows the west-ern sky,
While all a -round him waves the gold-en grain? And to each ser - vant
To young and old the gos - pel glad-ness bear; Re - deem the time; its
No arm so weak but may do ser - vice here; By fee - blest a - gents
Till the long shad-ows o'er our path-way lie, And a glad sound comes
does the Mas - ter say, "Go work to - day."
hours too swift - ly fly. The night draws nigh.
may our God ful - fill His righ - - teous will.
with the set - ting sun, "Well done, well done!"

O Master, Let Me Walk with Thee

MARYTON L.M.

Washington Gladden, 1880 — *H. Percy Smith, 1874*

1. O Mas - ter, let me walk with thee In low - ly paths of ser - vice free; Tell me thy se - cret, help me bear The strain of toil, the fret of care.
2. Help me the slow of heart to move By some clear, win - ning word of love; Teach me the way - ward feet to stay, And guide them in the home - ward way.
3. Teach me thy pa - tience; still with thee In clos - er, dear - er com - pa - ny, In work that keeps faith sweet and strong, In trust that tri - umphs o - ver wrong.
4. In hope that sends a shin - ing ray Far down the fu - ture's broad - 'ning way, In peace that on - ly thou canst give, With thee, O Mas - ter, let me live.

187

*O God of Earth and Altar

LLANGLOFFAN 7.6.7.6.D.
Traditional Welsh Melody

Gilbert K. Chesterton, 1906
D. Evans' Hymnau a Thonau, *1865*

1. O God of earth and al - tar, Bow down and hear our cry;
2. From all that ter - ror teach - es, From lies of tongue and pen,
3. Tie in a liv - ing teth - er The prince and priest and thrall;

Our earth-ly rul - ers fal - ter, Our peo - ple drift and die;
From all the eas - y speech - es That com - fort cru - el men,
Bind all our lives to - geth - er, Smite us and save us all;

The walls of gold en - tomb us, The swords of scorn di - vide;
From sale and prof - a - na - tion Of hon - or and the sword,
In ire and ex - ul - ta - tion A - flame with faith, and free,

Take not thy thun - der from us, But take a - way our pride.
From sleep and from dam - na - tion, De - liv - er us, good Lord!
Lift up a liv - ing na - tion, A sin - gle sword to thee.

*O Holy City, Seen of John

First Tune

Rev. 21:1-4
Walter Russell Bowie, 1910

SANCTA CIVITAS 8.6.8.6.8.6.
Herbert Howells, 1968

Unison

1. O ho - ly cit - y, seen of John, Where Christ, the Lamb, doth reign,
2. O shame to us who rest con - tent While lust and greed for gain
3. Give us, O God, the strength to build The cit - y that hath stood
4. Al - read - y in the mind of God That cit - y ris - eth fair;

With - in whose four-square walls shall come No night, nor need, nor pain,
In street and shop and ten - e - ment Wring gold from hu - man pain,
Too long a dream, whose laws are love, Whose ways are broth - er - hood,
Lo, how its splen-dor chal-leng - es The souls that great-ly dare,

And where the tears are wiped from eyes That shall not weep a - gain.
And bit - ter lips in blind de-spair Cry, "Christ hath died in vain."
And where the sun that shin-eth is God's grace for hu - man good.
Yea, bids us seize the whole of life And build its glo - ry there.

O Holy City, Seen of John

Second Tune

MORNING SONG 8.6.8.6.8.6.

Rev. 21:1-4
Walter Russell Bowie, 1910

Melody, Kentucky Harmony, *1816*
Harm. by C. Winfred Douglas, 1940

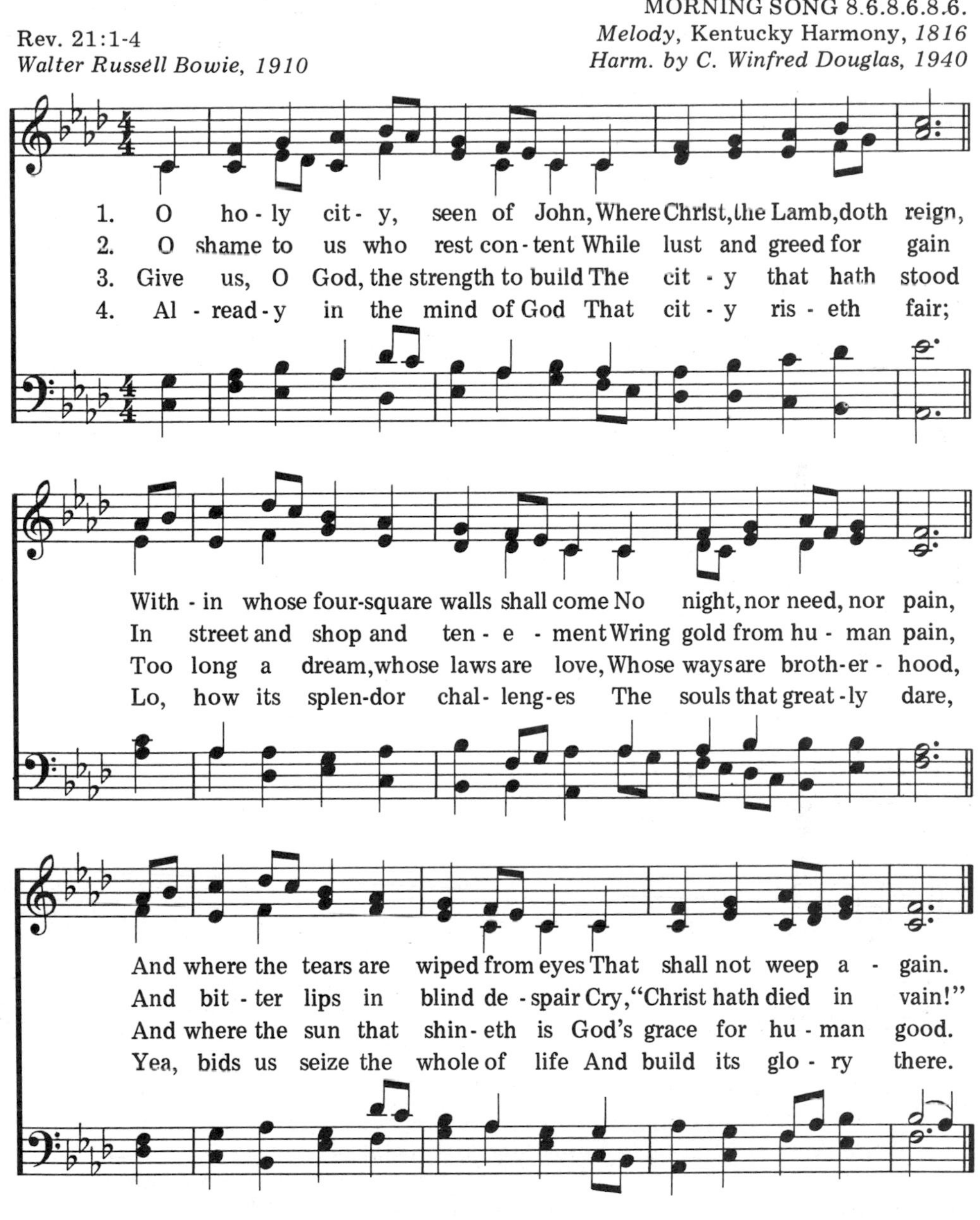

190

*Where Cross the Crowded Ways of Life

GERMANY L.M.

Frank Mason North, 1903

Gardiner's Sacred Melodies, *1815*

1. Where cross the crowded ways of life,
Where sound the cries of race and clan,
Above the noise of selfish strife,
We hear thy voice, O Son of man.

2. In haunts of wretchedness and need,
On shadowed thresholds dark with fears,
From paths where hide the lures of greed,
We catch the vision of thy tears.

3. O Master, from the mountain side,
Make haste to heal these hearts of pain;
Among these restless throngs abide,
O tread the city's streets again.

4. Till sons of men shall learn thy love
And follow where thy feet have trod,
Till glorious from thy heav'n above
Shall come the city of our God.

The Voice of God Is Calling

MEIRIONYDD 7.6.7.6.D.
Welsh Hymn Melody
Attr. to William Lloyd, 1840

John Haynes Holmes, 1913

1. The voice of God is call - ing Its sum-mons un - to men;
As once he spake in Zi - on, So now he speaks a - gain:
Whom shall I send to suc - cor My peo - ple in their need?
Whom shall I send to loos - en The bonds of shame and greed?

2. I hear my peo - ple cry - ing In cot and mine and slum;
No field or mart is si - lent, No cit - y street is dumb.
I see my peo - ple fall - ing In dark-ness and de - spair.
Whom shall I send to shat - ter The fet - ters which they bear?

3. We heed, O Lord, thy sum-mons, And an - swer: Here are we!
Send us up - on thine er - rand; Let us thy ser - vants be.
Our strength is dust and ash - es, Our years a pass - ing hour,
But thou canst use our weak-ness To mag - ni - fy thy power.

4. From ease and plen - ty save us; From pride of place ab - solve;
Purge us of low de - sire; Lift us to high re - solve;
Take us and make us ho - ly; Teach us thy will and way.
Speak and, be - hold! we an - swer; Command and we o - bey!

Lord God of Hosts, Whose Purpose

Shepherd Knapp, 1907

WELWYN 11.10.11.10.
Alfred Scott-Gatty, 1902

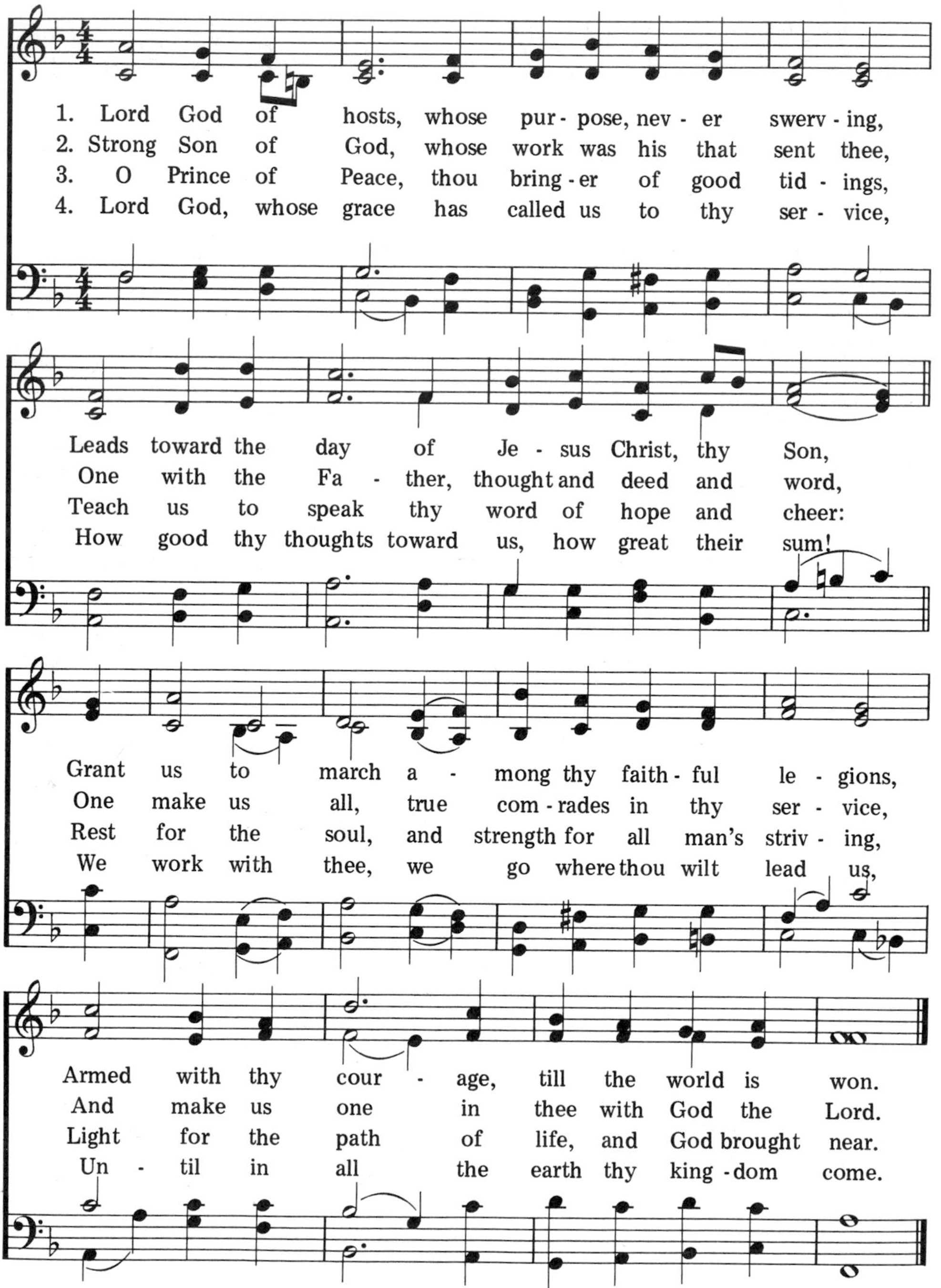
1. Lord God of hosts, whose pur-pose, nev-er swerv-ing,
2. Strong Son of God, whose work was his that sent thee,
3. O Prince of Peace, thou bring-er of good tid-ings,
4. Lord God, whose grace has called us to thy ser-vice,
Leads toward the day of Je-sus Christ, thy Son,
One with the Fa-ther, thought and deed and word,
Teach us to speak thy word of hope and cheer:
How good thy thoughts toward us, how great their sum!
Grant us to march a-mong thy faith-ful le-gions,
One make us all, true com-rades in thy ser-vice,
Rest for the soul, and strength for all man's striv-ing,
We work with thee, we go where thou wilt lead us,
Armed with thy cour-age, till the world is won.
And make us one in thee with God the Lord.
Light for the path of life, and God brought near.
Un-til in all the earth thy king-dom come.

Where Restless Crowds Are Thronging

NYLAND 7.6.7.6.D.
Finnish Hymn Melody
Harm. by David Evans, 1927

Thomas Curtis Clark, 1931

1. Where rest - less crowds are throng - ing A - long the cit - y ways,
2. In scenes of want and sor - row And haunts of fla - grant wrong,
3. O Christ, be - hold thy peo - ple They press on ev - ery hand!

Where pride and greed and tur - moil Con - sume the fe - ver'd days,
In homes where kind - ness fal - ters And strife and fear are strong,
Bring light to all the cit - ies Of our be - lov - ed land.

Where vain am - bi - tions ban - ish All thoughts of praise and prayer,
In bus - y street of bar - ter, In lone - ly thor - ough - fare,
May all our bit - ter striv - ing Give way to vi - sions fair

The peo - ple's spir - its wa - ver; But thou, O Christ, art there.
The peo - ple's spir - its lan - guish; But thou, O Christ, art there.
Of righ - teous - ness and jus - tice; For thou, O Christ, art there.

194

Teach Me, O Lord, Thy Holy Way

ROCKINGHAM L.M.

William Matson, 1866 *Adapted by Edward Miller, 1790*

1. Teach me, O Lord, thy ho - ly way, And give me
2. Help me, O Sav - ior, here to trace The sa - cred
3. Guard me, O Lord, that I may ne'er For - sake the
4. Bless me, in ev - ery task, O Lord, Be - gun, con -
an o - be - dient mind, That in thy ser - vice I may
foot - steps thou hast trod; And, meek - ly walk - ing with my
right or do the wrong; A - gainst temp - ta - tion make me
tin - ued, done for thee; Ful - fill thy per - fect work in
find My soul's de - light from day to day.
God, To grow in good - ness, truth, and grace.
strong And 'round me spread thy shel - t'ring care.
me, And thine a - bound - ing grace af - ford.

God of Earth and Sea and Heaven

LLANSANNAN 8.7.8.7.D.
Welsh Melody
Frank Edwards, 1958
Harm. by David Evans, 1927

1. God of earth and sea and heav - en, By thy power all things are made;
Man, cre - a - ted in thine im - age, Lives nor breathes with - out thine aid.
Thou who formed the earth's wide reach-es, Sum-moned forth its fruit and flower,
Teach our hearts to love thee on - ly; Help us know thy grace and power.

2. Thou hast blest us with thy fa - vor, Shown thy-self in saint and seer,
Borne thy wit - ness in all a - ges, In our hearts thou'rt ev - er near.
Purge our pride and our vain-glo - ry; Fill our hearts with prayer and praise;
May we of - fer for thy ser-vice All our wealth and all our days.

3. Thou hast giv'n thy Son to save us; We would give our lives to thee,
Naught with-hold-ing, free - ly yield-ing That all men thy love may see.
Now in grate - ful ded - i - ca - tion Our al - le- giance we would own,
Of - f'ring tal -ents, time, and trea-sure, For the mer- cy thou hast shown.

196

*Ye Servants of God, Your Master Proclaim

LYONS 10.10.11.11.
Arr. from J. Michael Haydn, 1737-1806
Charles Wesley, 1744, alt. *Gardiner's* Sacred Melodies, *1815*

1. Ye ser - vants of God, your Mas - ter pro - claim,
2. God rul - eth on high, al - might - y to save,
3. Sal - va - tion to God who sits on the throne!
4. Then let us a - dore and give him his right,
And pub - lish a - broad his won - der - ful name.
And still he is nigh, his pres - ence we have;
Let all cry a - loud and hon - or the Son;
All glo - ry and power, all wis - dom and might,
The name, all - vic - to - rious, of Je - sus ex - tol;
The great con - gre - ga - tion his tri - umph shall sing,
The prais - es of Je - sus the an - gels pro - claim,
All hon - or and bless - ing with an - gels a - bove,
His king - dom is glo - rious, he rules o - ver all.
As - crib - ing sal - va - tion to Je - sus, our King.
Fall down on their fa - ces and wor - ship the Lamb.
And thanks nev - er ceas - ing and in - fi - nite love.

Alternate tune, Hanover, No. 17

197

O Word of God Incarnate

MUNICH 7.6.7.6.D.

John 1:1
William W. How, 1867

Neu-vermehrtes Gesangbuch, *Meiningen, 1693*
Harm. by Felix Mendelssohn, 1847

1. O Word of God in - car - nate, O Wis - dom from on high,
2. The church from her dear Mas - ter Re - ceived the gift di - vine,
3. O make thy church, dear Sav - ior, A lamp of bur-nished gold,

O Truth un-changed, un - chang - ing, O Light of our dark sky,
And still that light she lift - eth O'er all the earth to shine.
To bear a - mong the na - tions Thy true light as of old!

We praise thee for the ra - diance That from the hal - lowed page,
It float - eth like a ban - ner Be - fore God's host un - furled;
O teach thy wan - dering pil - grims By this their path to trace,

A lan - tern to our foot - steps, Shines on from age to age.
It shin - eth like a bea - con A - bove the dark - ling world;
Till, clouds and dark - ness end - ed, They see thee face to face!

198

*God of Grace and God of Glory

CWM RHONDDA 8.7.8.7.8.7.7.

Harry Emerson Fosdick, 1930 | *John Hughes, 1907*

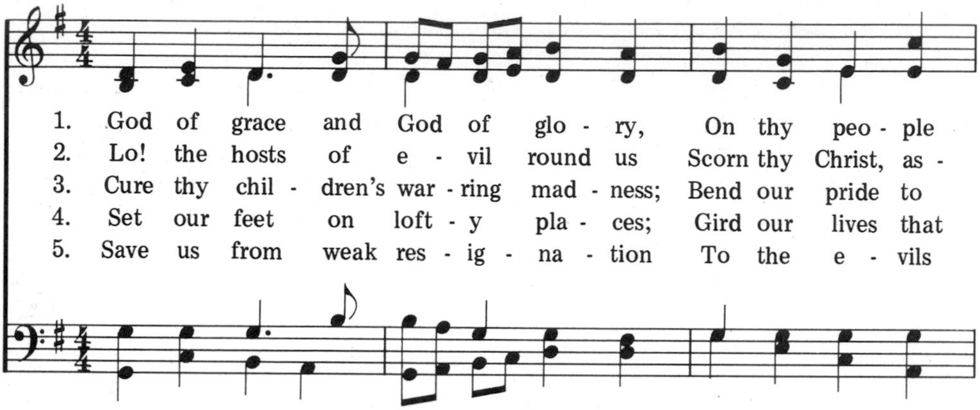

1. God of grace and God of glo - ry, On thy peo - ple
2. Lo! the hosts of e - vil round us Scorn thy Christ, as -
3. Cure thy chil - dren's war - ring mad - ness; Bend our pride to
4. Set our feet on loft - y pla - ces; Gird our lives that
5. Save us from weak res - ig - na - tion To the e - vils

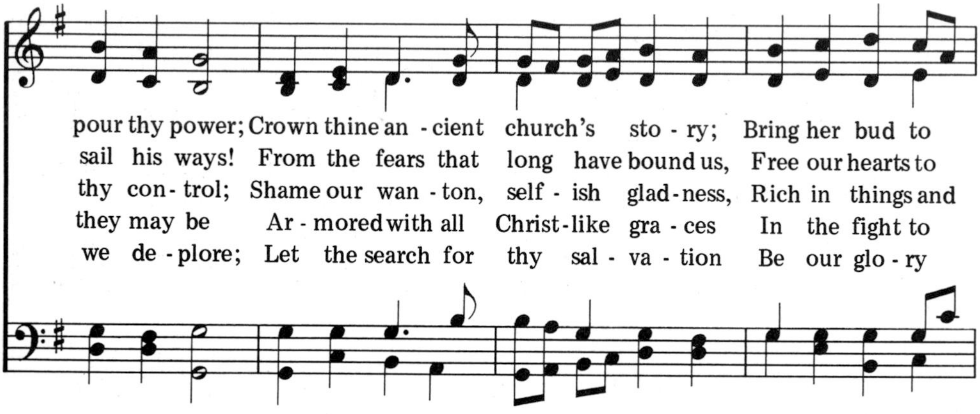

pour thy power; Crown thine an - cient church's sto - ry; Bring her bud to
sail his ways! From the fears that long have bound us, Free our hearts to
thy con - trol; Shame our wan - ton, self - ish glad - ness, Rich in things and
they may be Ar - mored with all Christ - like gra - ces In the fight to
we de - plore; Let the search for thy sal - va - tion Be our glo - ry

glo - rious flower. Grant us wis - dom, Grant us cour - age,
faith and praise. Grant us wis - dom, Grant us cour - age,
poor in soul. Grant us wis - dom, Grant us cour - age,
set men free. Grant us wis - dom, Grant us cour - age,
ev - er - more. Grant us wis - dom, Grant us cour - age,

For the fac - ing of this hour, For the fac - ing of this hour.
For the liv - ing of these days, For the liv - ing of these days.
Lest we miss thy king-dom's goal, Lest we miss thy king-dom's goal.
That we fail not man nor thee, That we fail not man nor thee.
Serv - ing thee whom we a - dore, Serv -ing thee whom we a - dore.

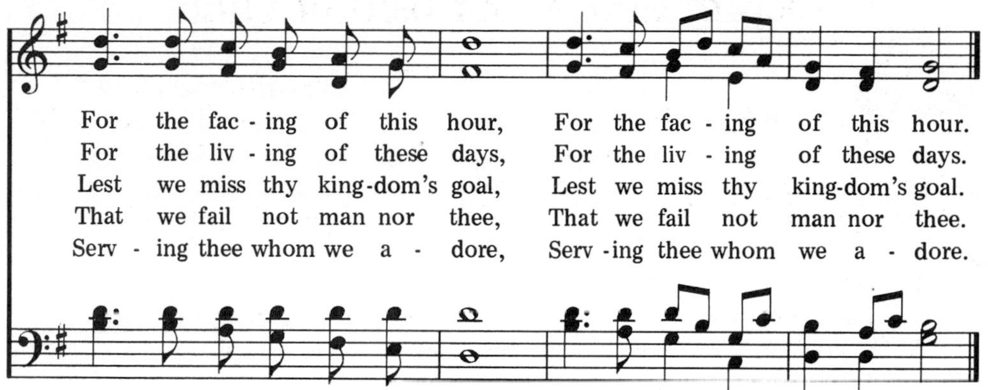

199

I Love to Tell the Story

HANKEY 7.6.7.6.D. *with Refrain*

Katherine Hankey, 1866; refrain added — *William G. Fischer, 1869*

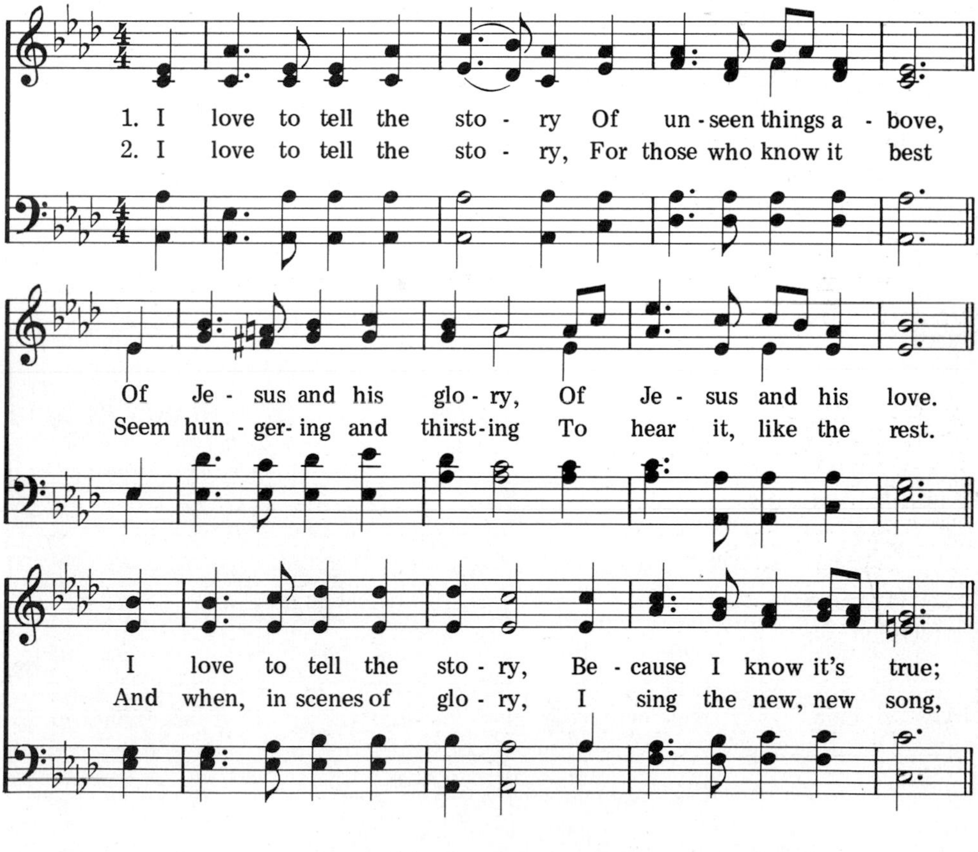

1. I love to tell the sto - ry Of un - seen things a - bove,
2. I love to tell the sto - ry, For those who know it best
Of Je - sus and his glo - ry, Of Je - sus and his love.
Seem hun - ger- ing and thirst-ing To hear it, like the rest.
I love to tell the sto - ry, Be - cause I know it's true;
And when, in scenes of glo - ry, I sing the new, new song,

It sat - is - fies my long- ings As noth -ing else would do.
'Twill be the old, old sto - ry That I have loved so long.

I love to tell the sto - ry; 'Twill be my theme in glo - ry

To tell the old, old sto - ry Of Je - sus and his love.

200

Speak Forth Your Word

DURROW 7.6.7.6.D.
Irish Traditional Melody
Harm. by William France, 1971

Attr. to Charles Jeffries, c.1925

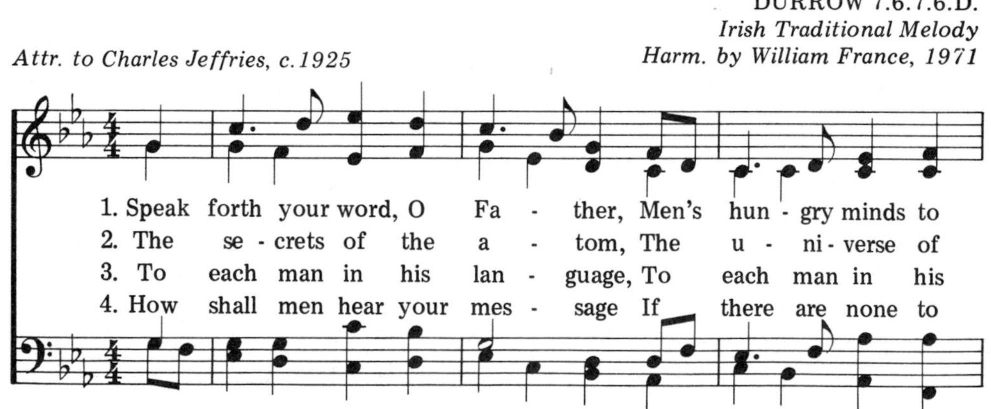

1. Speak forth your word, O Fa - ther, Men's hun - gry minds to
2. The se - crets of the a - tom, The u - ni - verse of
3. To each man in his lan - guage, To each man in his
4. How shall men hear your mes - sage If there are none to

feed; The peo - ple starve and per - ish, And
light, All won - ders of cre - a - tion Pro -
home, By man - y paths and chan - nels The
preach? How shall they learn your les - son If
can - not name their need; For so, Lord, you have
claim your bound- less might; But on - ly through the
faith of Christ may come: The print - ed word on
there are none to teach? Take us, then, Lord, and
made us That not a - lone by bread, But
wit - ness From man to man passed on Do
pa - per, The wave that spans the air, The
use us To tell what we have heard, And
by your word of com - fort Our hun - ger must be fed.
you re - veal in full - ness The gos - pel of your Son.
screen, the stage, the pic - ture, May all its truth de - clare.
all the minds of mil - lions Shall feed up - on your word.

201

I Am the Light of the World

John 8:12
Howard Thurman
and Jim Strathdee, 1969
LIGHT OF THE WORLD Irregular
Jim Strathdee, 1969
Refrain
"I am the light of the world! You peo-ple come and fol-low me!" If you fol - low and love You'll learn the mys - ter - y Of what you were meant to do and be.
Fine
1. When the song of the an - gels is stilled When the star in the sky is gone, When the kings and the shep-herds Have found their way home, The work of Christ-mas is be - gun:
2. To find the lost and lone - ly man, To heal his bro-ken soul with love, To feed the hun-gry chil - dren With warmth and good food, To feel the earth be - low, the sky a - bove!
3. To free the pris - 'ner from his chains, To make the pow-er - ful care, To re - build the na - tions With strength of good will, To call a man your broth-er ev - ery - where!
4. To bring hope to ev - ery task you do, To dance at a ba - by's new birth, To make mu - sic in An old man's heart, And sing to the col - ors of the earth!
Repeat refrain after each stanza

*Eternal God, Whose Power Upholds

WELLINGTON SQUARE C.M.D.

Henry Hallam Tweedy, 1929 *Guy Warrack, 1931*

1. E - ter - nal God, whose power up-holds Both flower and flam-ing star,
2. O God of love, whose spir - it wakes In ev - 'ry hu - man breast,
3. O God of truth, whom sci - ence seeks And rev- 'rent souls a - dore,

To whom there is no here nor there, No time, no near nor far,
Whom love, and love a - lone, can know, In whom all hearts find rest,
Who light - est ev - 'ry ear - nest mind Of ev - 'ry clime and shore,

No a - lien race, no for - eign shore, No child un-sought, un - known,
Help us to spread thy gra-cious reign, Till greed and hate shall cease,
Dis - pel the gloom of er - ror's night, Of ig - no-rance and fear,

O send us forth, thy proph-ets true, To make all lands thine own!
And kind - ness dwell in hu - man hearts, And all the earth find peace!
Un - til true wis - dom from a - bove Shall make life's path-way clear!

We Are Living, We Are Dwelling

IN BABILONE 8.7.8.7.D.
Traditional Dutch Melody
Arthur Cleveland Coxe, 1840, alt. *Harm. by T. Tertius Noble, 1918*

Unison
1. We are living, we are dwelling In a grand and awful time, In an age on ages telling; To be living is sublime.
2. Will ye play, then? will ye dally Far behind the battle line? Up! it is Jehovah's rally; God's own arm hath need of thine.
3. Sworn to yield, to waver, never; Consecrated, born again; Sworn to be Christ's soldiers ever, O for Christ at least be men.

An alternate setting may be found at No. 35.

Hark, the wak - ing up of na - tions, Hosts ad -
Worlds are charg - ing, heav'n be - hold - ing; Thou hast
O let all the soul with - in you For the
vanc - ing to the fray; Hark! what sound - eth
but an hour to fight; Now, the bla - zoned
truth's sake go a - broad! Strike! let ev - 'ry
is cre - a - tion's Groan - ing for the lat - ter day.
cross un - fold - ing, On, right on - ward for the right!
nerve and sin - ew Tell on a - ges, tell for God.

204

From the Shores of Many Nations

EBENEZER (TON-Y-BOTEL) 8.7.8.7.D.
James H. Hargett, 1971
Thomas J. Williams, 1890
Unison
1. From the shores of man-y na - tions Came your chil-dren, slave and free;
2. In the heart of this our na-tion, There are those in bond - age still;
Men es - cap-ing rank op - pres-sion, Sanc-tioned chat - tel slav - e - ry.
Bound in seeth-ing ghet-to plac - es, Cap- tives of a ruth - less will.
Yet was born a hope for free-dom, Born a - midst the groan of slaves.
Bring the pow'r of grace and judg-ment; From death's grip may life un - furl;
Christ, break through the cru - ci - fix - ion With your love that seeks to save.
Lib-er - at - ing res - ur - rec - tion, Serv-ing, shap-ing God's new world.

Onward, Christian Soldiers

ST. GERTRUDE 6.5.6.5.D. *with Refrain*

Sabine Baring-Gould, 1864 *Arthur S. Sullivan, 1871*

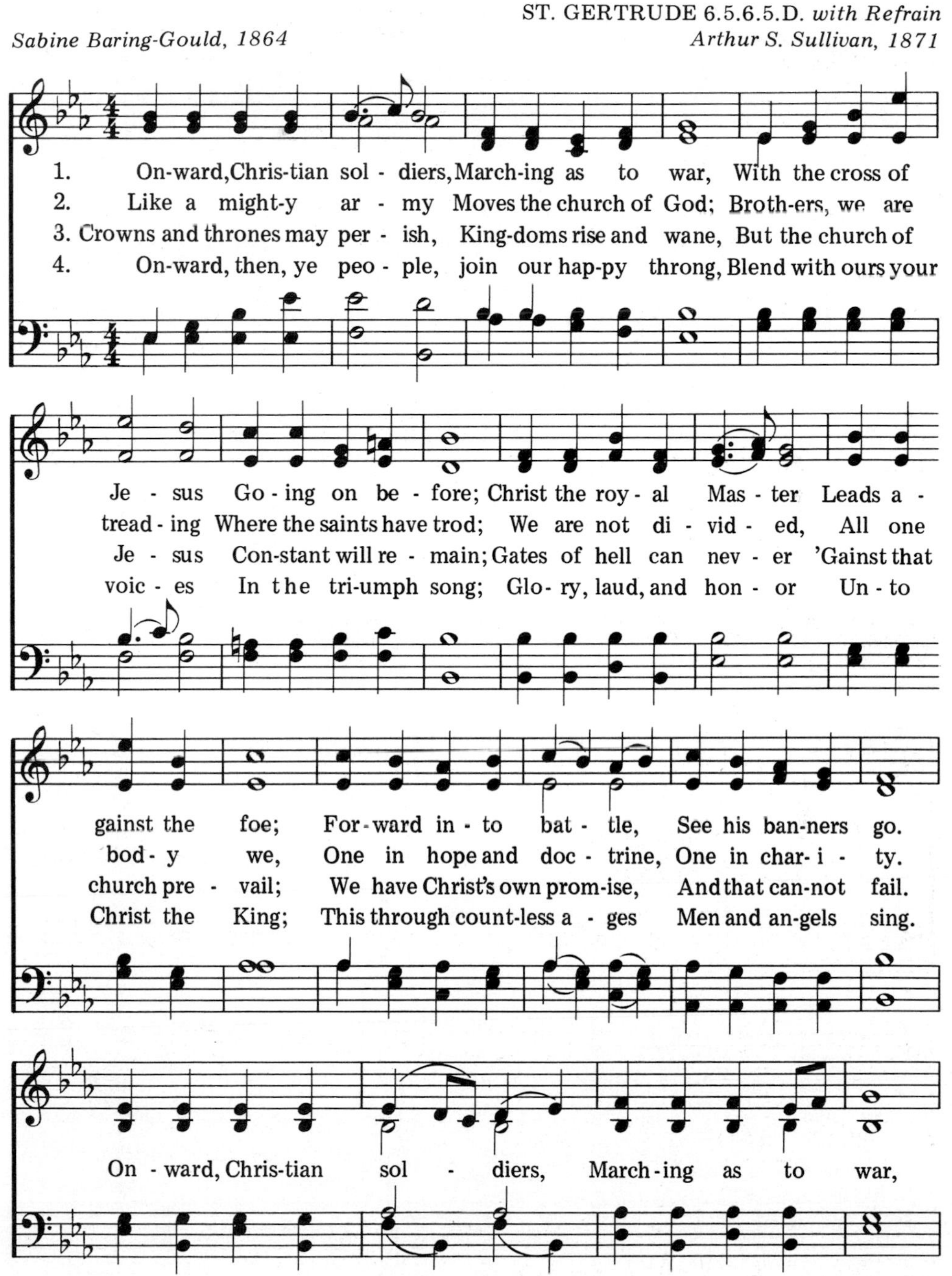
1. On-ward,Chris-tian sol - diers,March-ing as to war, With the cross of Je - sus Go - ing on be - fore; Christ the roy - al Mas - ter Leads a - gainst the foe; For-ward in - to bat - tle, See his ban-ners go.
2. Like a might-y ar - my Moves the church of God; Broth-ers, we are tread - ing Where the saints have trod; We are not di - vid - ed, All one bod - y we, One in hope and doc - trine, One in char- i - ty.
3. Crowns and thrones may per - ish, King-doms rise and wane, But the church of Je - sus Con-stant will re - main; Gates of hell can nev - er 'Gainst that church pre - vail; We have Christ's own prom-ise, And that can-not fail.
4. On-ward, then, ye peo - ple, join our hap-py throng, Blend with ours your voic - es In the tri-umph song; Glo- ry, laud, and hon - or Un - to Christ the King; This through count-less a - ges Men and an-gels sing.
On - ward, Chris-tian sol - diers, March - ing as to war,

With the cross of Je - sus Go - ing on be - fore.

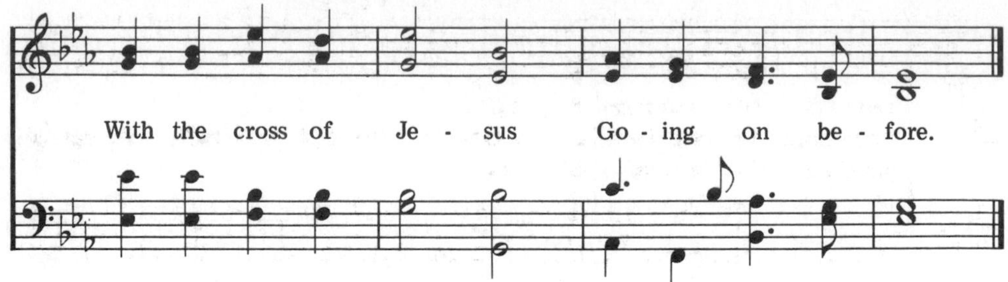

206

O Zion, Haste, Thy Mission High Fulfilling

Rom. 11:26
Mary A. Thomson, 1870

TIDINGS 11.10.11.10. *with Refrain*
James Walch, 1875

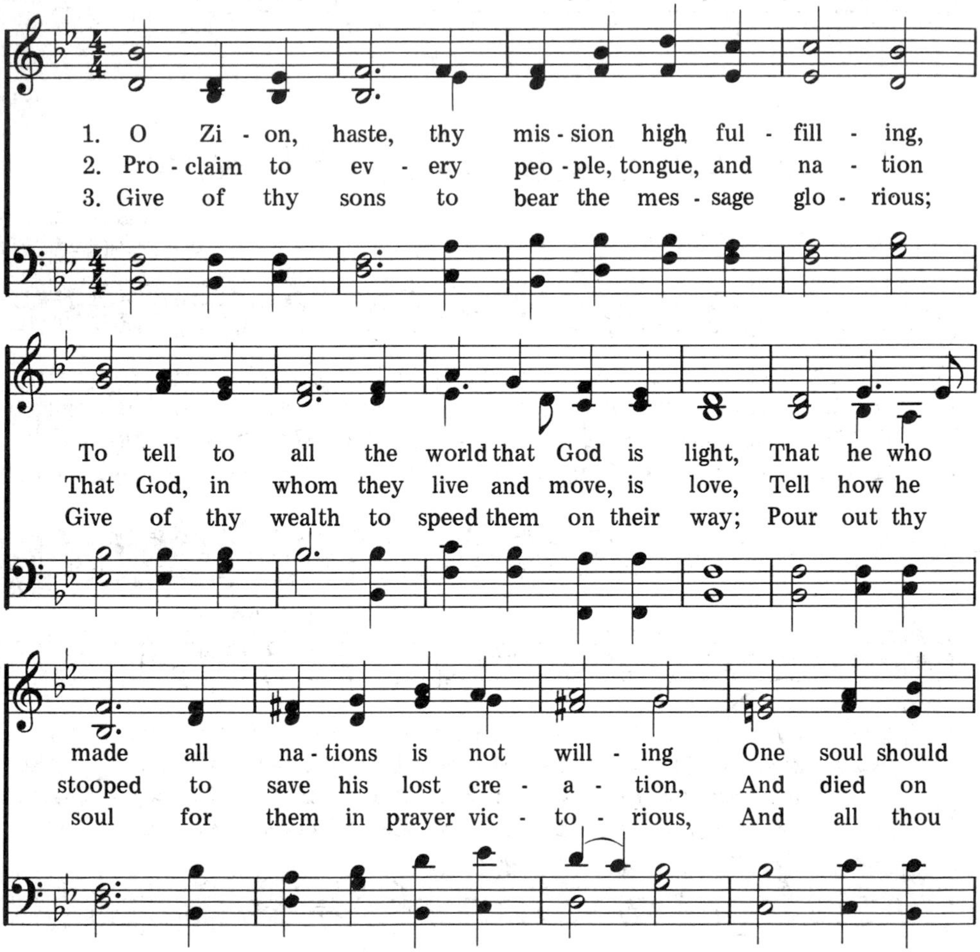

1. O Zi - on, haste, thy mis - sion high ful - fill - ing,
2. Pro - claim to ev - ery peo - ple, tongue, and na - tion
3. Give of thy sons to bear the mes - sage glo - rious;
To tell to all the world that God is light, That he who
That God, in whom they live and move, is love, Tell how he
Give of thy wealth to speed them on their way; Pour out thy
made all na - tions is not will - ing One soul should
stooped to save his lost cre - a - tion, And died on
soul for them in prayer vic - to - rious, And all thou

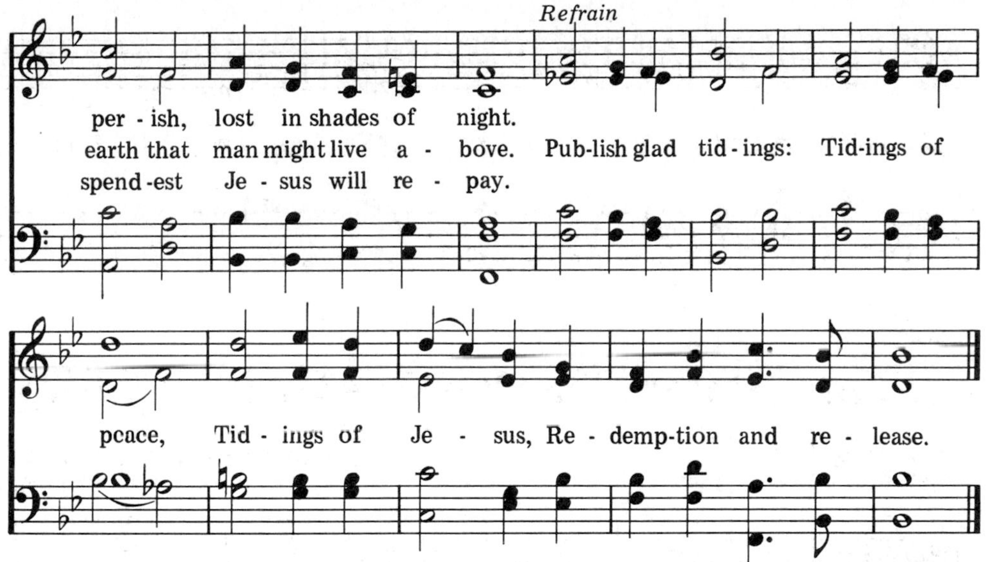
Refrain
per - ish, lost in shades of night.
earth that man might live a - bove. Pub-lish glad tid - ings: Tid-ings of
spend -est Je - sus will re - pay.
peace, Tid - ings of Je - sus, Re - demp-tion and re - lease.

207

Maker of All, to You We Give

ST. MAGNUS C.M.

Pamela-Rae Yeager Maloney, 1968 *Jeremiah Clark, 1709*

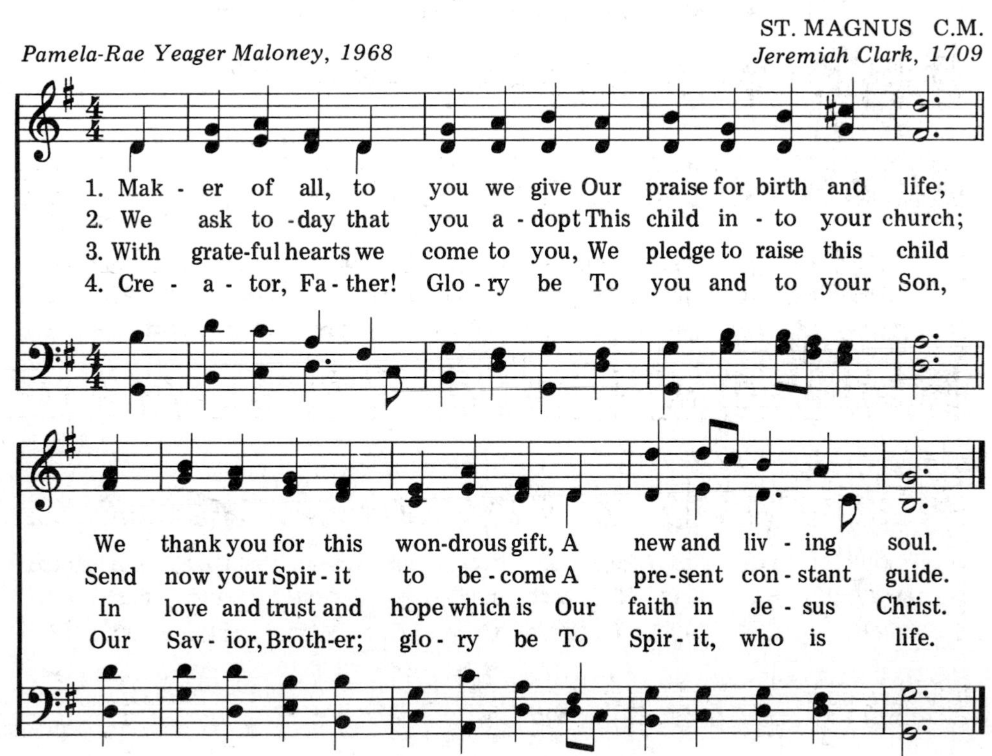
1. Mak - er of all, to you we give Our praise for birth and life;
2. We ask to - day that you a - dopt This child in - to your church;
3. With grate-ful hearts we come to you, We pledge to raise this child
4. Cre - a - tor, Fa - ther! Glo - ry be To you and to your Son,
We thank you for this won-drous gift, A new and liv - ing soul.
Send now your Spir - it to be - come A pre-sent con - stant guide.
In love and trust and hope which is Our faith in Je - sus Christ.
Our Sav - ior, Broth-er; glo - ry be To Spir - it, who is life.

208

Eternal God, We Consecrate

ST. FLAVIAN C.M.

Robert Dobbie, 1971 — Day's Psalter, *1562*

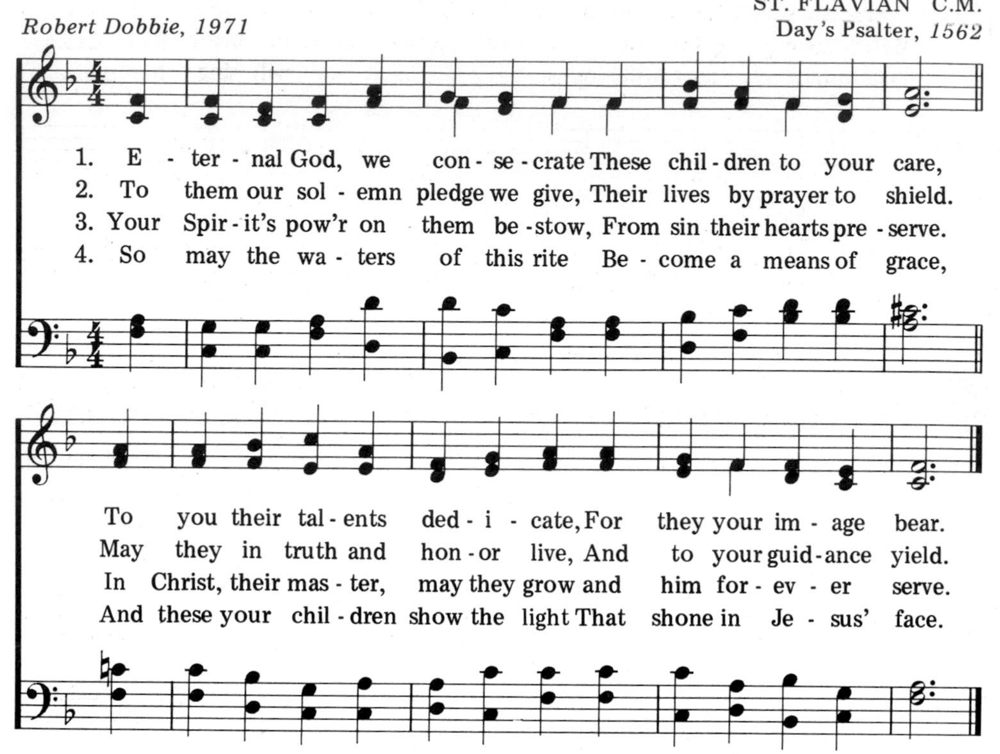

1. E - ter - nal God, we con - se - crate These chil - dren to your care,
2. To them our sol - emn pledge we give, Their lives by prayer to shield.
3. Your Spir - it's pow'r on them be - stow, From sin their hearts pre - serve.
4. So may the wa - ters of this rite Be - come a means of grace,
To you their tal - ents ded - i - cate, For they your im - age bear.
May they in truth and hon - or live, And to your guid - ance yield.
In Christ, their mas - ter, may they grow and him for - ev - er serve.
And these your chil - dren show the light That shone in Je - sus' face.

209

Broken Bread and Outpoured Wine

DELAWARE 7.6.8.6.D.

Scott McCormick, Jr., 1968 — *Joseph Willcox Jenkins, 1968*

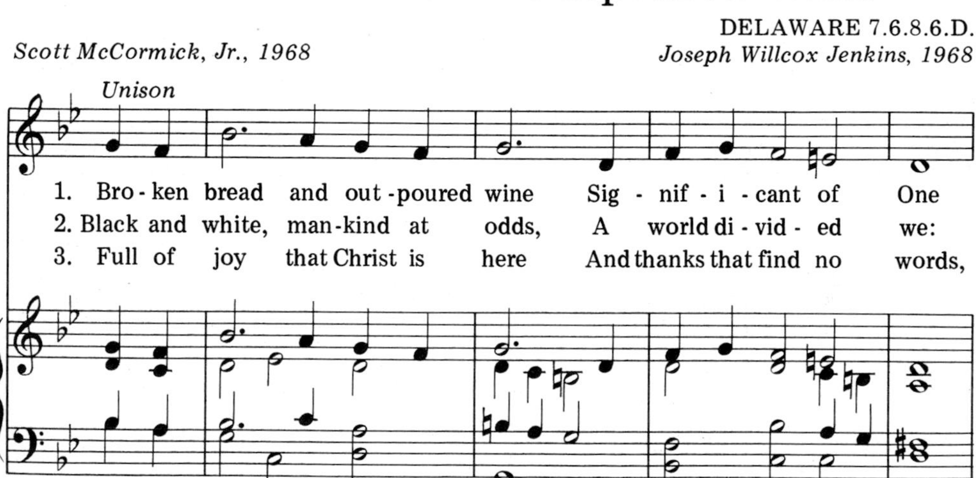

Unison
1. Bro - ken bread and out - poured wine Sig - nif - i - cant of One
2. Black and white, man-kind at odds, A world di - vid - ed we:
3. Full of joy that Christ is here And thanks that find no words,

Once bro- ken in o - be - di - ence To be the Man for us!
Let's take a - gain the gift of Christ To make us whole and free!
We look un - to the splen-did day When all will sing his praise!
Eat - ing, drink - ing with-out price God's good - ness at this board,
His one death is ours to share; His righ - teous - ness al - so.
Lest we lock our joy in- side And spoil this feast of love,
We thus pro - claim the death of Christ For- give-ness free to all!
O strength-en, God, this meal to mean Our be - ing one in him.
O lead us, God, in - to the world To suf -fer with the poor.

Let Us Break Bread Together

LET US BREAK BREAD 7.3.7.3. *with Refrain*

Negro Spiritual

Negro Melody

Unison
1. Let us break bread to - geth - er on our knees;
2. Let us drink wine to - geth - er on our knees;
3. Let us praise God to - geth - er on our knees;
Let us break bread to - geth - er on our knees.
Let us drink wine to - geth - er on our knees.
Let us praise God to - geth - er on our knees.
When I fall on my knees, with my face to the ris - ing sun,
O Lord, have mer - cy on me.

211

This Is the Hour

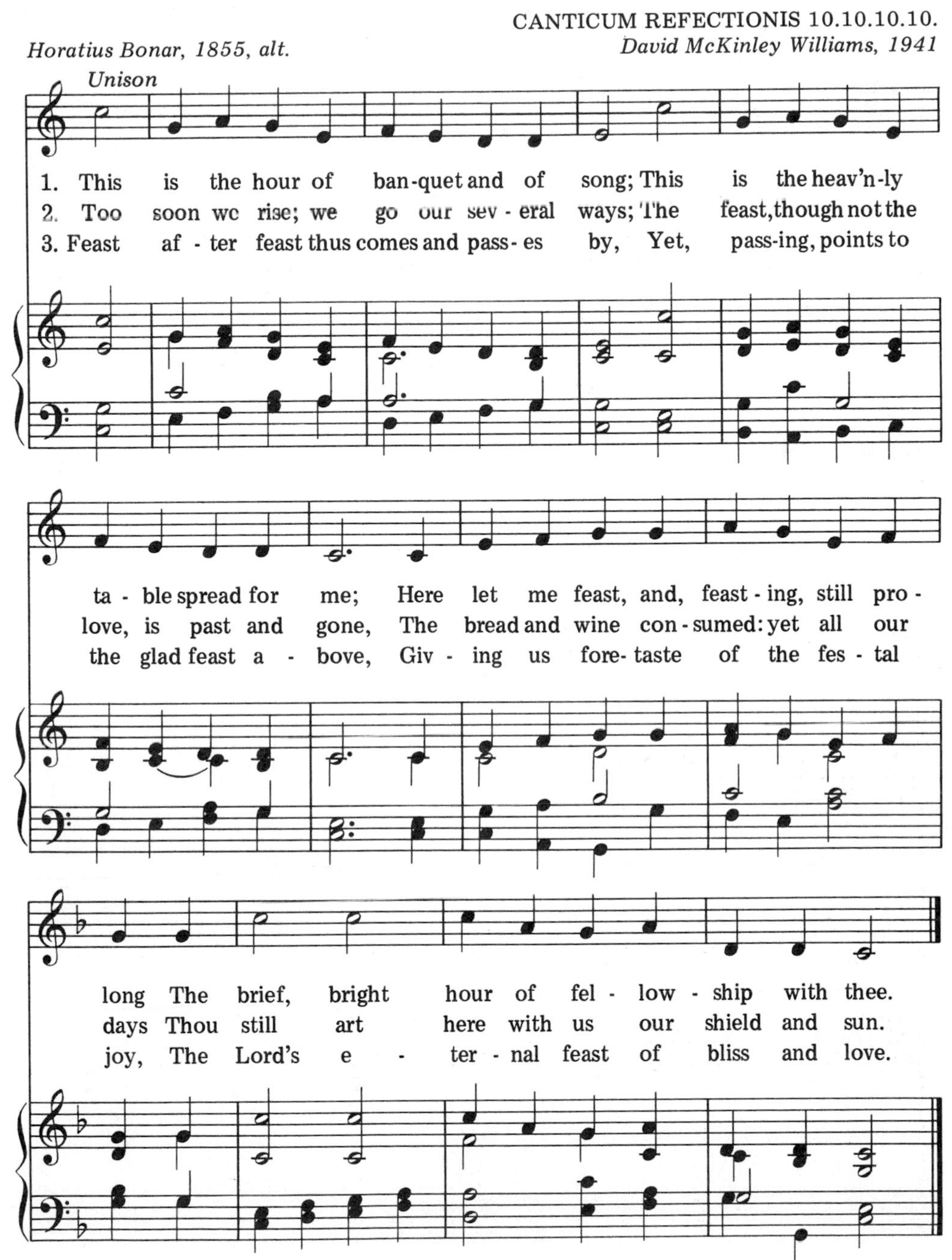
CANTICUM REFECTIONIS 10.10.10.10.
Horatius Bonar, 1855, alt.
David McKinley Williams, 1941
Unison
1. This is the hour of ban-quet and of song; This is the heav'n-ly ta - ble spread for me; Here let me feast, and, feast - ing, still pro - long The brief, bright hour of fel - low - ship with thee.
2. Too soon we rise; we go our sev - eral ways; The feast, though not the love, is past and gone, The bread and wine con - sumed: yet all our days Thou still art here with us our shield and sun.
3. Feast af - ter feast thus comes and pass - es by, Yet, pass-ing, points to the glad feast a - bove, Giv - ing us fore- taste of the fes - tal joy, The Lord's e - ter - nal feast of bliss and love.

*Bread of the World, in Mercy Broken

RENDEZ À DIEU 9.8.9.8.D.

Reginald Heber, 1827

Attr. to Louis Bourgeois, 1543

Bread of the world, in mer - cy bro - ken, Wine of the
soul, in mer - cy shed, By whom the words of life were spo - ken,
And in whose death our sins are dead, Look on the heart by sor - row
bro - ken, Look on the tears by sin - ners shed, And be thy

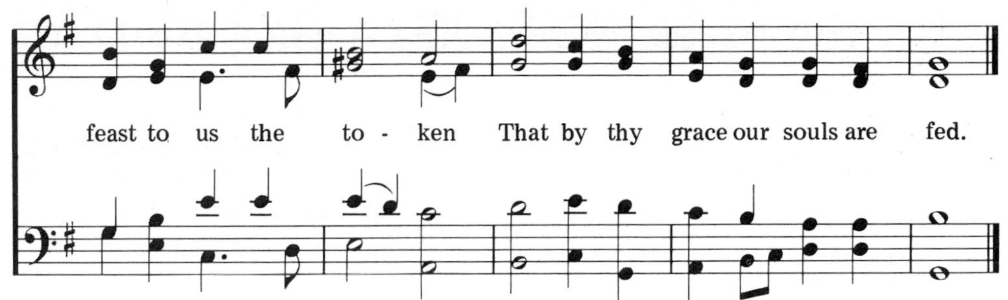

feast to us the to - ken That by thy grace our souls are fed.

213

This Do Remembering Me

NEW SONG 6.6.6.6.

R. B. Y. Scott, 1964 — *Lee Burswold, 1970*

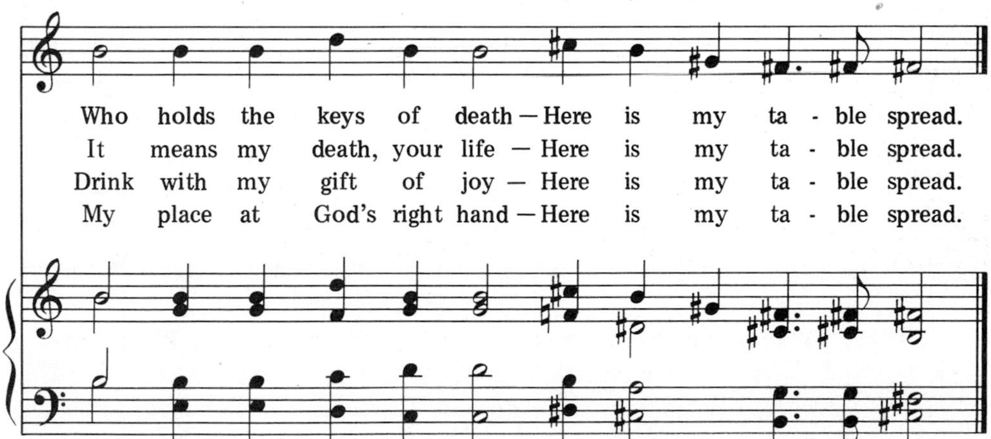

1. This do re - mem - bering me, The liv - ing who was dead,
Who holds the keys of death — Here is my ta - ble spread.

2. This do re - mem - bering me; Eat now this bro - ken bread,
It means my death, your life — Here is my ta - ble spread.

3. This do re - mem - bering me; Take this new wine blood-red,
Drink with my gift of joy — Here is my ta - ble spread.

4. This do re - mem - bering me, My wound - ing in your stead,
My place at God's right hand — Here is my ta - ble spread.

Accidentals apply only to the notes they precede. The absence of measure bars in this music encourages a free treatment of the hymn.

214

For the Bread, Which Thou Hast Broken

Louis F. Benson, 1924

KINGDOM 8.7.8.7.
V. Earle Copes, 1959

1. For the bread, which thou hast bro - ken, For the
2. By this pledge that thou dost love us, By thy
3. With our saint - ed ones in glo - ry Seat - ed
4. In thy ser - vice, Lord, de - fend us; In our
wine, which thou hast poured, For the words, which thou hast
gift of peace re - stored, By thy call to heav'n a -
at our Fa - ther's board, May the church that wait - eth
hearts keep watch and ward; In the world where thou dost
spo - ken, Now we give thee thanks, O Lord.
bove us, Hal - low all our lives, O Lord.
for thee Keep love's tie un - bro - ken, Lord.
send us Let thy king - dom come, O Lord.

Come, Risen Lord

Luke 24:28ff.
George W. Briggs, 1933
ROSEDALE 10.10.10.10.
Leo Sowerby, 1964
1. Come, ris - en Lord, and deign to be our guest; Nay, let us be thy guests; the feast is thine; Thy - self at thine own board make man - i - fest In this our sac - ra - ment of bread and wine.
2. We meet, as in that up - per room they met, Thou at the ta - ble, bless - ing, yet dost stand; "This is my bod - y"; so thou giv - est yet: Faith still re - ceives the cup as from thy hand.
3. One bod - y we, one bod - y who par - take, One church u - nit - ed in com - mu - nion blest; One name we bear, one bread of life we break, With all thy saints on earth and saints at rest.
4. One with each oth - er, Lord, for one in thee, Who art one Sav - ior and one liv - ing head; Then o - pen thou our eyes, that we may see; Be known to us in break - ing of the bread.

*Deck Thyself, My Soul, with Gladness

Johann Franck, c.1649
Tr. Catherine Winkworth, 1863

SCHMÜCKE DICH L.M.D.
Johann Crüger, 1649

1. Deck thy - self, my soul, with glad - ness, Leave the gloom-y haunts of
2. Sun, who all my life dost bright-en; Light, who dost my soul en-
3. Je - sus, Bread of life, I pray thee, Let me glad-ly here o-
sad - ness, Come in - to the day-light's splen-dor, There with
light - en; Joy, the sweet-est man e'er know-eth; Fount, whence
bey thee; Nev - er to my hurt in - vit - ed, Be thy
joy thy prais-es ren - der Un - to him whose grace un-bound - ed
all my be - ing flow - eth: At thy feet I cry, my Mak - er,
love with love re - quit - ed; From this ban - quet let me mea - sure,
Hath this won - drous ban-quet found - ed; High o'er all the heav'ns he
Let me be a fit par - tak - er Of this bless-ed food from
Lord, how vast and deep its trea - sure; Through the gifts thou here dost

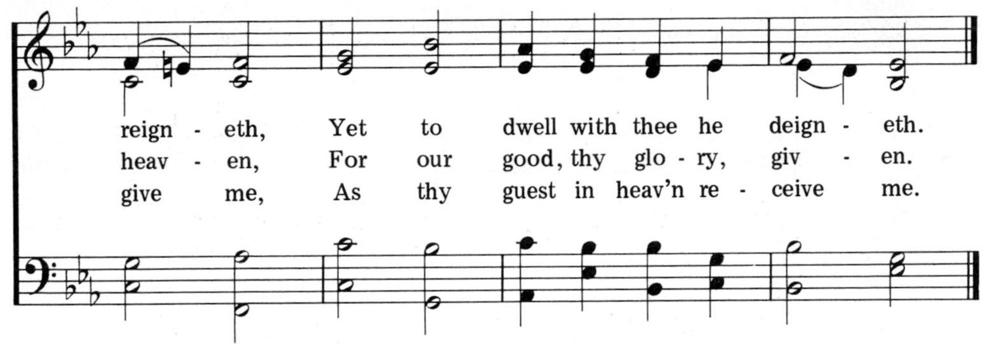
reign - eth, Yet to dwell with thee he deign - eth.
heav - en, For our good, thy glo - ry, giv - en.
give me, As thy guest in heav'n re - ceive me.

217

One Table Spread

ONE TABLE SPREAD 10.4.10.4.12.10.
Michael Ryan, 1971
Arr. by John Ferguson, 1972

Dalton E. McDonald, 1969

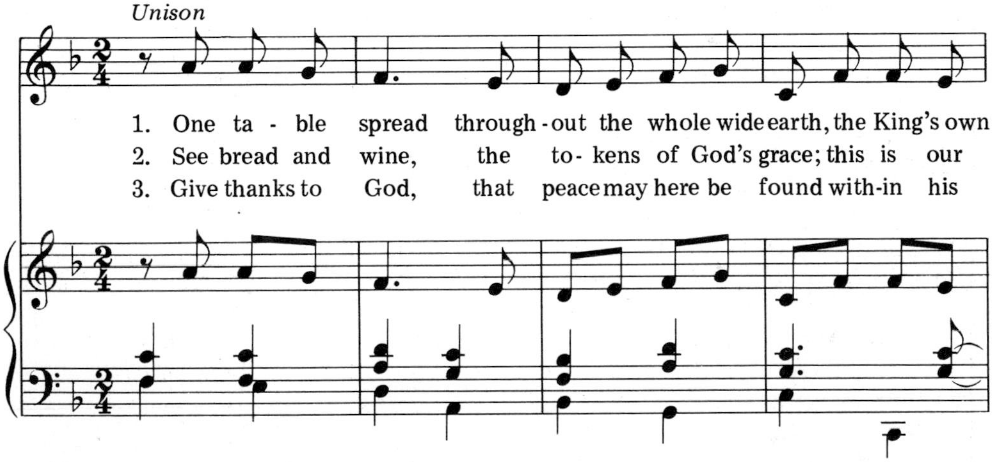

Unison

1. One ta - ble spread through-out the whole wide earth, the King's own
2. See bread and wine, the to- kens of God's grace; this is our
3. Give thanks to God, that peace may here be found with-in his

feast! From ev - 'ry na - tion men shall come to share from west and
meal. Here we re - call our Lord up - on the cross, his love is
plan; Our part to hear and heed his new com-mand: "Love God and

east. All now is read - y, and our host in -
real! Take it not light - ly; this is God's own
man!" Now is re - veal'd the glo - ry of the
vites us in: Both bad and good are guests. Let us be - gin.
sac - ri - fice For all our need, and his love will suf - fice.
Fa - ther, Son, And God the Ho - ly Spir - it, Three in One.

Draw Us in the Spirit's Tether

Matt. 18:20
Percy Dearmer, 1925

UNION SEMINARY 8.7.8.7.4.4.4.7.
Harold Friedell, 1957
Adapted by Jet Turner, 1967

Unison
1. Draw us in the Spir-it's teth-er, For when hum-bly in thy name, Two or three are met to-geth-er, Thou art in the midst of them; Al-le-lu-ya! Al-le-lu-ya! Touch we now thy gar-ment's hem.
2. As the breth-ren used to gath-er In the name of Christ to sup, Then with thanks to God the Fa-ther Break the bread and bless the cup, Al-le-lu-ya! Al-le-lu-ya, So knit thou our friend-ship up.
3. All our meals and all our liv-ing Make as sac-ra-ments of thee, That by car-ing, help-ing, giv-ing, We may true dis-ci-ples be. Al-le-lu-ya! Al-le-lu-ya, We will serve thee faith-ful-ly.

219

Here, O My Lord, I See Thee

First Tune

Horatius Bonar, 1855

ADORO TE 10.10.10.10.
Benedictine Plainsong, 13th century

Unison
1. Here, O my Lord, I see thee face to face;
2. Here would I feed up - on the bread of God,
3. I have no help but thine, nor do I need
Here would I touch and han - dle things un - seen;
Here drink with thee the roy - al wine of heav'n;
An - oth - er arm save thine to lean up - on.
Here grasp with firm - er hand e - ter - nal grace,
Here would I lay a - side each earth - ly load,
It is e - nough, my Lord, e - nough in - deed;
And all my wea - ri - ness up - on thee lean.
Here taste a - fresh the calm of sin for - given.
My strength is in thy might, thy might a - lone.

Here, O My Lord, I See Thee

Second Tune

MORECAMBE 10.10.10.10.

Horatius Bonar, 1855

Frederick C. Atkinson, 1870

1. Here, O my Lord, I see thee face to face;
2. Here would I feed up - on the bread of God,
3. I have no help but thine, nor do I need
Here would I touch and han - dle things un - seen,
Here drink with thee the roy - al wine of heav'n;
An - oth - er arm save thine to lean up - on.
Here grasp with firm - er hand e - ter - nal grace,
Here would I lay a - side each earth - ly load,
It is e - nough, my Lord, e - nough in - deed;
And all my wea - ri - ness up - on thee lean.
Here taste a - fresh the calm of sin for - given.
My strength is in thy might, thy might a - lone.

Now the Silence

NOW *Irregular*

Jaroslav J. Vajda, 1969 *Carl Schalk, 1969*

To capture the spirit of this hymn sing it joyfully.

Gm Cm F B♭ F Gm C
Now the blood Now the joy - ful cel - e - bra - tion
F Dm Gm C Am Gm Dm C
Now the wed-ding Now the songs Now the heart for - giv - en leap - ing
F Gm C Gm F Gm C Gm
Now the Spir - it's vis - i - ta - tion Now the Son's e - piph - a - ny
F Gm Dm C Gm C Gm C
Now the Fa - ther's bless - ing Now Now Now

*Jesus, Thou Joy of Loving Hearts

12th century
(possibly Bernard of Clairvaux, c.1150)
Tr. Ray Palmer, 1858

SONG 5 L.M.
Orlando Gibbons, 1623

1. Je - sus, thou joy of lov - ing hearts, Thou fount of life, thou light of men, From the best bliss that earth im - parts We turn un - filled to thee a - gain.
2. Thy truth un - changed hath ev - er stood; Thou sav - est those that on thee call; To them that seek thee, thou art good, To them that find thee, all in all.
3. We taste thee, O thou liv - ing bread, And long to feast up - on thee still; We drink of thee, the foun - tain - head, And thirst our souls from thee to fill.
4. O Je - sus, ev - er with us stay, Make all our mo - ments calm and bright; Chase the dark night of sin a - way, Shed o'er the world thy ho - ly light.

*Were You There

WERE YOU THERE *Irregular*

Negro Spiritual

Negro Melody

I Bind unto Myself Today

Attr. to Patrick, of Ireland, 4th century
Tr. Cecil Frances Alexander, 1889

ST. PATRICK L.M.D.
Traditional Irish Melody
Arr. by Charles V. Stanford, 1902

2. I bind this day to me for - ev - er, By pow-er of
3. I bind un - to my - self to - day The pow-er of
5. I bind un - to my - self the name, The strong name
faith, Christ's in - car - na - tion; His bap - - tism in
God to hold and lead, His eye to watch, his
of the Trin - i - ty, By in - vo - ca - tion
Jor - dan riv - er; His death on cross for my sal -
might to stay, His ear to hear - ken to my
of the same, The Three in One, and One in

va - tion; His burst - ing from the spic - ed tomb, His
need, The wis - dom of my God to teach, His
Three, Of whom all na - ture hath cre - a - tion, E -
rid - ing up the heav'n-ly way, His com - ing at the
hand to guide, his shield to ward, The word of God to
ter - nal Fa - ther, Spir - it, Word, Praise to the Lord of
day of doom, I bind un - to my - self to - day.
give me speech, His heav'n - ly host to be my guard.
my sal - va - tion; Sal - va - tion is of Christ the Lord.

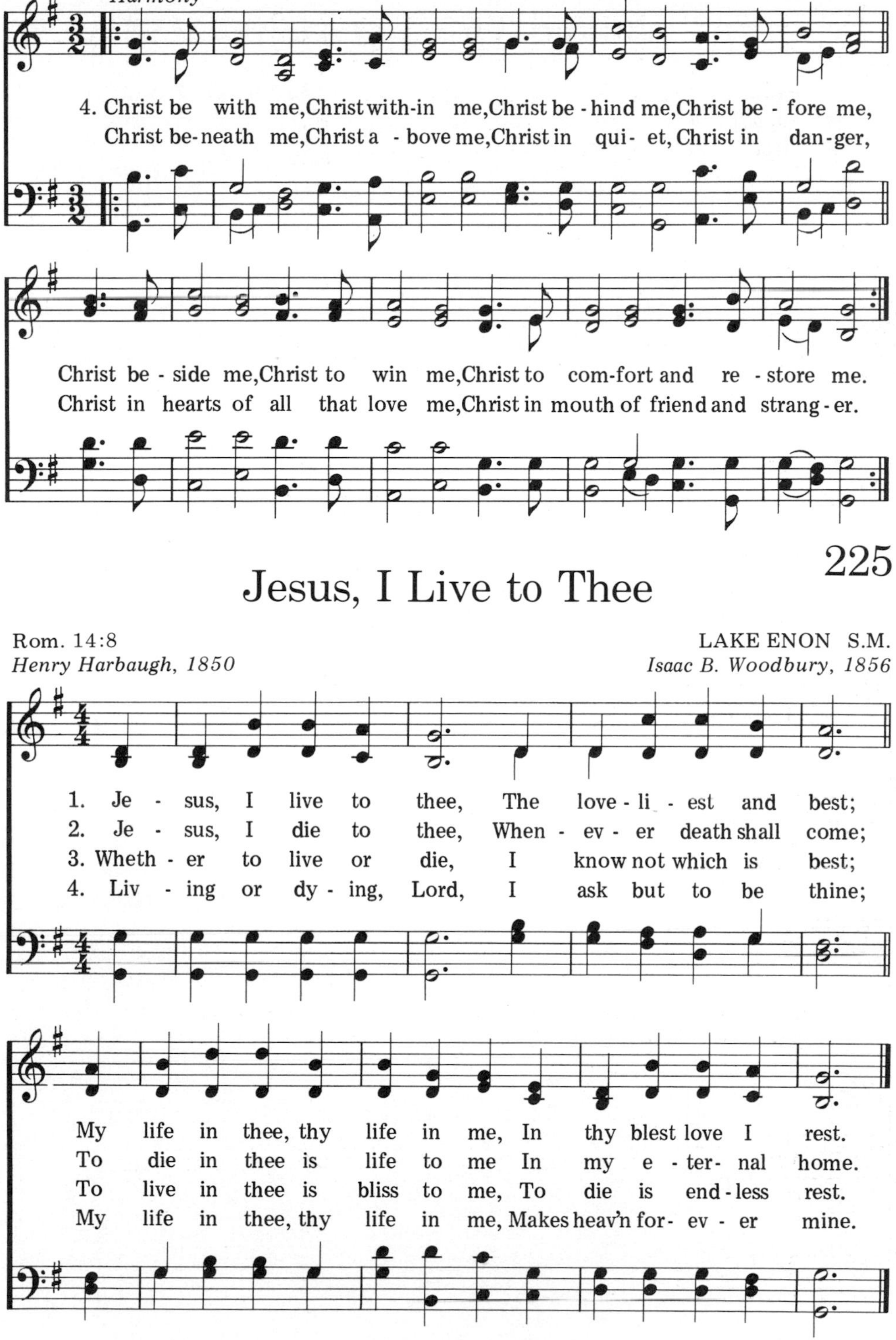
Harmony
4. Christ be with me, Christ with-in me, Christ be-hind me, Christ be-fore me,
Christ be-neath me, Christ a-bove me, Christ in qui-et, Christ in dan-ger,
Christ be-side me, Christ to win me, Christ to com-fort and re-store me.
Christ in hearts of all that love me, Christ in mouth of friend and strang-er.
225
Jesus, I Live to Thee
Rom. 14:8
Henry Harbaugh, 1850
LAKE ENON S.M.
Isaac B. Woodbury, 1856
1. Je-sus, I live to thee, The love-li-est and best;
2. Je-sus, I die to thee, When-ev-er death shall come;
3. Wheth-er to live or die, I know not which is best;
4. Liv-ing or dy-ing, Lord, I ask but to be thine;
My life in thee, thy life in me, In thy blest love I rest.
To die in thee is life to me In my e-ter-nal home.
To live in thee is bliss to me, To die is end-less rest.
My life in thee, thy life in me, Makes heav'n for-ev-er mine.

226

Jesus Walked This Lonesome Valley

LONESOME VALLEY 8.8.10.8.
American Spiritual
Collected by Gladys Jameson
American Spiritual
Harm. by John Ferguson, 1972
Unison
F
B♭
F
1. Je - sus walked this lone-some val - ley, He had to walk it
2. We must walk this lone-some val - ley, We have to walk it
3. You must go and stand your tri - al, You have to stand it
C
F
3
C
by him - self, Oh, no - bod - y else could walk it
by our - selves, Oh, no - bod - y else can walk it
by your - self, Oh, no - bod - y else can stand it
B♭
F
B
F
for him, He had to walk it by him - self.
for us, We have to walk it by our - selves.
for you, You have to stand it by your - self.

Lord Christ, When First Thou Cam'st

ALLEIN GOTT IN DER HÖH' 8.7.8.7.8.8.7.

W. Russell Bowie, 1928

Geistliche Lieder, *Leipzig, 1539*

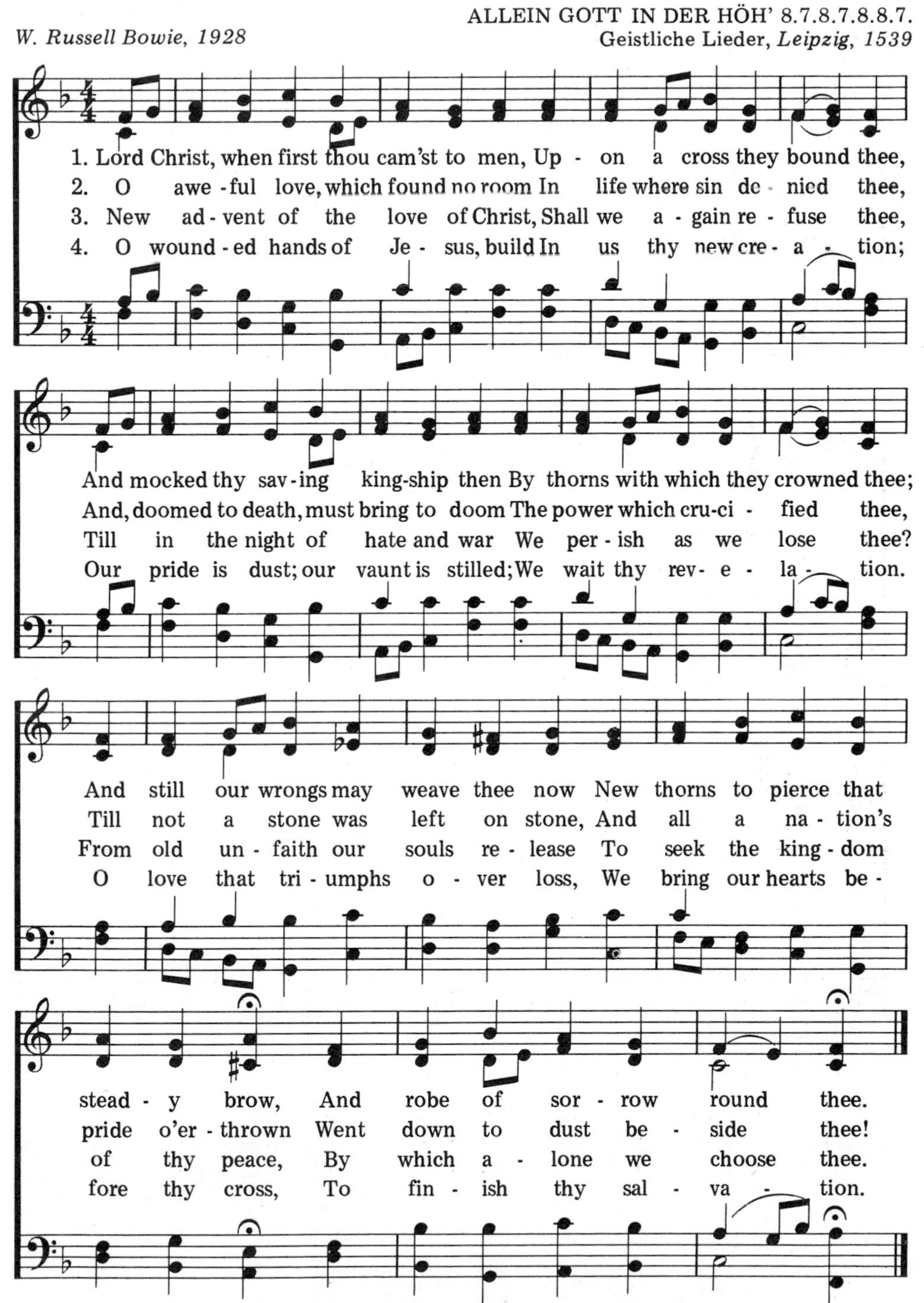
1. Lord Christ, when first thou cam'st to men, Upon a cross they bound thee,
2. O awe-ful love, which found no room In life where sin denied thee,
3. New advent of the love of Christ, Shall we again refuse thee,
4. O wounded hands of Jesus, build In us thy new creation;
And mocked thy saving kingship then By thorns with which they crowned thee;
And, doomed to death, must bring to doom The power which crucified thee,
Till in the night of hate and war We perish as we lose thee?
Our pride is dust; our vaunt is stilled; We wait thy revelation.
And still our wrongs may weave thee now New thorns to pierce that
Till not a stone was left on stone, And all a nation's
From old unfaith our souls release To seek the kingdom
O love that triumphs over loss, We bring our hearts be-
steady brow, And robe of sorrow round thee.
pride o'erthrown Went down to dust beside thee!
of thy peace, By which alone we choose thee.
fore thy cross, To finish thy salvation.

228

O Jesus, We Adore Thee

PASSION CHORALE 7.6.7.6.D.
Hans Leo Hassler, 1601
Harm. by Johann Sebastian Bach, 1729

Arthur T. Russell, 1851

1. O Je - sus, we a - dore thee, Up - on the cross, our King!
2. Yet doth the world dis - dain thee, Still pass - ing by the cross;
3. O glo-rious King, we bless thee, No lon- ger pass thee by;

We bow our hearts be - fore thee, Thy gra - cious name we sing.
Lord, may our hearts re - tain thee; All else we count but loss.
O Je - sus, we con - fess thee The Son en-throned on high.

That name hath brought sal - va - tion, That name in life our stay,
Ah, Lord, our sins ar - raigned thee, And nailed thee to the tree:
Lord, grant to us re - mis - sion; Life through thy death re - store;

Our peace, our con - so - la - tion When life shall fade a - way.
Our pride, our Lord, dis - dained thee; Yet deign our hope to be.
Yea, grant us the fru - i - tion Of life for - ev - er - more.

A lower setting may be found at No. 127.

Hope of the World

DONNE SECOURS 11.10.11.10.

Georgia Harkness, 1954 — Genevan Psalter, *1551*

1. Hope of the world, thou Christ of great com - pas - sion,
2. Hope of the world, God's gift from high - est heav - en,
3. Hope of the world, a - foot on dust - y high - ways,
4. Hope of the world, who by thy cross didst save us
Speak to our fear - ful hearts by con - flict rent.
Bring - ing to hun - gry souls the bread of life,
Show - ing to wan - dering souls the path of light,
From death and dark de - spair, from sin and guilt,
Save us, thy peo - ple, from con - sum - ing pas - sion,
Still let thy Spir - it un - to us be giv - en
Walk thou be - side us lest the tempt - ing by - ways
We ren - der back the love thy mer - cy gave us;
Who by our own false hopes and aims are spent.
To heal earth's wounds and end her bit - ter strife.
Lure us a - way from thee to end - less night.
Take thou our lives and use them as thou wilt.

I Know Not Where the Road Will Lead

KING'S HIGHWAY 8.6.8.6.7., 8.6.8.6., 8.6.8.6.7.
Herbert G. Draesel, Jr., 1964
Evelyn Atwater Cummins, 1922
Harm. by John Ferguson, 1973
Unison
Bm A Bm F♯
1. I know not where the road will lead I fol - low day by day,
2. The way is truth, the way is love, For light and strength I pray,
Bm F♯m G D Bm F♯ Bm Em
Or where it ends; I on - ly know I walk the King's high - way, Yes,
And through the eyes of life, to God, I walk the King's high - way, Yes,
Bm F♯ Bm A D
I walk the King's high - way. I know not if the way is long,
I walk the King's high - way, The count - less hosts lead on be - fore,

A D F#m Bm
And no one else can say; But rough or smooth, up hill or down,
I must not fear nor stray; With them, the pil - grims of the faith,
G A D F# Bm A
I walk the King's high - way. And some I love have reached the end,
I walk the King's high - way. Through light and dark the road leads on
Bm F# Bm F#m G D
And some with me may stay, Their faith and hope still guid - ing me:
Till dawns the end - less day, When I shall know why in this life
Bm F# G Em Bm F# Bm
I walk the King's high - way, Yes, I walk the King's high - way.
I walk the King's high - way, Yes, I walk the King's high - way.

Lead On, O King Eternal

LANCASHIRE 7.6.7.6.D.

Ernest W. Shurtleff, 1888 *Henry T. Smart, 1836*

1. Lead on, O King e - ter - nal, The day of march has come;
2. Lead on, O King e - ter - nal, Till sin's fierce war shall cease,
3. Lead on, O King e - ter - nal, We fol - low, not with fears,

Hence - forth in fields of con - quest Thy tents shall be our home.
And ho - li - ness shall whis - per The sweet a - men of peace.
For glad - ness breaks like morn - ing Wher - e'er thy face ap - pears.

Through days of prep - a - ra - tion Thy grace has made us strong,
For not with swords' loud clash - ing, Nor roll of stir - ring drums,
Thy cross is lift - ed o'er us; We jour - ney in its light;

And now, O King e - ter - nal, We lift our bat - tle song.
But deeds of love and mer - cy, The heav'n - ly king - dom comes.
The crown a - waits the con - quest; Lead on, O God of might.

A higher setting may be found at No. 87.

Lord, I Want to Be a Christian

I WANT TO BE A CHRISTIAN *Irregular*

Negro Spiritual *Negro Melody*

He Promises to All Who Trust Him Forgiveness of Sins and Fullness of Grace

Courage in the Struggle for Justice and Peace

His Presence in Trial and Rejoicing

And Eternal Life in His Kingdom Which Has No End

Amazing Grace! How Sweet the Sound

AMAZING GRACE C.M.
American Folk Hymn
John Newton, 1779 — *Arr. by Edwin O. Excell, 1900*

1. A - maz - ing gracc! How sweet the sound That
2. 'Twas grace that taught my heart to fear, And
3. Through man - y dan - gers, toils, and snares I
4. The Lord has prom - ised good to me, His
saved a wretch like me! I once was lost, but
grace my fears re - lieved; How pre - cious did that
have al - read - y come; 'Tis grace has brought me
word my hope se - cures; He will my shield and
now am found, Was blind, but now I see.
grace ap - pear The hour I first be - lieved!
safe thus far, And grace will lead me home.
por - tion be As long as life en - dures.

My Faith Looks Up to Thee

OLIVET 6.6.4.6.6.6.4.

Ray Palmer, 1830, alt. *Lowell Mason, 1832*

1. My faith looks up to thee, Thou Lamb of Cal - va - ry, Sav - ior di - vine! Now hear me while I pray; Take all my guilt a - way; Oh, let me from this day Be whol - ly thine.
2. May thy rich grace im - part Strength to my faint - ing heart, My zeal in - spire; As thou hast died for me, Oh, may my love to thee Pure, warm, and change-less be, A liv - ing fire.
3. While life's dark maze I tread, And griefs a - round me spread, Be thou my guide; Bid dark-ness turn to day; Wipe sor - row's tears a - way; Nor let me ev - er stray From thee a - side.
4. When ends life's tran - sient dream, When death's cold, sul - len stream Shall o'er me roll, Blest Sav - ior, then, in love, Fear and dis-trust re-move; Oh, bear me safe a - bove, A ran - somed soul.

There Is a Balm in Gilead

Jer. 8:22
Negro Spiritual

THERE IS A BALM *Irregular*
Negro Melody

Refrain
There is a balm in Gil-e-ad To make the wound-ed whole,
There is a balm in Gil-e-ad to heal the sin-sick soul.
1. Some-times I feel dis-cour-aged And think my work's in vain,
2. If you can-not preach like Pe-ter, If you can-not pray like Paul,
3. Don't ev-er feel dis-cour-aged, For Je-sus is your friend;
Repeat refrain after each stanza
But then the Ho-ly Spir-it Re-vives my soul a-gain.
You can tell the love of Je-sus, And say, "He died for all!"
And if you lack for knowl-edge He'll ne'er re-fuse to lend.

236

*Dear Lord and Father of Mankind

First Tune

HERMANN 8.6.8.8.6.

Melody by Nicholaus Hermann, 1554

John Greenleaf Whittier, 1872 — *Harm. by C. Winfred Douglas, 1940*

1. Dear Lord and Fa - ther of man-kind, For - give our fool - ish
2. In sim - ple trust like theirs who heard, Be - side the Syr - ian
3. Drop thy still dews of qui - et - ness, Till all our striv - ings
4. Breathe through the heats of our de - sire Thy cool-ness and thy

ways. Re - clothe us in our right- ful mind; In pur - er lives thy
sea, The gra - cious call - ing of the Lord, Let us, like them, with-
cease; Take from our souls the strain and stress, And let our or - dered
balm; Let sense be dumb, let flesh re- tire; Speak through the earth-quake,

ser - vice find, In deep - er rev - erence, praise.
out a word, Rise up and fol - low thee.
lives con - fess The beau - ty of thy peace.
wind, and fire, O still, small voice of calm.

Dear Lord and Father of Mankind

Second Tune

REST 8.6.8.8.6.

John Greenleaf Whittier, 1872 — *Frederick C. Maker, 1887*

1. Dear Lord and Fa - ther of man-kind, For - give our fool - ish ways.
2. In sim - ple trust like theirs who heard, Be - side the Syr- ian sea,
3. Drop thy still dews of qui - et - ness, Till all our striv-ings cease;
4. Breathe through the heats of our de - sire Thy cool - ness and thy balm;
Re - clothe us in our right - ful mind; In pur - er lives thy
The gra - cious call - ing of the Lord, Let us, like them, with -
Take from our souls the strain and stress, And let our or - dered
Let sense be dumb, let flesh re - tire: Speak through the earth-quake,
ser - vice find, In deep - er rev - erence, praise.
out a word, Rise up and fol - low thee.
lives con - fess The beau - ty of thy peace.
wind, and fire, O still, small voice of calm.

*All Praise to Thee, My God

Thomas Ken, 1692, alt.

TALLIS' CANON L.M.
Thomas Tallis, c.1567

1. All praise to thee, my God, this night, For all the bless - ings
2. For - give me, Lord, for thy dear Son, The ill that I this
3. O may my soul on thee re - pose, And may sweet sleep mine
4. Praise God, from whom all bless - ings flow; Praise him, all crea-tures
1. All praise to thee, my God, this night, For
2. For - give me, Lord, for thy dear Son, The
3. O may my soul on thee re - pose, And
4. Praise God, from whom all bless-ings flow; Praise
of the light! Keep me, O keep me, King of kings, Be -
day have done, That with the world, my - self, and thee, I,
eye - lids close, Sleep that may me more vig - orous make To
here be - low; Praise him a - bove, ye heav'n - ly host; Praise
all the bless - ings of the light! Keep me, O keep me,
ill that I this day have done, That with the world, my -
may sweet sleep mine eye - lids close, Sleep that may me more
him, all crea - tures here be - low; Praise him a - bove, ye

neath thine own al - might - y wings!
ere I sleep, at peace may be.
serve my God when I a - wake.
Fa - ther, Son, and Ho - ly Ghost.
King of kings, Be - neath thine own al - might - y wings!
self, and thee, I, ere I sleep, at peace may be.
vig - orous make To serve my God when I a - wake.
heav'n - ly host; Praise Fa - ther, Son, and Ho - ly Ghost.

239

*In the Cross of Christ I Glory

Gal. 6:14
John Bowring, 1825

RATHBUN 8.7.8.7.
Ithamar Conkey, 1851

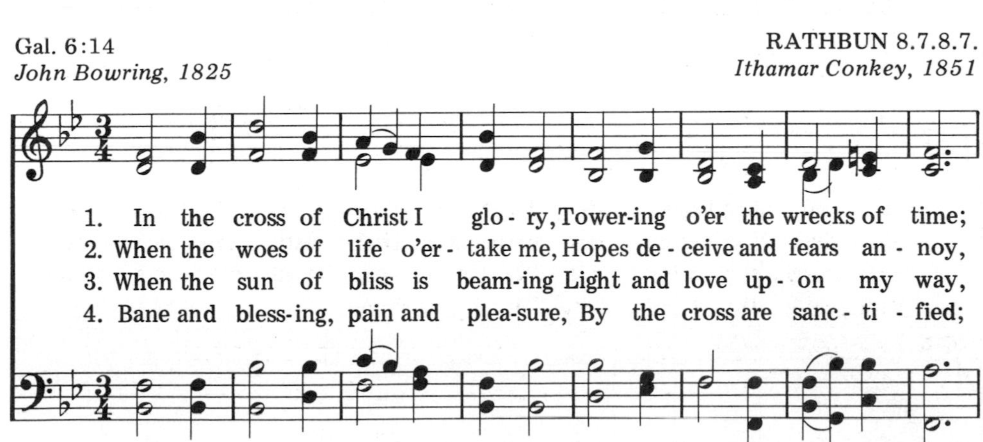

1. In the cross of Christ I glo - ry, Tower-ing o'er the wrecks of time;
2. When the woes of life o'er - take me, Hopes de - ceive and fears an - noy,
3. When the sun of bliss is beam-ing Light and love up - on my way,
4. Bane and bless-ing, pain and plea-sure, By the cross are sanc - ti - fied;

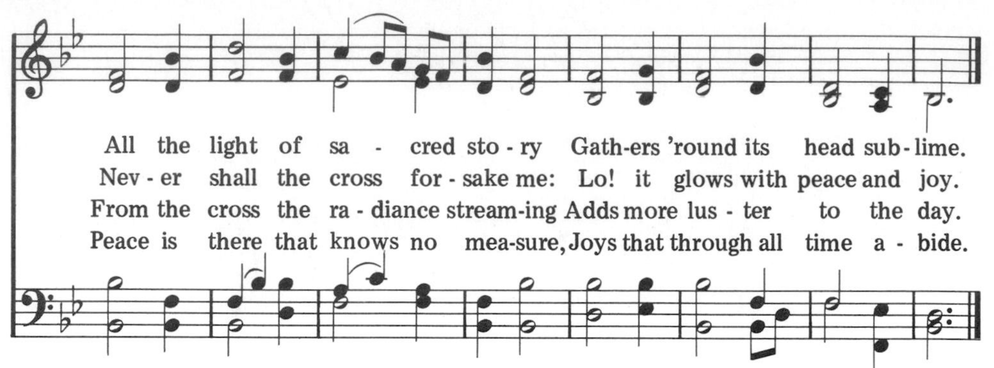
All the light of sa - cred sto - ry Gath-ers 'round its head sub - lime.
Nev - er shall the cross for - sake me: Lo! it glows with peace and joy.
From the cross the ra - diance stream-ing Adds more lus - ter to the day.
Peace is there that knows no mea-sure, Joys that through all time a - bide.

240 Good Is the Lord

Lam. 3
Para. by Donald Gowan, 1970

PILGRIMAGE 8.9.10.
John W. Neely, Jr., 1970

Unison

1. Good is the Lord to seek - ing hearts; Good is it to wait for God to save; Good for a young man to bear the Lord's yoke.
2. Si - lent - ly sit; the bur - den's his; Mouth in the dust, but hope still his; Smit - ten his cheek and no end to a - buse.
3. These things the Lord will not a - bide: Crush - ing one's pris - 'ners un - der foot; Al - so sub - vert - ing jus - tice in the court.
4. Search we our ways, re - turn to God; Lift up our hearts to the Lord of heav'n; For we've re - bell'd, still need him to for - give.

Beneath the Cross of Jesus

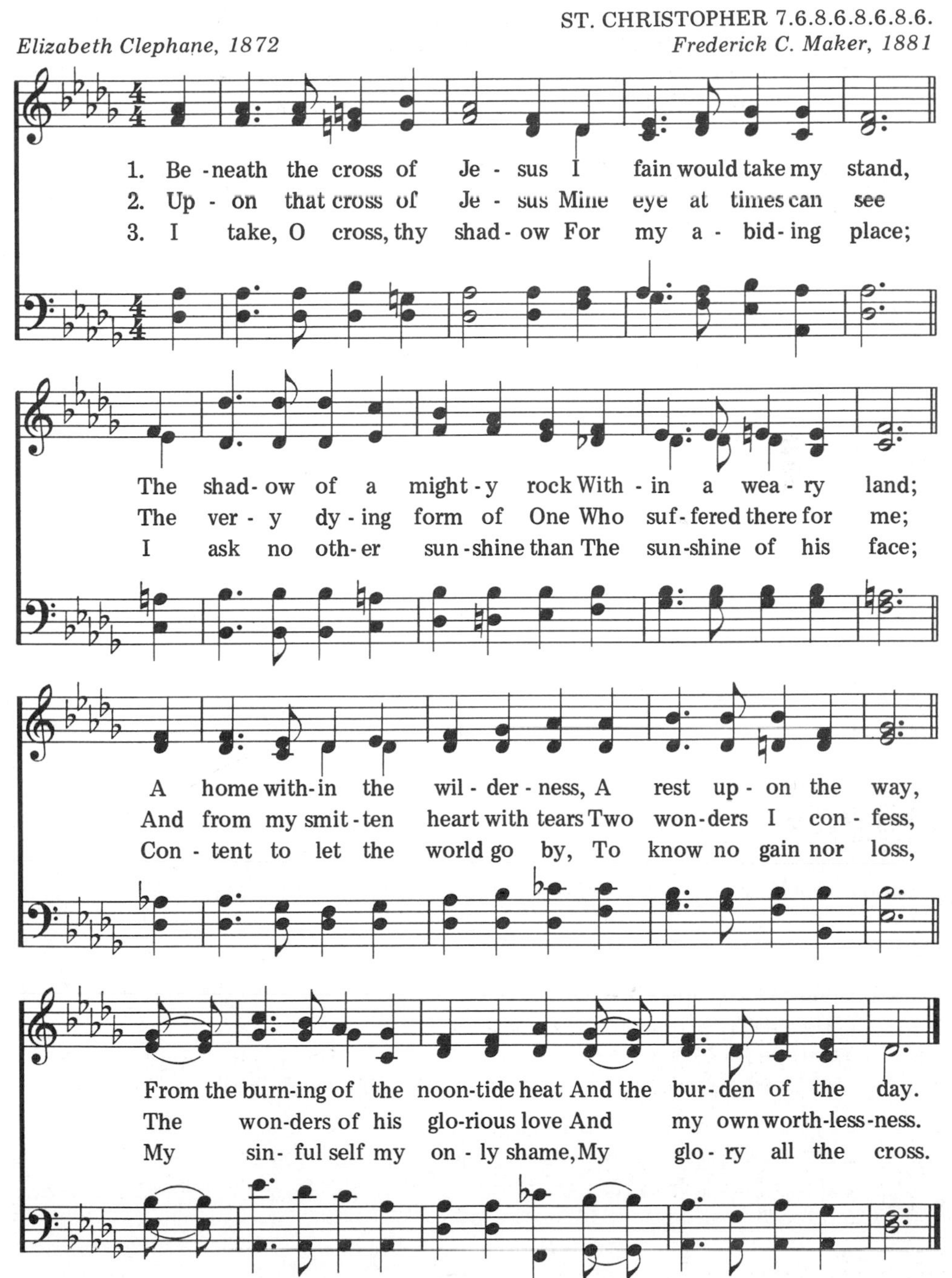
ST. CHRISTOPHER 7.6.8.6.8.6.8.6.
Elizabeth Clephane, 1872
Frederick C. Maker, 1881
1. Be - neath the cross of Je - sus I fain would take my stand,
2. Up - on that cross of Je - sus Mine eye at times can see
3. I take, O cross, thy shad - ow For my a - bid - ing place;
The shad - ow of a might - y rock With - in a wea - ry land;
The ver - y dy - ing form of One Who suf - fered there for me;
I ask no oth - er sun - shine than The sun - shine of his face;
A home with - in the wil - der - ness, A rest up - on the way,
And from my smit - ten heart with tears Two won - ders I con - fess,
Con - tent to let the world go by, To know no gain nor loss,
From the burn - ing of the noon - tide heat And the bur - den of the day.
The won - ders of his glo - rious love And my own worth - less - ness.
My sin - ful self my on - ly shame, My glo - ry all the cross.

242

Within the Maddening Maze of Things

ST. FLAVIAN C.M.

John Greenleaf Whittier, 1867 Day's Psalter, *1562*

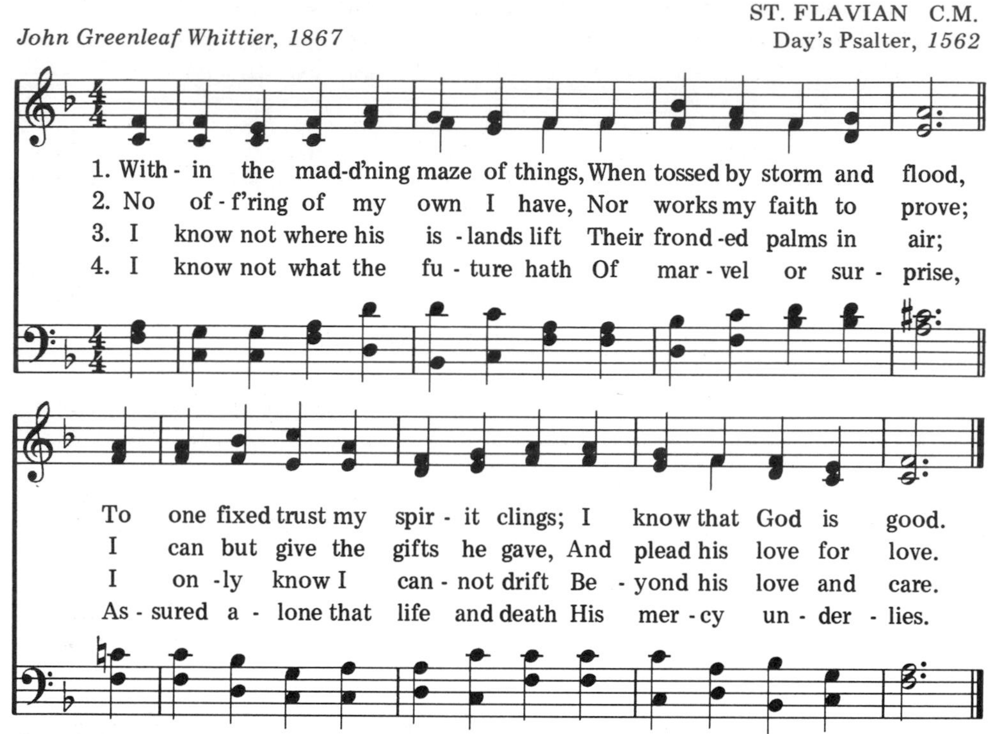
1. With - in the mad-d'ning maze of things, When tossed by storm and flood,
2. No of - f'ring of my own I have, Nor works my faith to prove;
3. I know not where his is - lands lift Their frond -ed palms in air;
4. I know not what the fu - ture hath Of mar - vel or sur - prise,
To one fixed trust my spir - it clings; I know that God is good.
I can but give the gifts he gave, And plead his love for love.
I on -ly know I can - not drift Be - yond his love and care.
As - sured a - lone that life and death His mer - cy un - der - lies.

243

Lord, Thy Mercy Now Entreating

RINGE RECHT 8.7.8.7.

Mary A. Sidebotham, 1881 Musikalischer Christen-Schatz, *Basel, 1745*

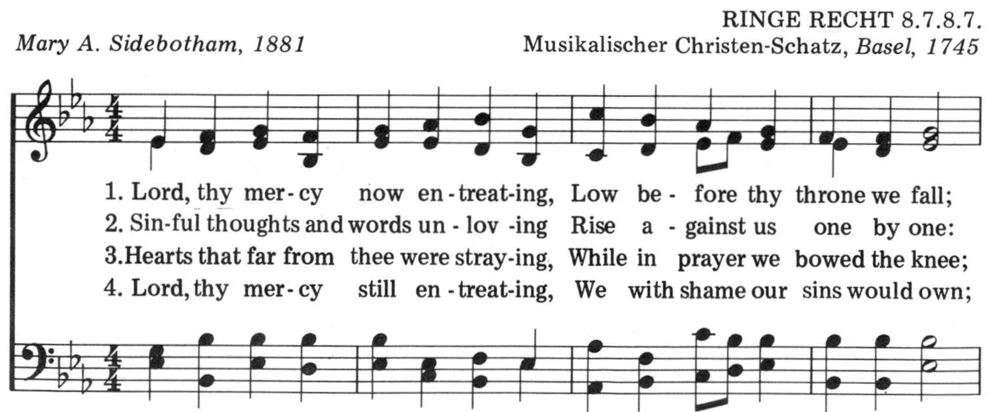
1. Lord, thy mer- cy now en - treat-ing, Low be - fore thy throne we fall;
2. Sin-ful thoughts and words un - lov -ing Rise a - gainst us one by one:
3.Hearts that far from thee were stray-ing, While in prayer we bowed the knee;
4. Lord, thy mer- cy still en - treat-ing, We with shame our sins would own;

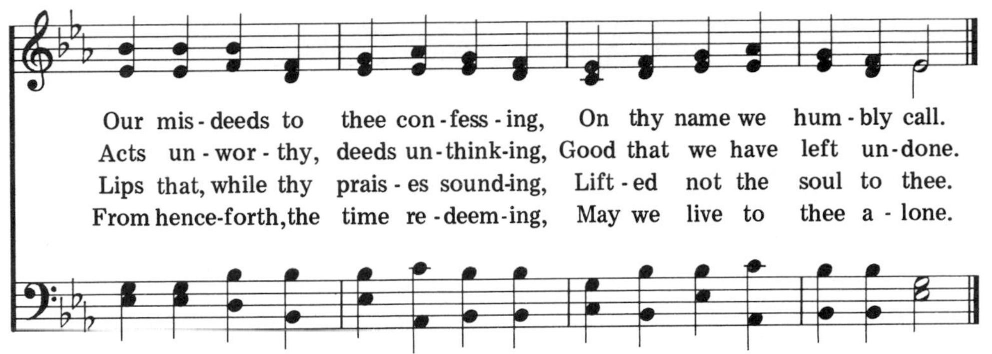

Our mis - deeds to thee con - fess - ing, On thy name we hum - bly call.
Acts un - wor - thy, deeds un - think - ing, Good that we have left un - done.
Lips that, while thy prais - es sound - ing, Lift - ed not the soul to thee.
From hence - forth, the time re - deem - ing, May we live to thee a - lone.

244

None Other Lamb

NONE OTHER LAMB 8.10.10.4.

Christina Rossetti, 1892 | *Charles Joseph Ridsdale, b. 1840*

1. None other lamb, none other name,
None other hope in heav'n or earth or sea,
None other hiding place from guilt and shame,
None beside thee.

2. My faith burns low, my hope burns low;
Only my heart's desire cries out in me,
By the deep thunder of its want and woe,
Cries out to thee.

3. Lord, thou art life, though I be dead;
Love's fire thou art, however cold I be:
Nor heav'n have I, nor place to lay my head,
Nor home, but thee.

245

O Christ, My God

SONG 24 10.10.10.10.
Christina Rossetti, 1885
Orlando Gibbons, 1623
1. O Christ, my God, who see - est the un - seen,
O Christ, my God, who know - est the un - known,
Thy might - y blood was poured forth to a - tone
For ev - ery sin that can be or hath been.
2. O thou who see - est what I can - not see,
Thou who didst love us all so long a - go,
O thou who know - est what I must not know,
Re - mem - ber all my hope, re - mem - ber me.

246

Lift Up Your Hearts

WOODLANDS 10.10.10.10.
Henry M. Butler, 1881, alt.
Walter Greatorex, 1916
Unison
1. "Lift up your hearts!" We lift them, Lord, to thee;
Here at thy feet none other may we see.
"Lift up your hearts!" E'en so, with one accord,
We lift them up, we lift them to the Lord.
2. Above the level of the former years,
The mire of sin, the weight of guilty fears,
The mist of doubt, the blight of love's decay,
O Lord of light, lift all our hearts today!
3. Lift every gift that thou thyself hast given;
Low lies the best till lifted up to heav'n;
Low lie the bounding heart, the teeming brain,
Till, sent from God, they mount to God again.
4. Then as the trumpet call, in after years,
"Lift up your hearts!" rings pealing in our ears,
Still shall those hearts respond, with full accord,
"We lift them up, we lift them to the Lord!"

An alternate setting may be found at No. 306.

247

Ask Ye What Great Thing I Know

Johann C. Schwedler, 1741
Tr. Benjamin H. Kennedy, 1863

HENDON 7.7.7.7.7.
H. A. César Malan, 1827

1. Ask ye what great thing I know
That delights and stirs me so?
What the high reward I win?
Whose the name I glory in?
Jesus Christ, the crucified.

2. Who defeats my fiercest foes?
Who consoles my saddest woes?
Who revives my fainting heart,
Healing all its hidden smart?
Jesus Christ, the crucified.

3. Who is life in life to me?
Who the death of death will be?
Who will place me on his right,
With the countless hosts of light?
Jesus Christ, the crucified.

4. This is that great thing I know;
This delights and stirs me so:
Faith in him who died to save,
Him who triumphed o'er the grave,
Jesus Christ, the crucified.

Somebody's Knockin' at Your Door

SOMEBODY'S KNOCKIN' *Irregular*

Negro Spiritual — *Negro Melody*

The style of many spirituals suggests that certain phrases be sung by a soloist or small group, with the congregation responding.

As the Bridegroom to His Chosen

John Tauler, 14th century
Para. by Emma Frances Bevan, 1827-1909

BRIDEGROOM 8.7.8.7.6.
Peter Cutts, 1964

Unison
1. As the bride-groom to his cho-sen, as the king un-to his realm,
2. As the foun-tain in the gar-den, as the can-dle in the dark,
3. As the ru-by in the set-ting, as the hon-ey in the comb,
4. As the sun-shine in the heav-ens, as the im-age in the glass,
As the keep un-to the cas-tle, as the pi-lot to the helm,
As the trea-sure in the cof-fer, as the man-na in the ark,
As the light with-in the lan-tern, as the fa-ther in the home,
As the fruit up-on the fig tree, as the dew up-on the grass,
Refrain
So, Lord, art thou to me.

Come, Thou Fount of Every Blessing

NETTLETON 8.7.8.7.D.
American Folk Tune
John Wyeth, 1812

Robert Robinson, 1758

1. Come, thou Fount of ev - ery bless - ing, Tune my heart to sing thy grace;
2. O to grace how great a debt - or Dai - ly I'm con-strained to be!
Streams of mer - cy, nev - er ceas - ing, Call for songs of loud-est praise.
Let thy good-ness, like a fet - ter, Bind my wan-dering heart to thee:
Teach me some me - lo - dious son - net, Sung by flam -ing tongues a - bove;
Prone to wan - der, Lord, I feel it, Prone to leave the God I love;
Praise the mount! I'm fixed up - on it, Mount of thy re - deem - ing love.
Here's my heart, O take and seal it, Seal it for thy courts a - bove.

251

In Boundless Mercy

Dietrich Bonhoeffer, 1942
Tr. F. L. Battles, 1965

HEATHERWOOD L.M.D.
David L. Thorburn, 1970

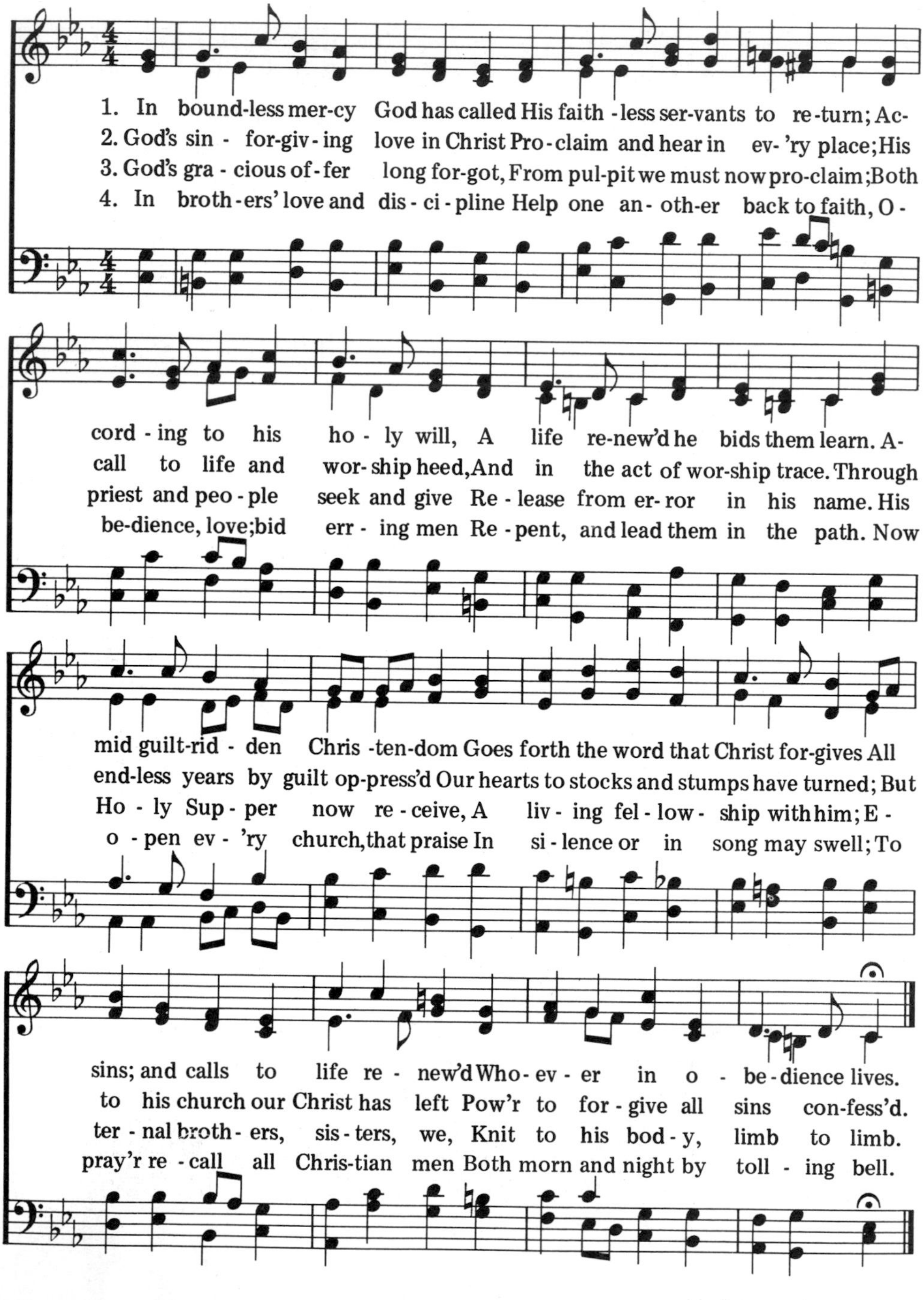

1. In bound-less mer-cy God has called His faith - less ser-vants to re-turn; Ac-
2. God's sin - for-giv - ing love in Christ Pro - claim and hear in ev- 'ry place; His
3. God's gra - cious of - fer long for-got, From pul-pit we must now pro-claim; Both
4. In broth - ers' love and dis - ci - pline Help one an- oth-er back to faith, O -

cord - ing to his ho - ly will, A life re-new'd he bids them learn. A-
call to life and wor- ship heed, And in the act of wor-ship trace. Through
priest and peo - ple seek and give Re - lease from er- ror in his name. His
be-dience, love; bid err - ing men Re - pent, and lead them in the path. Now

mid guilt-rid - den Chris -ten-dom Goes forth the word that Christ for-gives All
end-less years by guilt op-press'd Our hearts to stocks and stumps have turned; But
Ho - ly Sup - per now re - ceive, A liv - ing fel - low - ship with him; E -
o - pen ev - 'ry church, that praise In si - lence or in song may swell; To

sins; and calls to life re - new'd Who- ev - er in o - be - dience lives.
to his church our Christ has left Pow'r to for - give all sins con-fess'd.
ter - nal broth - ers, sis - ters, we, Knit to his bod - y, limb to limb.
pray'r re - call all Chris-tian men Both morn and night by toll - ing bell.

Once to Every Man and Nation

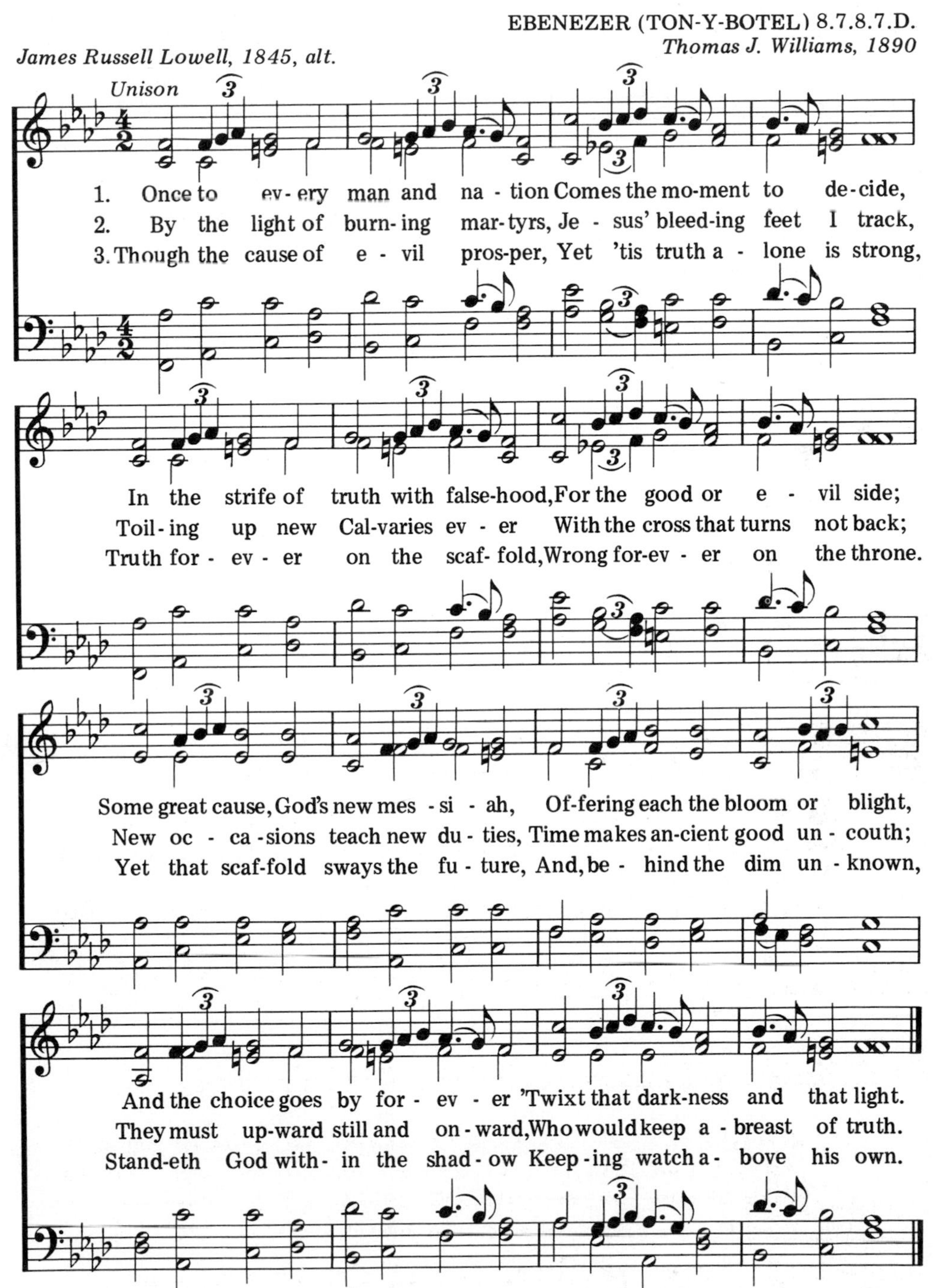
EBENEZER (TON-Y-BOTEL) 8.7.8.7.D.
Thomas J. Williams, 1890
James Russell Lowell, 1845, alt.
Unison
1. Once to ev-ery man and na-tion Comes the mo-ment to de-cide,
2. By the light of burn-ing mar-tyrs, Je-sus' bleed-ing feet I track,
3. Though the cause of e-vil pros-per, Yet 'tis truth a-lone is strong,
In the strife of truth with false-hood, For the good or e-vil side;
Toil-ing up new Cal-varies ev-er With the cross that turns not back;
Truth for-ev-er on the scaf-fold, Wrong for-ev-er on the throne.
Some great cause, God's new mes-si-ah, Of-fering each the bloom or blight,
New oc-ca-sions teach new du-ties, Time makes an-cient good un-couth;
Yet that scaf-fold sways the fu-ture, And, be-hind the dim un-known,
And the choice goes by for-ev-er 'Twixt that dark-ness and that light.
They must up-ward still and on-ward, Who would keep a-breast of truth.
Stand-eth God with-in the shad-ow Keep-ing watch a-bove his own.

253

March On, O Soul, with Strength

ARTHUR'S SEAT 6.6.6.6.8.8.
George T. Coster, 1900, alt.
Arr. from John Goss, 1874
1. March on, O soul, with strength, Like those strong men of old
2. The sons of fa - thers we By whom our faith is taught
3. March on, O soul, with strength, As strong the bat - tle rolls;
Who 'gainst en - thron - ed wrong Stood con - fi - dent and bold,
To fear no ill, to fight The ho - ly fight they fought;
'Gainst lies and lusts and wrongs, Let cour - age rule our souls;
Who, thrust in prison or cast to flame,
He - ro - ic war - riors, ne'er from Christ
In keen - est strife, Lord, may we stand,
Still made their glo - ry in thy name.
By an - y lure or guile en - ticed.
Up - held and strength - ened by thy hand.

*God of Our Fathers, Whose Almighty Hand

NATIONAL HYMN 10.10.10.10.

Daniel C. Roberts, 1876

George W. Warren, 1892

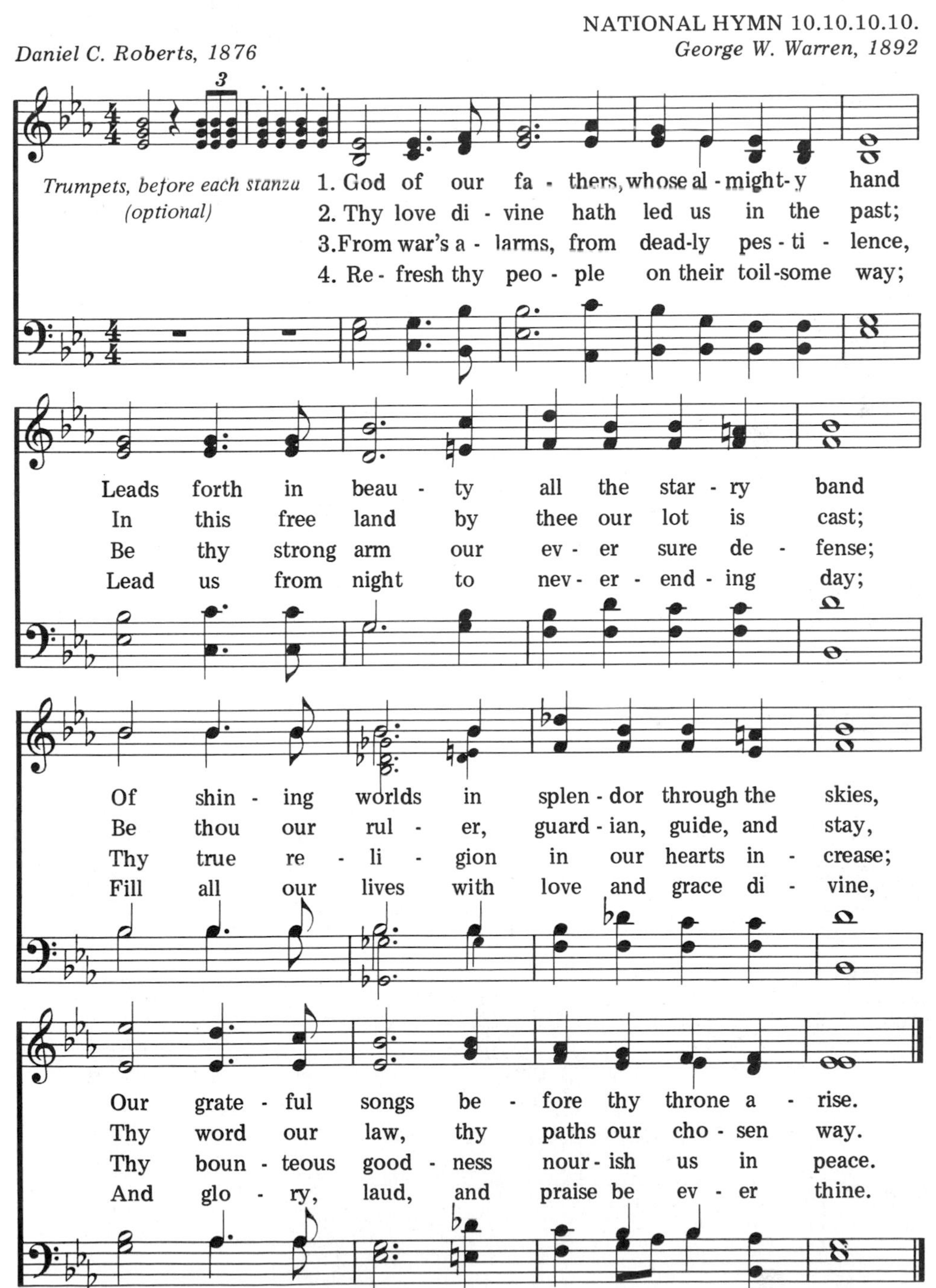
Trumpets, before each stanza
(optional)
1. God of our fa - thers, whose al - might - y hand
2. Thy love di - vine hath led us in the past;
3. From war's a - larms, from dead-ly pes - ti - lence,
4. Re - fresh thy peo - ple on their toil-some way;
Leads forth in beau - ty all the star - ry band
In this free land by thee our lot is cast;
Be thy strong arm our ev - er sure de - fense;
Lead us from night to nev - er - end - ing day;
Of shin - ing worlds in splen - dor through the skies,
Be thou our rul - er, guard - ian, guide, and stay,
Thy true re - li - gion in our hearts in - crease;
Fill all our lives with love and grace di - vine,
Our grate - ful songs be - fore thy throne a - rise.
Thy word our law, thy paths our cho - sen way.
Thy boun - teous good - ness nour - ish us in peace.
And glo - ry, laud, and praise be ev - er thine.

255

Let There Be Light

PENTECOST L.M.

William M. Vories, 1908, alt.

William Boyd, 1864

1. Let there be light, Lord God of hosts! Let there be wis - dom on the earth! Let broad hu - man - i - ty have birth! Let there be deeds in - stead of boasts!
2. With - in our pas - sioned hearts in still The calm that end - eth strain and strife; Make us thy min - is - ters of life; Purge us from lusts that curse and kill!
3. Give us the peace of vi - sion clear To see our broth - ers' good our own, To joy and suf - fer not a - lone: The love that cast - eth out all fear!
4. Let woe and waste of war - fare cease, That use - ful la - bor yet may build Its homes with love and laugh - ter filled! God, give thy way - ward chil - dren peace!

*God the Omnipotent

Henry F. Chorley, 1842, St. 1, alt.
John Ellerton, 1870, Sts. 2, 3, 4, alt.

RUSSIAN HYMN 11.10.11.9.
Alexis F. Lvov, 1833

1. God the om - nip - o - tent! King, who or - dain - est
2. God the all - righ-teous one! man hath de - fied thee,
3. God the all - wise! By the fire of thy chast' - ning
4. So shall thy chil - dren with thank - ful de - vo - tion
Great winds thy clar - i - ons, light - nings thy sword;
Yet to e - ter - ni - ty stand - eth thy word;
Earth shall to free - dom and truth be re - stored;
Praise him who saved them from per - il and sword,
Show forth thy pit - y on high where thou reign - est:
False - hood and wrong shall not tar - ry be - side thee:
Through the thick dark - ness thy king - dom is hast' - ning:
Sing - ing in cho - rus from o - cean to o - cean:
Give to us peace in our time, O Lord.
Give to us peace in our time, O Lord.
Thou wilt give peace in thy time, O Lord.
"Peace to the na - tions and praise to the Lord."

257

By the Babylonian Rivers

LATVIAN MELODY 8.7.8.7.
Ps. 137:1-4
Ewald Bash, 1964
Latvian Melody
Arr. by Ewald Bash, 1964
Harm. by Paul Abels, 1966
Unison
Dm Gm Dm7 Gm
A7 Dm Gm C
F Gm A7 Dm
1. By the Bab - y - lo - nian riv - ers We sat down in grief and wept; Hanged our harps up - on a wil - low, Mourned for Zi - on when we slept.
2. There our cap - tors in de - ri - sion Did re - quire of us a song; So we sat with star - ing vi - sion, And the days were hard and long.
3. How shall we sing the Lord's song In a strange and bit - ter land? Can our voic - es veil the sor - row? Lord God, help thy lone - ly band.
4. Let thy cross be ben - e - dic - tion For men bound in tyr - an - ny; By the power of res - ur - rec - tion Loose them from cap - tiv - i - ty.

When Israel Was in Egypt's Land

GO DOWN MOSES *Irregular*

Negro Spiritual *Negro Melody*

(I)
(II)
1. When Is - rael was in E - gypt's land,
2. Thus saith the Lord, bold Mo - ses said, Let my peo- ple go,
3. No more in bond age shall they toil,
(I)
(II)
Op - pressed so hard they could not stand,
If not I'll smite your first - born dead, Let my peo- ple go.
Let them come out with E - gypt's spoil,
Refrain (I + II)
Go down, Mo - ses, 'Way down in E - gypt's land,
Tell old Pha - raoh, To let my peo-ple go.

The style of many spirituals suggests that certain phrases (marked I) be sung by a soloist or small group, with the congregation responding (II).

Sing We of the Modern City

GENEVA 8.7.8.7.D.

Frederick Herman Kaan, c.1968 *George Henry Day, 1940*

Unison
1. Sing we of the mod - ern cit - y, Scene a - like of
2. In the cit - y full of peo - ple, World of speed and
3. God is not re - mote in heav - en, But on earth to
joy and stress; Sing we of its name-less peo - ple, In their
hec- tic days, In the ev - er - chang-ing set - ting Of the
share our shame, Chang - ing graph and mass and num - bers In - to
ur - ban wil - der - ness. In - to end- less rows of hous-es
lat - est trend and craze, Christ is pres- ent and a - mong us;
per - sons with a name. Christ has shown, be - yond sta - tis - tics,

Life is set a mil - lion - fold, Life ex - pressed in hu - man be - ings Dai - ly born and grow - ing old.
In the crowd we see him stand. In the bus - tle of the cit - y Je - sus Christ is ev - ery man.
Hu - man life with glo - ry crowned, By his time - less pres - ence prov - ing Peo - ple mat - ter, peo - ple count.

260

O Day of God, Draw Nigh

ST. MICHAEL S.M.
Genevan Psalter, *1551*
Adapted by William Crotch, 1836

R. B. Y. Scott, 1937, alt.

1. O Day of God, draw nigh In beau - ty and in power,
2. Bring to our trou - bled minds, Un - cer - tain and a - fraid,
3. Bring jus - tice to our land, That all may dwell se - cure,
4. Bring to our world of strife Thy sov - ereign word of peace,
5. O Day of God, draw nigh As at cre - a - tion's birth;

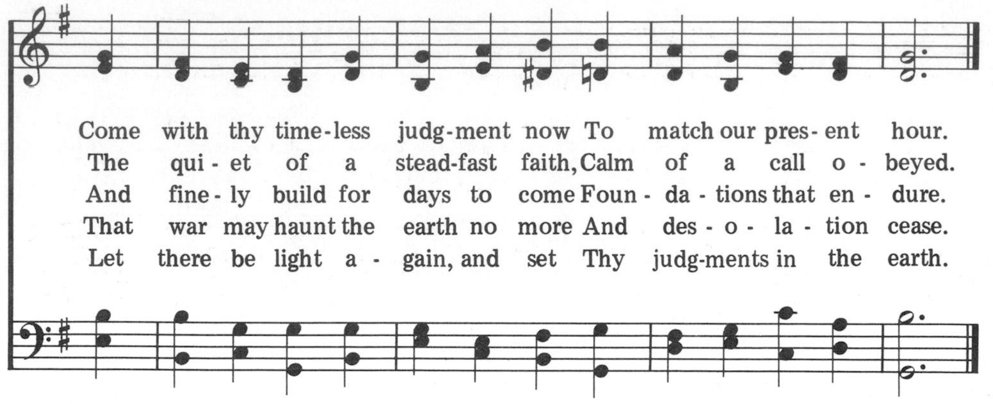
Come with thy time-less judg-ment now To match our pres-ent hour.
The qui-et of a stead-fast faith, Calm of a call o-beyed.
And fine-ly build for days to come Foun-da-tions that en-dure.
That war may haunt the earth no more And des-o-la-tion cease.
Let there be light a-gain, and set Thy judg-ments in the earth.

261

Thou Whose Purpose Is to Kindle

LADUE CHAPEL 8.7.8.7.D.

Elton Trueblood, 1966 *Ronald Arnatt, 1968*

Unison

1. Thou whose pur-pose is to kin-dle, Now ig-nite us with thy fire; While the earth a-waits thy burn-ing,
2. Thou who, in thy ho-ly gos-pel, Wills that man should tru-ly live, Make us sense our share of fail-ure,
3. Lord, who still a sword de-liv-ers Rath-er than a plac-id peace, With thy sharp-ened word dis-turb us,

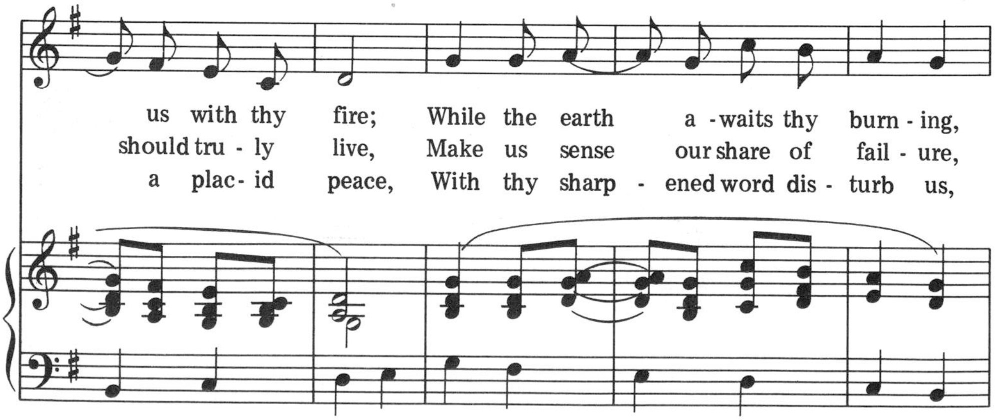

With thy pas - sion us in - spire. O - ver - come our sin - ful
Our tran - quil - li - ty for - give. Teach us cour - age as we
From com - pla - cen - cy re - lease! Save us now from sat - is -
calm - ness, Rouse us with re - demp - tive shame; Bap - tize with
strug - gle In all lib - er - a - ting strife; Lift the small-
fac - tion, When we pri - vate - ly are free, Yet are un -
thy fi - ery spir - it, Crown our lives with tongues of flame.
ness of our vi - sion By thine own a - bun - dant life.
dis - turbed in spir - it By our broth - er's mis - er - y.

262

O God of Love, O King of Peace

HESPERUS L.M.
Henry W. Baker, 1861
Henry W. Baker, 1854
1. O God of love, O King of peace, Make wars through-
2. Re - mem - ber, Lord, thy works of old, The won - ders
3. Whom shall we trust but thee, O Lord? Where rest but
out the world to cease; The wrath of sin - ful man re -
that our fa - thers told; Re - mem - ber not our sin's dark
on thy faith - ful word? None ev - er called on thee in
strain: Give peace, O God, give peace a - gain!
stain: Give peace, O God, give peace a - gain!
vain: Give peace, O God, give peace a - gain!

An alternate setting may be found at No. 48.

*A Mighty Fortress

First Version

Ps. 46
Martin Luther, 1529
Tr. Frederick H. Hedge, 1853

EIN' FESTE BURG 8.7.8.7.6.6.6.6.7.
Martin Luther, 1529

1. A might - y for - tress is our God, A bul - wark nev - er fail - ing;
2. Did we in our own strength con - fide, Our striv - ing would be los - ing,
3. And though this world, with dev - ils filled, Should threat - en to un - do us,
4. That word a - bove all earth - ly powers, No thanks to them, a - bid - eth;
Our help - er he a - mid the flood Of mor - tal ills pre - vail - ing.
Were not the right man on our side, The man of God's own choos - ing.
We will not fear, for God hath willed His truth to tri - umph through us.
The Spir - it and the gifts are ours Through him who with us sid - eth.
For still our an - cient foe Doth seek to work us woe; His craft and power are
Dost ask who that may be? Christ Je - sus, it is he; Lord Sab - a - oth his
The prince of dark - ness grim, We trem - ble not for him; His rage we can en -
Let goods and kin - dred go, This mor - tal life al - so; The bod - y they may
great, And armed with cru - el hate, On earth is not his e - qual.
name. From age to age the same, And he must win the bat - tle.
dure, For lo, his doom is sure: One lit - tle word shall fell him.
kill; God's truth a - bid - eth still, His king - dom is for - ev - er.

*A Mighty Fortress

Second Version

Ps. 46
Martin Luther, 1529
Tr. F. Samuel Janzow, 1970

EIN' FESTE BURG 8.7.8.7.5.5.5.6.7.
Martin Luther, 1529

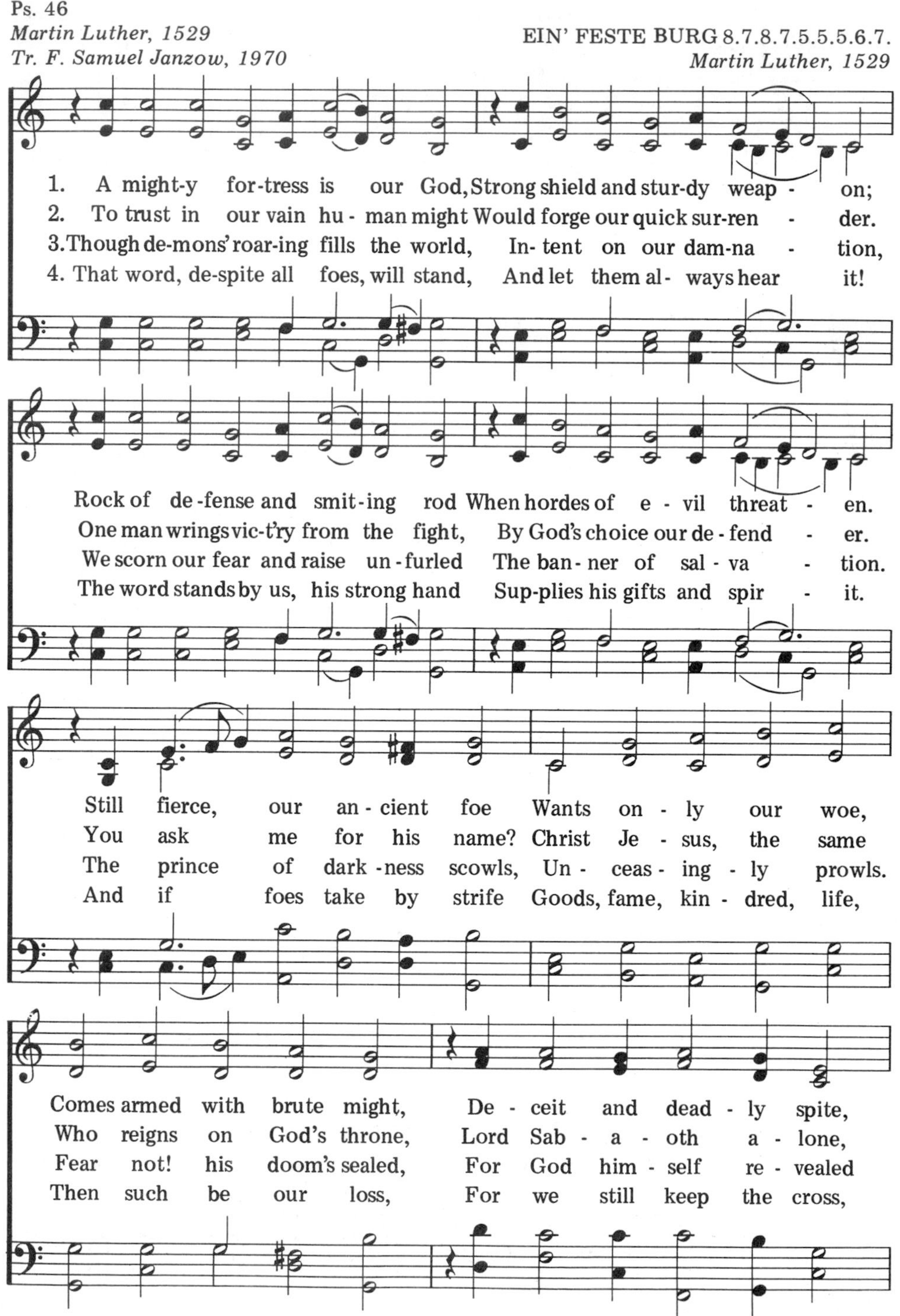
1. A might-y for-tress is our God, Strong shield and stur-dy weap - on;
2. To trust in our vain hu - man might Would forge our quick sur-ren - der.
3. Though de-mons' roar-ing fills the world, In- tent on our dam-na - tion,
4. That word, de-spite all foes, will stand, And let them al- ways hear it!
Rock of de-fense and smit-ing rod When hordes of e - vil threat - en.
One man wrings vic-t'ry from the fight, By God's choice our de - fend - er.
We scorn our fear and raise un-furled The ban- ner of sal - va - tion.
The word stands by us, his strong hand Sup-plies his gifts and spir - it.
Still fierce, our an - cient foe Wants on - ly our woe,
You ask me for his name? Christ Je - sus, the same
The prince of dark - ness scowls, Un - ceas - ing - ly prowls.
And if foes take by strife Goods, fame, kin - dred, life,
Comes armed with brute might, De - ceit and dead - ly spite,
Who reigns on God's throne, Lord Sab - a - oth a - lone,
Fear not! his doom's sealed, For God him - self re - vealed
Then such be our loss, For we still keep the cross,

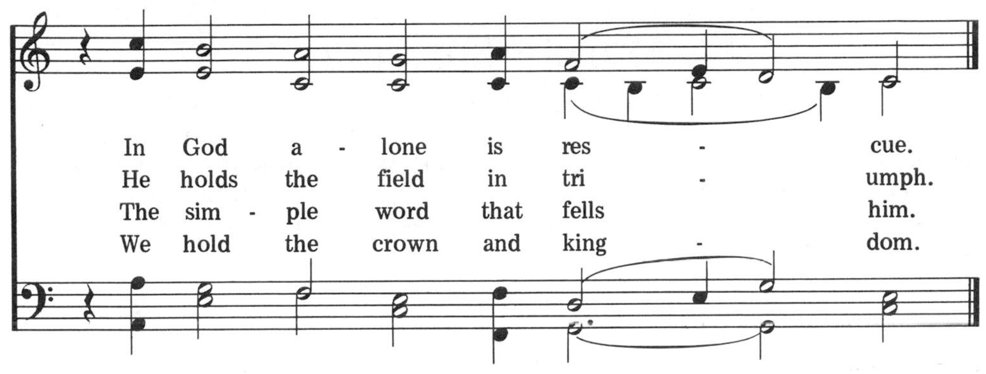
In God a - lone is res - cue.
He holds the field in tri - umph.
The sim - ple word that fells him.
We hold the crown and king - dom.

265

Jesus, Savior, Pilot Me

PILOT 7.7.7.7.7.7.

Edward Hopper, 1871 *John E. Gould, 1871*

1. Je - sus, Sav - ior, pi - lot me O - ver life's tem - pes - tuous sea;
2. As a moth-er stills her child, Thou canst hush the o - cean wild;
3. When at last I near the shore, And the fear - ful break-ers roar

Un-known waves be - fore me roll, Hid - ing rock and treach-erous shoal;
Bois-terous waves o - bey thy will When thou sayest to them, "Be still."
'Twixt me and the peace-ful rest, Then, while lean - ing on thy breast,

Chart and com - pass come from thee; Je - sus, Sav - ior, pi - lot me.
Won-drous Sov-ereign of the sea, Je - sus, Sav - ior, pi - lot me.
May I hear thee say to me, "Fear not, I will pi - lot thee."

How Firm a Foundation

2 Tim. 2:19; Heb. 13:5; Isa. 43:1-2
"K"' in John Rippon's
A Selection of Hymns, *1787, alt.*

FOUNDATION 11.11.11.11.
Early American Melody
Harm. by Charles H. Heaton, 1928-

Unison

1. How firm a foundation, ye saints of the Lord,
Is laid for your faith in his excellent word!
What more can he say than to you he hath said,

2. "Fear not, I am with thee, oh, be not dismayed,
For I am thy God, and will still give thee aid.
I'll strengthen thee, help thee, and cause thee to stand,

3. "When through the deep waters I call thee to go,
The rivers of woe shall not thee overflow;
For I will be near thee, thy troubles to bless,

4. "The soul that on Jesus hath leaned for repose,
I will not, I will not desert to his foes,
That soul, though all hell should endeavor to shake,

Alternate tune, Adeste Fidelis, No. 89

To you who for refuge to Jesus have fled?
Upheld by my righteous, omnipotent hand.
And sanctify to thee thy deepest distress.
I'll never, no never, no never forsake!"

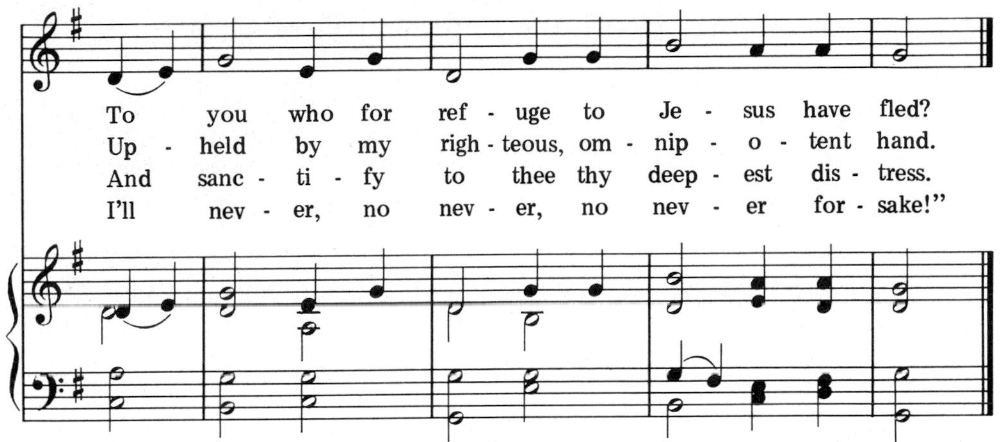

267

Jesus, the Very Thought of Thee

Latin: 12th century (Bernard of Clairvaux?)
Tr. Edward Caswall, 1849, alt.

ST. AGNES C.M.
John B. Dykes, 1866

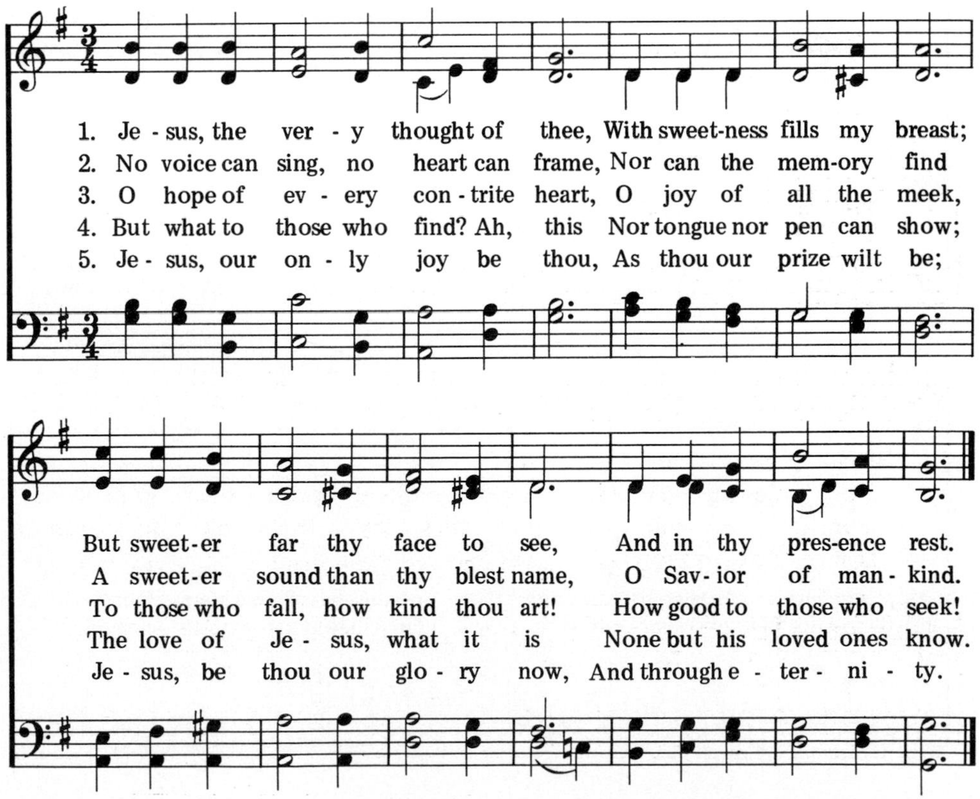

1. Jesus, the very thought of thee, With sweetness fills my breast; But sweeter far thy face to see, And in thy presence rest.
2. No voice can sing, no heart can frame, Nor can the memory find A sweeter sound than thy blest name, O Savior of mankind.
3. O hope of every contrite heart, O joy of all the meek, To those who fall, how kind thou art! How good to those who seek!
4. But what to those who find? Ah, this Nor tongue nor pen can show; The love of Jesus, what it is None but his loved ones know.
5. Jesus, our only joy be thou, As thou our prize wilt be; Jesus, be thou our glory now, And through eternity.

268

Lift Thy Head, O Zion, Weeping

MAGYAR 8.7.8.7.7.7.8.8.

Karoly Jeszensky, c.1674 — *Hymn of the Hungarian Galley Slaves, 1674*

Tr. William Toth, 1938 — *Metrical Version, G. J. Neumann, 1938*

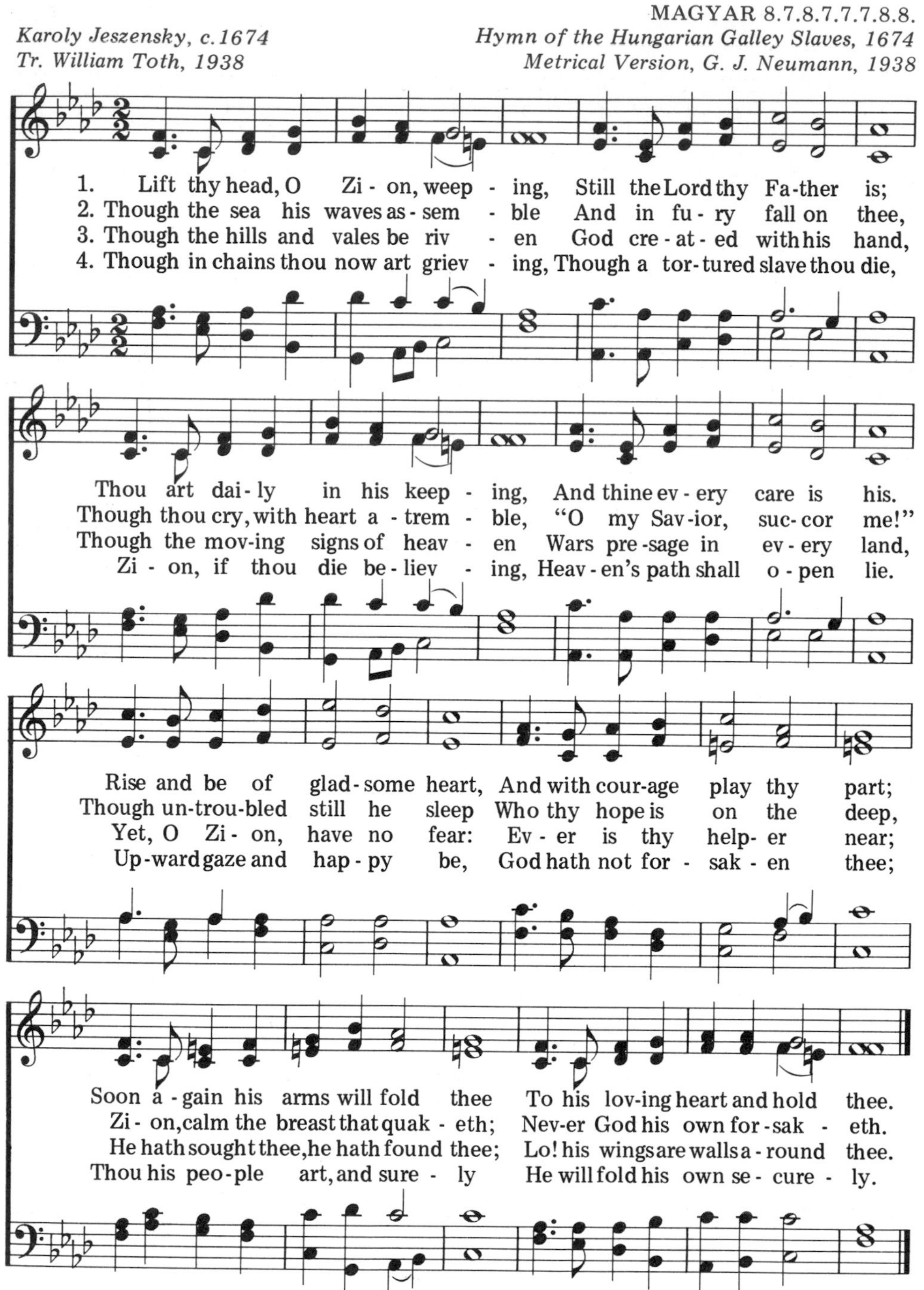

1. Lift thy head, O Zi - on, weep - ing, Still the Lord thy Fa-ther is;
2. Though the sea his waves as - sem - ble And in fu - ry fall on thee,
3. Though the hills and vales be riv - en God cre - at - ed with his hand,
4. Though in chains thou now art griev - ing, Though a tor- tured slave thou die,
Thou art dai - ly in his keep - ing, And thine ev - ery care is his.
Though thou cry, with heart a - trem - ble, "O my Sav-ior, suc- cor me!"
Though the mov-ing signs of heav - en Wars pre-sage in ev - ery land,
Zi - on, if thou die be - liev - ing, Heav - en's path shall o - pen lie.
Rise and be of glad - some heart, And with cour-age play thy part;
Though un-trou-bled still he sleep Who thy hope is on the deep,
Yet, O Zi - on, have no fear: Ev - er is thy help- er near;
Up-ward gaze and hap - py be, God hath not for - sak - en thee;
Soon a - gain his arms will fold thee To his lov-ing heart and hold thee.
Zi - on, calm the breast that quak - eth; Nev-er God his own for - sak - eth.
He hath sought thee, he hath found thee; Lo! his wings are walls a - round thee.
Thou his peo-ple art, and sure - ly He will fold his own se - cure - ly.

Every Time I Feel the Spirit

EVERYTIME *Irregular*

Negro Spiritual *Negro Melody*

Refrain
Ev - 'ry time I feel the Spir - it mov - in' in my heart, I will pray.
Oh ev - 'ry time I feel the Spir - it mov - in' in my heart, I will pray.
Unison
1. Up - on the moun - tain, when my Lord spoke,
Looked all a - round me, it looked so fine,
2. Oh, I have sor - rows and I have woe,
But my Lord leads me, I'm in his care,
Repeat refrain after each stanza
Out of his mouth came fire and smoke;
'Til I asked my Lord if it were mine.
And I have heart - aches here be - low;
And I can feel him ev' - ry - where.

270

The Man Who Once Has Found Abode

Ps. 91
Anon.
United Presbyterian Book of Psalms U.S.A., 1871, alt.
TALLIS' CANON L.M.
Thomas Tallis, c.1567
1. The man who once has found a - bode With -
2. I of the Lord my God will say, "He
3. He shall with all - pro - tect - ing care Pre -
4. His out - spread pin - ions shall thee hide; Be -
5. No night - ly ter - rors shall a - larm No
6. Be - cause thy trust is God a - lone, Thy
in the se - cret place of God, Shall with al - might - y
is my ref - uge and my stay; To him for safe - ty
serve thee from the fowl - er's snare; When fear - ful plagues a -
neath his wings shalt thou a - bide; His faith - ful - ness shall
dead - ly shaft by day shall harm, Nor pes - ti - lence that
dwell - ing place the high - est one, No e - vil shall up -
God a - bide, And in his shad - ow safe - ly hide.
I will flee; My God, in him my trust shall be."
round pre - vail, No fa - tal stroke shall thee as - sail.
ev - er be A shield and buck - ler un - to thee.
walks by night, Nor plagues that waste in noon - day light.
on thee come, Nor plague ap - proach thy guard - ed home.

*In Heavenly Love Abiding

NYLAND 7.6.7.6.D.
Traditional Finnish Melody
Harm. by David Evans, 1927

Anna L. Waring, 1850

1. In heav'n-ly love a - bid - ing, No change my heart shall fear,
2. Wher - ev - er he may guide me, No want shall turn me back;
3. Green pas - tures are be - fore me, Which yet I have not seen;

And safe is such con - fid - ing, For noth-ing chang-es here.
My shep-herd is be - side me, And noth-ing can I lack.
Bright skies will soon be o'er me, Where the dark clouds have been.

The storm may roar with - out me, My heart may low be laid,
His wis - dom ev - er wak - eth; His sight is nev - er dim;
My hope I can - not mea-sure; The path to life is free;

But God is round a - bout me, And can I be dis - mayed?
He knows the way he tak - eth, And I will walk with him.
My Sav - ior has my trea - sure, And he will walk with me.

*There's a Wideness in God's Mercy

Rom. 11:33
Frederick W. Faber, 1862

GOTT WILL'S MACHEN 8.7.8.7.
Johann Ludwig Steiner, 1735

1. There's a wide - ness in God's mer - cy like the wide - ness of the sea; There's a kind - ness in his jus - tice which is more than lib - er - ty.
2. Souls of men, why will ye scat - ter like a crowd of fright-ened sheep? Fool - ish hearts, why will ye wan - der from a love so true and deep?
3. For the love of God is broad - er than the mea - sure of man's mind, And the heart of the E - ter - nal is most won - der - ful - ly kind.

*Eternal Father, Strong to Save

Mark 4:36-41
William Whiting, 1860, alt.
MELITA 8.8.8.8.8.8.
John B. Dykes, c.1861
1. E - ter - nal Fa - ther, strong to save, Whose arm has bound the
2. O Christ, whose voice the wa - ters heard, And hushed their rag - ing
3. O Ho - ly Spir - it, who does brood Up - on the cha - os
4. O Tri - ni - ty of love and pow'r, Our broth-ers shield in
rest - less wave, Who bids the might - y o - cean deep Its
at thy word, Who walked up - on the foam - ing deep, And
dark and rude, And bids the an - gry tu - mult cease, And
dan - ger's hour. From rock and tem - pest, fire and foe, Pro -
own ap - point - ed lim - its keep: O hear us when we
calm a - mid the storm did sleep: O hear us when we
gives for wild con - fu - sion peace: O hear us when we
tect them where - so - e'er they go: Thus ev - er - more shall
cry to thee For those in per - il on the sea.
cry to thee For those in per - il on the sea.
cry to thee For those in per - il on the sea.
rise to thee Glad hymns of praise from land and sea.

274

*Love Divine, All Loves Excelling

First Tune

HYFRYDOL 8.7.8.7.D.

Charles Wesley, 1747, alt. *Melody by Rowland H. Prichard, 1855*

275

Love Divine, All Loves Excelling

Second Tune

BEECHER 8.7.8.7.D.

Charles Wesley, 1747, alt. *John Zundel, 1870*

1. Love di - vine, all loves ex - cel - ling, Joy of heav'n to earth come down,
2. Breathe, O breathe thy lov - ing spir - it In - to ev - ery trou - bled breast;
3. Come, al - might - y to de - liv - er, Let us all thy life re - ceive;
4. Fin - ish, then, thy new cre - a - tion; Pure and spot - less let us be;

Fix in us thy hum - ble dwell - ing, All thy faith - ful mer - cies crown;
Let us all in thee in - her - it, Let us find thy prom - ised rest;
Sud - den - ly re - turn and nev - er, Nev - er - more thy tem - ples leave.
Let us see thy great sal - va - tion Per - fect - ly re - stored in thee;

Je - sus, thou art all com - pas - sion; Pure, un - bound - ed love thou art;
Take a - way the love of sin - ning; Al - pha and O - me - ga be;
Thee we would be al - ways bless - ing, Serve thee as thy hosts a - bove,
Changed from glo - ry in - to glo - ry, Till in heav'n we take our place,

Vis - it us with thy sal - va - tion, En - ter ev - ery trem - bling heart.
End of faith, as its be - gin - ning, Set our hearts at lib - er - ty.
Pray and praise thee, with - out ceas - ing, Glo - ry in thy pre - cious love.
Till we cast our crowns be - fore thee, Lost in won - der, love, and praise.

276

*Guide Me, O Thou Great Jehovah

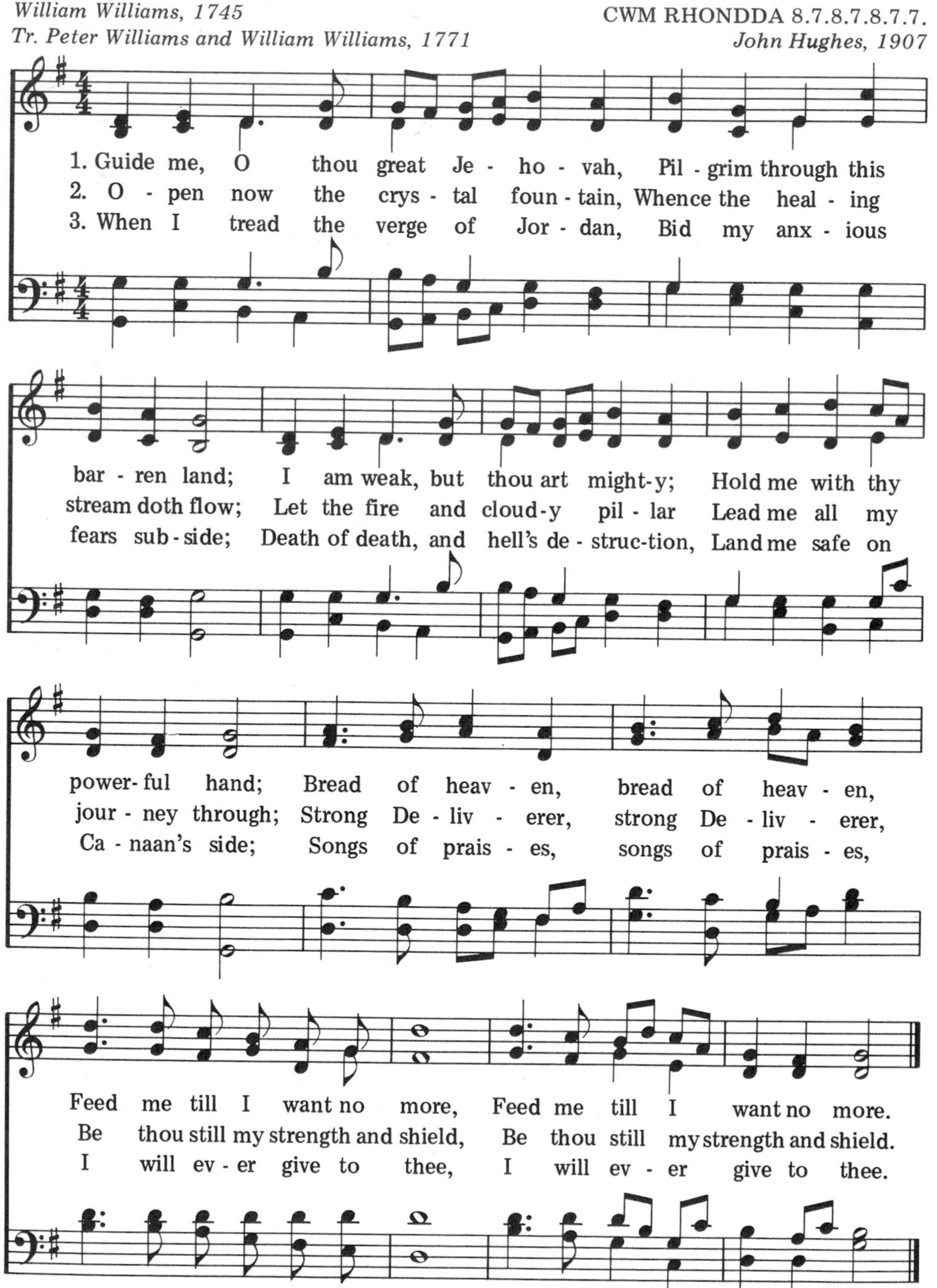
William Williams, 1745
Tr. Peter Williams and William Williams, 1771
CWM RHONDDA 8.7.8.7.8.7.7.
John Hughes, 1907
1. Guide me, O thou great Je - ho - vah, Pil - grim through this
2. O - pen now the crys - tal foun - tain, Whence the heal - ing
3. When I tread the verge of Jor - dan, Bid my anx - ious
bar - ren land; I am weak, but thou art might-y; Hold me with thy
stream doth flow; Let the fire and cloud-y pil - lar Lead me all my
fears sub-side; Death of death, and hell's de - struc-tion, Land me safe on
power-ful hand; Bread of heav - en, bread of heav - en,
jour - ney through; Strong De - liv - erer, strong De - liv - erer,
Ca - naan's side; Songs of prais - es, songs of prais - es,
Feed me till I want no more, Feed me till I want no more.
Be thou still my strength and shield, Be thou still my strength and shield.
I will ev - er give to thee, I will ev - er give to thee.

Spirit of God, Descend upon My Heart

MORECAMBE 10.10.10.10.

Attr. to George Croly, 1867 — *Frederick C. Atkinson, 1870*

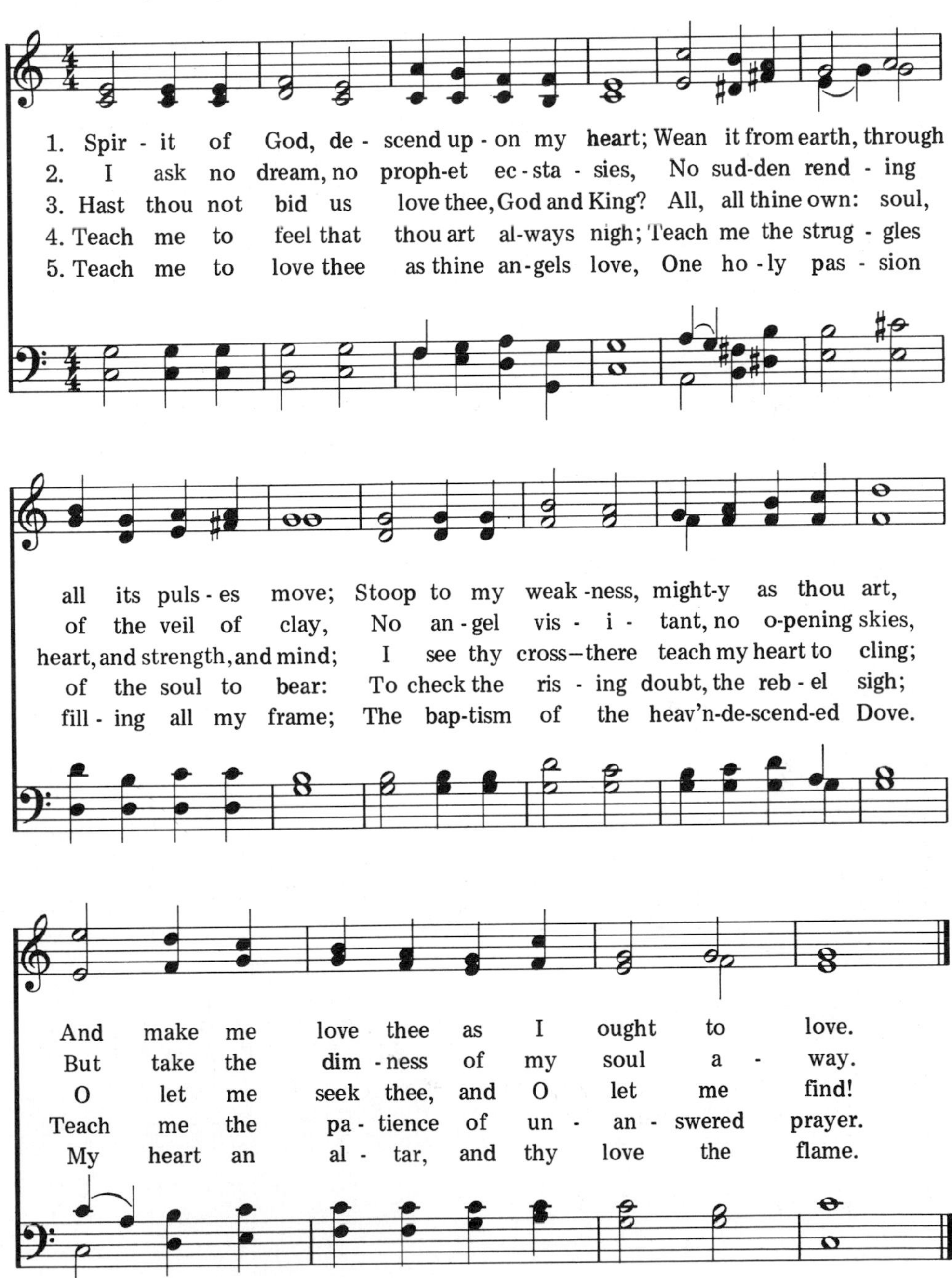
1. Spir - it of God, de - scend up - on my heart; Wean it from earth, through all its puls - es move; Stoop to my weak-ness, might-y as thou art, And make me love thee as I ought to love.
2. I ask no dream, no proph-et ec - sta - sies, No sud-den rend - ing of the veil of clay, No an - gel vis - i - tant, no o-pening skies, But take the dim - ness of my soul a - way.
3. Hast thou not bid us love thee, God and King? All, all thine own: soul, heart, and strength, and mind; I see thy cross—there teach my heart to cling; O let me seek thee, and O let me find!
4. Teach me to feel that thou art al-ways nigh; Teach me the strug - gles of the soul to bear: To check the ris - ing doubt, the reb - el sigh; Teach me the pa - tience of un - an - swered prayer.
5. Teach me to love thee as thine an-gels love, One ho - ly pas - sion fill - ing all my frame; The bap-tism of the heav'n-de-scend-ed Dove. My heart an al - tar, and thy love the flame.

278

The Lord's My Shepherd

BROTHER JAMES' AIR 8.6.8.6.8.6.
James Leith Macbeth Bain, c.1840-1925
Adapted from Gordon Jacob, 1934
by Walter W. Felton, 1955

Ps. 23
Scottish Psalter, *1650*

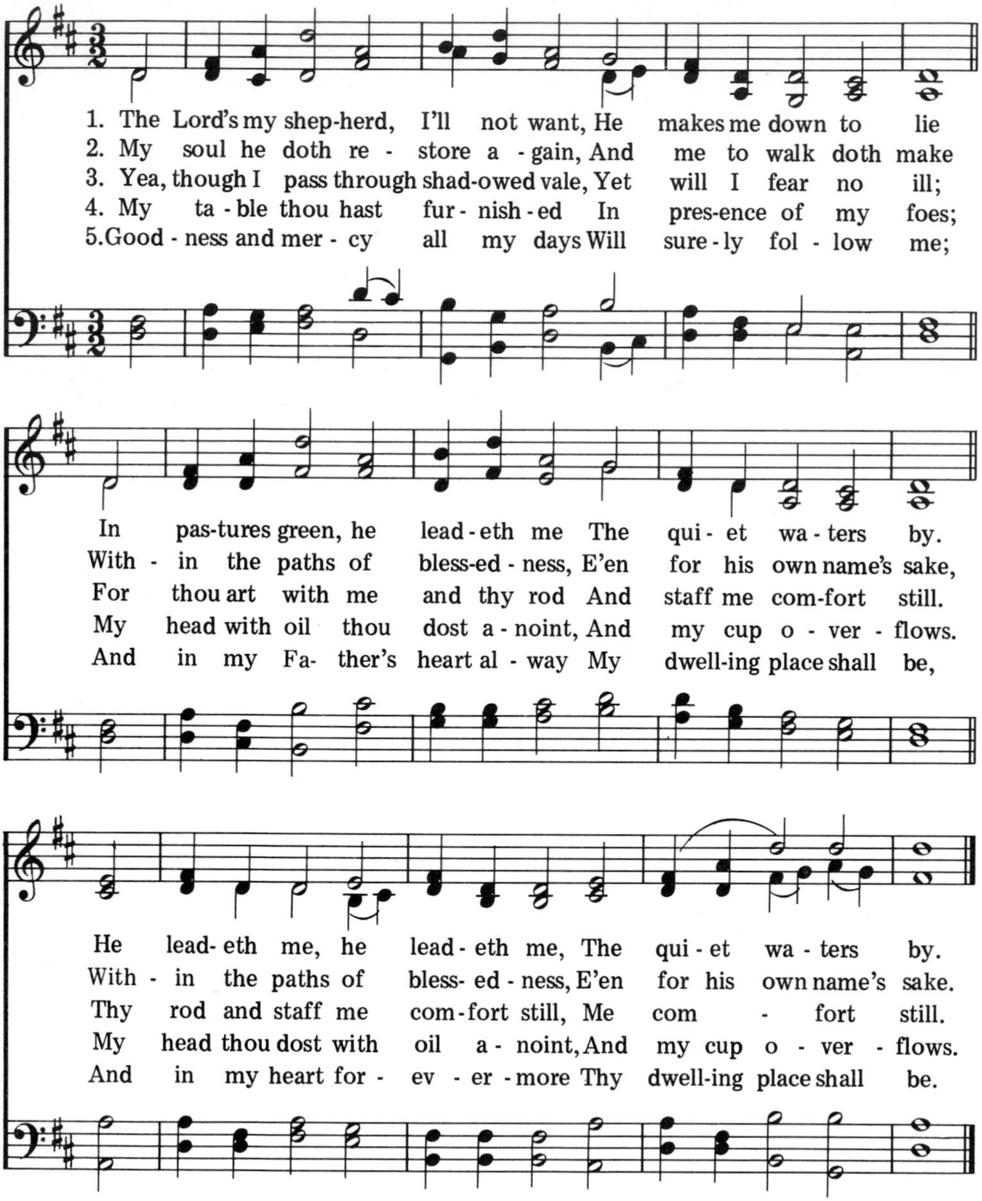

1. The Lord's my shep-herd, I'll not want, He makes me down to lie
2. My soul he doth re - store a - gain, And me to walk doth make
3. Yea, though I pass through shad-owed vale, Yet will I fear no ill;
4. My ta - ble thou hast fur - nish - ed In pres-ence of my foes;
5. Good - ness and mer - cy all my days Will sure - ly fol - low me;

In pas-tures green, he lead - eth me The qui - et wa - ters by.
With - in the paths of bless-ed - ness, E'en for his own name's sake,
For thou art with me and thy rod And staff me com-fort still.
My head with oil thou dost a - noint, And my cup o - ver - flows.
And in my Fa- ther's heart al - way My dwell-ing place shall be,

He lead- eth me, he lead - eth me, The qui - et wa - ters by.
With - in the paths of bless- ed - ness, E'en for his own name's sake.
Thy rod and staff me com-fort still, Me com - fort still.
My head thou dost with oil a - noint, And my cup o - ver - flows.
And in my heart for - ev - er - more Thy dwell-ing place shall be.

279

My Shepherd Will Supply My Need

RESIGNATION C.M.D.

Ps. 23 | Southern Harmony, *1835*

Para. by Isaac Watts, 1719 | *Harm. in* Hymnal for Colleges and Schools, *1956*

C G Em G C Dm Am Em C

1. My shep - herd will sup - ply my need; Je - ho - vah
2. When I walk through the shades of death Thy pres - ence
3. The sure pro - vi - sions of my God At - tend me

Am G C G Em C Dm Am

is his name: In pas - tures fresh he makes me feed, Be -
is my stay; One word of thy sup - port - ing breath Drives
all my days; O may thy house be my a - bode, And

G C G C Am F Dm C

side the liv - ing stream. He brings my wan - dering spir - it
all my fears a - way. Thy hand, in sight of all my
all my work be praise. There would I find a set - tled

G C Am Em C Dm C G

back, When I for - sake his ways; And leads me,
foes, Doth still my ta - ble spread; My cup with
rest, While oth - ers go and come; No more a

C G C Em Am G C G C
for his mer - cy's sake, In paths of truth and grace.
bless - ings o - ver - flows, Thine oil a - noints my head.
stran - ger, nor a guest, But like a child at home.

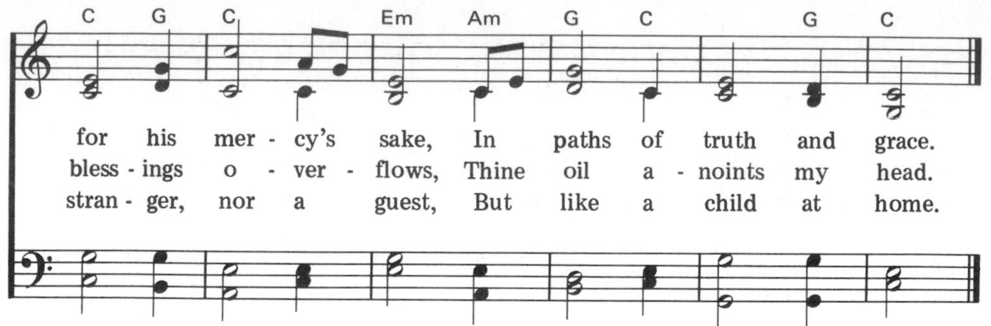

280

*Jesus, Priceless Treasure

First Tune

Johann Franck, 1653
Tr. Catherine Winkworth, 1863

LINDEMAN 6.6.5.6.6.5.7.8.6.
Ludvig M. Lindeman, 1840

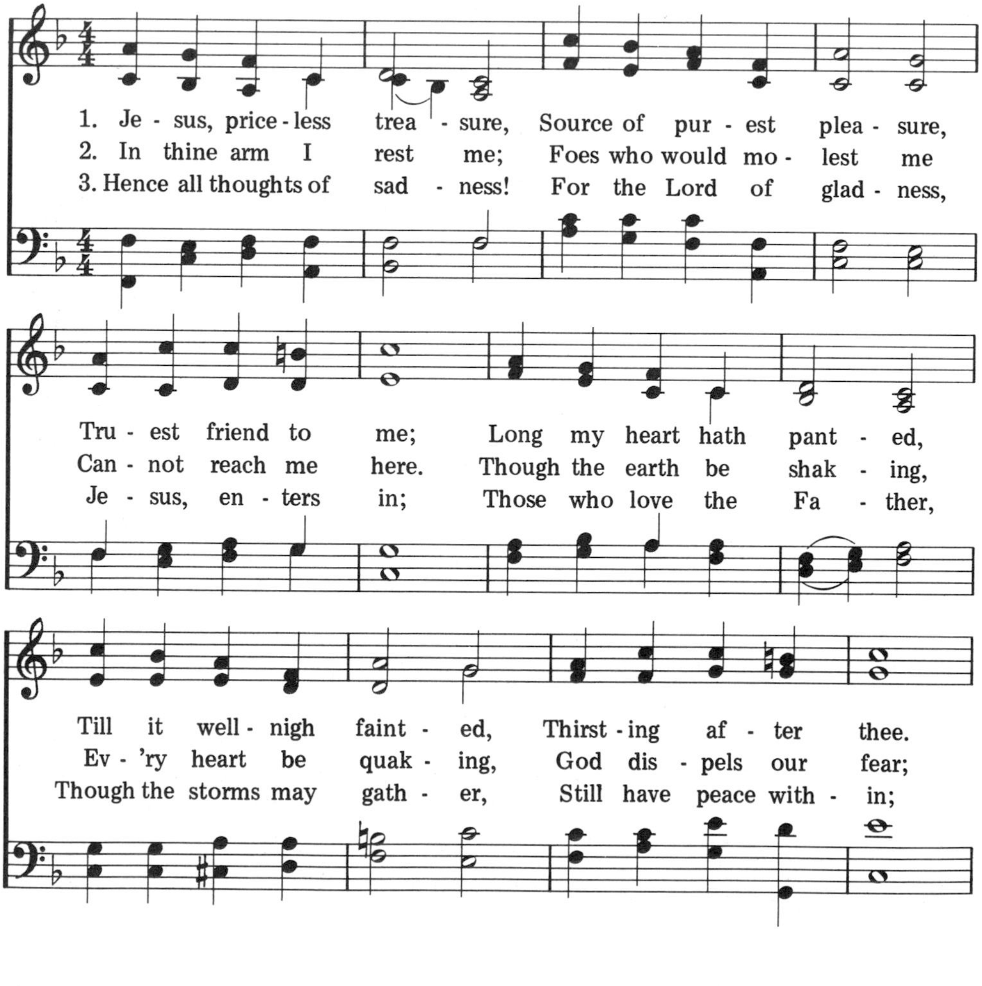

1. Je - sus, price - less trea - sure, Source of pur - est plea - sure,
2. In thine arm I rest me; Foes who would mo - lest me
3. Hence all thoughts of sad - ness! For the Lord of glad - ness,
Tru - est friend to me; Long my heart hath pant - ed,
Can - not reach me here. Though the earth be shak - ing,
Je - sus, en - ters in; Those who love the Fa - ther,
Till it well - nigh faint - ed, Thirst - ing af - ter thee.
Ev - 'ry heart be quak - ing, God dis - pels our fear;
Though the storms may gath - er, Still have peace with - in;

Thine I am, O spot - less Lamb, I will suf - fer
Sin and hell in con - flict fell With their heavi - est
Yea, what - e'er we here must bear, Still in thee lies
nought to hide thee, Ask for nought be - side thee.
storms as - sail us; Je - sus will not fail us.
pur - est plea - sure, Je - sus, price - less trea - sure!

281

Jesus, Priceless Treasure

Second Tune

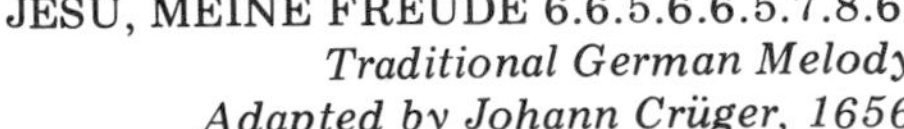
JESU, MEINE FREUDE 6.6.5.6.6.5.7.8.6.

Johann Franck, 1653
Tr. Catherine Winkworth, 1863

Traditional German Melody
Adapted by Johann Crüger, 1656

1. Je - sus, price - less trea - sure, Source of pur - est plea - sure,
2. In thine arm I rest me; Foes who would mo - lest me
3. Hence all thoughts of sad - ness! For the Lord of glad - ness,
Tru - est friend to me; Long my heart hath pant - ed, Till it well - nigh
Can-not reach me here. Though the earth be shak - ing, Ev - 'ry heart be
Je - sus, en - ters in; Those who love the Fa-ther, Though the storms may

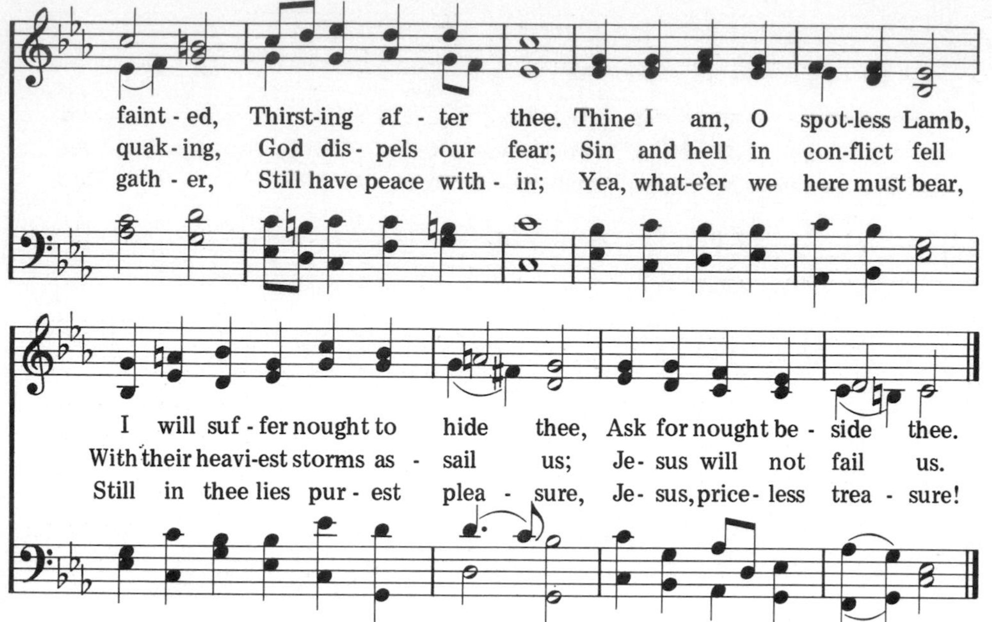
faint - ed, Thirst-ing af - ter thee. Thine I am, O spot-less Lamb,
quak - ing, God dis - pels our fear; Sin and hell in con-flict fell
gath - er, Still have peace with - in; Yea, what-e'er we here must bear,
I will suf - fer nought to hide thee, Ask for nought be - side thee.
With their heavi-est storms as - sail us; Je- sus will not fail us.
Still in thee lies pur - est plea - sure, Je- sus, price - less trea - sure!

282

God Himself Is with Us

Gerhard Tersteegen, 1729
Tr. Composite

WUNDERBARER KÖNIG 6.6.8.6.6.8.3.3.6.6.
Joachim Neander's Bundes-Lieder, *1680*

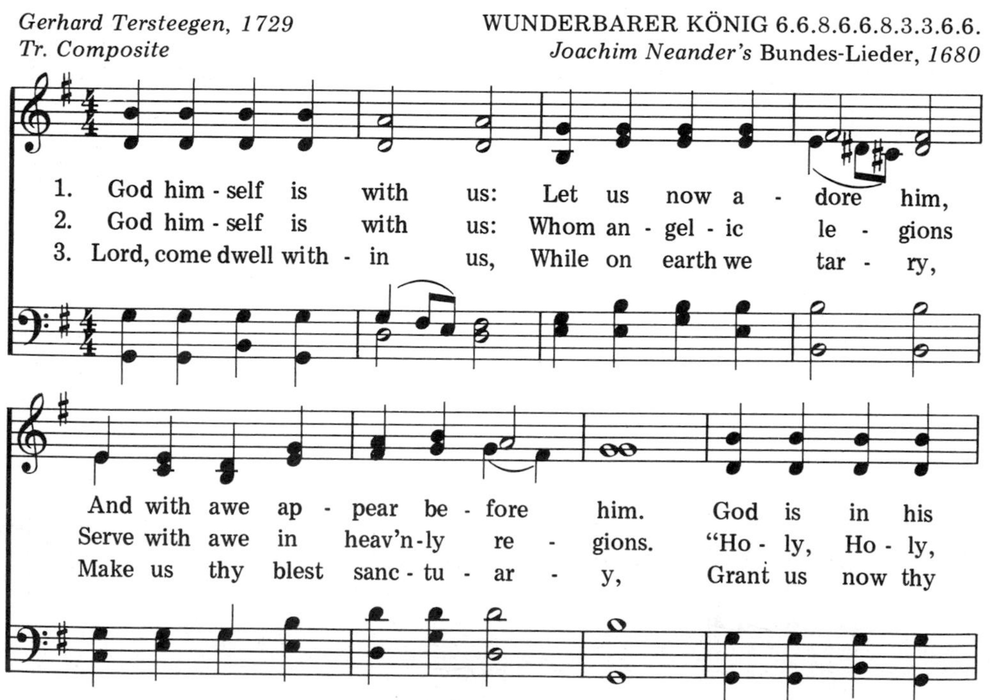
1. God him - self is with us: Let us now a - dore him,
2. God him - self is with us: Whom an - gel - ic le - gions
3. Lord, come dwell with - in us, While on earth we tar - ry,
And with awe ap - pear be - fore him. God is in his
Serve with awe in heav'n-ly re - gions. "Ho - ly, Ho - ly,
Make us thy blest sanc - tu - ar - y, Grant us now thy

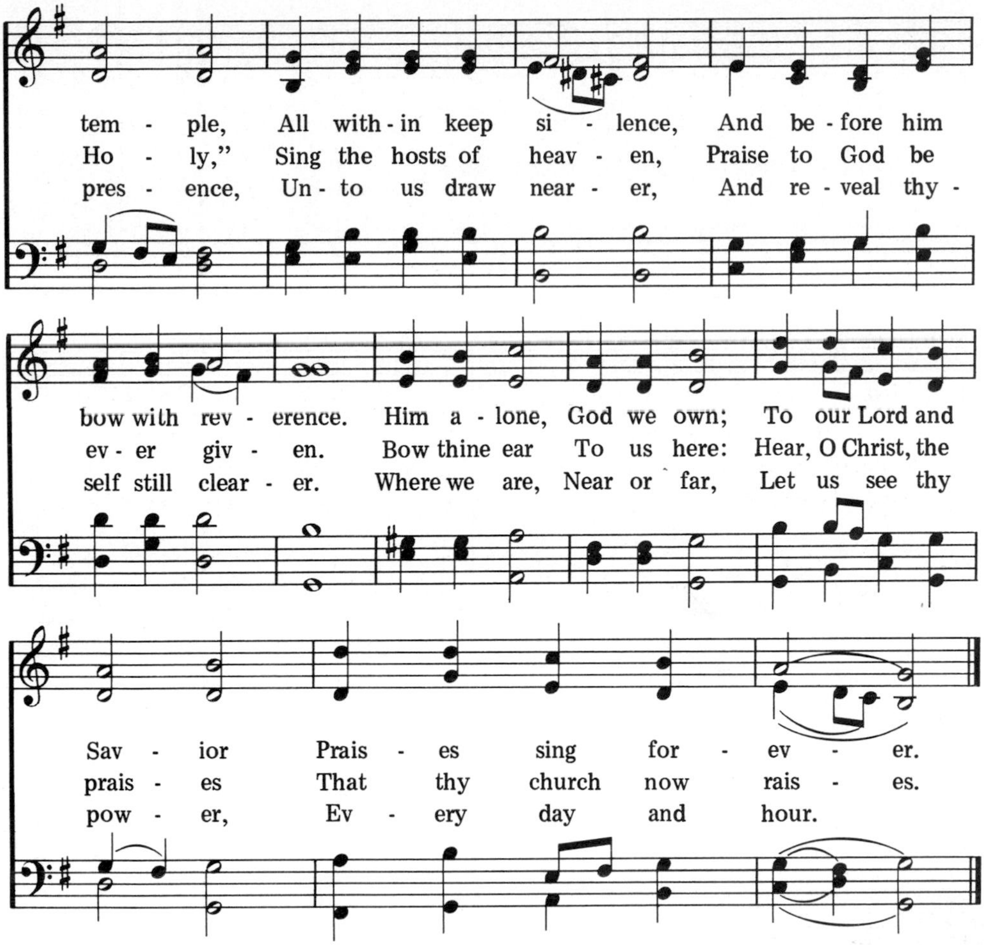

tem - ple, All with-in keep si - lence, And be-fore him
Ho - ly," Sing the hosts of heav - en, Praise to God be
pres - ence, Un-to us draw near - er, And re-veal thy-
bow with rev - erence. Him a - lone, God we own; To our Lord and
ev-er giv - en. Bow thine ear To us here: Hear, O Christ, the
self still clear - er. Where we are, Near or far, Let us see thy
Sav - ior Prais - es sing for - ev - er.
prais - es That thy church now rais - es.
pow - er, Ev - ery day and hour.

283

I Want a Song

HORNING ROAD 11.10.11.10.10.

Dalton E. McDonald, 1945, alt. *John Ferguson, 1972*

Unison
1. I want a song, a mel-o-dy so might-y It bears a
star to turn my eyes to heav - en To guide me,
Sav - ior, for my life un-wor-thy Re-flects the

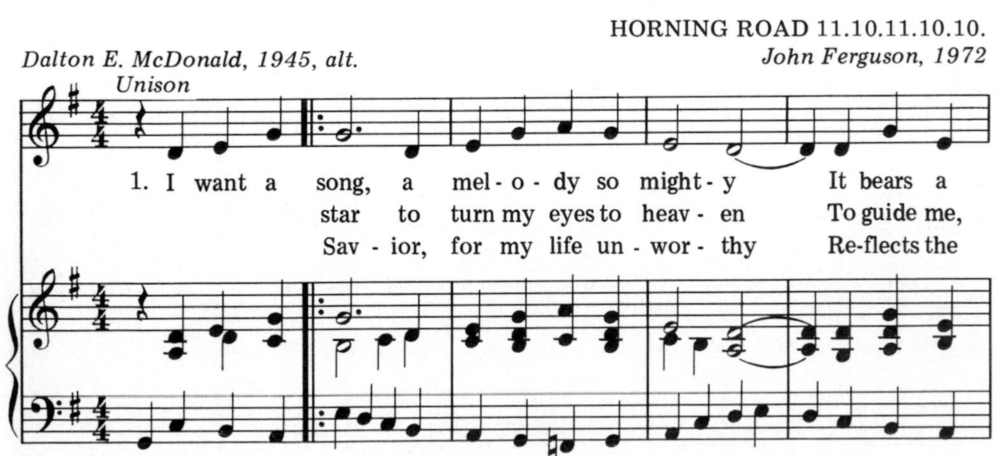

feel - ing and con-veys a thought. It must be true, yet
for I know I must be led. No night will ev - er
world's great lust and sin and greed. It must be God; no
stir my heart to dream-ing, And set my life to sing-ing as it ought.
pass in ut - ter dark - ness If some bright star shall lead the way a - head.
man could give the an - swer, The faith and hope and love to fill my need.
rit.
Sts. 1, 2
St. 3
"Glo-ry to God on high, and peace on earth!" 2. I want a
"Hap - py were they when they saw the star!" 3. I need a
"God so loved the world that he gave his Son!"

*Abide with Me

Luke 24:29
Henry F. Lyte, 1847, alt.
EVENTIDE 10.10.10.10.
William H. Monk, 1861
1. A - bide with me; fast falls the e - ven - tide; The dark-ness deep-ens, Lord, with me a - bide; When oth - er help - ers fail, and com - forts flee, Help of the help - less, O a - bide with me.
2. Swift to its close ebbs out life's lit - tle day; Earth's joys grow dim, its glo - ries pass a - way; Change and de - cay in all a - round I see; O thou who chang-est not, a - bide with me.
3. I need thy pres-ence ev - ery pass-ing hour; What but thy grace can foil the temp-ter's power? Who like thy - self my guide and stay can be? Through cloud and sun - shine, O a - bide with me.
4. I fear no foe, with thee at hand to bless; Ills have no weight, and tears no bit - ter - ness; Where is death's sting? where, grave, thy vic - to - ry? I tri - umph still if thou a - bide with me.
5. Hold thou thy cross be - fore my clos - ing eyes; Shine through the gloom, and point me to the skies; Heav'n's morn-ing breaks, and earth's vain shad-ows flee; In life, in death, O Lord, a - bide with me.

285

Just as I Am, Without One Plea

WOODWORTH L.M.

Charlotte Elliott, 1836 *William B. Bradbury, 1849*

1. Just as I am, with - out one plea But
2. Just as I am, though tossed a - bout With
3. Just as I am, poor, wretch - ed, blind; Sight,
4. Just as I am, thou wilt re - ceive, Wilt
that thy blood was shed for me, And that thou bidd'st me
man-y a con - flict, man- y a doubt, Fight - ings and fears with -
rich - es, heal - ing of the mind; Yea, all I need in
wel-come, par - don, cleanse, re - lieve; Be - cause thy prom - ise
come to thee, O Lamb of God, I come, I come!
in, with - out, O Lamb of God, I come, I come!
thee to find, O Lamb of God, I come, I come!
I be - lieve, O Lamb of God, I come, I come!

*Faith of Our Fathers

ST. CATHERINE 8.8.8.8.8.8.
Henri F. Hemy, 1864
Frederick W. Faber, 1849, alt. *Adapted by James G. Walton, 1874*

1. Faith of our fa - thers! liv - ing still In spite of dun - geon,
2. Our fa - thers, chained in pris - ons dark, Were still in heart and
3. Faith of our fa - thers! faith and prayer Shall win all na - tions
4. Faith of our fa - thers! we will love Both friend and foe in

fire, and sword: O how our hearts beat high with joy,
con - science free: And tru - ly blest would be our fate,
un - to thee; And through the truth that comes from God,
all our strife: And preach thee, too, as love knows how,

When-e'er we hear that glo - rious word:
If we, like them, should die for thee.
Man-kind shall then in - deed be free.
By kind - ly word and vir - tuous life.

Refrain

Faith of our fa - thers,

ho - ly faith, We will be true to thee till death.

287

Lighten the Darkness

2 Cor. 4:4
Frances M. Owen, 1868

SONG 24 10.10.10.10.
Orlando Gibbons, 1623

1. Light - en the dark - ness of our life's long night, Through which we
2. Light - en the dark - ness of our self - con - ceit, The sub - tle
3. Light - en our dark - ness when we bow the knee To all the
blind-ly stum- ble to the day. Shad-ows mis - lead us; Fa - ther,
dark-ness that we love so well, Which shrouds the path of wis - dom
gods we ig - no - rant - ly make And wor - ship, dream - ing that we
send thy light To set our foot - steps in the home-ward way.
from our feet, And lulls our spir - its with its bane - ful spell.
wor - ship thee, Till clear - er light our slum-bering souls a - wake.

Be Thou My Vision

Ancient Irish
Tr. Mary E. Byrne, 1905
Versified by Eleanor H. Hull, 1912

SLANE 10.10.9.10.
Traditional Irish Melody
Harm. by David Evans, 1927

Unison
1. Be thou my vi - sion, O Lord of my heart;
2. Be thou my wis - dom, and thou my true word;
3. Rich - es I heed not, nor man's emp - ty praise,
4. High King of heav - en, my vic - to - ry won,
Nought be all else to me save that thou art.
I ev - er with thee and thou with me, Lord;
Thou mine in - her - i - tance, now and al - ways;
May I reach heav'n's joys, O bright heav - en's Sun!
Thou my best thought, by day or by night,
Thou my great Fa - ther, I thy true son;
Thou and thou on - ly, first in my heart,
Heart of my own heart, what - ev - er be - fall,
Wak - ing or sleep - ing, thy pres - ence my light.
Thou in me dwell - ing, and I with thee one.
High King of heav - en, my trea - sure thou art.
Still be my vi - sion, O Rul - er of all.

What a Friend We Have in Jesus

ERIE 8.7.8.7.D.

Joseph Scriven, 1855 *Charles C. Converse, 1868*

1. What a friend we have in Je - sus, All our sins and griefs to bear! What a priv - i - lege to car - ry Ev - ery-thing to God in prayer! Oh, what peace we of - ten for - feit, Oh, what need-less pain we bear, All be-cause we do not car - ry Ev - ery-thing to God in prayer.

2. Have we tri - als and temp - ta - tions? Is there trou-ble an - y - where? We should nev - er be dis - cour - aged; Take it to the Lord in prayer! Can we find a friend so faith - ful, Who will all our sor-rows share? Je - sus knows our ev - ery weak - ness; Take it to the Lord in prayer!

3. Are we weak and heav - y lad - en, Cum - bered with a load of care? Pre - cious Sav - ior, still our ref - uge, Take it to the Lord in prayer! Do thy friends de-spise, for - sake thee? Take it to the Lord in prayer! In his arms he'll take and shield thee, Thou wilt find a sol - ace there.

What a Fellowship

Deut. 33:27
E. A. Hoffman, 1888

LEANING 5.5.9.D. *with Refrain*
A. J. Showalter, 1888

1. What a fel - low-ship, what a joy di - vine, Lean - ing on the
2. Oh, how sweet to walk in this pil - grim way, Lean - ing on the
3. What have I to dread, what have I to fear, Lean - ing on the

ev - er - last - ing arms. What a bless-ed - ness, what a peace is mine, Lean-ing on the
ev - er-last-ing arms. Oh, how bright the path grows from day to day, Lean-ing on the
ev - er - last - ing arms? I have blessed peace with my Lord so near, Lean-ing on the

ev - er - last - ing arms.
ev - er - last - ing arms.
ev - er - last - ing arms.

Refrain

Lean-ing, lean - ing, Safe and se-cure from all a-larms;
Lean - ing, lean - ing, lean- ing on the ev - er - last - ing arms.

291

We Shall Overcome

WE SHALL OVERCOME *Irregular*

American Freedom Song *American Freedom Song*

1. We shall o - ver - come! We shall o - ver - come!
2. We'll walk hand in hand, We'll walk hand in hand,
3. We are not a - fraid, We are not a - fraid,
4. We shall live in peace, We shall live in peace,
5. We shall o - ver - come! We shall o - ver - come!
We shall o - ver - come some day.
We'll walk hand in hand some day.
We are not a - fraid to - day.
We shall live in peace some day.
We shall o - ver - come some day.
Refrain
Oh, deep in my heart I do be - lieve that we shall o - ver - come some day.

Lead, Kindly Light

LUX BENIGNA 10.4.10.4.10.10.
John H. Newman, 1833, alt.
John B. Dykes, 1865
1. Lead, kind-ly Light, a - mid the en-cir-cling gloom, Lead thou me on;
2. I was not ev - er thus, nor prayed that thou Shouldst lead me on;
3. So long thy power has blest me, sure it still Will lead me on
The night is dark, and I am far from home; Lead thou me on!
I loved to choose and see my path, but now Lead thou me on.
O'er moor and fen, o'er crag and tor - rent, till The night is gone;
Keep thou my feet; I do not ask to see
I loved the gar - ish day, and, spite of fears,
And with the morn those an - gel fac - es smile
The dis - tant scene: one step e - nough for me.
Pride ruled my will: re - mem - ber not past years.
Which I have loved long since, and lost a - while.

293

Unto the Hills I Lift Mine Eyes

Ps. 121
The Psalter, *1912*

DUNFERMLINE C.M.
Scottish Psalter, *1615*

1. Un - to the hills I lift mine eyes; O
2. He will not let thy foot be moved, Thy
3. Thy faith - ful keep - er is the Lord, Thy
4. From e - vil he will keep thee safe, For
whence shall come my aid? My help is from the
guard - ian nev - er sleeps; With watch - ful and un -
shel - ter and thy shade; 'Neath sun or moon, by
thee he will pro - vide; Thy go - ing out, thy
Lord a - lone, Who heav'n and earth has made.
slum - bering care His own he safe - ly keeps.
day or night, Thou shalt not be a - fraid.
com - ing in, For - ev - er he will guide.

Unto the Hills Around Do I Lift Up

Ps. 121
John Campbell,
Duke of Argyll, 1877

SANDON 10.4.10.4.10.10.
Charles H. Purday, 1860

1. Un - to the hills a - round do I lift up My long - ing eyes;
2. He will not suf - fer that thy foot be moved: Safe shalt thou be.
3. Je - ho - vah is him - self thy keep - er true, Thy change - less shade;
4. From ev - 'ry e - vil shall he keep thy soul, From ev - 'ry sin;
O whence for me shall my sal - va - tion come, From whence a - rise?
No care - less slum - ber shall his eye - lids close, Who keep - eth thee.
Je - ho - vah thy de - fense on thy right hand Him - self hath made.
Je - ho - vah shall pre - serve thy go - ing out, Thy com - ing in.
From God the Lord doth come my cer - tain aid, From
Be - hold, he sleep - eth not. He slum - b'reth ne'er, Who
And thee no sun by day shall ev - er smite; No
A - bove thee watch - ing, he whom we a - dore Shall
God the Lord who heav'n and earth hath made.
keep - eth Is - rael in his ho - ly care.
moon shall harm thee in the si - lent night.
keep thee hence - forth, yea, for - ev - er - more.

295

*If Thou but Suffer God to Guide Thee

Georg Neumark, 1657
Tr. Catherine Winkworth, 1863

NEUMARK 9.8.9.8.8.8.
Melody by Georg Neumark, 1657

1. If thou but suf - fer God to guide thee, And hope in
2. On - ly be still and wait his lei - sure In cheer - ful
3. Sing, pray, and keep his ways un - swerv - ing; In all thy

him through all thy ways, He'll give thee strength, what-e'er be - tide thee,
hope, with heart con - tent To take what - e'er thy Fa - ther's plea-sure
la - bor faith - ful be, And trust his word; though un - de - serv - ing,

And bear thee through the e - vil days; Who trusts in God's un-
And all - de - serv - ing love have sent; Nor doubt our in - most
Thou yet shall find it true for thee; God nev - er will for-

chang - ing love Builds on the rock that nought can move.
wants are known To him who chose us for his own.
sake in need The soul that trusts in him in - deed.

*For All the Saints

SINE NOMINE 10.10.10.4.

William W. How, 1864, alt. *R. Vaughan Williams, 1906*

Unison

1. For all the saints who from their la - bors rest, Who thee by
2. Thou wast their rock, their for - tress, and their might: Thou, Lord, their
3. O may thy sol - diers, faith - ful, true, and bold, Fight as the
4. O blest com - mu - nion, fel - low - ship di - vine! We fee - bly
5. And when the strife is fierce, the war - fare long, Steals on the

faith be - fore the world con - fessed, Thy name O Je - sus, be for - ev - er
cap - tain in the well-fought fight; Thou, in the dark-ness drear, their one true
saints who no - bly fought of old, And win with them the vic-tor's crown of
strug - gle, they in glo - ry shine; Yet all are one in thee, for all are
ear the dis - tant tri - umph song, And hearts are brave a - gain, and arms are

blest.
light.
gold. Al - le - lu - ia! Al - le - lu - ia!
thine.
strong.

297

O, Rise and Shine

Isa. 40:11; Matt. 25:1-13
Negro Spiritual

RISE AND SHINE *Irregular*
Negro Melody

Refrain
O, rise and shine and give God the glo-ry, glo-ry,
Rise and shine and give God the glo-ry, glo-ry, Rise and
shine and give God the glo-ry, glo-ry For the year of ju-bi-lee.
1. Je-sus car-ry the young lambs in his bo-som, bo-som, Car-ry the
young lambs in his bo-som, bo-som, Car-ry the young lambs
2. O, come on, mourn-ers, get you read-y, read-y, Come on,
mourn-ers, get you read-y, read-y, Come on, mourn-ers,
3. O, come on, chil-dren, don't be wea-ry, wea-ry, Come on,
chil-dren, don't be wea-ry, wea-ry Come on, chil-dren,

in his bo-som, bo-som, For the year of ju-bi-lee. Je-sus
get you read-y, read-y, For the year of ju-bi-lee. You may
don't be wea-ry, wea-ry, For the year of ju-bi-lee. O,
lead the old sheep by still wa-ters, wa-ters, Lead the
keep your lamps trimmed and burn-ing, burn-ing, Keep your
don't you hear them bells a-ring-ing, ring-ing, Don't you
old sheep by still wa-ters, wa-ters, Lead the old sheep
lamps trimmed and burn-ing, burn-ing, Keep your lamps
hear them bells a-ring-ing, ring-ing, Don't you hear them
Repeat refrain after each stanza
by still wa-ters, wa-ters, For the year of ju-bi-lee.
trimmed and burn-ing, burn-ing, For the year of ju-bi-lee.
bells a-ring-ing, ring-ing, For the year of ju-bi-lee.

298

I Sing a Song of the Saints of God

GRAND ISLE *Irregular*

Lesbia Scott, 1929, alt. *John H. Hopkins, 1940*

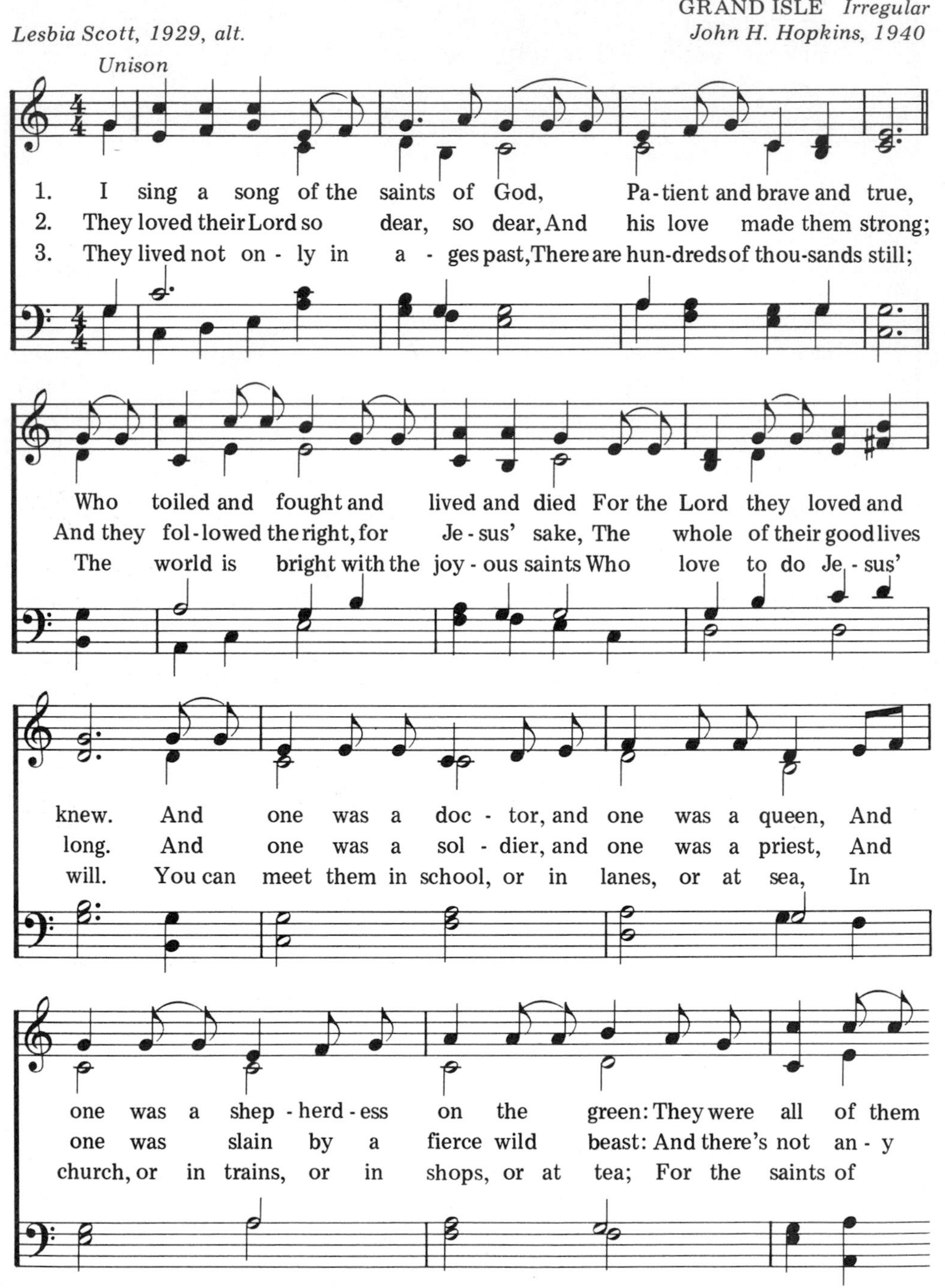

Unison
1. I sing a song of the saints of God, Pa-tient and brave and true,
2. They loved their Lord so dear, so dear, And his love made them strong;
3. They lived not on - ly in a - ges past, There are hun-dreds of thou-sands still;
Who toiled and fought and lived and died For the Lord they loved and
And they fol-lowed the right, for Je - sus' sake, The whole of their good lives
The world is bright with the joy - ous saints Who love to do Je - sus'
knew. And one was a doc - tor, and one was a queen, And
long. And one was a sol - dier, and one was a priest, And
will. You can meet them in school, or in lanes, or at sea, In
one was a shep - herd - ess on the green: They were all of them
one was slain by a fierce wild beast: And there's not an - y
church, or in trains, or in shops, or at tea; For the saints of

saints of God, and I mean, God help- ing, to be one too.
rea - son, no, not the least, Why I shouldn't be one too.
God are just folk like me, And I mean to be one too.

299

Sooner or Later

Christina Rossetti, 1881

DUNFERMLINE C.M.
Scottish Psalter, *1615*

1. Soon - er or lat - er: yet at last The Jor - dan must be past.
2. When mys - ter - ies shall be re-vealed, All se - crets be un - sealed:
Soon - er or lat - er: yet one day We all must pass that way.
Lord God of mer - cy and of men, Show mer - cy on us then.

I Want to Be Ready

Rev. 21:1-4
Traditional

I WANT TO BE READY *Irregular*
Traditional

E Refrain
A
E
I want to be read - y, I want to be read - y,
B7
E
A
I want to be read - y To walk in Je - ru - sa - lem
E
just like John. 1. John said that Je - ru - sa - lem was four-square,
2. When Pe - ter was preach-in' at Pen - te - cost,
E
A
E
Walk in Je - ru - sa - lem just like John, I hope, good Lord, I'll
O he was filled with the
Repeat refrain after each stanza
E
A
E
meet you there, Walk in Je - ru - sa - lem just like John.
Ho - ly Ghost,

A solo voice or the choir should sing the stanzas with the congregation answering: "Walk in Jerusalem just like John."

Blessing and Honor,
Glory and Power
Be unto Him

Blessing and Honor

Rev. 7:12-14
Horatius Bonar, 1808-1889

O QUANTA QUALIA 10.10.10.10.
La Feillée's Methode du Plain-chant, *1808*

1. Blessing and honor and glory and power,
Wisdom and riches and strength evermore
Give ye to him who our battle hath won,
Whose are the kingdom, the crown, and the throne.

2. Ever ascendeth the song and the joy;
Ever descendeth the love from on high;
Blessing and honor and glory and praise—
This is the theme of the hymns that we raise.

3. Give we the glory and praise to the Lamb;
Take we the robe and the harp and the palm;
Sing we the song of the Lamb that was slain,
Dying in weakness, but rising to reign.

*Holy God, We Praise Thy Name

German: 18th century
Tr. Clarence Walworth, 1820-1900, alt.

GROSSER GOTT WIR LOBEN DICH 7.8.7.8.7.7.
Katholisches Gesangbuch, *Vienna, c.1774*

1. Ho - ly God, we praise thy name; Lord of all, we bow be - fore thee; All on earth thy scep - ter claim, All in heav-en a - bove a - dore thee. In - fi - nite thy vast do - main, Ev - er - last - ing is thy reign.
2. Hark, the loud ce - les - tial hymn, An - gel choirs a - bove are rais - ing; Cher - u - bim and ser - a - phim, In un - ceas - ing cho - rus prais - ing, Fill the heav-ens with sweet ac - cord: Ho - ly, ho - ly, ho - ly Lord.
3. Ho - ly Fa - ther, ho - ly Son, Ho - ly Spir - it: Three we name thee, While in es - sence on - ly One; Un - di - vid - ed God we claim thee, And a - dor - ing bend the knee While we own the mys - ter - y.

*Let All the World

ST. TEILO 10.4.6.6.6.6.10.4.
George Herbert, 1633
William Mathias, 1967
1. & 2. Let all the world in ev - 'ry cor - ner sing, My God and King.
1. The heav'ns are not too high, His praise may thith - er fly: The earth is not too low, His prais-es there may grow.
2. The church with psalms must shout, No door can keep them out: But a - bove all the heart Must bear the long - est part.
Let all the world in ev - 'ry cor - ner sing, My God and King.

*Glorious Things of Thee Are Spoken

Ps. 87:1-3; Isa. 33:20-21
John Newton, 1779, alt.
AUSTRIAN HYMN 8.7.8.7.D.
Franz J. Haydn, 1797
1. Glo-rious things of thee are spo - ken, Zi - on, cit - y of our God;
2. See, the streams of liv - ing wa - ters, Spring-ing from e - ter - nal love,
3. Round each hab - i - ta - tion hov-'ring, See the cloud and fire ap - pear
He whose word can - not be bro - ken Formed thee for his own a - bode.
Well sup - ply thy sons and daugh-ters, And all fear of want re - move.
For a glo - ry and a cov-'ring, Show-ing that the Lord is near!
On the Rock of A - ges found-ed, What can shake thy sure re - pose?
Who can faint, while such a riv - er Ev - er will their thirst as - suage?
Thus de - riv - ing from their ban - ner Light by night and shade by day,
With sal - va -tion's walls sur-round-ed, Thou may'st smile at all thy foes.
Grace, which like the Lord, the Giv - er, Nev - er fails from age to age.
Safe they feed up - on the man - na Which he gives them when they pray.

*O for a Thousand Tongues to Sing

AZMON C.M.
Carl G. Gläser, 1784-1839
Mason's Modern Psalmody, *1839*

Charles Wesley, 1739, alt.

1. O for a thou-sand tongues to sing My great Re-deem-er's praise,
2. My gra-cious Mas-ter and my God, As-sist me to pro-claim,
3. Glo-ry to God and praise and love Be ev-er, ev-er giv'n
The glo-ries of my God and King, The tri-umphs of his grace.
To spread through all the earth a-broad The hon-ors of thy name.
By saints be-low and saints a-bove, The church in earth and heav'n.

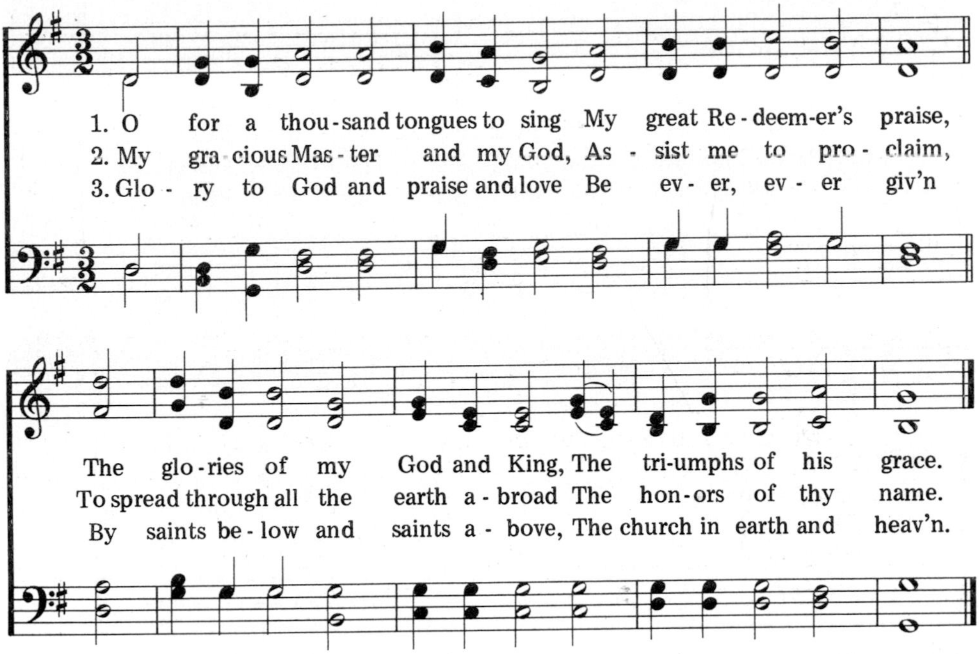

Tell Out, My Soul

Luke 1:46-55
Timothy Dudley-Smith, 1969

WOODLANDS 10.10.10.10.
Walter Greatorex, 1916

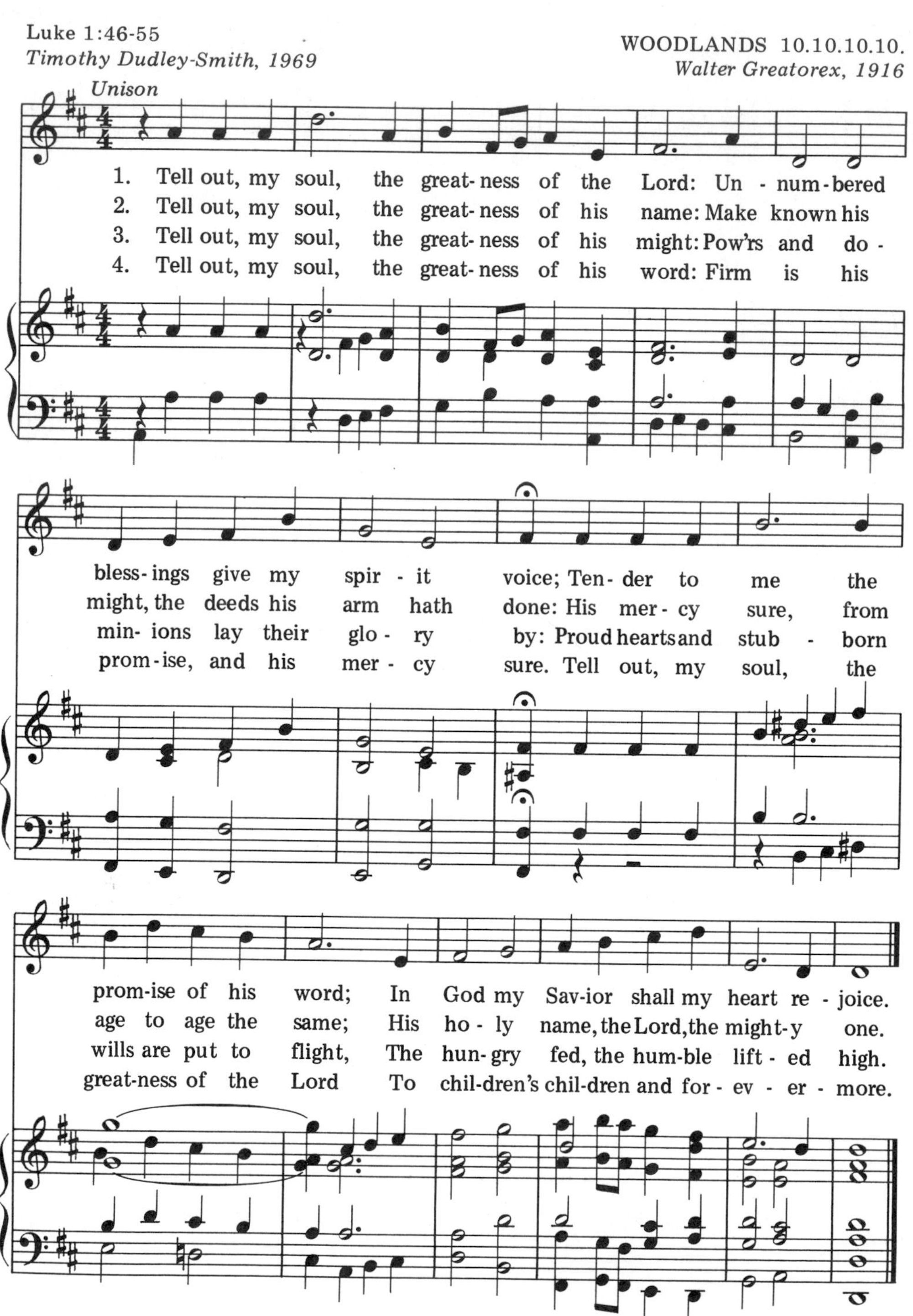
Unison
1. Tell out, my soul, the great-ness of the Lord: Un - num-bered bless-ings give my spir - it voice; Ten- der to me the prom-ise of his word; In God my Sav-ior shall my heart re - joice.
2. Tell out, my soul, the great-ness of his name: Make known his might, the deeds his arm hath done: His mer- cy sure, from age to age the same; His ho - ly name, the Lord, the might-y one.
3. Tell out, my soul, the great-ness of his might: Pow'rs and do - min- ions lay their glo - ry by: Proud hearts and stub - born wills are put to flight, The hun-gry fed, the hum-ble lift - ed high.
4. Tell out, my soul, the great-ness of his word: Firm is his prom-ise, and his mer - cy sure. Tell out, my soul, the great-ness of the Lord To chil-dren's chil-dren and for - ev - er - more.

An alternate setting may be found at No. 125.

*Now Thank We All Our God

NUN DANKET 6.7.6.7.6.6.6.6.
Melody by Johann Crüger, 1648
Alt. by Felix Mendelssohn, 1840

Martin Rinckart, c.1636
Tr. Catherine Winkworth, 1858

1. Now thank we all our God With heart and hands and voic - es,
2. O may this boun-teous God Through all our life be near us,
3. All praise and thanks to God The Fa - ther now be giv - en,
Who won-drous things hath done, In whom his world re - joic - es,
With ev - er - joy - ful hearts And bless - ed peace to cheer us,
The Son, and him who reigns With them in high - est heav - en,
Who, from our moth - ers' arms, Hath blessed us on our way
And keep us in his grace, And guide us when per - plexed,
The one e - ter - nal God, Whom earth and heav'n a - dore,
With count-less gifts of love, And still is ours to - day.
And free us from all ills In this world and the next.
For thus it was, is now, And shall be ev - er - more.

Let the Whole Creation Cry

SALZBURG 7.7.7.7.D.
Ps. 148
Melody by Jacob Hintze, 1652
Stopford A. Brooke, 1881
Harm. by Johann Sebastian Bach, 1685-1750
1. Let the whole cre - a - tion cry, "Glo - ry to the Lord on high."
2. War-riors fight - ing for the Lord, Proph-ets burn - ing with his word,
3. Men and wom-en, young and old, Raise the an - them man - i - fold;
Heav'n and earth, a - wake and sing, "God is good and there - fore king."
Those to whom the arts be - long, Add their voic - es to the song.
And let chil-dren's hap - py hearts In this wor - ship bear their parts;
Praise him, all ye hosts a - bove, Ev - er bright and fair in love;
Kings of knowl-edge and of law, To the glo - rious cir - cle draw;
From the north to south-ern pole Let the might-y cho - rus roll:
Sun and moon, up - lift your voice, Night and stars, in God re - joice!
All who work and all who wait, Sing, "The Lord is good and great!"
"Ho - ly, ho - ly, ho - ly One, Glo - ry be to God a - lone!"

*Crown Him with Many Crowns

Matthew Bridges, 1851
Godfrey Thring, 1823-1903, St. 2

DIADEMATA S.M.D.
George J. Elvey, 1868

1. Crown him with man - y crowns, The Lamb up - on his throne;
2. Crown him the Lord of life, Who tri - umphed o'er the grave,
3. Crown him the Lord of love; Be - hold his hands and side,
4. Crown him the Lord of years, The po - ten - tate of time,

Hark! how the heaven-ly an - them drowns All mu - sic but its own;
And rose vic - to - rious in the strife For those he came to save;
Rich wounds, yet vis - i - ble a - bove, In beau - ty glo - ri - fied;
Cre - a - tor of the roll - ing spheres, In - ef - fa - bly sub - lime.

A - wake, my soul, and sing Of him who died for thee,
His glo - ries now we sing Who died and rose on high,
No an - gel in the sky Can ful - ly bear that sight,
All hail, Re - deem - er, hail! For thou hast died for me;

And hail him as thy match-less king Through all e - ter - ni - ty.
Who died, e - ter - nal life to bring, And lives that death may die.
But down-ward bends his burn - ing eye At mys - ter - ies so bright.
Thy praise shall nev - er, nev - er fail Through-out e - ter - ni - ty.

A higher setting may be found at No. 47.

All Hail the Power of Jesus' Name

Rev. 19
Edward Perronet, 1779
Alt. by John Rippon, 1787

First Tune

CORONATION C.M.
Oliver Holden, 1792

1. All hail the power of Je - sus' name! Let an - gels pros - trate fall;
2. Crown him, ye mar - tyrs of our God, Who from his al - tar call;
3. Ye seed of Is - rael's cho - sen race, Ye ran - somed of the fall;
4. O that, with yon - der sa - cred throng, We at his feet may fall;

Bring forth the roy - al di - a - dem, And crown him Lord of all.
Ex - tol the stem of Jes - se's rod, And crown him Lord of all.
Hail him who saves you by his grace, And crown him Lord of all.
We'll join the ev - er - last - ing song, And crown him Lord of all.

Bring forth the roy - al di - a - dem, And crown him Lord of all.
Ex - tol the stem of Jes - se's rod, And crown him Lord of all.
Hail him who saves you by his grace, And crown him Lord of all.
We'll join the ev - er - last - ing song, And crown him Lord of all.

All Hail the Power of Jesus' Name

Second Tune

Rev. 19
Edward Perronet, 1779, alt.
Alt. by John Rippon, 1787
MILES LANE C.M.
William Shrubsole, 1779
1. All hail the power of Je - sus' name! Let an - gels pros - trate fall; Bring forth the roy - al di - a - dem,
2. Crown him, ye mar - tyrs of our God, Who from his al - tar call; Ex - tol the stem of Jes - se's rod,
3. Ye seed of Is - rael's cho - sen race, Ye ran - somed of the fall, Hail him who saves you by his grace,
4. O that, with yon - der sa - cred throng, We at his feet may fall; We'll join the ev - er - last - ing song,
Refrain
And crown him, crown him, crown him, crown him Lord of all!

*Jesus Shall Reign Where'er the Sun

Ps. 72
Isaac Watts, 1719

DUKE STREET L.M.
John Hatton, d. 1793

1. Je - sus shall reign wher - e'er the sun Doth his suc - ces - sive jour - neys run; His king - dom stretch from shore to shore Till moons shall wax and wane no more.
2. Peo - ple and realms of ev - 'ry tongue Dwell on his love with sweet - est song, And in - fant voic - es shall pro - claim Their ear - ly bless - ings on his name.
3. Bless - ings a - bound wher - e'er he reigns; The pris - 'ner leaps to lose his chains; The wea - ry find e - ter - nal rest, And all the sons of want are blest.
4. Let ev - 'ry crea - ture rise and bring Pe - cu - liar hon - ors to our king; An - gels de - scend with songs a - gain, And earth re - peat the loud a - men.

313

*Joy to the World

ANTIOCH C.M.
Ps. 98:5-9
Isaac Watts, 1719
Attr. to Georg F. Handel, 1742
Arr. by Lowell Mason, 1839
1. Joy to the world! the Lord is come: Let earth re -
2. Joy to the earth! the Sav - ior reigns: Let men their
3. He rules the world with truth and grace, And makes the
ceive her king; Let ev - 'ry heart pre - pare him room,
songs em - ploy; While fields and floods, rocks, hills, and plains
na - tions prove The glo - ries of his righ - teous - ness,
And heav'n and na - ture sing, And heav'n and na - ture
Re - peat the sound - ing joy, Re - peat the sound - ing
And won - ders of his love, And won - ders of his
And heav'n and na - ture sing, And
Re - peat the sound - ing joy, Re -
And won - ders of his love, And
sing, And heav'n and heav'n and na - ture sing.
joy, Re - peat, re - peat the sound - ing joy.
love, And won - ders, won - ders of his love.
heav'n and na - ture sing.
peat the sound - ing joy,
won - ders of his love,

Service Music

314 Lord, Have Mercy on Us

KYRIE

Traditional: 6th century *Ronald A. Nelson, 1971*

Unison

Lord, have mer-cy on us. Lord, have mer-cy on us.

Christ, have mer-cy on us. Christ, have mer-cy on us.

Lord, have mer-cy on us. Lord, have mer-cy on us.

This Kyrie may be sung responsively.

315 Glory to God in Heaven

GLORIA IN EXCELSIS

2d century Canticle *Ronald A. Nelson, 1971*

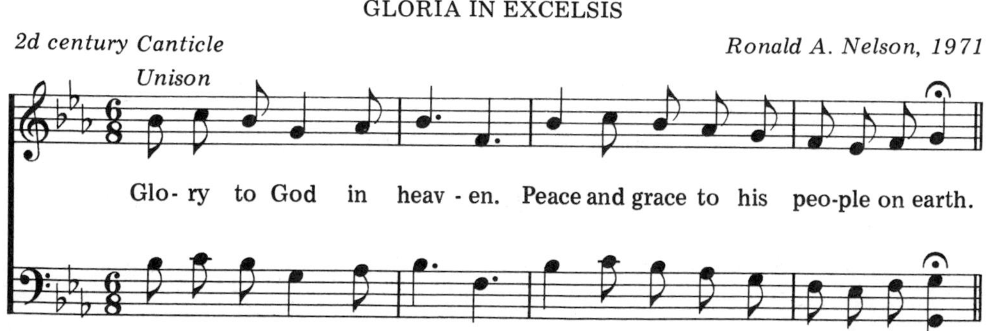

We praise you for your great glo - ry. We wor-ship you, we
give you thanks, Lord God, heav-en-ly King, Al - might-y God and
Fa - ther. Lord Je-sus Christ, Lamb of God, on - ly Son of the
Fa - ther, you take a - way the sin of the world, have mer-cy on
us. You sit at the right hand of the Fa - ther. Hear our

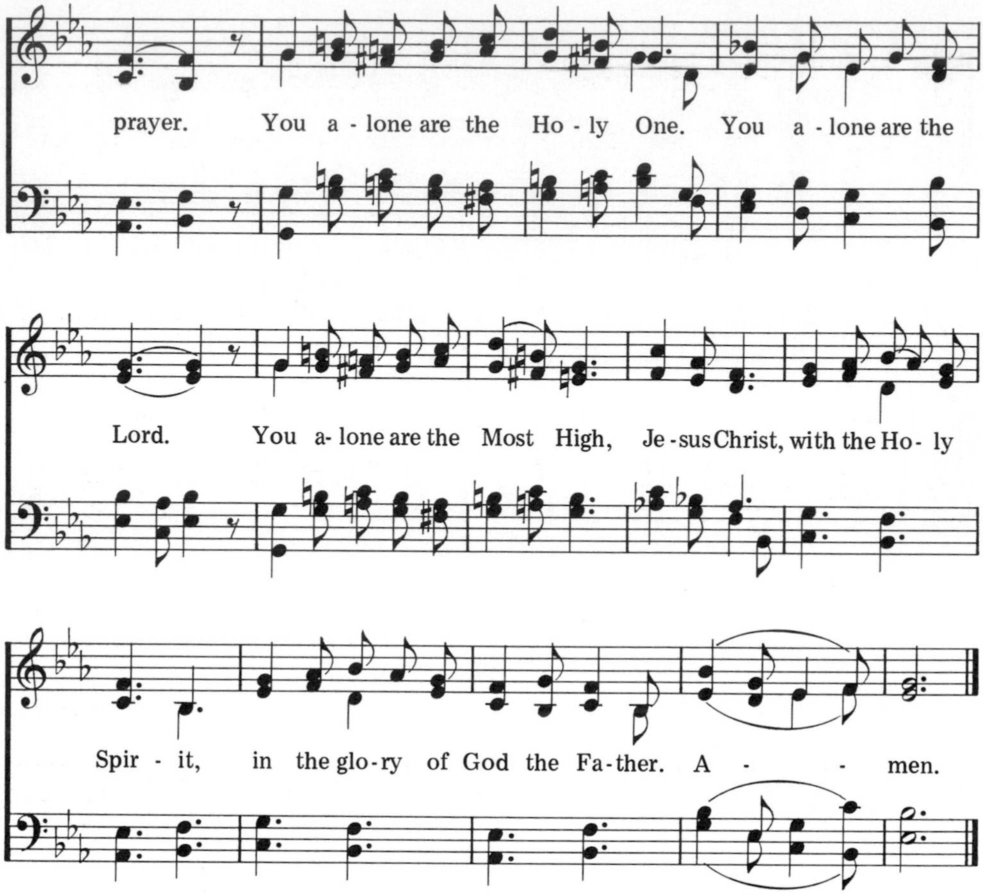

prayer. You a - lone are the Ho - ly One. You a - lone are the
Lord. You a- lone are the Most High, Je - sus Christ, with the Ho- ly
Spir - it, in the glo - ry of God the Fa - ther. A - - men.

316 Glory to the Father

GLORIA PATRI

Traditional
Adapted by F. L. Battles, 1971

Ronald A. Nelson, 1971

Unison
Glo - ry to the Fa - ther!

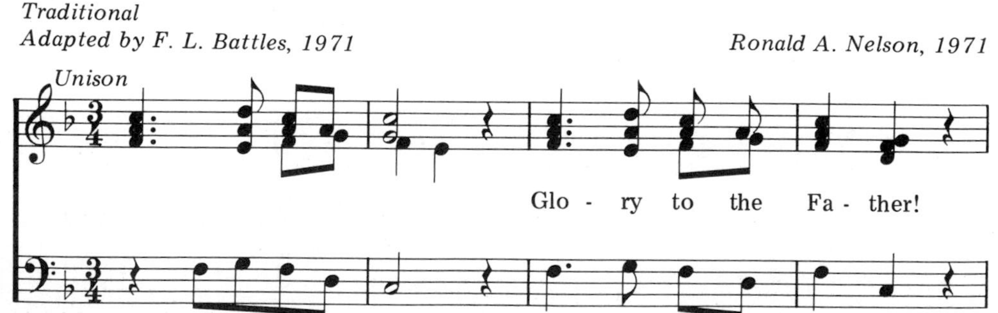

Glo - ry to the Son! Glo - ry to the Spi - rit, both
now and al - ways and to all e - ter - ni - ty! So be it!

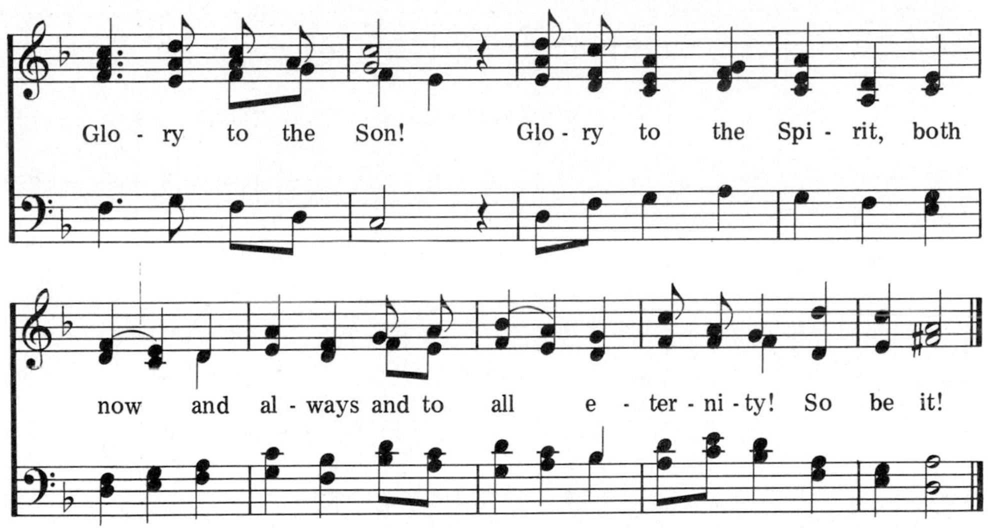

Praise the Father

317

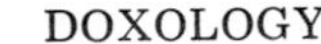

DOXOLOGY

F. L. Battles, 1971 | *Ronald A. Nelson, 1971*

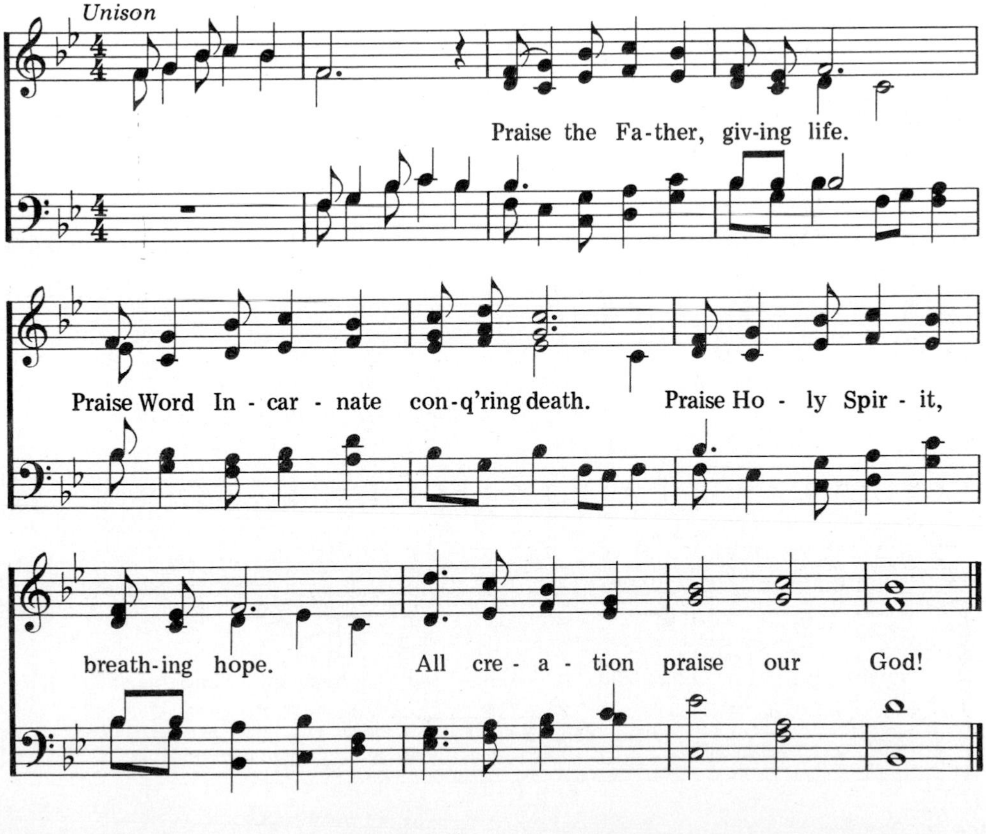

Unison
Praise the Fa-ther, giv-ing life.
Praise Word In - car - nate con-q'ring death. Praise Ho - ly Spir - it,
breath-ing hope. All cre - a - tion praise our God!

318 Lift Up Your Hearts

SURSUM CORDA

Traditional: 3d century *Ronald A. Nelson, 1971*

The Sursum Corda traditionally is sung or said responsively between minister and congregation. Therefore in this setting parts "a" could be sung by minister or choir, the congregation responding at parts "b."

319 Holy, Holy, Holy

SANCTUS

Isa. 6:3; Mark 11:9-10 *Ronald A. Nelson, 1971*

Our Father 320

Matt. 6:9-13 *Ronald A. Nelson, 1971*

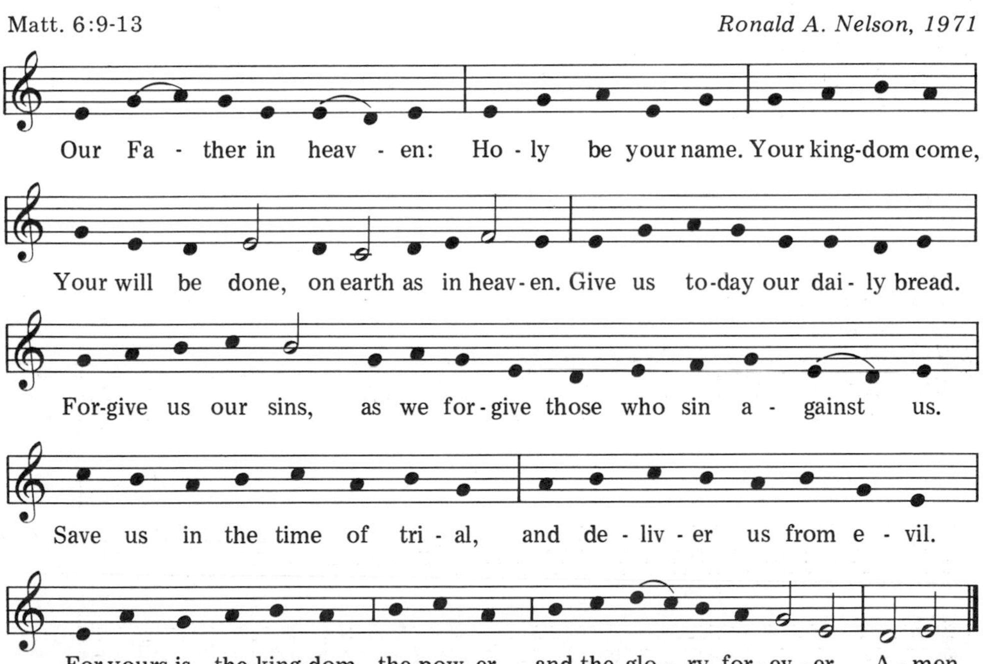

This setting of the Lord's Prayer should be sung freely. The black note (•) implies a free rhythmic syllable, length depending upon speech rhythm. The stemmed white note (𝅗𝅥) is sustained about twice as long as a black note. The full bar-line indicates a slight pause for breath, the half bar-line a lesser pause for punctuation.

321 As You Have Promised, Lord

NUNC DIMITTIS

Luke 2:29-32
Adapted by F. L. Battles, 1971

Ronald A. Nelson, 1971

Lord, Have Mercy on Us 322

KYRIE

Traditional: 6th century *John Ylvisaker, 1971*

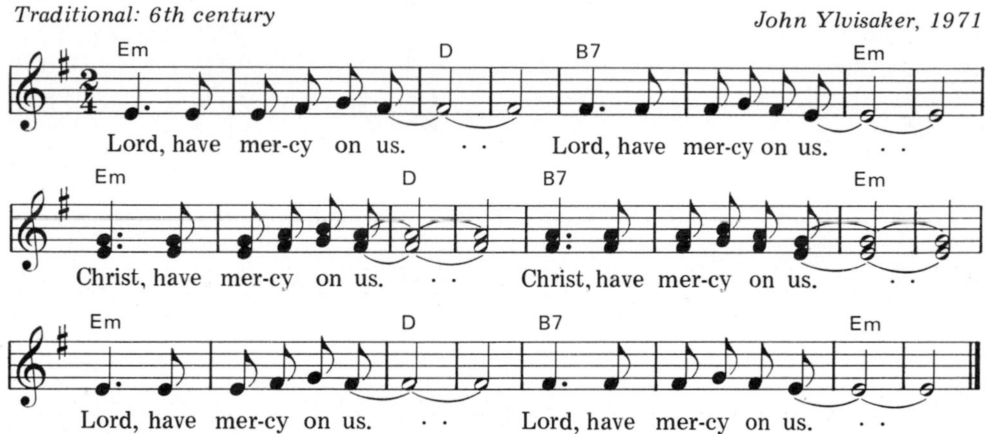
Em
D
B7
Em
Lord, have mer-cy on us. . .
Lord, have mer-cy on us. . .
Christ, have mer-cy on us. . .
Christ, have mer-cy on us. . .
Lord, have mer-cy on us. . .
Lord, have mer-cy on us. . .

This Kyrie may be sung responsively.

Glory Be to Our God in Heaven 323

GLORIA IN EXCELSIS

2d century Canticle
Adapted by F. L. Battles, 1971 *John Ylvisaker, 1971*

C G C Am F G
1. Glo-ry be to our God in heav'n Peace and grace to his
2. Glo-ry be to the on-ly Son, the Lamb, You who should-er the
3. You a-lone are the Ho-ly One, You a-lone are our
C Am F Em Am Em
peo-ple on earth. We praise you, God, for your great glo-ry,
sins of men. Have mercy on us, Lord Je-sus Christ; At the
Lord in-deed; A-lone you are the Lord Most High
F G C Am F Em Am
wor-ship you and give you thanks, heav'n-ly King.
right hand of God your Fa-ther. Hear our prayer.
Jesus the Christ with the Ho-ly Spirit in God's glory.

In stanzas 2 and 3 certain notes have more than one syllable. Sing these extra syllables in free, natural speech rhythm.

324 Glory to the Father

GLORIA PATRI

Traditional
Adapted by F. L. Battles, 1971

John Ylvisaker, 1971

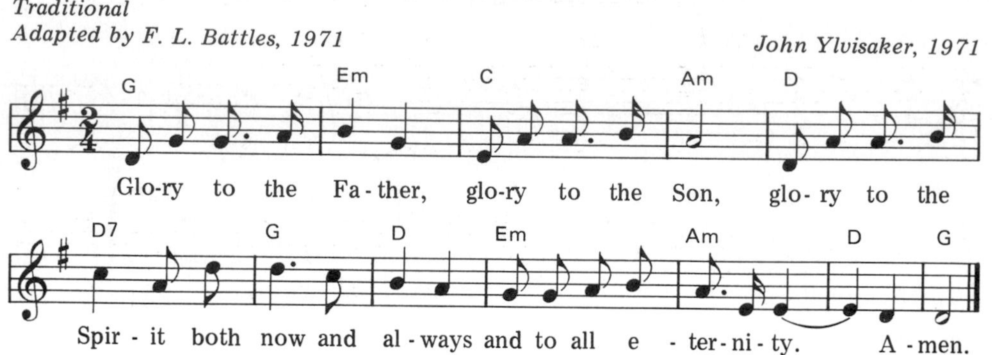

325 Lift Up Your Hearts

SURSUM CORDA

Traditional: 3d century

John Ylvisaker, 1971

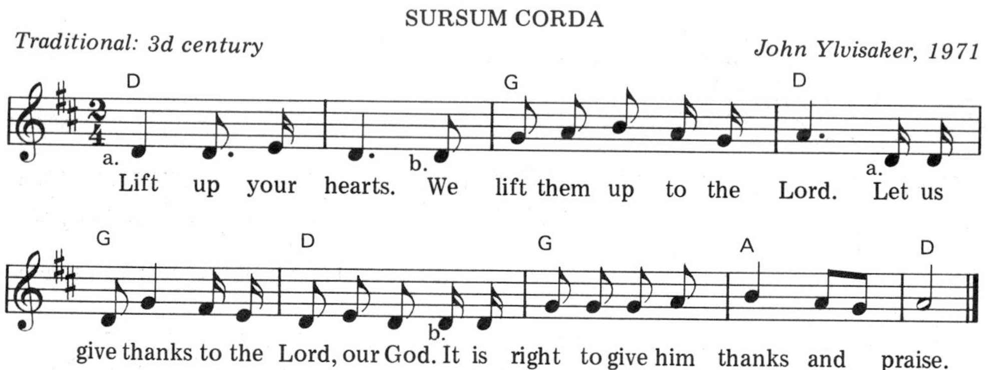

The Sursum Corda traditionally is sung or said responsively between minister and congregation. Therefore in this setting parts "a" could be sung by minister or choir, the congregation responding at parts "b."

326 Holy, Holy, Holy

SANCTUS

Isa. 6:3; Mark 11:9-10

John Ylvisaker, 1971

Am E Am G Dm Em Am
glo - ry fills all heav'n and earth. Ho - san - na in the high - est.
F G Dm Em Am G
Bless - ed is he who comes in the name of the Lord. Ho -
F Em Am G F Em Am
san - na in the high - est! Ho - san - na in the high - est.

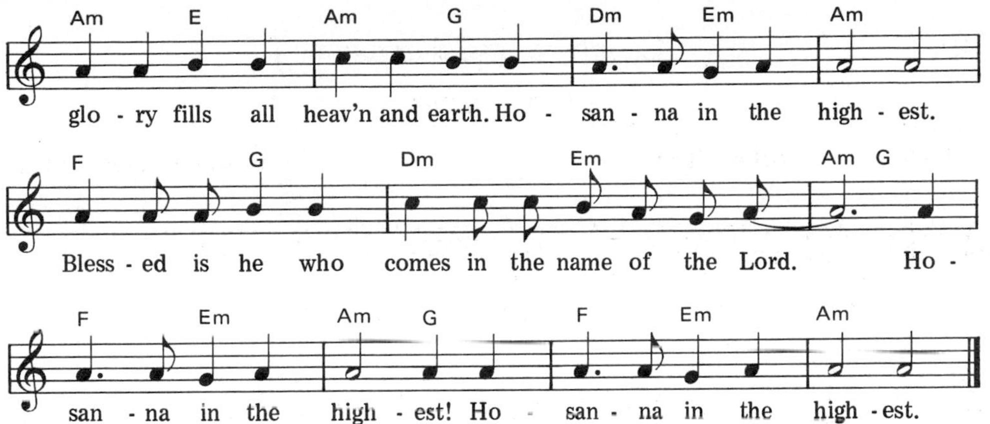

Our Father

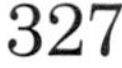

327

Matt. 6:9-13

John Ylvisaker, 1971

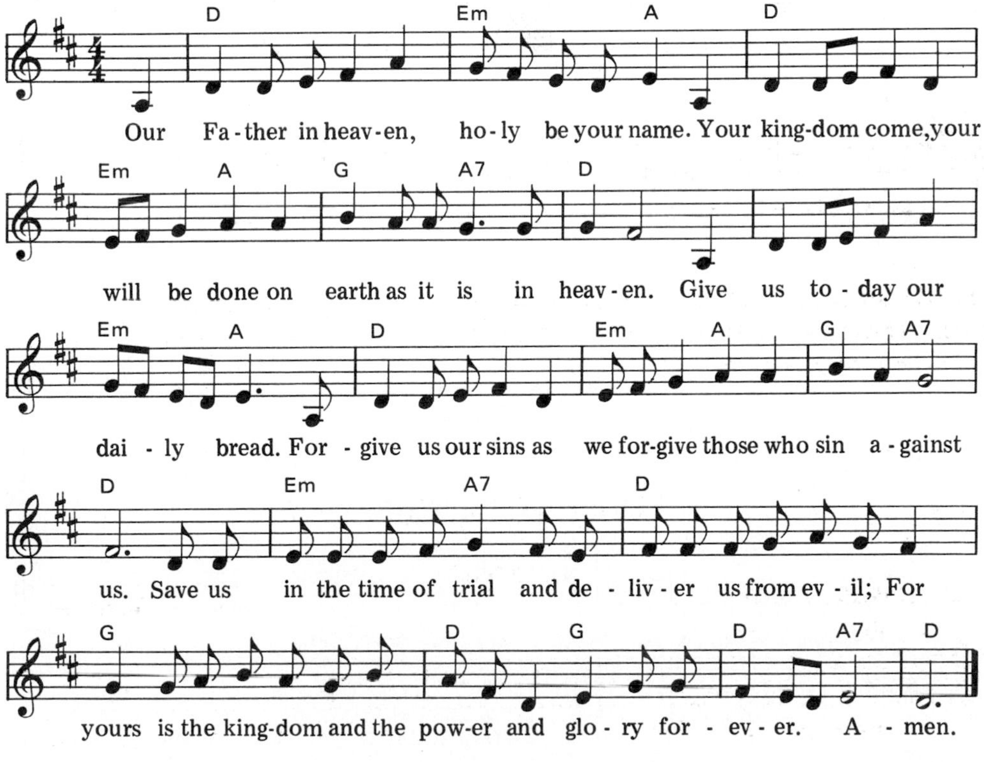

D Em A D
Our Fa - ther in heav - en, ho - ly be your name. Your king - dom come, your
Em A G A7 D
will be done on earth as it is in heav - en. Give us to - day our
Em A D Em A G A7
dai - ly bread. For - give us our sins as we for - give those who sin a - gainst
D Em A7 D
us. Save us in the time of trial and de - liv - er us from ev - il; For
G D G D A7 D
yours is the king - dom and the pow - er and glo - ry for - ev - er. A - men.

328 As You Have Promised, Lord

NUNC DIMITTIS

Luke 2:29-32
Adapted by F. L. Battles, 1971

John Ylvisaker, 1971

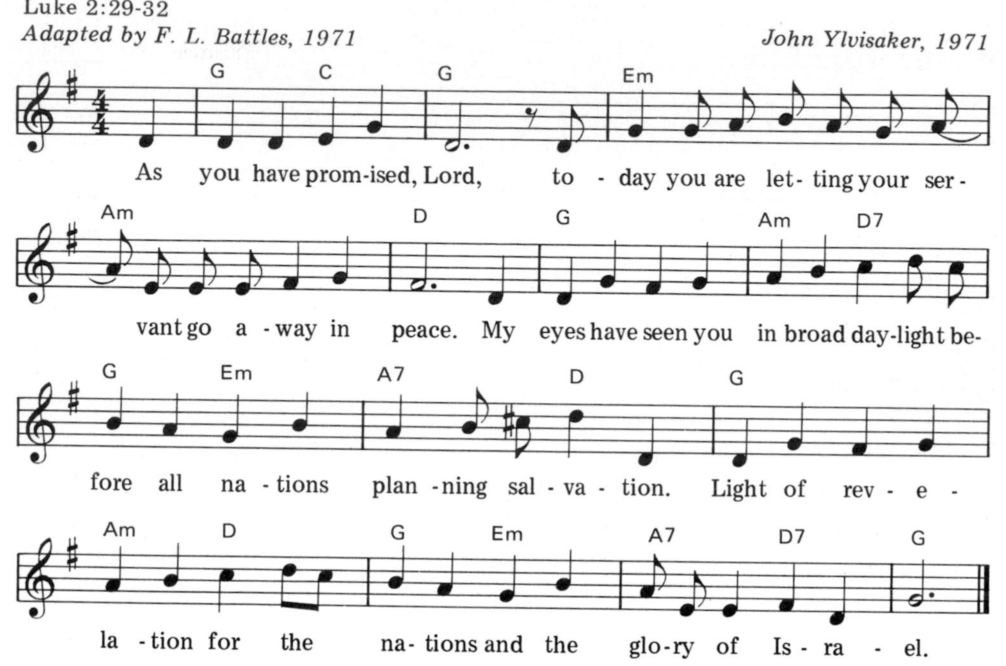

329 The Lord Is in His Holy Temple

Hab. 2:20

Lindsey Merrill, 1971

Jesus, Stand Among Us 330

BEMERTON 6.5.6.5.

William Pennefather, 1873

Friedrich Filitz, 1847

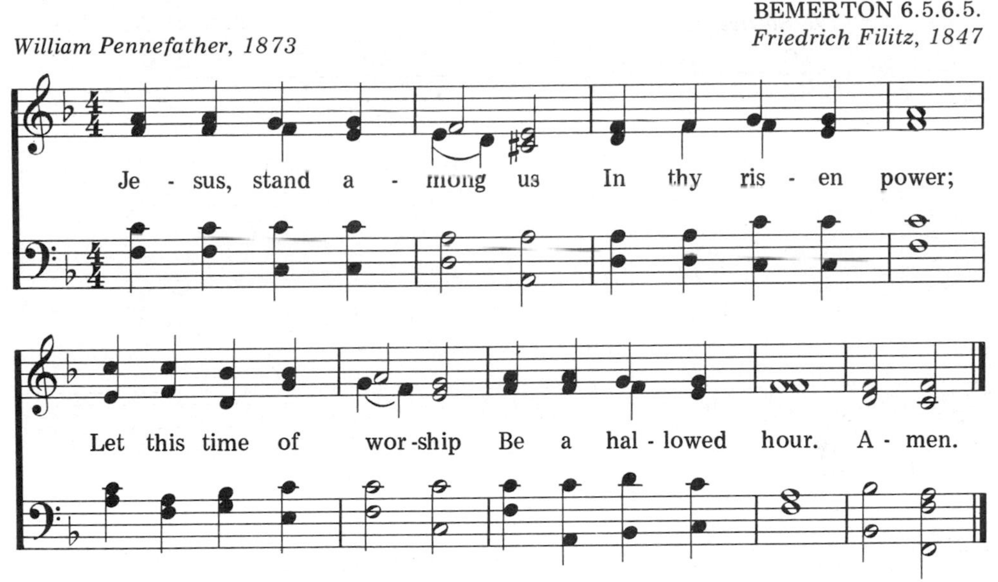

This Is the Day the Lord Hath Made 331

Ps. 118:24

Isaac Watts, 1719

TWENTY-FOURTH C.M.

Probably by Lucius Chapin, 1760-1842

This is the day the Lord hath made; He calls the hours his own.

Let heav'n re - joice, let earth be glad, And praise sur-round the throne.

332 Come, Bless the Lord

Ps. 134:2

Austin C. Lovelace, 1956

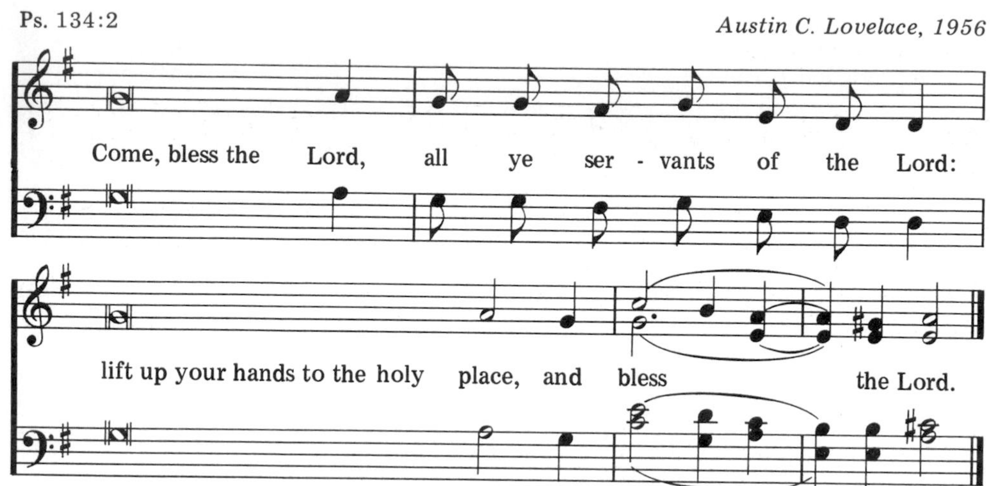

333 Lord, Have Mercy upon Us

KYRIE

Traditional: 6th century

From the American Lutheran Hymnal

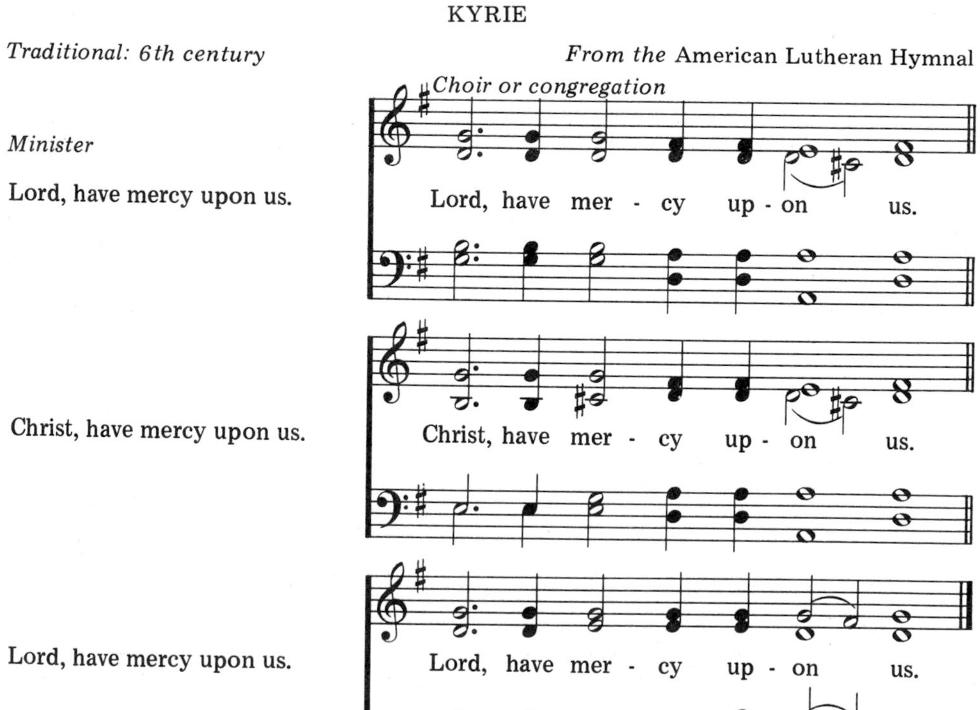

Minister

Lord, have mercy upon us.

Christ, have mercy upon us.

Lord, have mercy upon us.

Lord, Have Mercy upon Us 334

KYRIE

Traditional: 6th century — *John Merbecke, 1550*

Unison

Lord, have mer-cy up-on us; Christ, have mer-cy up-on us; Lord, have mer-cy up-on us.

Lord, Have Mercy on Us 335

KYRIE

Lee Burswold, 1971

This Kyrie may be sung responsively. See additional versions of the Kyrie at Nos. 314 and 322.

Glory Be to God on High

GLORIA IN EXCELSIS

2d century Canticle *Old Scottish Chant*

1. Glory be to God on high, and on earth peace, good will toward men.
2. We praise thee, we bless thee, we wor - ship thee, we glorify thee, we give thanks to thee for thy great glo - ry.
3. O Lord God, heaven - ly King, God the Father Al - might - y.
4. O Lord, the only begotten Son,
5. That takest away the
6. Thou that takest away the
7. Thou that sittest at the right hand of
Je - sus Christ; O Lord God, Lamb of God, Son of the Fa - ther,
sins of the world, have mercy up - on us.
sins of the world, re - ceive our prayer.
God the Father, have mercy up - on us.

See additional versions of the Gloria in Excelsis at Nos. 315 and 323.

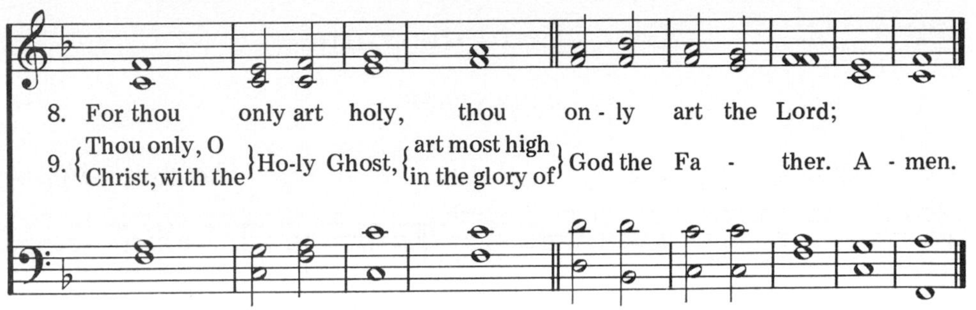
8. For thou only art holy, thou on-ly art the Lord;
9. {Thou only, O Christ, with the} Ho-ly Ghost, {art most high in the glory of} God the Fa - ther. A - men.

Glory Be to the Father 337

GLORIA PATRI

Traditional *Old Scottish Chant*

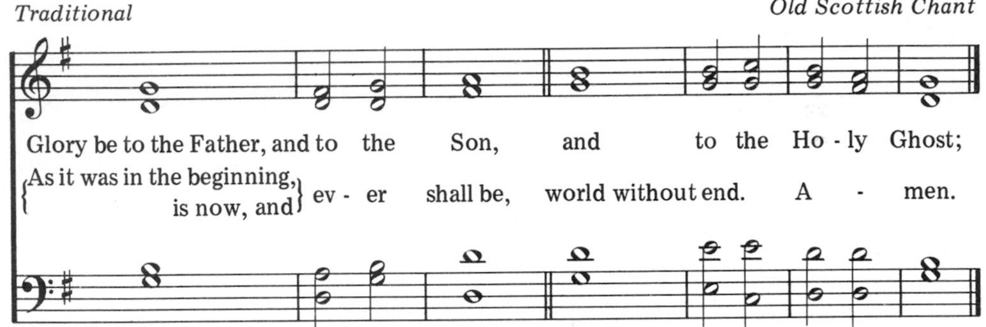
Glory be to the Father, and to the Son, and to the Ho-ly Ghost;
{As it was in the beginning, is now, and} ev - er shall be, world without end. A - men.

Glory Be to the Father 338

GLORIA PATRI

Traditional *Henry W. Greatorex, 1851*

Glo-ry be to the Fa-ther, and to the Son, and to the Ho-ly Ghost; As it
was in the be-gin-ning, is now, and ev-er shall be, world with-out end. A-men. A-men.

339 Glory Be to the Father

GLORIA PATRI

Traditional *Charles Meineke, 1844*

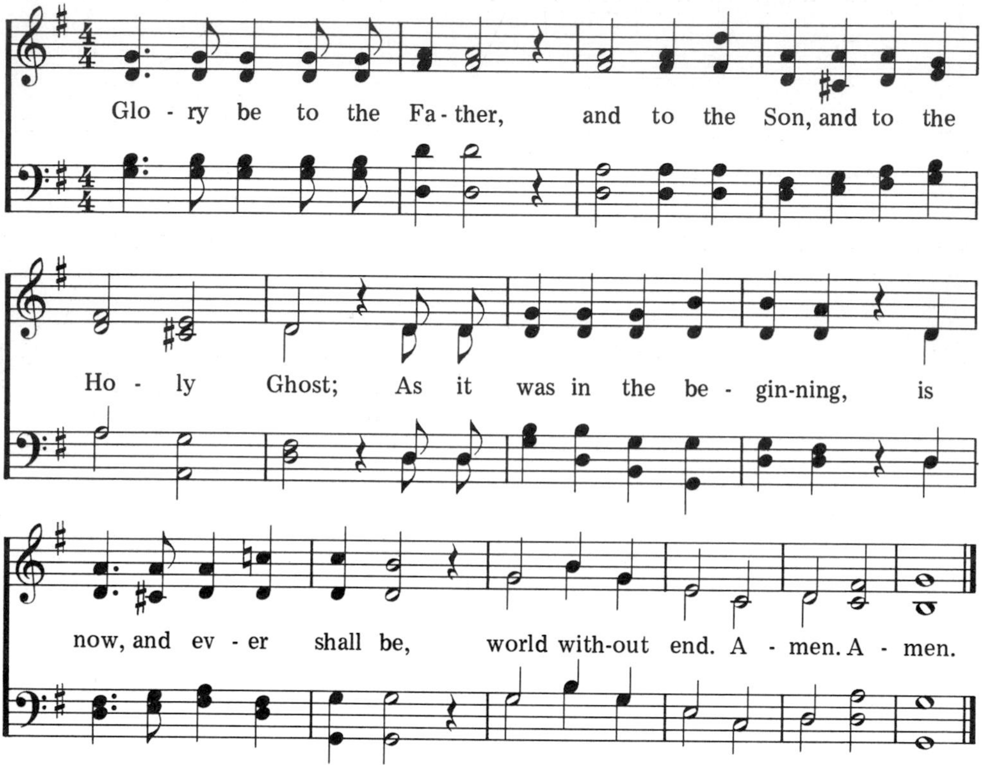

Glo - ry be to the Fa - ther, and to the Son, and to the
Ho - ly Ghost; As it was in the be - gin-ning, is
now, and ev - er shall be, world with-out end. A - men. A - men.

340 Glory Be to God the Father

GLORIA PATRI

TONUS PEREGRINUS
Plainsong

Traditional *Setting by Johann Sebastian Bach, c.1740*

Unison
Glo - ry be to God the Fa - ther, and the Son,

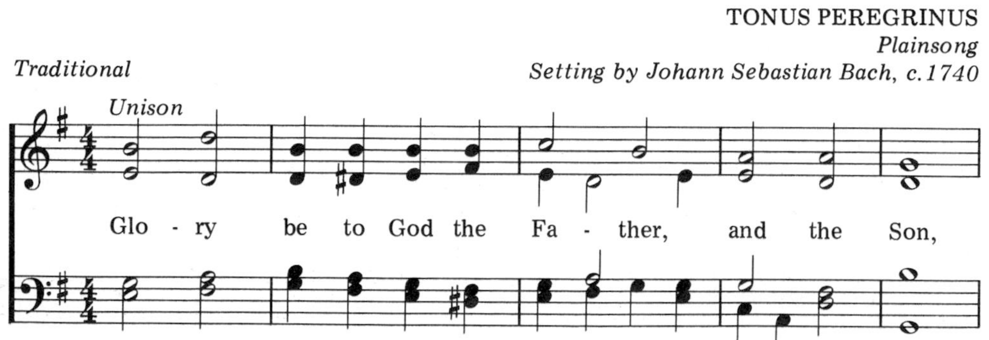

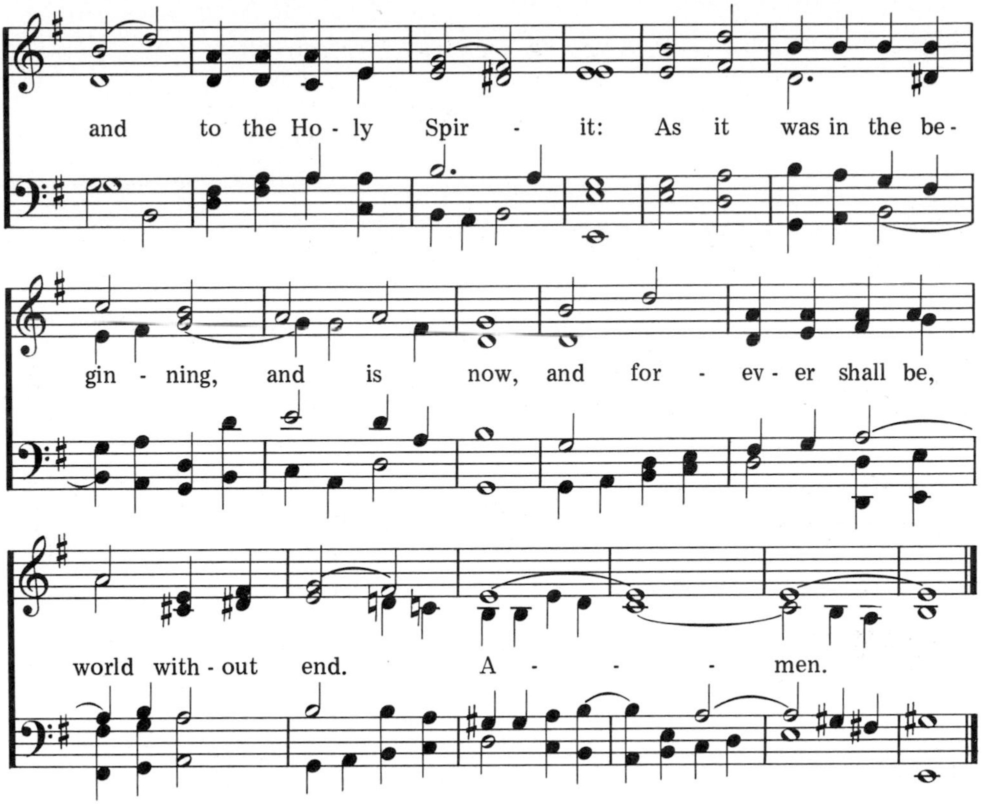

and to the Ho - ly Spir - it: As it was in the be -
gin - ning, and is now, and for - ev - er shall be,
world with - out end. A - - - men.

See additional versions of the Gloria Patri at Nos. 316 and 324.

Responses to Scripture 341

GLORIA TIBI
(Before the Gospel)

Glo - ry be to thee, O Lord.

LAUS TIBI
(After the Gospel)

J. Playford, 1674-1730

Praise be to thee, O Christ.

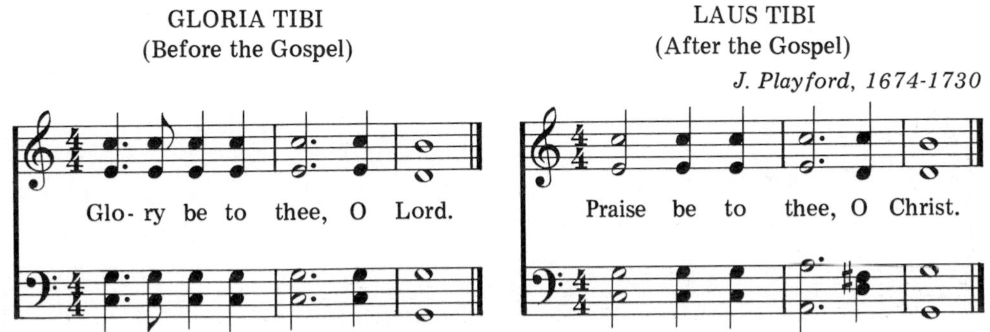

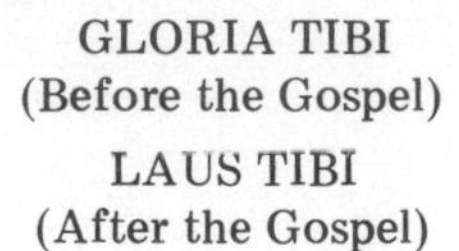

GLORIA TIBI
(Before the Gospel)
LAUS TIBI
(After the Gospel)

Traditional

Glo- ry be to thee, O Lord.
(Praise be to thee, O Christ.)

GLORIA TIBI
(Before the Gospel)
LAUS TIBI
(After the Gospel)

Ancient Chant

Glo - ry be to thee, O Lord.
(Praise be to thee, O Christ.)

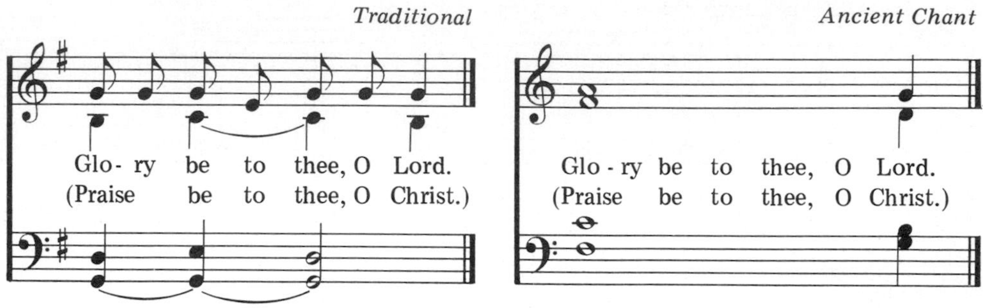

342 The Lord Be with You

Book of Common Prayer, *1549*

Thomas Tallis, c.1564

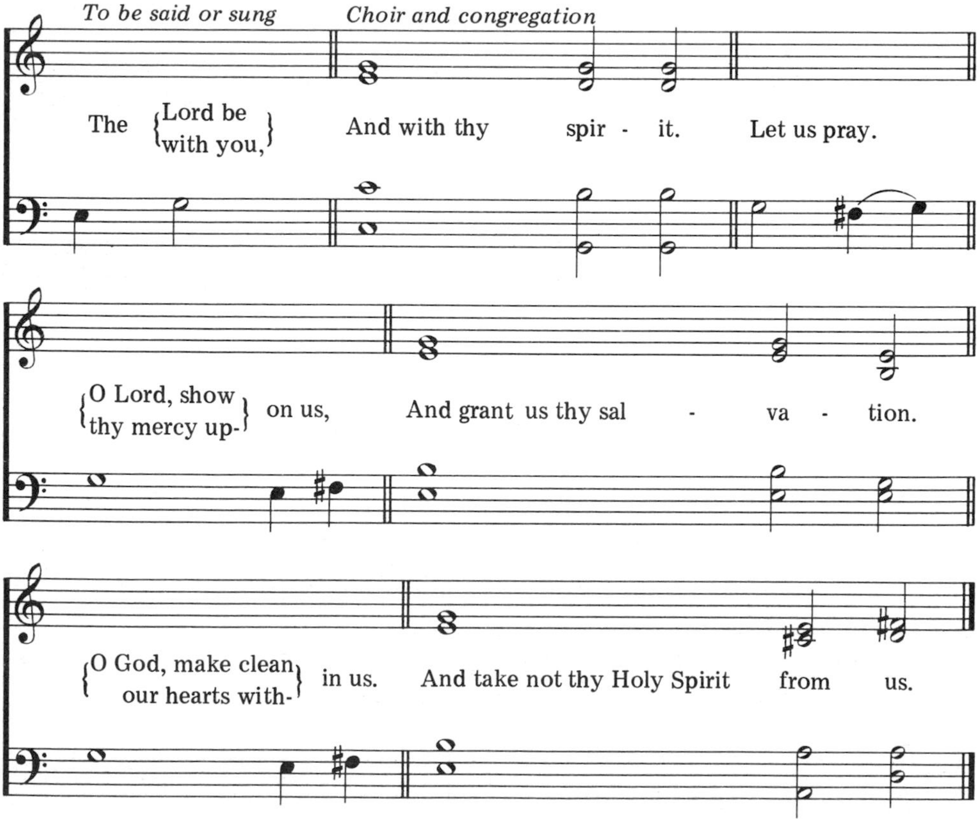

To be said or sung
Choir and congregation
The Lord be with you,
And with thy spir - it.
Let us pray.
O Lord, show thy mercy up- on us,
And grant us thy sal - va - tion.
O God, make clean our hearts with- in us.
And take not thy Holy Spirit from us.

The Lord Be with You 343

Book of Common Prayer, *1549* | *Thomas Tallis, c.1564*

To be said or sung *Choir and congregation*

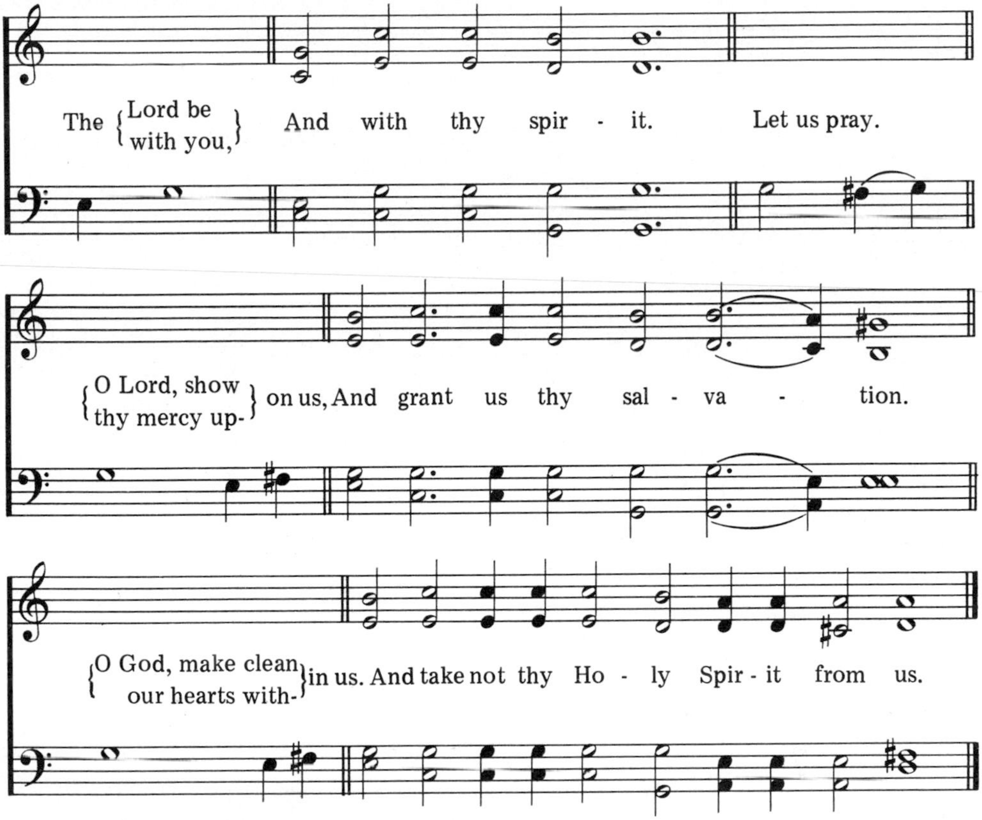

The {Lord be with you,} And with thy spir - it. Let us pray.

{O Lord, show thy mercy up-} on us, And grant us thy sal - va - tion.

{O God, make clean our hearts with-} in us. And take not thy Ho - ly Spir - it from us.

Let the Words of My Mouth 344

Ps. 19:14 | *Joseph Barnby, 1838-1896*

Let the words of my mouth and the med- itation
of my heart
be acceptable in thy sight, O Lord, my strength and
my Re - deem - er. A - men.

345 Enrich, Lord, Heart, Mouth, Hands in Me

WULFRUN 8.8.8.

George Herbert, 1633, alt.

George W. Briggs, 1929

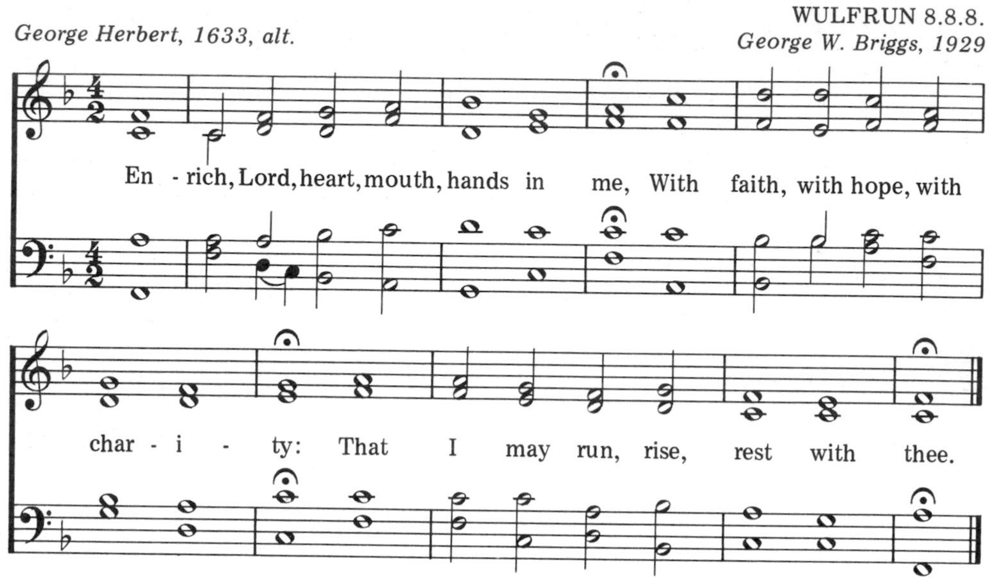
En - rich, Lord, heart, mouth, hands in me, With faith, with hope, with
char - i - ty: That I may run, rise, rest with thee.

346 To My Humble Supplication

MON DIEU, PRÊTE-MOI L'OREILLE 8.8.7.7.

Joseph Bryan, 17th century

Genevan Psalter, *1543*

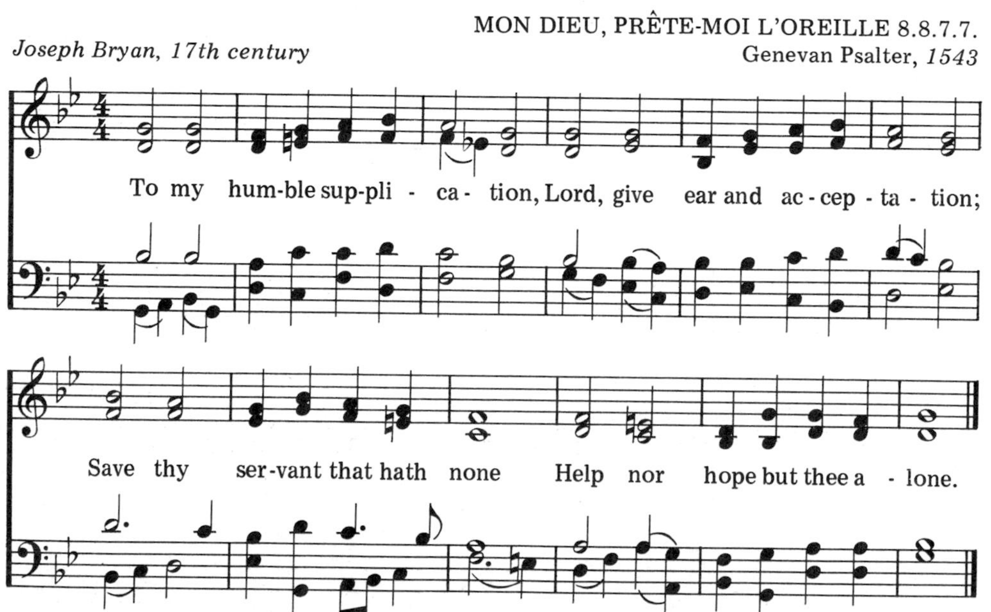
To my hum-ble sup-pli - ca - tion, Lord, give ear and ac - cep - ta - tion;
Save thy ser-vant that hath none Help nor hope but thee a - lone.

May the Words of Our Mouths 347

Ps. 19:14, *alt.* — *Alan Walker, 1958*

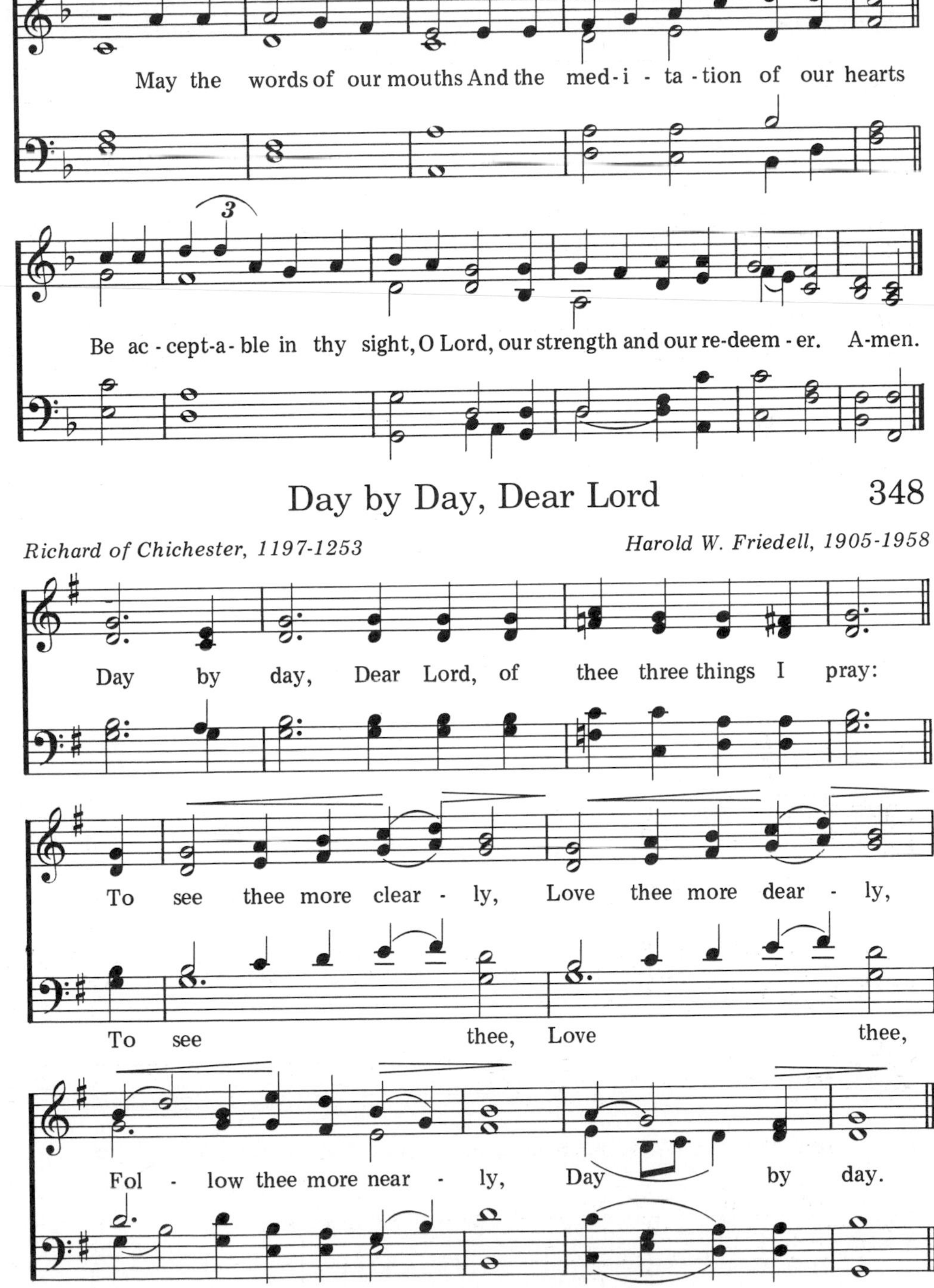
Unison
May the words of our mouths And the med-i-ta-tion of our hearts
Be ac-cept-a-ble in thy sight, O Lord, our strength and our re-deem-er. A-men.
3
Day by Day, Dear Lord 348
Richard of Chichester, 1197-1253
Harold W. Friedell, 1905-1958
Day by day, Dear Lord, of thee three things I pray:
To see thee more clear-ly, Love thee more dear-ly,
To see thee, Love thee,
Fol-low thee more near-ly, Day by day.

349 Let Thy Word Abide

Col. 3:16

D. Tait Patterson *John Ferguson, 1971*

Let thy word a - bide in us, O Lord.

350 Our Father

West Indies Tune

Matt. 6:9-13 *Collected by Olive Pattison, 1945*

Adapted by Ewald Bash, 1964 *Arr. by Paul Abels, 1964*

E B7 E B7
1. Our Fa - ther who art in heav - en,
2. As in heav - en, so on the earth;
3. And for - give us, Fa - ther, all our debts;
4. And lead us not into temp-ta - tion;
5. For thine is the king-dom, pow-er, and glory;
6. A - men, a - men, it shall be so;
E B7 E
Hal - low - ed be thy name;
E A E B7
Thy king-dom come, thy will be done.
Give us this day our dai - ly bread.
As we for - give our debt - ors.
But de - liv - er us from all e - vil.
For - ev - er and for - ev - er and ev - er.
A - men, a - men it shall be so.
E B7 E
Hal - low - ed be thy name.

See additional versions of the Lord's Prayer at Nos. 320 and 327.

We Give Thee but Thine Own 351

SCHUMANN S.M.
Mason and Webb's Cantica Laudis, *Boston, 1850*

William Walsham How, 1864

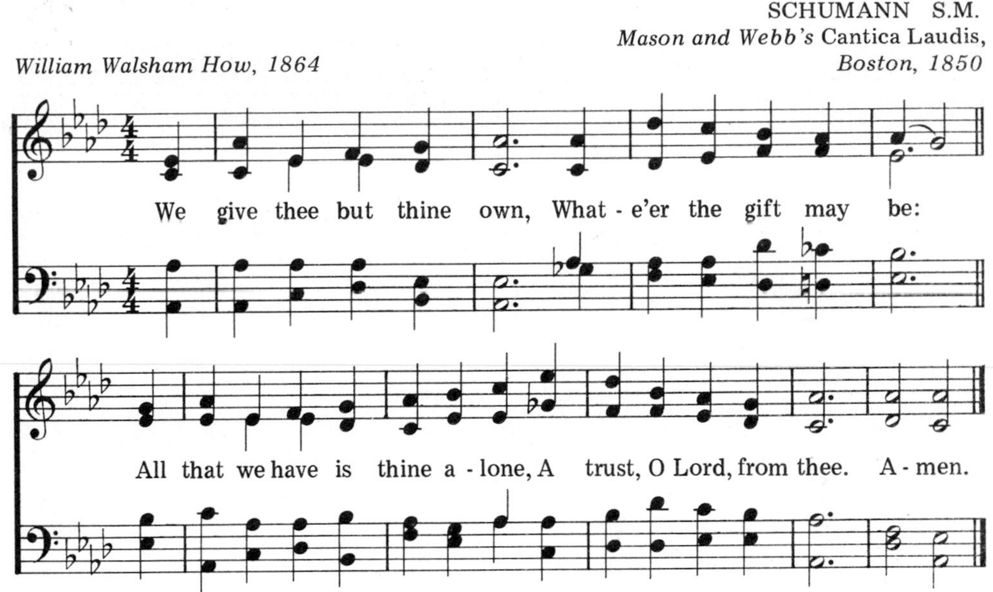

All Things Are Thine 352

HERR JESU CHRIST L.M.
John Greenleaf Whittier, 1843
Pensum Sacrum, *1648*

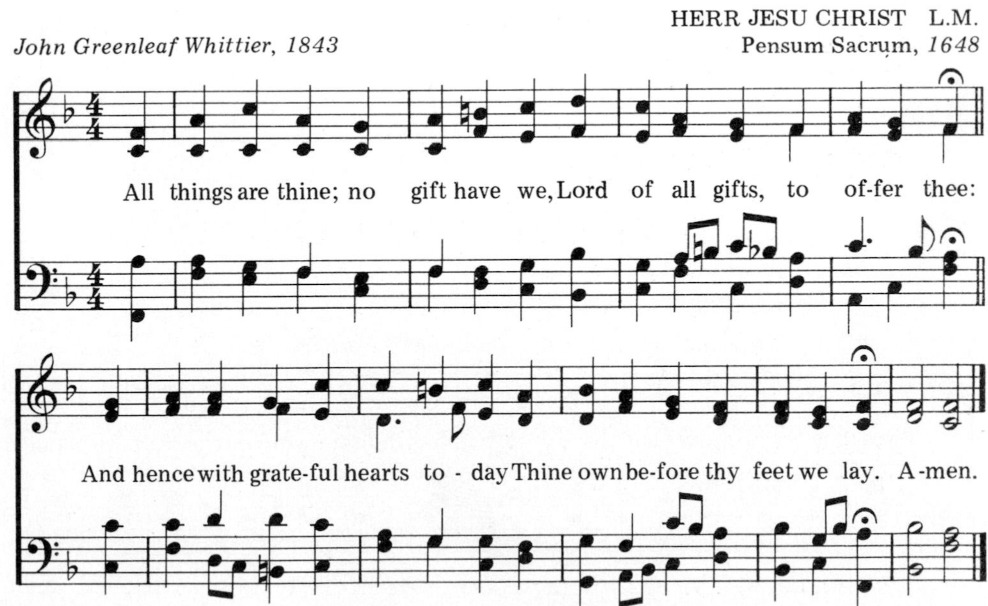

353 Bless Thou the Gifts

CANONBURY L.M.

Samuel Longfellow, 1886 *Arr. from Robert A. Schumann, 1839*

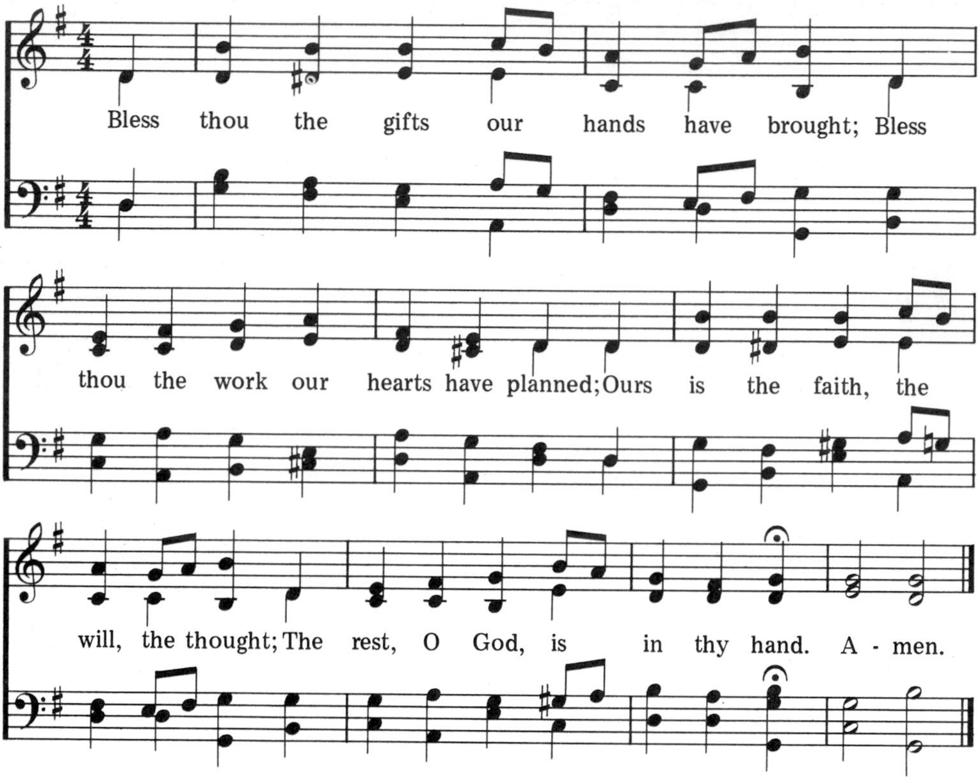

Bless thou the gifts our hands have brought; Bless
thou the work our hearts have planned; Ours is the faith, the
will, the thought; The rest, O God, is in thy hand. A - men.

354 Bless Thou the Gifts

Samuel Longfellow, 1886 *Walter Watson, 1971*

Bless thou the gifts our hands have brought; Bless thou the work our hearts have planned;

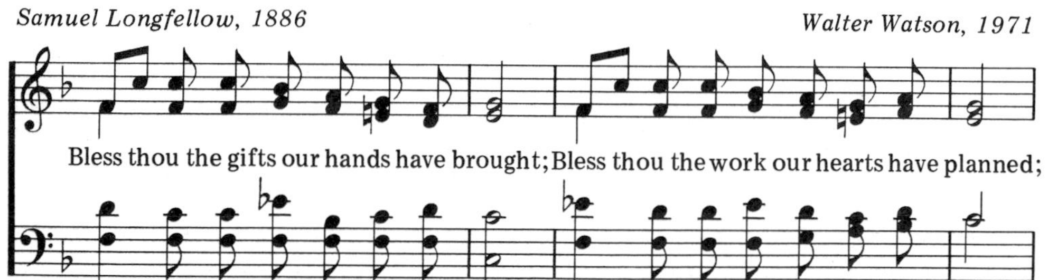

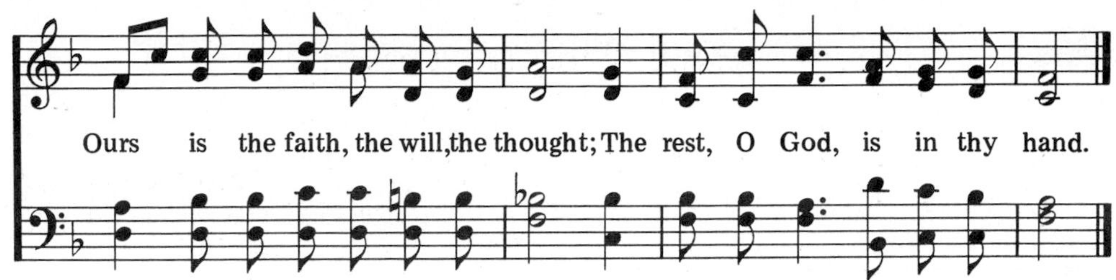

Praise God from Whom All Blessings Flow 355

OLD HUNDREDTH L.M.
Attr. to Louis Bourgeois,
Genevan Psalter, *1551*

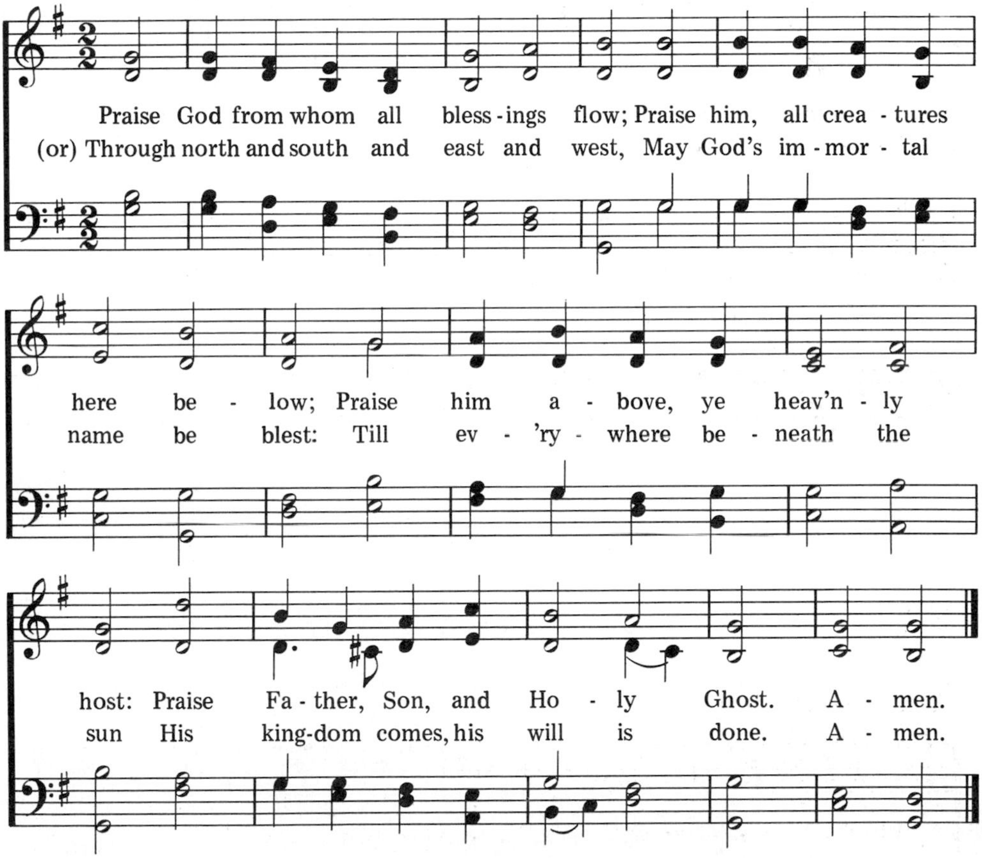

1st version, Thomas Ken, 1692
2d version, Percy Dearmer, 1931

Praise God from whom all bless-ings flow; Praise him, all crea - tures
(or) Through north and south and east and west, May God's im - mor - tal

here be - low; Praise him a - bove, ye heav'n - ly
name be blest: Till ev - 'ry - where be - neath the

host: Praise Fa - ther, Son, and Ho - ly Ghost. A - men.
sun His king-dom comes, his will is done. A - men.

The text "Through North and South" is an alternate Doxology for use in place of the better known Thomas Ken Doxology. See an additional version of the Doxology at No. 317.

356 Praise God from Whom All Blessings Flow

OLD HUNDREDTH L.M. *(altered rhythm)*

1st version, Thomas Ken, 1692
2d version, Percy Dearmer, 1931

Attr. to Louis Bourgeois,
Genevan Psalter, *1551*

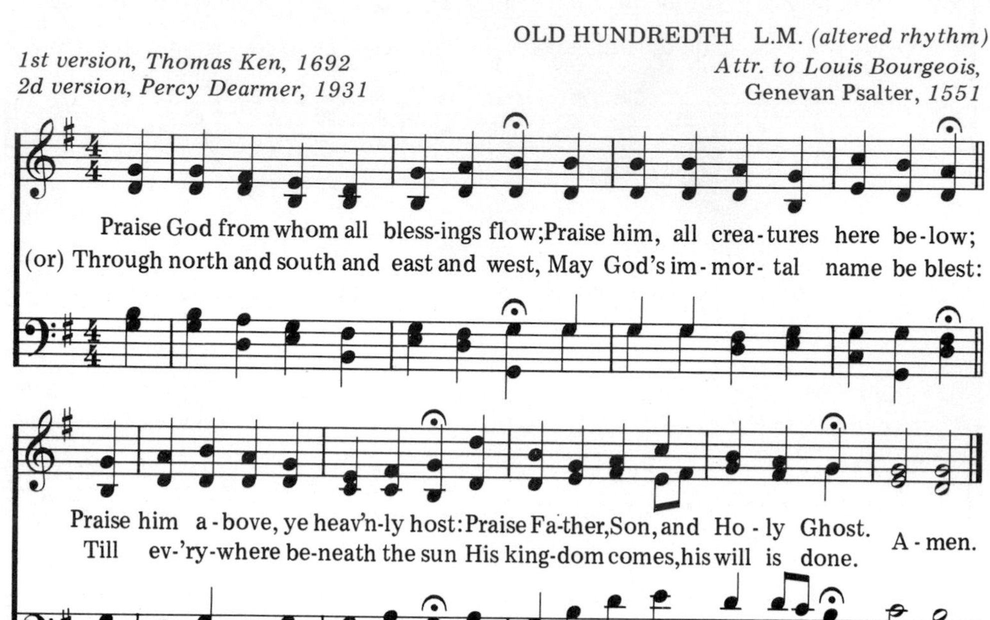

357 Praise God from Whom All Blessings Flow

LASST UNS ERFREUEN L.M. *with Alleluias*

1st version, Thomas Ken, 1692
2d version, Percy Dearmer, 1931

Geistliche Kirchengesäng, *Cologne, 1623*
Harm. by R. Vaughan Williams, 1906

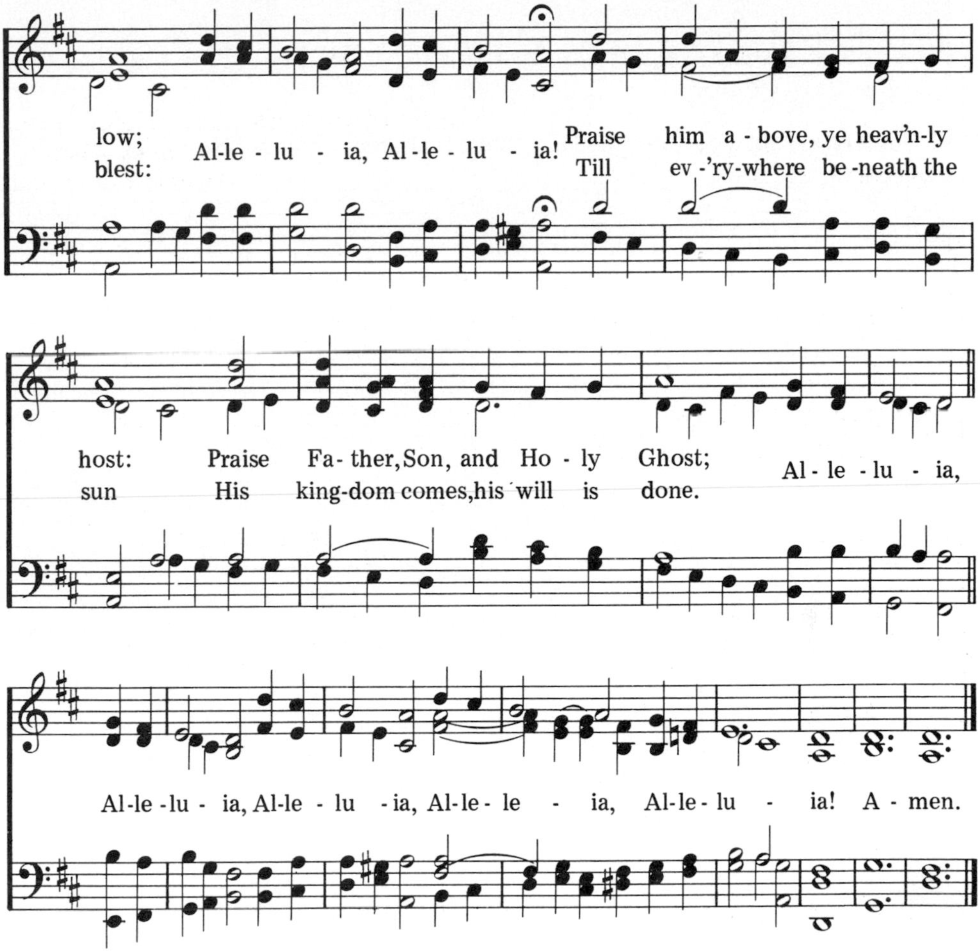

low; Al-le - lu - ia, Al-le - lu - ia! Praise him a - bove, ye heav'n-ly
blest: Till ev -'ry-where be -neath the
host: Praise Fa- ther, Son, and Ho - ly Ghost; Al - le - lu - ia,
sun His king-dom comes, his will is done.
Al-le -lu - ia, Al-le - lu - ia, Al-le- le - ia, Al-le- lu - ia! A - men.

A higher setting may be found at No. 30.

Praise God from Whom All Blessings Flow 358

Tamil Melody (Usani)
Arr. by John Milton Kelly, 1962
Adapted and harm. by Mary L. VanDyke
and John Ferguson, 1973

Traditional
Adapted by D. T. Niles

Unison
Praise God from whom all bless-ings flow: Praise him! Al - le - lu - ia in the

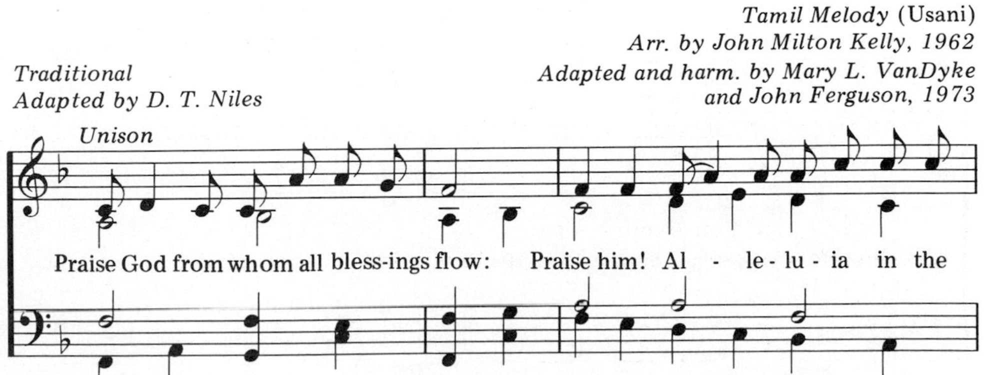

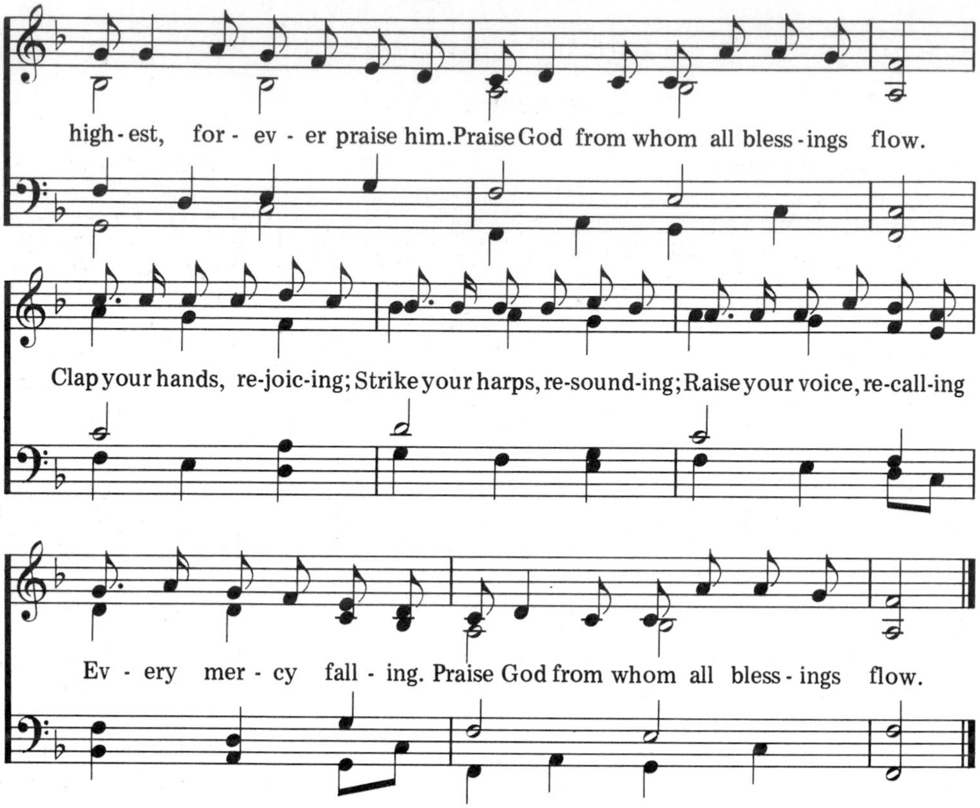

high-est, for-ev-er praise him. Praise God from whom all bless-ings flow.
Clap your hands, re-joic-ing; Strike your harps, re-sound-ing; Raise your voice, re-call-ing
Ev-ery mer-cy fall-ing. Praise God from whom all bless-ings flow.

359 Praise the Father Giving Life

F. L. Battles, 1971 *Lee Burswold, 1971*

Unison
Praise the Fa-ther giv-ing life; praise Word In-car-nate con-q'ring death;
Praise Ho-ly Spir-it breath-ing hope; all cre-a-tion praise our God.

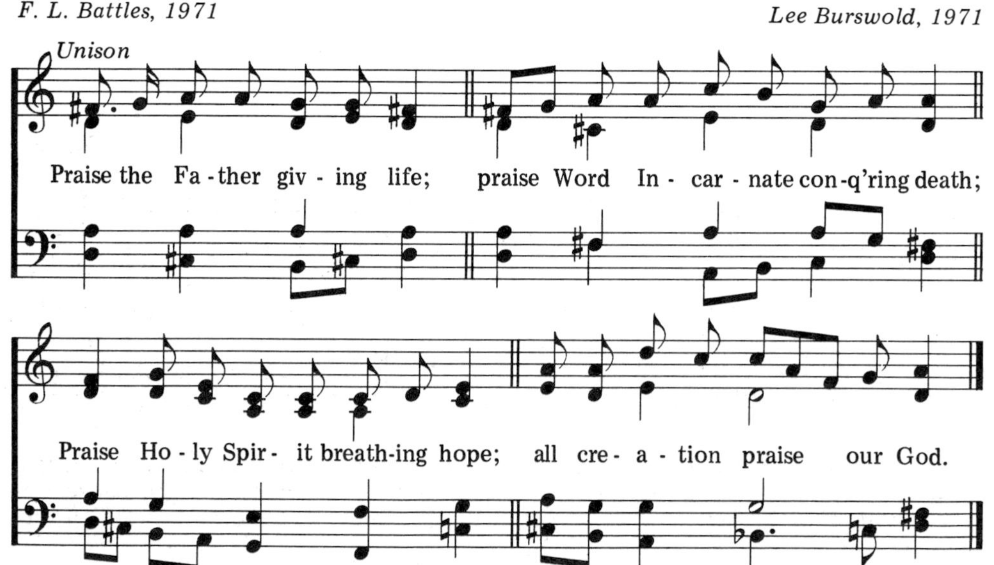

Lift Up Your Hearts 360

SURSUM CORDA

Traditional: 3d century *Lee Burswold, 1971*

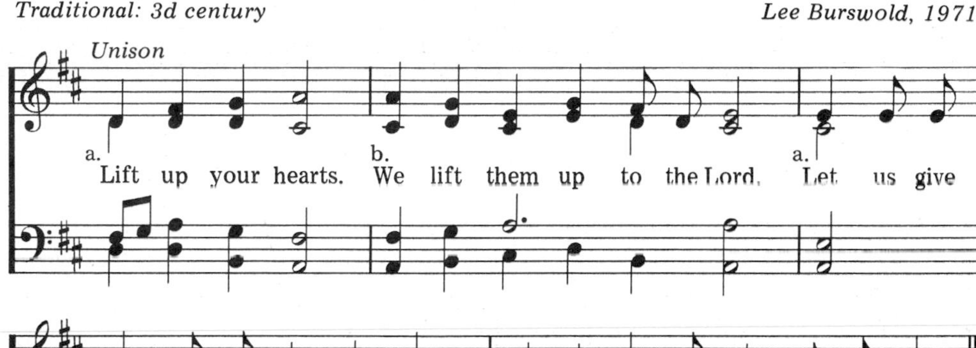

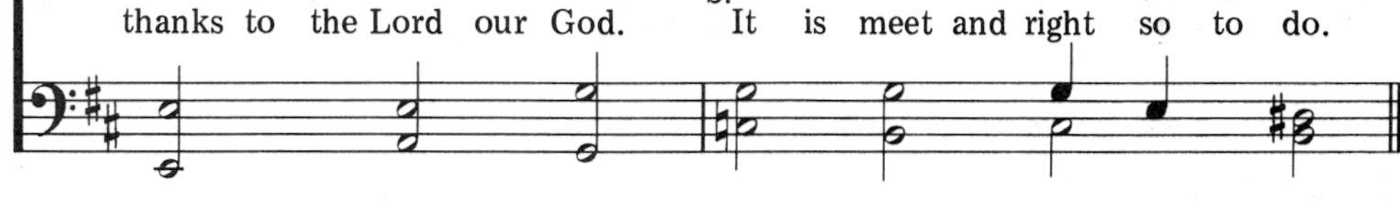

The Sursum Corda traditionally is sung or said responsively between minister and congregation. Therefore in this setting parts "a" could be sung by minister or choir, the congregation responding at parts "b."

Lift Up Your Hearts 361

SURSUM CORDA

Traditional: 3d century *John W. Neely, Jr., 1971*

The Sursum Corda traditionally is sung or said responsively between minister and congregation. Therefore in this setting parts "a" could be sung by minister or choir, the congregation responding at parts "b". See additional versions of the Sursum Corda at Nos. 318 and 325.

b.
thanks to the Lord our God. It is meet and right so to do.

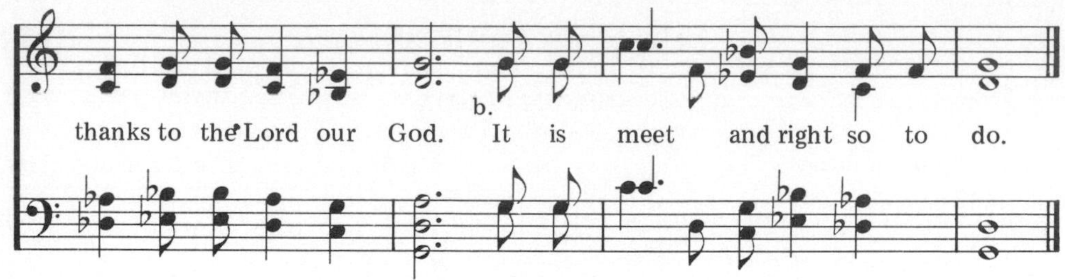

362 Holy, Holy, Holy

SANCTUS

Isa. 6:3; Mark 11:9-10 *Lee Burswold, 1971*

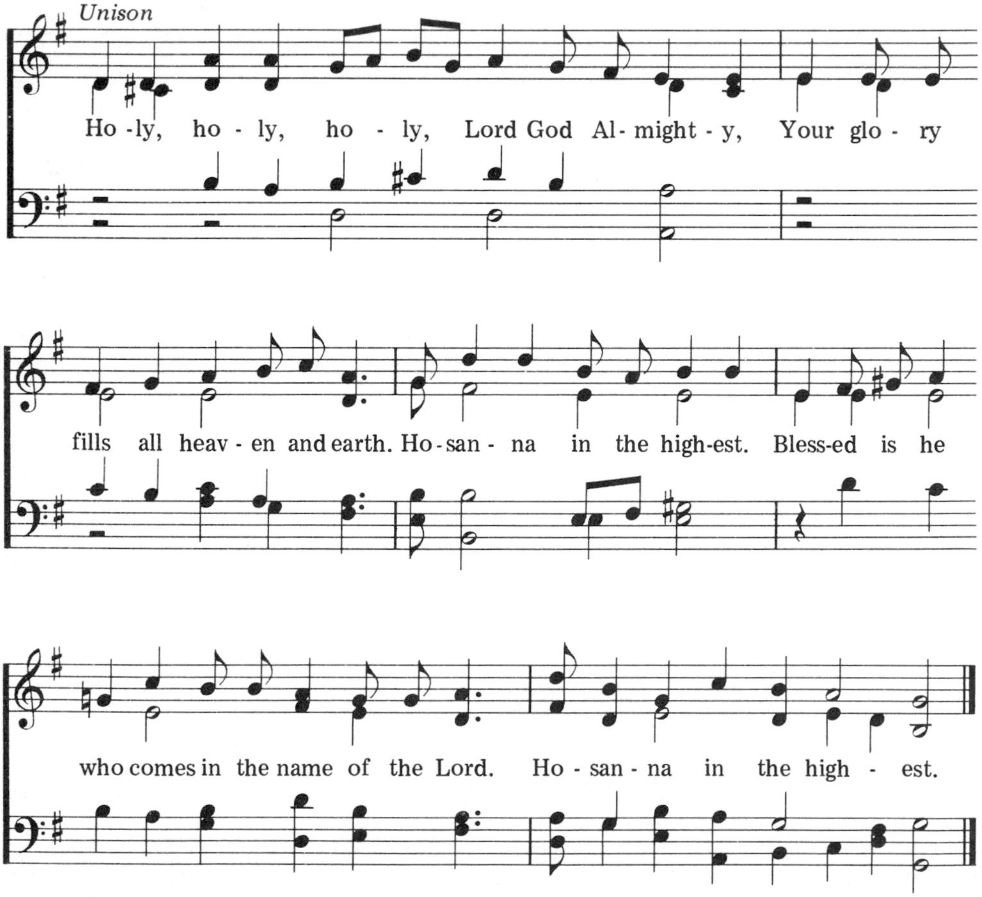

Unison
Ho-ly, ho - ly, ho - ly, Lord God Al-might-y, Your glo - ry
fills all heav - en and earth. Ho-san - na in the high-est. Bless-ed is he
who comes in the name of the Lord. Ho - san - na in the high - est.

Holy, Holy, Holy

SANCTUS

Isa. 6:3; Mark 11: 9-10

John W. Neely, Jr., 1971

Holy, Holy, Holy

SANCTUS

Isa. 6:3; Mark 11:9-10

Alonzo P. Howard, 1838-1902

Holy, Holy, Holy

SANCTUS

Isa. 6:3

Vincent Persichetti, 1956

See additional versions of the Sanctus at Nos. 319 and 326.

O Christ, Thou Lamb of God

AGNUS DEI

John 1:29
7th century Liturgy

CHRISTE, DU LAMM GOTTES
Arr. by Healey Willan, 1880-1968

Father, Give Thy Benediction 367

RINGE RECHT 8.7.8.7.

Samuel Longfellow, 1864

Musikalischer Christen-Schatz, *Basel, 1745*

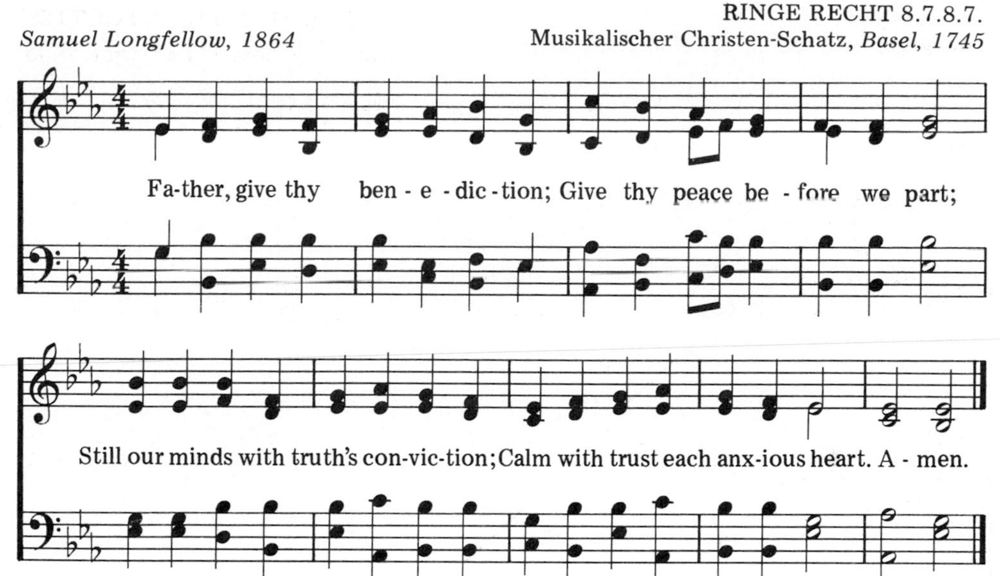

Shalom 368

Ancient Hebrew
English version by Paul Abels, 1937-

Israeli Round

"Shalom" means "peace" in Hebrew.

369 We Praise Thee, O God

TE DEUM LAUDAMUS

Composite of
Apostles' Creed, Gloria, Sanctus, and Psalms — *Edwin G. Monk, 1819-1900*

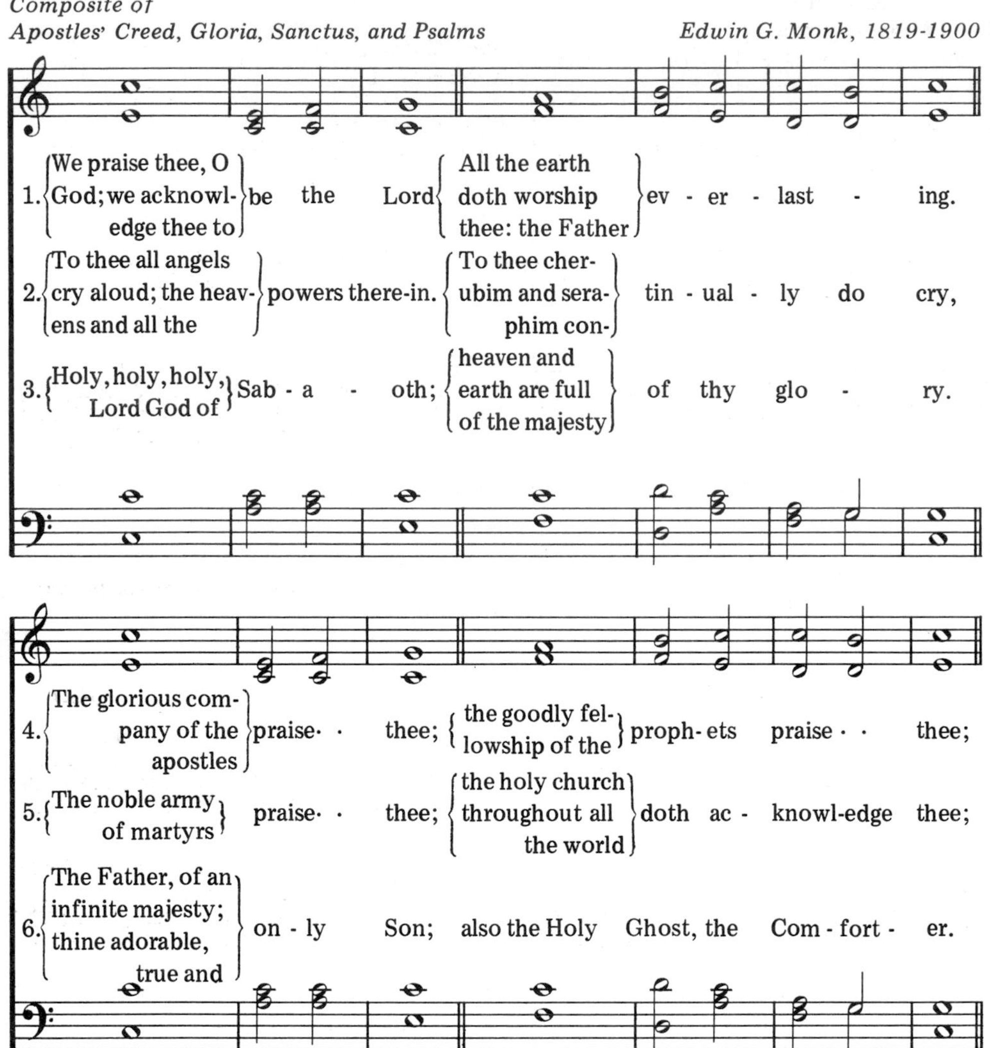

The canticle may end with the twelfth verse. Verses 13 to 16 may be sung either by themselves, or with the other verses.

William Croft, 1678-1727
7. Thou art the King of glory, O Christ, Thou art the everlasting Son of the Fa - ther.
8. When thou tookest upon thee to deliv - er man, Thou didst humble thyself to be born of a vir - gin.
9. When thou hadst overcome the sharpness of death, Thou didst open the kingdom of heaven to all be - liev - ers.
10. Thou sittest at the right hand of God, in the glory of the Fa - ther.
11. We believe that thou shalt come to be our judge; we therefore pray thee, help thy servants whom thou hast redeemed with thy pre-cious blood;
12. Make them to be numbered with thy saints in glory ev - er - last - ing.
E. G. Monk
13. O Lord, save thy people and bless thine her - it - age: govern them and lift them up for - ev - er.
14. Day by day we magni - fy thee, and we worship thy name ever, world with - out end.
15. Vouchsafe, O Lord, to keep us this day without · · sin. O Lord, have mercy upon us, have mercy up - on · · us.
16. O Lord, let thy mercy be upon us, as our trust is in thee; O Lord, in thee have I trusted, let me never be con - found - ed.

370 O Come, Let Us Sing

VENITE

Ps. 95
The Book of Common Prayer, *1789*

William Boyce, 1710-1779

1. O come, let us sing unto the Lord; let us heartily rejoice in the strength of our sal - va - tion.
3. For the Lord is a great · · God; and a great King a - bove all gods.
5. The sea is his and he made · · it; and his hands pre-pared the dry · · land.
7. For he is the Lord our God; and we are the people of his pasture, and the sheep of his · · hand.
Glory be to the Father, and to the Son, and to the Ho - ly Ghost;

2. Let us come before his presence with thanks - giving; and show ourselves glad in him with psalms.
4. In his hand are all the corners of the earth; and the strength of the hills is his · · al - so.
6. O come, let us worship and fall · · down, and kneel before the Lord our mak - er.
8. O worship the Lord in the beauty of holiness; let the whole earth stand in awe of him.
9. For he cometh, for he cometh to judge the earth; and with righteousness to judge the world, and the peo-ples with his truth.
As it was in the beginning, is now, and ev - er shall be, world without end. · · A - men.

O Be Joyful in the Lord

JUBILATE DEO

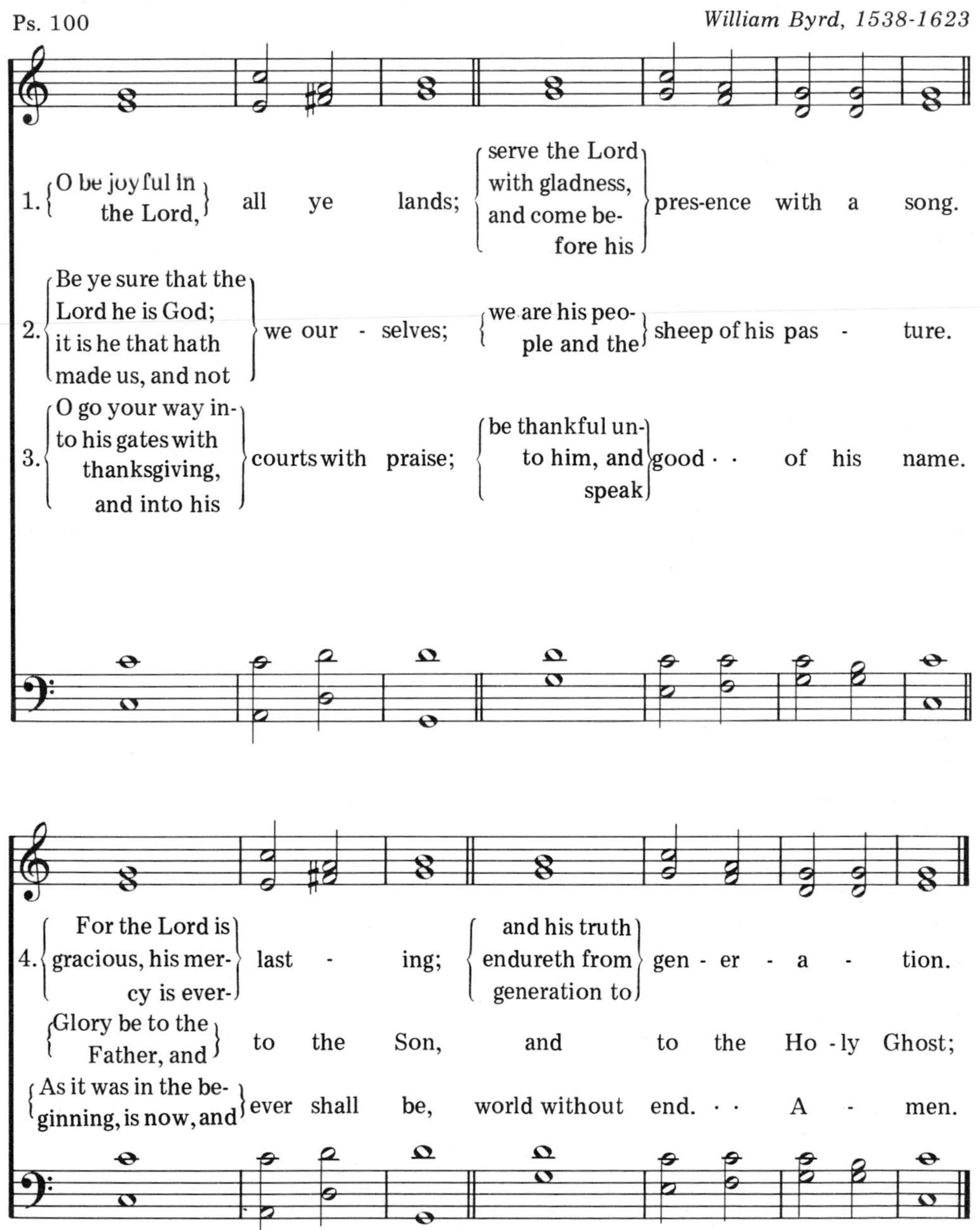
Ps. 100
William Byrd, 1538-1623
1. O be joyful in the Lord, all ye lands; serve the Lord with gladness, and come before his presence with a song.
2. Be ye sure that the Lord he is God; it is he that hath made us, and not we our - selves; we are his people and the sheep of his pas - ture.
3. O go your way into his gates with thanksgiving, and into his courts with praise; be thankful unto him, and speak good · · of his name.
4. For the Lord is gracious, his mercy is ever-last - ing; and his truth endureth from generation to gen - er - a - tion.
Glory be to the Father, and to the Son, and to the Ho - ly Ghost;
As it was in the beginning, is now, and ever shall be, world without end. · · A - men.

See Nos. 2, 12, 37, and 38 which are a paraphrase of this Canticle.

372 Blessed Be the Lord God

BENEDICTUS

Luke 1:68-79

Joseph Barnby, 1838-1896

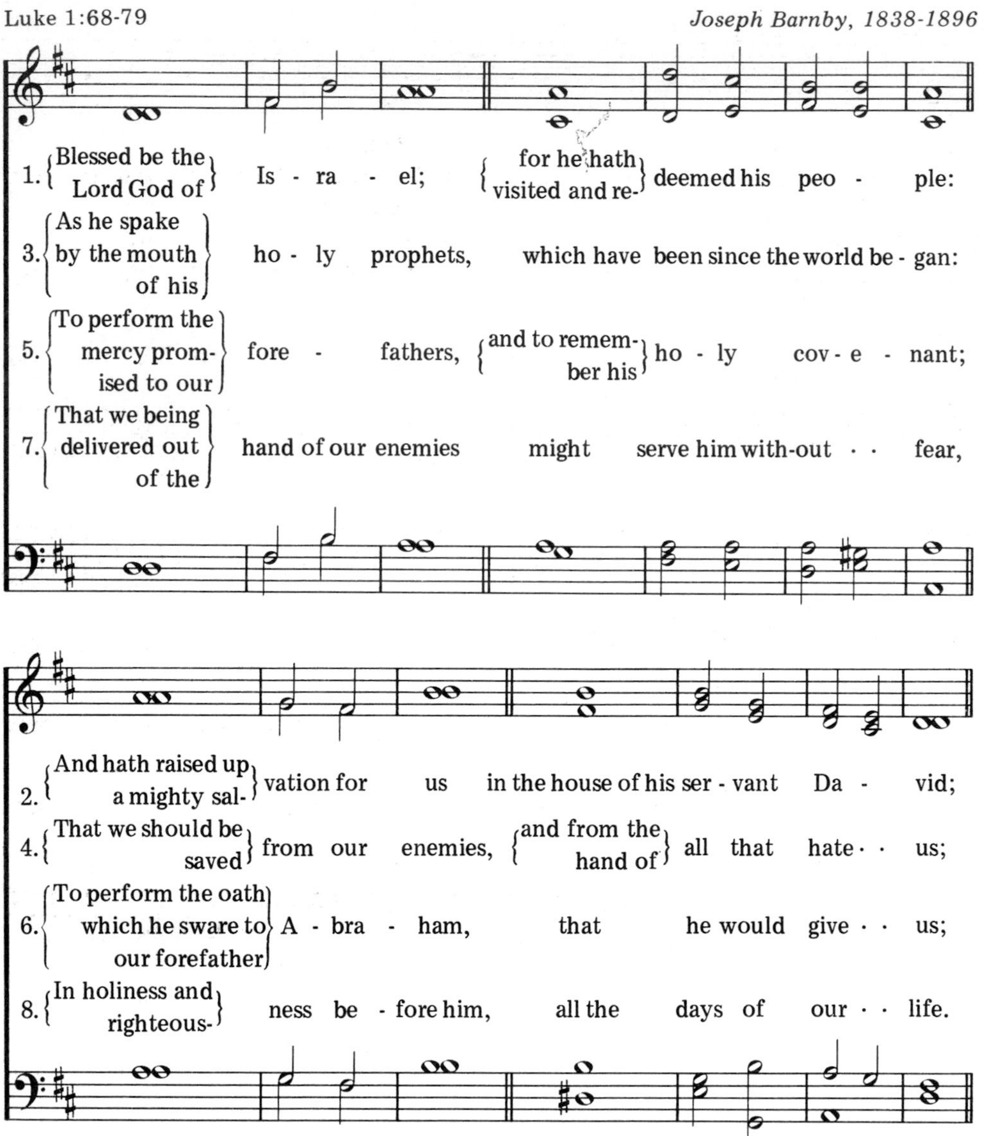
1. Blessed be the Lord God of Is - ra - el; for he hath visited and redeemed his peo - ple:
3. As he spake by the mouth of his ho - ly prophets, which have been since the world be - gan:
5. To perform the mercy promised to our fore - fathers, and to remember his ho - ly cov - e - nant;
7. That we being delivered out of the hand of our enemies might serve him with-out fear,
2. And hath raised up a mighty salvation for us in the house of his ser - vant Da - vid;
4. That we should be saved from our enemies, and from the hand of all that hate us;
6. To perform the oath which he sware to our forefather A - bra - ham, that he would give us;
8. In holiness and righteousness be - fore him, all the days of our life.

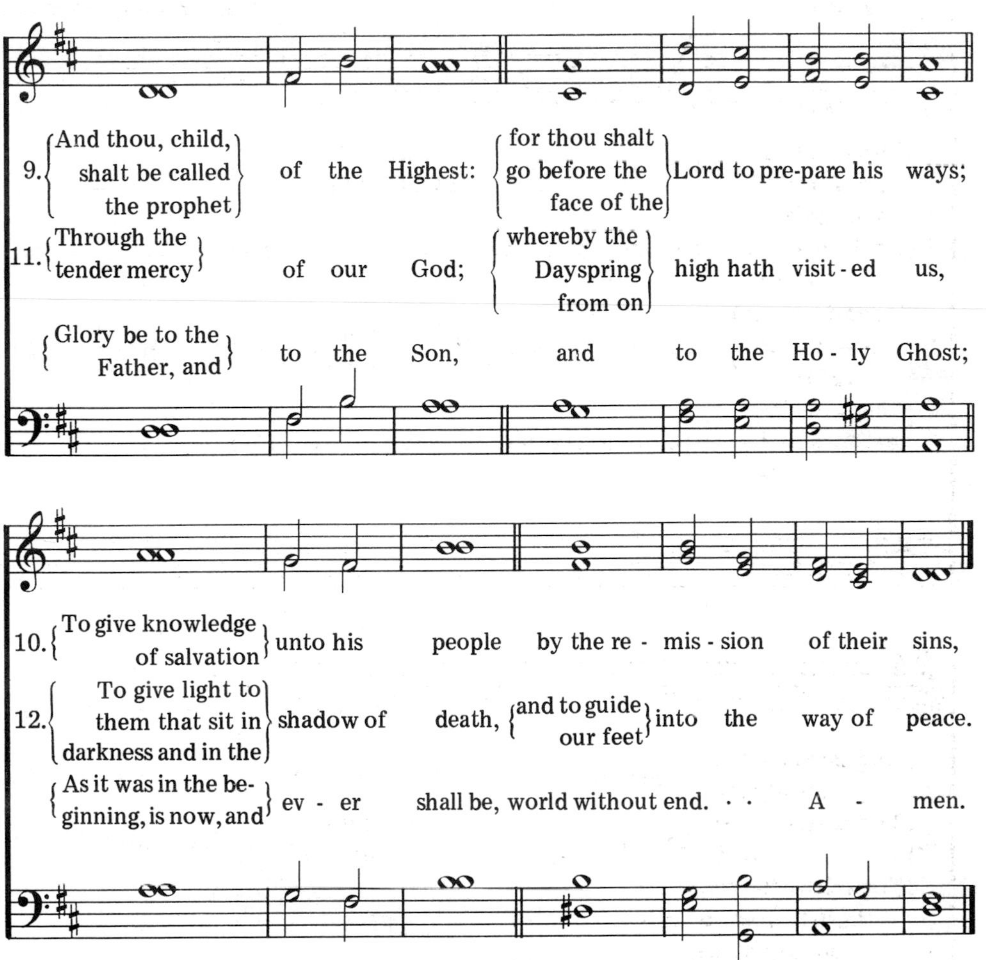
9. And thou, child, shalt be called the prophet of the Highest: for thou shalt go before the face of the Lord to pre-pare his ways;
11. Through the tender mercy of our God; whereby the Dayspring from on high hath visit-ed us,
Glory be to the Father, and to the Son, and to the Ho - ly Ghost;
10. To give knowledge of salvation unto his people by the re - mis - sion of their sins,
12. To give light to them that sit in darkness and in the shadow of death, and to guide our feet into the way of peace.
As it was in the be-ginning, is now, and ev - er shall be, world without end. · · A - men.

373 Blessed Art Thou, O Lord

BENEDICTUS ES, DOMINE

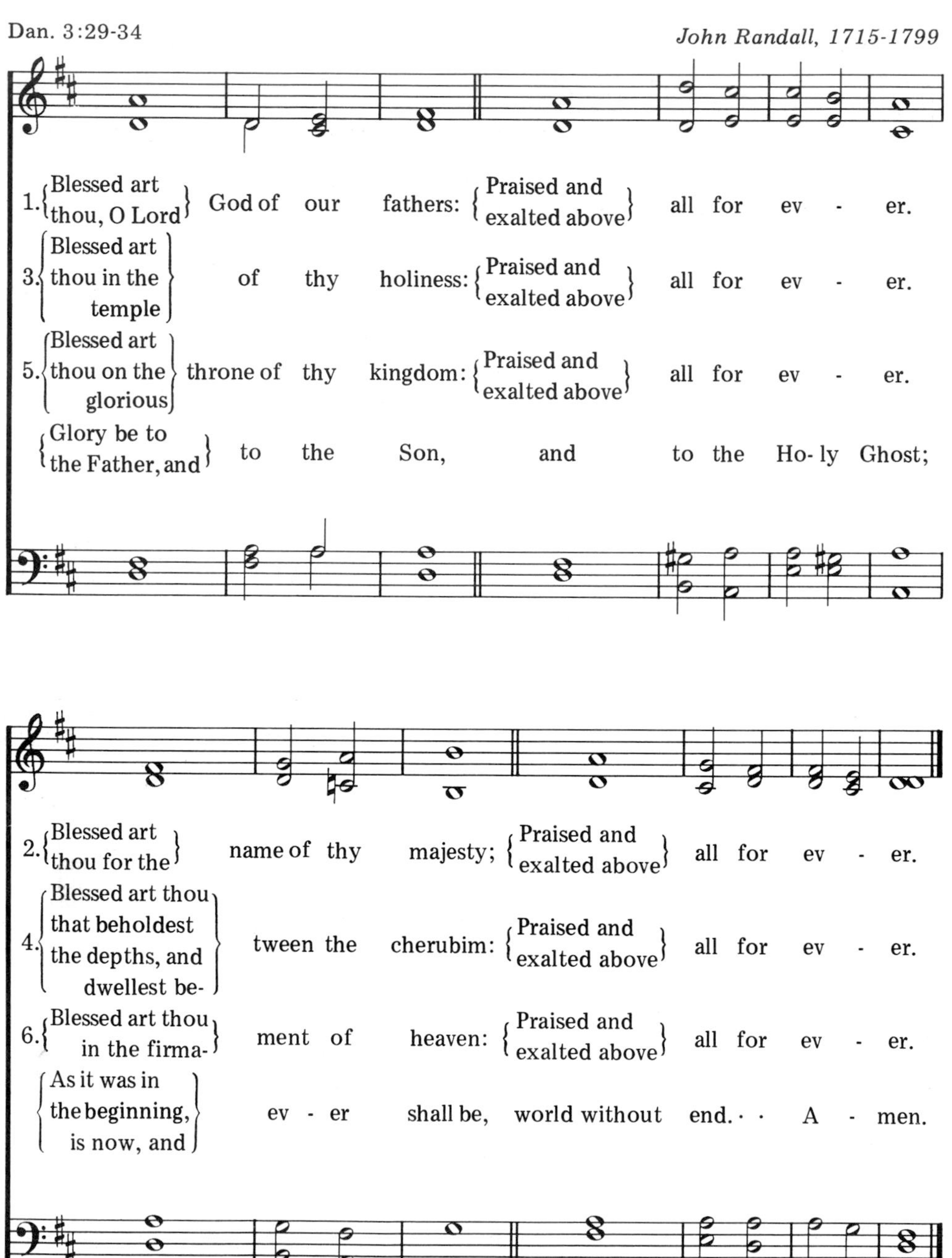
Dan. 3:29-34
John Randall, 1715-1799
1. Blessed art thou, O Lord God of our fathers: Praised and exalted above all for ev - er.
3. Blessed art thou in the temple of thy holiness: Praised and exalted above all for ev - er.
5. Blessed art thou on the glorious throne of thy kingdom: Praised and exalted above all for ev - er.
Glory be to the Father, and to the Son, and to the Ho-ly Ghost;
2. Blessed art thou for the name of thy majesty; Praised and exalted above all for ev - er.
4. Blessed art thou that beholdest the depths, and dwellest be- tween the cherubim: Praised and exalted above all for ev - er.
6. Blessed art thou in the firma- ment of heaven: Praised and exalted above all for ev - er.
As it was in the beginning, is now, and ev - er shall be, world without end. · · A - men.

My Soul Doth Magnify the Lord

MAGNIFICAT

Luke 1:46-55 *John Robinson, 1682-1762*

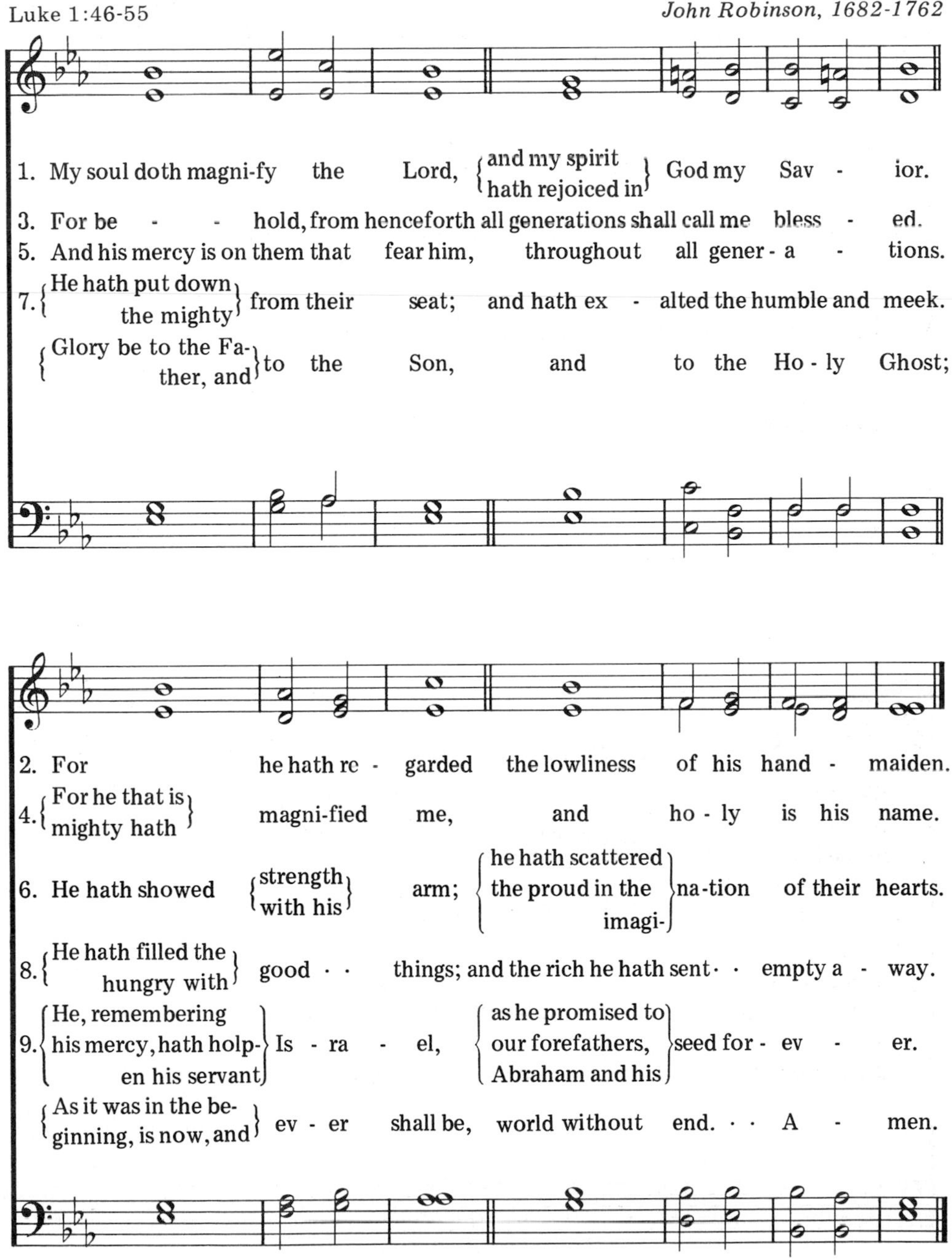
1. My soul doth magni-fy the Lord, and my spirit hath rejoiced in God my Sav - ior.
3. For be - - hold, from henceforth all generations shall call me bless - ed.
5. And his mercy is on them that fear him, throughout all gener - a - tions.
7. He hath put down the mighty from their seat; and hath ex - alted the humble and meek.
Glory be to the Father, and to the Son, and to the Ho - ly Ghost;
2. For he hath re - garded the lowliness of his hand - maiden.
4. For he that is mighty hath magni-fied me, and ho - ly is his name.
6. He hath showed strength with his arm; he hath scattered the proud in the imagi- na-tion of their hearts.
8. He hath filled the hungry with good · · things; and the rich he hath sent · · empty a - way.
9. He, remembering his mercy, hath holpen his servant Is - ra - el, as he promised to our forefathers, Abraham and his seed for - ev - er.
As it was in the beginning, is now, and ev - er shall be, world without end. · · A - men.

See No. 306 which is a paraphrase of this Canticle.

375 Lord, Now Lettest Thou Thy Servant Depart

NUNC DIMITTIS

Luke 2:29-32

Joseph Barnby, 1838-1896

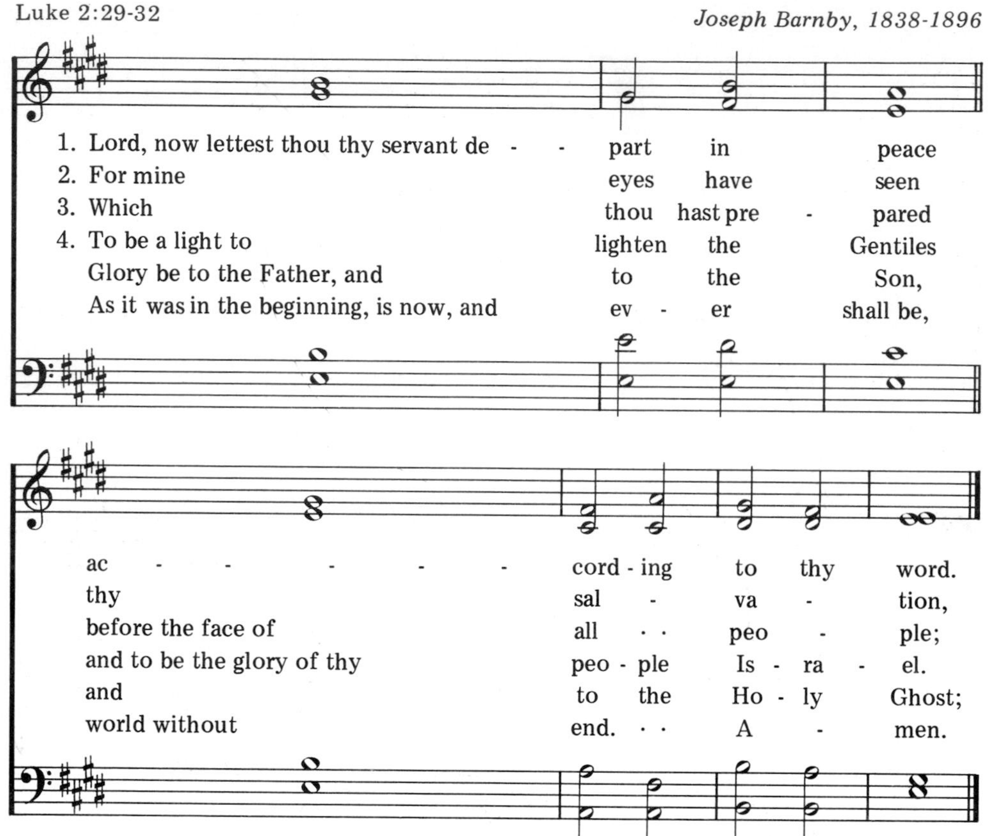

See additional versions of the Nunc Dimittis at Nos. 321 and 328.

Out of the Depths

DE PROFUNDIS

Ps. 130

J. F. Petri, 1831

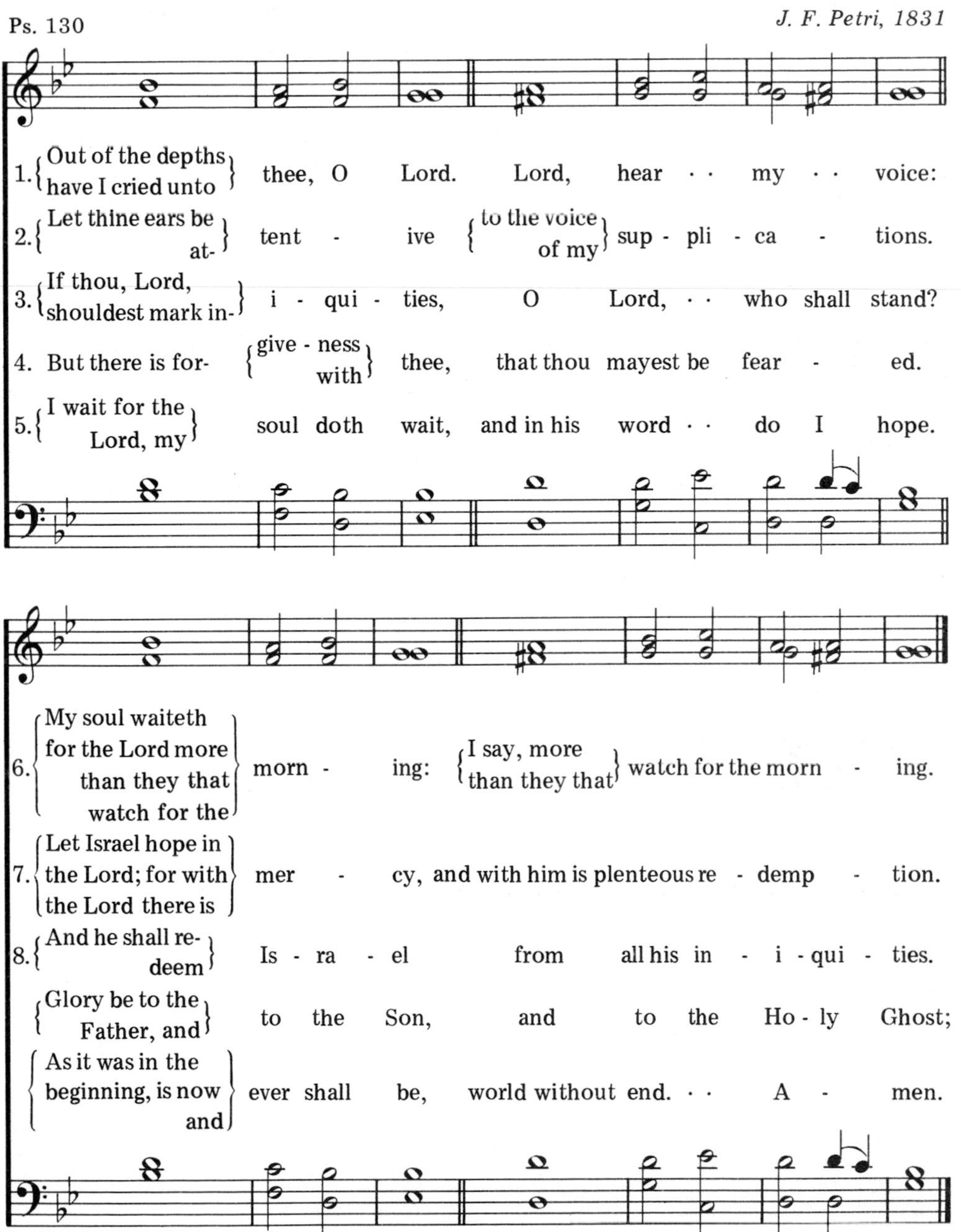

377 Have Mercy upon Me, O God

MISERERE MEI DEUS

Ps. 51 — *Richard Langdon, 1774*

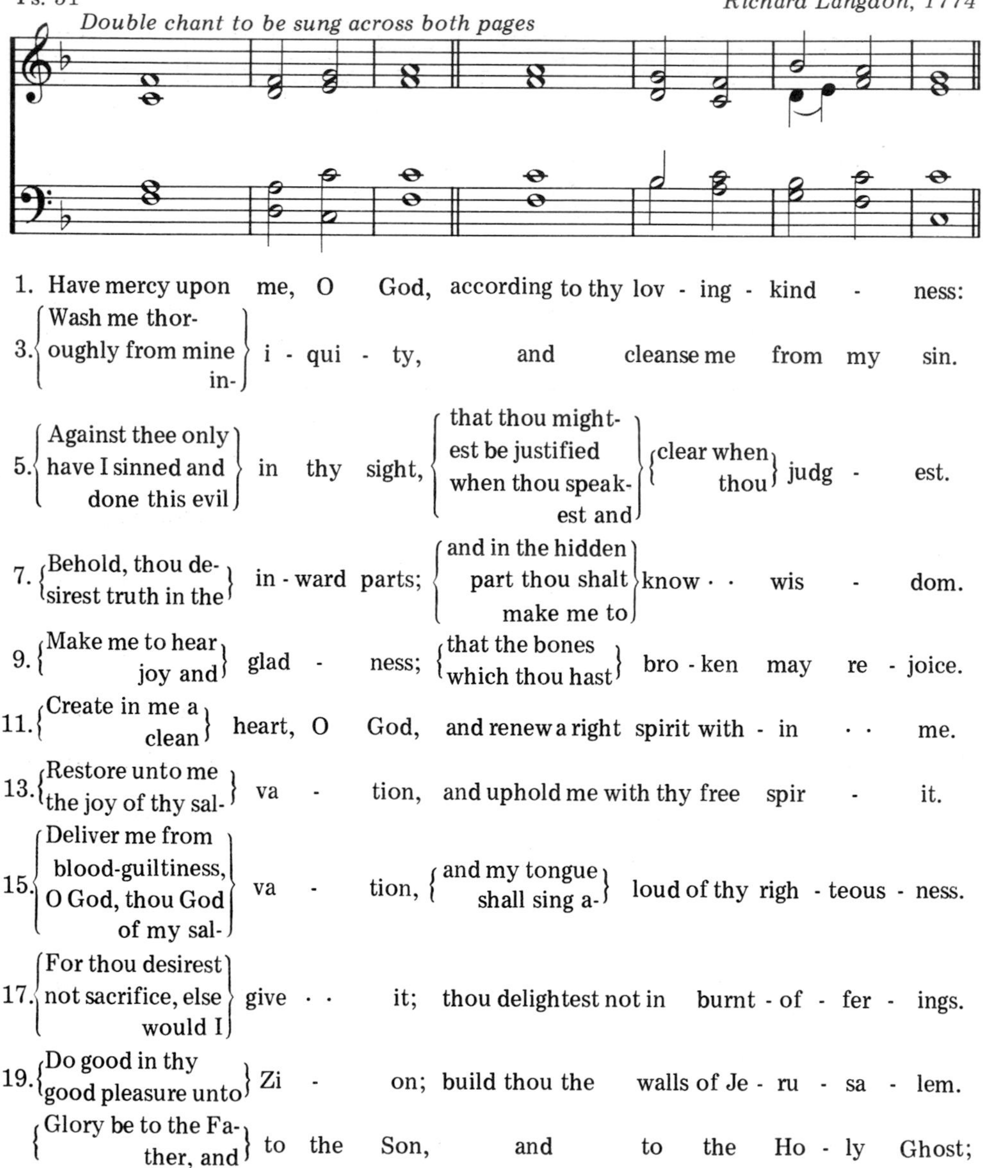
Double chant to be sung across both pages
1. Have mercy upon me, O God, according to thy lov - ing - kind - ness:
3. Wash me thoroughly from mine in- i - qui - ty, and cleanse me from my sin.
5. Against thee only have I sinned and done this evil in thy sight, that thou mightest be justified when thou speakest and clear when thou judg - est.
7. Behold, thou desirest truth in the in - ward parts; and in the hidden part thou shalt make me to know · · wis - dom.
9. Make me to hear joy and glad - ness; that the bones which thou hast bro - ken may re - joice.
11. Create in me a clean heart, O God, and renew a right spirit with - in · · me.
13. Restore unto me the joy of thy sal- va - tion, and uphold me with thy free spir - it.
15. Deliver me from blood-guiltiness, O God, thou God of my sal- va - tion, and my tongue shall sing a- loud of thy righ - teous - ness.
17. For thou desirest not sacrifice, else would I give · · it; thou delightest not in burnt - of - fer - ings.
19. Do good in thy good pleasure unto Zi - on; build thou the walls of Je - ru - sa - lem.
Glory be to the Father, and to the Son, and to the Ho - ly Ghost;

2. According to the multitude of thy tender mer - cies, blot out my trans - gres - sions.

4. For I acknowledge my trans- gres - sions and my sin is ever be - fore · · me.

6. Behold, I was shapen in in- i - qui - ty, and in sin did my mother con - ceive · · me.

8. Purge me with hyssop and I shall be clean; wash me and I shall be whiter than snow.

10. Hide thy face from my sin; and blot out all mine in - i - qui - ty.

12. Cast me not away from thy pre - sence, and take not thy Ho - ly Spirit from me.

14. Then will I teach trans- gressors thy ways, And sinners shall be con- vert - ed un - to thee.

16. O Lord, open thou my lips, and my mouth shall show forth thy praise.

18. The sacrifices of God are a broken spir - it; a broken and a contrite heart, O God, thou wilt not des - pise.

20. Then shalt thou be pleased with the sacrifice of righteousness, with burnt-offering and whole burnt- of - fer - ing; then shall they offer bullocks up- on thine al - tar.

As it was in the beginning, is now, and ever shall be, world without end. · · A - men.

378

Vincent Persichetti, 1956

379

Vincent Persichetti, 1956

380

Orlando Gibbons, 1583-1625

381

William Smith, ?-1645

382

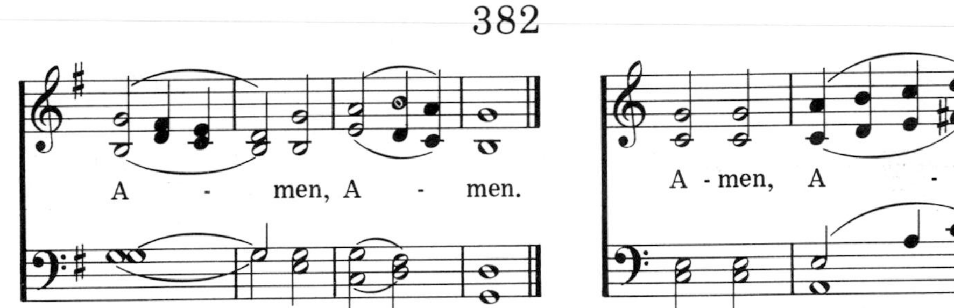

383

384

John Ferguson, 1968

385

386

Preface to the Readings and Litanies

The biblical readings that follow have been selected and arranged for use in contemporary corporate worship. Verbs and pronouns common in everyday language are used when appropriate. In a few instances of well-known passages, traditional language has been preserved. A primary objective has been to provide effective instruments for worship.

A variety of arrangements of the biblical readings is intended to encourage some experimentation, not for the sake of variety or novelty, but to bring new dimensions of participation, insight, and understanding. Variety and change increase interest and intensify experiential perception. Responsive readings, for example, may be used in several ways. Traditionally, they have moved between the minister and the congregation; but they can be used antiphonally with one half of the congregation responding to the other half; or men and women may read responsively; or a speaking choir and congregation may read antiphonally. In these and other ways the biblical readings are enhanced by a choral style that lifts the spirit of the worshiper.

Since so much in creative and innovative worship is being done, and worship resources are numerous and accessible, only a minimum of litanies is provided here. Many congregations and pastors find the writing of prayers and litanies to be a meaningful part of the church's total life of worship. A few examples are offered here.

An ecumenical lectionary, prepared by scholars from several traditions and used widely in Presbyterian, Episcopal, and Roman Catholic churches, is included to assist pastors and people in a systematic use of the scriptures.

Readings

387

Fear the Lord and serve him perfectly and sincerely; put away the gods that your ancestors served, . . . and serve the Lord. But if you will not serve the Lord, choose today whom you wish to serve. . . . As for me and my House, we will serve the Lord.

We have no intention of deserting the Lord and serving other gods!

You cannot serve the Lord, because he is a holy God, he is a jealous God. . . .

No; it is the Lord we wish to serve.

You are witnesses against yourselves that you have chosen the Lord, to serve him.

We are witnesses.

Then cast away the alien gods among you and give your hearts to the Lord the God of Israel!

It is the Lord our God we choose to serve; it is his voice that we will obey.

—Joshua 24:14–16, 19, 21–24, JB
(*See No. 252.*)

388

Lord, our Lord, how great your name throughout the earth!

I look up at your heavens, made by your fingers, at the moon and stars you set in place . . .

What is man that you should spare a thought for him, the son of man that you should care for him?

Yet you have made him little less than a god, you have crowned him with glory and splendor,

Made him lord over the work of your hands, set all things under his feet,

Sheep and oxen, all these, yes, wild animals too,

Birds in the air, fish in the sea traveling the paths of the ocean.

Lord, our Lord, how great your name throughout the earth!

—Psalm 8:1, 3–9, JB
(*See Nos. 35, 40.*)

389

I How clearly the sky reveals God's glory!

II **How plainly it shows what he has done!**

I Each day announces it to the following day;

II **Each night repeats it to the next.**

I No speech or words are used,

II **No sound is heard;**

Unison **Yet their voice goes out to all the world, their message reaches the ends of the earth.**

I God set up a tent in the sky for the sun;

II **It comes out like a bridegroom striding from his house, like an athlete, eager to run a race.**

I It starts at one end of the sky and goes around to the other.

II **Nothing can hide from its heat.**

Unison **Glory be to the Father, and to the Son, and to the Holy Ghost. As it was in the beginning, is now and ever shall be, world without end. Amen.**

—Psalm 19:1–6, TEV
(*See Nos. 36, 312.*)

The congregation may speak or sing the Gloria Patri or respond with a hymn of praise.

390

The law of the Lord is perfect;
It gives new life.
The commands of the Lord are trustworthy,
Giving wisdom to those who lack it.
The rules of the Lord are right,
And those who obey them are happy.
His commandments are completely just
And give understanding to the mind.
The worship of the Lord is good;
It will continue forever.
The judgments of the Lord are just,
They are always fair.
They are more desirable than gold,
Even the finest gold.
They are sweeter than honey,
Even the purest honey.
They give knowledge to me, your servant;
I am rewarded for obeying them.
No one can see his own errors;
Deliver me from hidden faults!
Keep me safe, also, from open sins;
Don't let them rule over me.
Then I shall be perfect
And free from terrible sin.

Unison **May my words and my thoughts be acceptable to you, O Lord, my refuge and my redeemer!**

—Psalm 19:7–14, TEV
(*See Nos. 344, 347.*)

391

I O God, why have you left me? Why are you so far from me?
II **I can no longer feel you near. I reach desperately for you, but I cannot find you.**
I I know you are holy and all-righteous and everywhere present.
II **The saints of past years believed in you and trusted you. You responded to their cries.**
I They sought for you and they found you.
II **It is no wonder that your praises were constantly on their lips.**

Solo 1 *But I feel as empty and insignificant as a bag full of wind.*

Solo 2 ***Even my friends fail to support me and they actually turn against me.***

Solo 1 *I believe that you were with me from the very beginning of my life.*

Solo 2 ***I know that you have cared for me through these many years.***

Unison **But, God, I need you now.**

I I am in trouble, and I can't find you or feel you to be near.

II **O God, I feel in this moment as if I am falling apart. Nothing seems to make sense anymore.**

I Everything I attempt to do ends in failure. I feel inferior and weak.

II **Those I have tried to serve are actually gloating over my flops and failures.**

Unison **I know, O God, that much of it is a matter of my foolish feelings.**

I The fact is, you are not far off. You know both my feelings and my failings. Yet you love me and accept me. You will save me—even from myself.

II **Thus I will continue to sing your praises.**

I Your love is personal, and it is eternal.

II **Your sons and your servants are precious to you.**

I Even when they fail you, you will never fail them.

II **You hear their cries and feel their pain and are ever ready to support them in their conflicts.**

Unison **I dedicate myself anew to you, O Lord. I will serve you whatever the cost or the consequence. You are my God.**

—Psalm 22, BRANDT

392

Unison **The Lord is my shepherd; I have everything I need. He lets me rest in fields of green grass and leads me to quiet pools of fresh water. He gives me new strength. He guides me in the right way, as he has promised. Even if that way goes through deepest darkness, I will not be afraid, Lord, because you are with me! Your shepherd's rod and staff keep me safe.**

You prepare a banquet for me, where all my enemies can see me; you welcome me by pouring ointment on my head and filling my cup to the brim. Certainly your goodness and love will be with me as long as I live; and your house will be my home forever.

—Psalm 23, TEV

(*See Nos. 271, 278–279.*)

393

Unison **The Lord is my shepherd; I shall not want. He maketh me to lie down in green pastures: he leadeth me beside the still waters. He restoreth my soul: he leadeth me in the paths of righteousness for his name's sake. Yea, though I walk through the valley of the shadow of death, I will fear no evil: for thou art with me; thy rod and thy staff they comfort me. Thou preparest a table before me in the presence of mine enemies: thou anointest my head with oil; my cup runneth over. Surely goodness and mercy shall follow me all the days of my life: and I will dwell in the house of the Lord for ever.**

—Psalm 23, KJV

394

Unison **My shepherd is the God of creation; there is nothing I lack. He lets me lie down in high pastures; he guides me to the water of peace. He opens my life in liberty to walk in the ways of justice. Although I go through death valley I am not afraid of wickedness; for you are walking beside me, the way of my leader guides me. You set a table before me in the face of all my oppressors; my brow is bright with the olive, my cup is filled overflowing. Joy and gentleness follow me all the days of my life; I make my home in God's keeping until the end of all days.**

—Psalm 23, *The Covenant of Peace: A Liberation Prayer Book*

395

The Lord is my light and my salvation;
I will fear no one.
The Lord protects me from all danger;
I will not be afraid.
Unison **When evil men attack me and try to kill me, they stumble and fall.**
Even if a whole army surrounds me,
I will not be afraid;
Even if my enemies attack me,
I will still trust God.
I have asked the Lord for one thing;
One thing only do I want;

To live in the Lord's house all my life,
To marvel at his goodness, and to ask his guidance there.
In times of trouble he will protect me in his shelter;
He will keep me safe in his temple, and place me securely on a high rock.
So I will triumph over my enemies around me.
Unison **With shouts of joy I will offer sacrifices in his temple; I will sing, I will praise the Lord!**

—Psalm 27:1–6, TEV
(*See No. 295.*)

396

Hear me, Lord, when I call to you!
Be merciful and answer me!
"Come to me," you said.
I will come to you, Lord; don't hide yourself from me!
Don't be angry with me;
Don't turn your servant away.
You have been my help;
Don't leave me, don't abandon me, God, my Savior!
My father and mother may abandon me,
But the Lord will take care of me.
Teach me, Lord, what you want me to do and lead me along a safe path, because I have many enemies.
Do not abandon me to my enemies, who attack me with lies and threats.
Certainly I will live to see the Lord's goodness to his people.
Trust in the Lord!
Have faith, don't despair.
Unison **Trust in the Lord!**

—Psalm 27:7–14, TEV

397

Unison **I feel at times as if I could never cease praising God. Come and rejoice with me over his goodness!**
I I reached out for him out of my inner conflicts, and he was there to give me inner strength and courage.
II **I wept in utter frustration over my troubles, and he was near to help and support me.**
I What he has done for me he can do for you.

II **Turn to him; he will not turn away from you.**

Unison **His loving presence encompasses those who yield to him.**

I He is with them even in the midst of their troubles and conflicts.

II **He meets their emptiness with his abundance and shores up their weakness with his divine power.**

I Listen to me; I know whereof I speak. I have learned through experience that this is the way to happiness.

II **God is ever alert to the cries of his children; he feels and bears with them their pains and problems.**

I He is very near to those who suffer

II **And reaches out to help those who are battered down with despair.**

Unison **Even the children of God must experience affliction, but they have a loving God who will keep them and watch over them. The godless suffers in loneliness and without hope; the servant of God finds meaning and purpose even in the midst of his suffering and conflict.**

—Psalm 34, BRANDT

398

As a deer longs for a stream of cool water, so I long for you, God.

I thirst for you, the living God; when can I go and worship in your presence?

Day and night I cry, and tears are my only food;

All the time my enemies ask me, "Where is your God?"

My heart breaks when I remember the past, when I went with the crowds to the house of God,

And led them as they walked along, a happy crowd, singing and shouting praise to God.

Unison **Why am I so sad? Why am I troubled? I will put my hope in God, and once again I will praise him, my Savior and my God.**

—Psalm 42:1–5, TEV

399

The ocean depths call out to each other, and the waterfalls of God are roaring!

They are like the waves of sorrow with which he floods my soul.

May the Lord show his constant love every day!

May I sing praise to him every night, and pray to God who gives me life.

To God, my defender, I say, "Why have you forgotten me? Why must I go on suffering from the cruelty of my enemies?"

I am crushed by their insults, as they keep on asking me "Where is your God?"

Unison **Why am I so sad? Why am I troubled? I will put my hope in God, and once again I will praise him, my Savior and my God.**

—Psalm 42:7–11, TEV

400

Send your light and your truth;

May they lead me and bring me back to Zion, your sacred hill, and to your temple, where you live!

Then I will go to your altar, God, because you give me joy and happiness;

I will play my harp and sing praise to you, God, my God!

Unison **Why am I so sad? Why am I troubled? I will put my hope in God, and once again I will praise him, my Savior and my God.**

—Psalm 43:3–5, TEV

401

God is our refuge and strength,

A very present help in trouble.

Therefore we will not fear though the earth should change,

Though the mountains shake in the heart of the sea;

Though its waters roar and foam,

Though the mountains tremble with its tumult.

There is a river whose streams make glad the city of God,

The holy habitation of the Most High.

God is in the midst of her, she shall not be moved;

God will help her right early.

The nations rage, the kingdoms totter;

He utters his voice, the earth melts.

The Lord of hosts is with us;

The God of Jacob is our refuge.

Come, behold the works of the Lord,

How he has wrought desolations in the earth.

He makes wars cease to the end of the earth;

He breaks the bow, and shatters the spear, he burns the chariots with fire!

"Be still, and know that I am God.

I am exalted among the nations, I am exalted in the earth!"
The Lord of hosts is with us;
The God of Jacob is our refuge.

—Psalm 46, RSV
(*See Nos. 262–264.*)

402

Be merciful to me, God, because of your constant love; wipe away my sins, because of your great mercy!
Wash away my evil, and make me clean from my sin! . . .
Create a pure heart in me, God, and put a new and loyal spirit in me.
Do not banish me from your presence; do not take your holy spirit away from me.
Give me again the joy that comes from your salvation, and make my spirit obedient.
Then I will teach sinners your commands, and they will turn back to you.
Spare my life, God my Savior, and I will gladly proclaim your righteousness.
Help me to speak, Lord, and I will praise you.
You do not want sacrifices, or I would offer them;
You are not pleased with burnt offerings.
My sacrifice is a submissive spirit, God;
A submissive and obedient heart you will not reject.

—Psalm 51:1–2, 10–19, TEV
(*See Nos. 305, 377.*)

403

God, be merciful to us and bless us;
Look on us with kindness, that the whole world may know your will; that all nations may know your salvation.
Unison **May the peoples praise you, God; may all peoples praise you!**
May the nations be glad and sing for joy,
Because you judge the peoples with justice and guide all the nations.
Unison **May the peoples praise you, God; may all peoples praise you!**
The land has produced its harvest;
God, our God, has blessed us.
Unison **God has blessed us; may all people everywhere honor him.**

—Psalm 67, TEV
(*See Nos. 42–43, 198.*)

404

How I love your temple, Almighty God! How I want to be there!

I long for the courts of the Lord's temple. With my whole being I sing with joy to the living God.

Even the sparrows have built a nest, and the swallows have their own home; they keep their young near your altars.

Lord Almighty, my king and my God, how happy are those who live in your temple, always singing praise to you!

How happy are those whose strength comes from you, who are eager to make the pilgrimage to Mount Zion.

As they pass through the dry valley it becomes a place of springs; the early rain fills it with pools.

They grow stronger as they go; they will see the God of gods on Zion!

One day in your temple is better than a thousand anywhere else;

I would rather stand at the gate of the house of my God than live in the homes of the wicked.

The Lord is our protector and glorious king, blessing us with kindness and honor.

He does not refuse any good thing to those who do what is right.

Happy are those who trust in you, Almighty God!

—Psalm 84, TEV

405

Lord, you have always been our home.

Before the hills were created, before you brought the world into being, you are eternally God, without beginning or end.

You tell men to return to what they were: you change them back to soil.

A thousand years to you are like one day; they are like yesterday, already gone, like a short hour in the night.

You carry men away like a flood; they last no longer than a dream.

They are like weeds that sprout in the morning, that grow and burst into bloom, then dry up and die in the evening.

We are destroyed by your anger; we are terrified by your fury.

You place our sins before you, our secret sins where you can see them.

Our lifetime is cut short by your anger;
Our life comes to an end like a whisper.
Seventy years is all we have—
Eighty years, if we are strong;
Yet all they bring us is worry and trouble;
Life is soon over, and we are gone.
Who really knows the full power of your anger? Who knows what fear your fury can bring?
Teach us how short our life is, so that we may become wise....

Unison **Fill us each morning with your constant love, that we may sing and be glad all our life.**

—Psalm 90:1–12, 14, TEV
(*See Nos. 9, 165.*)

406

God, you have been a home for us from one age of man to another.
Before the mountains were pushed up, or the planet gave birth to the continents, from before time and until after time, you are the Power of Being.
You turn man back into dust, and then say, "Rise up, children of Adam."
For a thousand years in your eyes are as yesterday or a night watch. You sweep them away with your floods. They are remembered as a dream.
They are grass that springs up in the morning; in the evening it withers and dries
For we came to an end by your outrage, we draw back at your indignation. You have set our complicity before you, our crimes in the blaze of your features.
All the days fade away at your sentence; our years pass at the snap of your finger.
Our days are seventy years, or eighty in our farthest strength; their breadth is labor and trouble, soon it is gone and we are blown away.

Unison **Make us learn so to count our days that we bring our hearts to wisdom.**

—Psalm 90, *The Covenant of Peace: A Liberation Prayer Book*

407

O come, let us sing to the Lord;
Let us make a joyful noise to the rock of our salvation!
Let us come into his presence with thanksgiving;
Let us make a joyful noise to him with songs of praise!
For the Lord is a great God,
And a great King above all gods.
In his hand are the depths of the earth;
The heights of the mountains are his also.
The sea is his, for he made it;
For his hands formed the dry land.
O come, let us worship and bow down,
Let us kneel before the Lord, our Maker!
Unison **For he is our God, and we are the people of his pasture, and the sheep of his hand.**

—Psalm 95:1–7, RSV
(*See No. 370.*)

408

O sing to the Lord a new song; sing to the Lord, all the earth!
Sing to the Lord, bless his name; tell of his salvation from day to day.
Declare his glory among the nations, his marvelous works among all the peoples!
For great is the Lord, and greatly to be praised; he is to be feared above all gods.
For all the gods of the peoples are idols; but the Lord made the heavens.
Honor and majesty are before him; strength and beauty are in his sanctuary.
Ascribe to the Lord, O families of the peoples, ascribe to the Lord glory and strength!
Ascribe to the Lord the glory due his name; bring an offering, and come into his courts!
Worship the Lord in holy array; tremble before him, all the earth!
Say among the nations, "The Lord reigns! Yea, the world is established, it shall never be moved; he will judge the peoples with equity."
Let the heavens be glad, and let the earth rejoice; let the sea roar, and all that fills it; let the field exult, and everything in it!
Then shall all the trees of the wood sing for joy before the Lord, for he comes, for he comes to judge the earth. He will judge the world with righteousness, and the peoples with his truth.

—Psalm 96, RSV
(*See No. 24.*)

409

Sing a new song to the Lord; he has done wonderful things!
By his own power and holy strength, he has won the victory.
The Lord announced his victory;
He made his saving power known to the nations.
He kept his promise to the people of Israel, with constant love and loyalty for them.
All people everywhere have seen the victory of our God!
Sing for joy to the Lord, all the earth;
Praise him with songs and shouts of joy!
Sing praises to the Lord with harps; play music on the harps!
With trumpets and horns, shout for joy before the Lord, the king!
Roar, sea, and all creatures in you;
Sing, earth, and all who live there!
Clap your hands, oceans;
Hills, sing together with joy before the Lord, because he comes to rule the earth!

Unison **He will rule all peoples of the world with justice and fairness.**

—Psalm 98, TEV

(*See No. 313.*)

410

Unison **Men have proclaimed God's praises throughout the ages. Now it is our turn to worship the Lord and to announce God's presence and his loving concern for the inhabitants of this world. His power is as great today as it ever was. He continues to reign over his universe and the creatures that move in this world. He alone is the true God. He offers to all men his salvation. He is close to his sons and servants and fills the hearts of his children with joy. Now, as his sons and servants, let us express this joy. With voice and musical instruments, with lovely melodies and joyful sounds, let us proclaim the glory of God. Let us fill our homes and sanctuaries, our halls of learning, our factories and marketplaces, even the streets of our city with sounds of celebration. God is here; God is now!**

—Psalm 98, BRANDT

411

I	Make a joyful noise to the Lord, all the lands!
II	**Serve the Lord with gladness!**
III	***Come into his presence with singing!***
I	Know that the Lord is God!
II	**It is he that made us, and we are his;**
III	***We are his people and the sheep of his pasture.***
I	Enter his gates with thanksgiving, and his courts with praise!
II	**Give thanks to him,**
III	***Bless his name!***
Unison	**For the Lord is good; his steadfast love endures for ever, and his faithfulness to all generations.**

—Psalm 100, RSV

(*See Nos. 2, 37–38, 371.*)

412

Bless the Lord, O my soul; and all that is within me, bless his holy name!

Bless the Lord, O my soul, and forget not all his benefits,

Who forgives all your iniquity, who heals all your diseases,

Who redeems your life from the Pit, who crowns you with steadfast love and mercy,

Who satisfies you with good as long as you live so that your youth is renewed like the eagle's.

The Lord works vindication and justice for all who are oppressed.

He made known his ways to Moses, his acts to the people of Israel.

The Lord is merciful and gracious, slow to anger and abounding in steadfast love.

He will not always chide, nor will he keep his anger for ever.

He does not deal with us according to our sins, nor requite us according to our iniquities.

For as the heavens are high above the earth, so great is his steadfast love toward those who fear him;

As far as the east is from the west, so far does he remove our transgressions from us.

As a father pities his children, so the Lord pities those who fear him.

For he knows our frame; he remembers that we are dust.

As for man, his days are like grass; he flourishes like a flower of the field;

For the wind passes over it, and it is gone, and its place knows it no more.

But the steadfast love of the Lord is from everlasting to everlasting upon those who fear him, and his righteousness to children's children,

To those who keep his covenant and remember to do his commandments.

The Lord has established his throne in the heavens, and his kingdom rules over all.

Bless the Lord, O you his angels, you mighty ones who do his word, hearkening to the voice of his word!

Bless the Lord, all his hosts, his ministers that do his will!

Bless the Lord, all his works, in all places of his dominion. Bless the Lord, O my soul.

—Psalm 103, RSV

(*See Nos. 7, 23, 25, 196.*)

413

My heart is bursting with praises to God;

Every fiber of my being reaches out in rejoicing!

How can I ever forget his many blessings?

He forgives all my sins;

He touches my afflictions with healing;

He snatches me back from the gaping jaws of hell;

He covers me with concern and love;

He fulfills my deepest desires and gives me meaning for life and purpose for living.

God is a God of justice and judgment,

But he is on the side of those who need his help.

He is angry with those who persistently rebel against him,

But he pours out his love upon those who turn to him.

He does not give us our just deserts

Or pay us what we well deserve.

He is grieved when we so miserably fail,

But he quickly draws us to his forgiving heart

And accepts us just as if it never happened.

He looks with tenderness upon his faltering children;

He knows and understands our fallible natures.

Man by himself is a pitiful picture of weakness.

Now and then one will, like a streaking meteor, blaze out across the skies of time,

Only to become a smoking cinder at the end of his short journey.

But those who tie on to God's loving will and purposes

Become the objects of his eternal mercy and righteousness.

Rejoice with me, you who are his invisible servants

And you who hear and obey his voice.

Shout his praises, you who are his children.

And you who serve as his ministers and priests.
There is no time for despair and discouragement.
Whoever and wherever you are, lift your hearts in praises to God.

—Psalm 103, BRANDT

414

Unison **I will lift up mine eyes unto the hills, from whence cometh my help. My help cometh from the Lord, which made heaven and earth. He will not suffer thy foot to be moved: he that keepeth thee will not slumber. Behold, he that keepeth Israel shall neither slumber nor sleep. The Lord is thy keeper: the Lord is thy shade upon thy right hand. The sun shall not smite thee by day, nor the moon by night. The Lord shall preserve thee from all evil: he shall preserve thy soul. The Lord shall preserve thy going out and thy coming in from this time forth, and even for evermore.**

—Psalm 121, KJV
(*See Nos. 293–294.*)

415

I Where should I look for help in my need?

II **To the majestic mountain peaks that probe our skies or the giants of industry that hem in our cities?**

III ***To the satellites that circle our world or the computers that store up our knowledge?***

Unison **The answer to my problems, the fulfillment of my needs must come from God himself, from him who created the skies and the mountains and man to dwell in their midst.**

I He is a great God who knows our every desire, whose watchful eye is upon us night and day.

II **We can make no move without his knowledge.**

III ***His concern for his children is constant; his love for them is eternal.***

I And thus the Lord will keep you, shielding you from the forces of evil as a shade tree shields you from the rays of the blazing sun.

I & II **He does care for you, and he will fight with you against the enemies of your soul.**

Unison **Whether you be coming or going, he knows the course you take; and he will go before you.**

—Psalm 121, BRANDT

416

In my despair I call to you, Lord.
Hear my cry, Lord, listen to my call for help!
If you kept a record of our sins, who could escape being condemned?
But you forgive us, so that we should fear you.
I wait eagerly for the Lord's help, and in his word I trust.
I wait for the Lord, more eagerly than watchmen wait for the dawn, than watchmen wait for the dawn.
Israel, trust in the Lord, because his love is constant, and he is always willing to save.
He will save his people Israel from all their sins.

—Psalm 130, TEV
(*See No. 376.*)

417

Minister (or leader) O Lord, you have searched me and known me!
I **You know when I sit down and when I rise up;**
II ***You discern my thoughts from afar.***
I **You search out my path and my lying down,**
II ***And are acquainted with all my ways.***
I **Even before a word is on my tongue,**
II ***Lo, O Lord, you know it altogether.***
I **You beset me behind and before,**
II ***And lay your hand upon me.***
I **Such knowledge is too wonderful for me;**
II ***It is high, I cannot attain it.***
Minister Whither shall I go from your Spirit?
I **Or whither shall I flee from your presence?**
Minister If I ascend to heaven, you are there!
I **If I make my bed in Hell, you are there!**
Minister If I take the wings of the morning and dwell in the uttermost parts of the sea,
II ***Even there your hand shall lead me, and your right hand shall hold me.***
Minister If I say, "Let only darkness cover me, and the light about me be night,"
II ***Even the darkness is not dark to you, the night is bright as the day;***
Unison **For darkness is as light with you.**

II *How precious to me are your thoughts, O God!*

I **How vast is the sum of them!**

II ***If I would count them, they are more than the sand.***

I **Were I to come to the end I would still be with you.**

Unison **Search me, O God, and know my heart! Try me and know my thoughts! And see if there be any wicked way in me, and lead me in the way everlasting!**

—Psalm 139:1–12, 17, RSV

(*See No. 284.*)

418

I will proclaim your greatness, my God and king; I will thank you forever and ever. Every day I will thank you; I will praise you forever and ever.

The Lord is great and must be highly praised; his greatness is beyond understanding.

What you have done will be praised from one generation to the next; they will proclaim your mighty acts.

Men will speak of your glory and majesty, and I will meditate on your wonderful deeds.

Men will speak of your mighty acts, and I will proclaim your greatness.

They will tell about all your goodness, and sing about your kindness.

The Lord is loving and merciful, slow to become angry and full of constant love.

He is good to everyone and has compassion on all he made.

All your creatures, Lord, will praise you,

And your people will give you thanks!

They will speak of the glory of your kingdom, and tell of your might,

So that all men will know your mighty acts, and the glorious majesty of your kingdom.

Your kingdom is eternal,

And you are king forever.

The Lord is faithful to his promises, and good in all he does.

He helps all who are in trouble; he raises all who are humbled.

All living things look hopefully to him and he gives them food when they need it.

He gives them enough and satisfies the needs of all.

The Lord is righteous in all he does,

Merciful in all his acts.
He is near to all who call to him,
Who call to him with sincerity.
He supplies the needs of all who fear him;
He hears their cry and saves them.
He protects all who love him,
But he will destroy all the wicked.

Unison **I will always praise the Lord; let all creatures praise his holy name forever!**

—Psalm 145, TEV

419

Praise God!
As long as I have breath in my body, I will praise God!
Don't pin your hopes on the genius of man. His ultimate end is the same as yours.
And he becomes once more like the dust from which he came.
That person is secure who draws his strength from God.
He who created the earth and all that abides on it, he is that One who can heal the wounds and mend the fractures of this disjointed world.
He can break the bonds of obsession and pierce man's stupor with visions of truth.
He tenderly reaches out to those who are oppressed and reveals his concern for those who are lost and lonely.
He watches over his own while the paths of the godless lead to their own destruction.
This is the God who cannot die!
Praise God!
Amen.

—Psalm 146, BRANDT

420

Praise the Lord!
It is good to sing praise to our God; it is pleasant and right to praise him.
The Lord is restoring Jerusalem; he is bringing back the exiles.
He heals the brokenhearted, and bandages their wounds.
He has determined the number of the stars and calls each one by name.
Great and almighty is our Lord; his knowledge cannot be measured.

He raises the humble, but crushes the wicked to the ground.

Sing hymns of praise to the Lord; play music to our God on the harp.

He spreads clouds over the sky; he provides rain for the earth, and makes grass to grow on the hills.

He gives animals their food, and feeds the young ravens when they call.

His pleasure is not in strong horses, nor his delight in brave soldiers;

But he takes pleasure in those who fear him, in those who trust in his constant love.

Unison **Praise the Lord, Jerusalem! Praise your God, Zion!**

—Psalm 147:1–12, TEV

(*See No. 156.*)

421

Alleluia!

Alleluia!

Let heaven praise the Lord:

Praise him, heavenly heights,

Praise him, all his angels,

Praise him, all his armies!

Praise him, sun and moon,

Praise him, shining stars,

Praise him, highest heavens,

And waters above the heavens!

Let them all praise the name of the Lord, at whose command they were created;

He has fixed them in their place for ever, by an unalterable statute.

Let earth praise the Lord: sea-monsters and all the deeps,

Fire and hail, snow and mist, gales that obey his decree,

Mountains and hills, orchards and forests,

Wild animals and farm animals, snakes and birds,

All kings on earth and nations, princes, all rulers in the world,

Young men and girls, old people, and children too!

Let them all praise the name of the Lord, for his name and no other is sublime,

Transcending earth and heaven in majesty,

Raising the fortunes of his people,

To the praises of the devout, of Israel, the people dear to him.

—Psalm 148, JB

(*See Nos. 8, 22, 30.*)

422

Unison **Praise the Lord!**
Praise God in his temple!
Praise his strength in heaven!
Praise him for the mighty things he has done!
Praise his supreme greatness!
Praise him with trumpets!
Praise him with harps and lyres!
Praise him with drums and dancing!
Praise him with harps and flutes!
Praise him with cymbals!
Praise him with loud cymbals!
Praise the Lord, all living creatures!
Praise the Lord!

—Psalm 150, TEV
(*See Nos. 25–26, 358.*)

423

Do you not know,
Have you not heard?
The Lord, the everlasting God, creator of the wide world, grows neither weary nor faint;
No man can fathom his understanding.
He gives vigour to the weary,
New strength to the exhausted.
Young men may grow weary and faint,
Even in their prime they may stumble and fall;
But those who look to the Lord will win new strength,
They will grow wings like eagles;
They will run and not be weary,
They will march on and never grow faint.

—Isaiah 40:28–31, NEB

424

Who could have believed what we have heard,
And to whom has the power of the Lord been revealed?
He grew up before the Lord like a young plant whose roots are in parched ground;
He had no beauty, no majesty to draw our eyes, no grace to make us delight in him;

His form, disfigured, lost all the likeness of a man, his beauty changed beyond human semblance.

He was despised, he shrank from the sight of men, tormented and humbled by suffering;

Unison **We despised him, we held him of no account, a thing from which men turn away their eyes.**

Yet on himself he bore our sufferings,

Our torments he endured, while we counted him smitten by God, struck down by disease and misery;

But he was pierced for our transgressions,

Tortured for our iniquities;

The chastisement he bore is health for us

And by his scourging we are healed.

We had all strayed like sheep,

Each of us had gone his own way;

Unison **But the Lord laid upon him the guilt of us all.**

—Isaiah 53:1–7, NEB

(*See Nos. 127–128.*)

425

Seek the Lord while he may be found, call upon him while he is near;

Let the wicked forsake his way, and the unrighteous man his thoughts;

Let him return to the Lord, that he may have mercy on him.

And to our God, for he will abundantly pardon.

For my thoughts are not your thoughts,

Neither are your ways my ways, says the Lord.

For as the heavens are higher than the earth,

So are my ways higher than your ways and my thoughts than your thoughts.

For as the rain and the snow come down from heaven, and return not thither but water the earth,

Making it bring forth and sprout, giving seed to the sower and bread to the eater,

So shall my word be that goes forth from my mouth; it shall not return to me empty,

But it shall accomplish that which I purpose, and prosper in the thing for which I sent it.

—Isaiah 55:6–11, RSV

(*See No. 57.*)

426

The Lord's true love is surely not spent, nor has his compassion failed;

They are new every morning, so great is his constancy.

The Lord, I say, is all that I have; therefore I will wait for him patiently.

The Lord is good to those who look for him, to all who seek him; . . .

The Lord will not cast off his servants for ever.

He may punish cruelly, yet he will have compassion in the fullness of his love;

Unison **He does not willingly afflict or punish any mortal man. To trample underfoot any prisoner in the land, to deprive a man of his rights in defiance of the Most High, to pervert justice in the courts—**

Such things the Lord has never approved.

Let us examine our ways and put them to the test and turn back to the Lord;

Unison **Let us lift up our hearts, not our hands, to God in heaven.**

—Lamentations 3:22–25, 31–36, 40–41, NEB

(*See No. 240.*)

427

Blessed are the poor in spirit,

For theirs is the kingdom of heaven.

Blessed are those who mourn,

For they shall be comforted.

Blessed are the meek,

For they shall inherit the earth.

Blessed are those who hunger and thirst for righteousness,

For they shall be satisfied.

Blessed are the merciful,

For they shall obtain mercy.

Blessed are the pure in heart,

For they shall see God.

Blessed are the peacemakers,

For they shall be called sons of God.

Blessed are those who are persecuted for righteousness' sake,

For theirs is the kingdom of heaven.

Blessed are you when men revile you and persecute you and utter all kinds of evil against you falsely on my account.

Rejoice and be glad, for your reward is great in heaven, for so men persecuted the prophets who were before you.

—Matthew 5:3–12, RSV

428

How happy are the humble-minded,
For they already own the kingdom of heaven!
How happy are those who know what sorrow means,
For they will be given courage and comfort!
Happy are those who claim nothing,
For the whole earth will belong to them!
Happy are those who are hungry and thirsty for goodness,
For they will be fully satisfied!
Happy are the kind-hearted,
For they will have kindness shown to them!
Happy are the pure in heart,
For they will see God!
Happy are those who make peace,
For they will be known as sons of God!
Happy are those who have suffered persecution for the cause of goodness,
For the kingdom of heaven belongs to them!
And what happiness will be yours when people blame you and say all kinds of slanderous things against you for my sake!
Be glad then, yes, be tremendously glad—for your reward in heaven is magnificent. They persecuted the prophets before your time in exactly the same way.

—Matthew 5:3–12, PHILLIPS

429

I In the beginning was the Word:
II **The Word was with God**
III ***And the Word was God.***
I He was with God in the beginning.
II **Through him all things came to be,**
III ***Not one thing had its being but through him.***
I All that came to be had life in him
II **And that life was the light of men,**
III ***A light that shines in the dark,***

Unison **A light that darkness could not overpower.**

I A man came, sent by God. His name was John.

II **He came as a witness,**

III ***As a witness to speak for the light,***

I So that everyone might believe through him.

II **He was not the light,**

III ***Only a witness to speak for the light.***

I The Word was the true light that enlightens all men; and he was coming into the world.

II **He was in the world that had its being through him, and the world did not know him.**

III ***He came to his own domain and his own people did not accept him.***

Unison **But to all who did accept him he gave power to become children of God,**

I To all who believe in the name of him who was born not out of human stock

II **Or urge of the flesh**

III ***Or will of man***

Unison **But of God himself.**

I The Word was made flesh,

II **He lived among us,**

III ***And we saw his glory,***

Unison **The glory that is his as the only Son of the Father, full of grace and truth.**

—John 1:1–14, JB

(*See Nos. 14, 72, 116, 143, 197.*)

430

I consider that what we suffer at this present time cannot be compared at all with the glory that is going to be revealed to us.

All of creation waits with eager longing for God to reveal his sons.

Faced with all this, what can we say?

If God is for us, who can be against us?

He did not even keep back his own Son, but offered him for us all!

He gave us his Son . . . will he not also freely give us all things?

Who, then, can separate us from the love of Christ?

Can trouble do it, or hardship, or persecution?

Or hunger, or poverty, or danger, or death?

No, in all these things we have complete victory through him who loved us!

I am certain that nothing can separate us from his love: neither death nor life;

Neither angels nor other heavenly rulers or powers;

Neither the present nor the future;

Neither the world above nor the world below.

Unison **There is nothing in all creation that will ever be able to separate us from the love of God which is ours through Christ Jesus our Lord.**

—Romans 8:18–19, 31–32, 35, 37–39, TEV

(*See No. 54.*)

431

In my opinion whatever we may have to go through now is less than nothing compared with the magnificent future God has planned for us.

The whole creation is on tiptoe to see the wonderful sight of the sons of God coming into their own. . . .

If God is for us, who can be against us?

He that did not hesitate to spare his own Son but gave him up for us all—can we not trust such a God to give us, with him, everything else that we can need? . . .

Can anything separate us from the love of Christ? Can trouble, pain or persecution?

Can lack of clothes and food, danger to life and limb, the threat of force of arms? . . .

No, in all these things we win an overwhelming victory through him who has proved his love for us.

Unison **I have become absolutely convinced that neither death nor life, neither messenger of heaven nor monarch of earth, neither what happens today nor what may happen tomorrow, neither a power from on high nor a power from below, nor anything else in God's whole world has any power to separate us from the love of God in Jesus Christ our Lord!**

—Romans 8:18–19, 31–32, 35, 37–39, PHILLIPS

432

Leader With eyes wide open to the mercies of God, I beg you, my brothers, as an act of intelligent worship, to give him your bodies, as a living sacrifice, consecrated to him and acceptable by him. Don't let the world around you squeeze you into its own mold, but let God remold your minds from within, so that you may prove in practice that the plan of God for you is good, meets all his demands and moves toward the goal of true maturity.

I **Let us have no imitation Christian love.**

II ***Let us have a genuine break with evil and a real devotion to good.***

I **Let us have real warm affection for one another as between brothers, and a willingness to let the other man have the credit.**

II ***Let us not allow slackness to spoil our work and let us keep the fires of the spirit burning, as we do our work for the Lord.***

Leader Base your happiness on your hope in Christ.

I **When trials come endure them patiently: steadfastly maintain the habit of prayer.**

II ***Give freely to fellow Christians in want, never grudging a meal or a bed to those who need them.***

Leader And as for those who try to make your life a misery, bless them. Don't curse, bless.

I **Share the happiness of those who are happy, and the sorrow of those who are sad.**

II ***Live in harmony with one another.***

I **Don't become snobbish but take a real interest in ordinary people.**

II ***Don't become set in your own opinions.***

I **Don't pay back a bad turn by a bad turn, to anyone.**

II ***See that your public behavior is above criticism.***

I **As far as your responsibility goes, live at peace with everyone.**

Leader Never take vengeance into your own hands, my dear friends: stand back and let God punish if he will. . . .

Unison **Don't allow yourself to be overpowered with evil. Take the offensive—overpower evil by good!**

—Romans 12:1–2, 9–19, 21, PHILLIPS

433

I If I speak in the tongues of men and of angels, but have not love, I am a noisy gong or a clanging cymbal.

II **And if I have prophetic powers, and understand all mysteries and all knowledge, and if I have all faith, so as to remove mountains, but have not love, I am nothing.**

III ***If I give away all I have, and if I deliver my body to be burned, but have not love, I gain nothing.***

I Love is patient and kind;

II **Love is not jealous or boastful;**

III ***It is not arrogant or rude.***

I Love does not insist on its own way;

II **It is not irritable or resentful;**

III ***It does not rejoice at wrong, but rejoices in the right.***

Unison **Love bears all things, believes all things, hopes all things, endures all things.**

I Love never ends;

II **As for prophecy, it will pass away;**

III ***As for tongues, they will cease;***

II & III **As for knowledge, it will pass away.**

I For our knowledge is imperfect and our prophecy is imperfect;

II & III **But when the perfect comes, the imperfect will pass away.**

I When I was a child, I spoke like a child, I thought like a child, I reasoned like a child;

II & III **When I became a man, I gave up childish ways.**

I For now we see in a mirror dimly, but then face to face.

II & III **Now I know in part; then I shall understand fully, even as I have been fully understood.**

Unison **So faith, hope, love abide, these three; but the greatest of these is love.**

—1 Corinthians 13, RSV

434

Leader Your attitude must be that of Christ:

I **Though he was in the form of God, he did not deem equality with God something to be grasped at.**

II ***Rather, he emptied himself and took the form of a slave, being born in the likeness of men.***

I **He was known to be of human estate,**

II ***And it was thus that he humbled himself, obediently accepting even death,***

Unison **Death on a cross!**
Leader Because of this, God highly exalted him and bestowed on him the name above every name, so that at Jesus' name every knee must bend in the heavens
I **On the earth**
II ***And under the earth***
Leader And every tongue proclaim to the glory of God the Father:
Unison **Jesus Christ is Lord!**

—Philippians 2:5–11, *New American Bible*
(*See Nos. 69–70, 310–311.*)

435

I **Then I saw a new heaven and a new earth;**
II ***For the first heaven and the first earth had passed away, . . .***
I **And I saw the holy city, new Jerusalem, coming . . . out of heaven from God,**
II ***Prepared as a bride adorned for her husband;***
Minister And I heard a loud voice from the throne saying,
Unison **"Behold, the dwelling of God is with men.**
Minister He will dwell with them,
I **And they shall be his people,**
II ***And God himself will be with them;***
Minister He will wipe away every tear from their eyes,
I **And death shall be no more,**
II ***Neither shall there be mourning nor crying nor pain any more,***
Unison **For the former things have passed away."**
Minister And he who sat upon the throne said,
Unison **"Behold, I make all things new. . . . I am the Alpha and the Omega, the beginning and the end.**
I **To the thirsty I will give water without price from the fountain of the water of life.**
II ***He who conquers shall have this heritage, and I will be his God and he shall be my son." . . .***
Minister Then he showed me the river of the water of life,
I **Bright as crystal,**
II ***Flowing from the throne of God and of the Lamb. . . .***
Minister And night shall be no more;
I **They need no light of lamp or sun,**
II ***For the Lord God will be their light,***
Unison **And they shall reign for ever and ever.**

—Revelation 21:1–7; 22:1, 5, RSV
(*See Nos. 188–189, 304.*)

436

A LITANY OF THANKSGIVING

Almighty God, from whom comes each good gift of life, we remember your loving-kindness and your uncounted mercies and we join in grateful praise.

For all your gifts to us and to our human race; for our life and the world in which we live,
We give you thanks, O God.
For the order and constancy of nature; for the beauty and bounty of the world; for day and night, summer and winter, seed-time and harvest; for the varied joys which every season brings,
We give you thanks, O God.
For the work we are enabled to do, and the truth we are permitted to discover; for whatever of good there has been in our past lives, and for all the hopes which lead us on toward better things,
We give you thanks, O God.
For all the joys and comforts of life; for homes and families; for our friends; for the love, sympathy, and good will of persons near and far,
We give you thanks, O God.
For all civilization, wise government and laws which order our common life; for education and all the treasures of literature, science, and art,
We give you thanks, O God.
For prophets, pioneers, and all earnest seekers after a dream; for all lovers and helpers of humankind; for the aid and counsel of those who are wiser than ourselves,
We give you thanks, O God.
For all the discipline of life; for the tasks and trials which train us to know ourselves and which bring us to accept one another,
We give you thanks, O God.
For the desire and power to help others; for every opportunity of serving our generation in ways large or small,
We give you thanks, O God.
For all true knowledge of you and the world in which we live; for the life of truth and right to which you have called us,
We give you thanks, O God.

For the gift of Jesus Christ, and everything which is ours as his disciples; for the presence and inspiration of your Holy Spirit throughout our day,

We give you thanks, O God.

For the tender ties which bind us to the unseen world; for the faith which dispels the shadows of earth and fills the closing years of life with the light of hope.

We give you thanks, O God.

Unison **God of all grace and love, we have praised you with our lips for all the richness and meaning that life holds for us. Now send us into the world to praise you with our lives; through Jesus Christ our Lord. Amen.**

437

A LITANY FOR THOSE WHO SERVE

O God, who has made us a royal priesthood, that we might offer to you prayer and intercession for all sorts and conditions of people, hear us as we pray.

For all who toil in the burden and heat of the day, that they may enjoy the rewards of their industry, that they may not be defrauded of their due, and that we may never cease to be mindful of our debt to them;

We ask your grace and pledge our concern, O God.

For those who have authority and power over others, that they may not use it for selfish advantage, but be guided to do justice and to love mercy;

We ask your grace and pledge our concern, O God.

For rulers of the nations, that they may act wisely and without pride, may seek to promote peace among the peoples and establish justice in our common life;

We ask your grace and pledge our concern, O God.

For teachers and ministers of the word, for artists and interpreters of our spiritual life, that they may rightly divide the word of truth, and not be tempted by pride or greed or any ignoble passion to corrupt the truth to which they are committed;

We ask your grace and pledge our concern, O God.

For prophets and seers and saints, who awaken us from our sloth, that they may continue to hold their torches high in a world darkened by prejudice and sin, and ever be obedient to the heavenly vision;

We ask your grace and pledge our concern, O God.

Unison **O Lord, who has bound us together in this bundle of life, give us grace to understand how our lives depend upon the courage, the industry, the honesty and integrity of others; that we may be mindful of their needs, grateful for their faithfulness, and faithful in our responsibilities to them; through Jesus Christ, our Lord. Amen.**

—Harry Emerson Fosdick

438

A LITANY OF INTERCESSION

Almighty God, our heavenly Father, who loves all and forgets none, we bring to you our prayers for all your children.

For all whom we love, and for whom we watch and care;
Hear us, O God.
For all prisoners and captives, and all who suffer from oppression, that you will manifest your mercy toward them, and make all hearts as merciful as your own;
Hear us, O God.
For all who bear the cross of suffering, the sick in body or mind;
Hear us, O God.
For all those who are troubled by the sin or suffering of those they love;
Hear us, O God.
For all who are absorbed in their own grief, that they may be raised to share the sorrows of others, and know the secret and blessed fellowship of the cross;
Hear us, O God.
For all perplexed by the deeper questions of life and overshadowed with doubt, that light may arise in their darkness;
Hear us, O God.
For all who are tried by passionate temptations or mean suggestions, that your mercy may be their salvation;
Hear us, O God.
For all who are lonely and sad in the midst of others' joy, that they may know you as their friend and comforter;
Hear us, O God.
For the infirm and aged and for all who are passing through the valley of death, that they may find their strength in you and light at evening time;
Hear us, O God.
For all forgotten by us, but dear to you;

Hear us, O God.

Unison **O compassionate God, have regard to our intercessions, answer them according to your will, and make us channels of your infinite grace; through Jesus Christ, our Lord. Amen.**

439

A LITANY OF CONFESSION

Let us confess to God our sins as members of this congregation.

For coming into your presence with unclean lips and impure hearts;
Forgive us, we pray.
For bringing jealousies and resentments into our life as a congregation;
Forgive us, we pray.
For wasting time we have set aside for your service;
Forgive us, we pray.
For accepting help from others without giving, and for offering help to others in the hope of receiving;
Forgive us, we pray.
For praising you here more fervently than in our daily living;
Forgive us, we pray.
For every unChristlike attitude that corrupts our worship and weakens our witness;
Forgive us, we pray.
Accept us and use us in your service, we ask you in Christ's name. **Amen.**

440

A LITANY FOR THE HUMAN FAMILY

O God, the Father of us all, we offer our prayers for the human family: We pray for those who have given up praying for themselves, because experience has made them cynical or wary of asking; for those who dislike what they have become but will not turn to you for forgiveness; and for those who have made an uneasy truce with conscience.
Lord, hear our prayer and strengthen us that we may strengthen others.
We pray for those who are weakened by selfishness and poisoned by resentment, for those who see everyone's hand against them, and for those who are intent on spoiling the peace of others.
Lord, hear our prayer and make us instruments of your judgment.

We pray for the disgruntled, the weak-minded, those who bury their gifts, the sick who have taken refuge in invalidism, and the bereaved who have lost the power of making new friends.

Lord, hear our prayer and make us instruments of renewal.

We pray for those who refuse to be discouraged by failure, for those who live in the midst of negative thought, pessimism, and hopelessness yet remain undaunted.

Lord, hear our prayer and enable us to join their ranks.

Finally, we pray for ourselves, that in the name and power of Christ we may bring healing to the sick, hope to the defeated, and confidence to the disheartened.

Unison **Lord, hear our prayer and make us children of your love; through Jesus Christ, our Lord. Amen.**

441

A LITANY OF REMEMBRANCE AND COMMITMENT

Eternal God, you have given us knowledge of yourself through your Son; help us by faith to join the company of his disciples and to learn from him personally.

Help us to do so, O Lord.

We remember with thankfulness our Lord's love of life, his identity with ordinary people, his joy in companionship, and his appreciation of the beauty and grandeur of this world.

Increase our joy, O Lord.

We remember how he used his freedom to do your will regardless of the consequences; how he chose the way of sacrificial love rather than the way of personal convenience and moral compromise.

Increase our love, O Lord.

We remember how his faithfulness led him from Galilee to Jerusalem, and from Jerusalem to the cross, where he died for us.

Increase our loyalty, O Lord.

We remember that you did not forsake your Son on the cross, nor leave him in the tomb, but raised him in the victory of the resurrection.

Increase our faith, O Lord.

Our time is one of despair and expectation: despair because of our inability to save ourselves, of expectation because of our hope that you will make us a loyal and courageous people.

Increase our hope, O Lord.

Redeem our times and guide us into the way of truth and peace.

Increase our desire to serve you, O Lord.

You are our God and we are your people, therefore help us to be faithful to you at all times.

And to your name be glory and praise evermore. Amen.

442

A LITANY FOR UNITY AND PEACE

O God, our Father, who showed forth your love by sending your only-begotten Son into the world that all might live through him: pour your Spirit upon your church that it may fulfill his command to preach the gospel to every creature;

Hear us, O God.

Look upon the sickness of the world and stretch forth your hand to heal. Make your church one and fill it with your Spirit, that it may be the instrument of your reconciling power among the nations, and that all people may be drawn to you and to one another by the bands of your love;

For this we pray.

Give your peace, your help, and your love to us your servants, that we may be united in the bond of peace and love, in one body and one Spirit, in one hope of our calling;

Make us one in the unity of your Holy Spirit.

We pray for all those who are seeking for the nations of the world a way whereby order and freedom may be maintained and the differences of peoples be justly resolved. Establish their purpose on sure foundations, and prosper their work by your Holy Spirit;

Help us to follow the Prince of Peace.

Out of the darkness of our divided world we cry to you, O God. Let not the hopes of people perish, nor their sacrifice be vain. Turn to yourself the hearts of rulers and peoples, that a new world may arise where all live as your children; through Jesus Christ our Lord.

Hear us, O God. Amen.

443

A LITANY OF DELIVERANCE

Almighty God, who delivered your ancient people from slavery and in the fullness of time sent your Son Jesus Christ to rescue the people from their sins, hear us as we pray for deliverance from our bondage and lead us forth into the glorious liberty of your children.

Hear our prayer, O Lord, and let our cry come to you.

Deliver us from habits that enslave, from willing bondage to the flesh, from contentment with mediocrity, and from our reluctance to enter your kingdom.

Hear our prayer, O Lord, and lead us into the land of promise.

Deliver us from fragmentary living, from divided aims and rival loyalties, and from failure to seek and achieve wholeness in thought, word, and deed.

Teach us to remember the words of Jesus, "Seek first the kingdom of God and all else shall be added to you."

Deliver us from counterfeit humility, from the modesty that calls attention to itself, from the arrogance which creates the world in our own image, and will not bow to the authority of truth as it meets us in Jesus Christ.

Hear our prayer, O Lord, and save us from ourselves.

Deliver us from religious selfishness, from the piety that is centered upon safety rather than service, from seeking peace of mind instead of reconciliation with you and with all people.

Teach us to remember the words of Jesus, "Whoever loses his life for my sake shall find it."

Deliver us from being sorry for ourselves and not for our sins, for esteeming reputation above character and the show of righteousness above the reality of it.

O God, create in us a clean heart, and renew a right spirit within us.

Deliver us, above all, from substituting religion for Christ, from taking refuge in systems and ceremonies that bring us comfort and security rather than encountering his disturbing presence.

Unison **Restore to us the joy of your salvation, and uphold us with a willing spirit. Amen.**

Lectionary for the Christian Year

This lectionary provides readings for a cycle of three years. The designations A, B, and C are used for the first, second, and third years. Each Christian year in the three-year cycle begins, of course, at Advent of one year and continues to the Lord's Day just before the beginning of Advent in the next year.

Because other Christian churches are using this lectionary, congregations may wish to follow the cycle in the same pattern as the others. The general practice is such that those years whose last two digits are divisible by three are years in which the lessons designated B are employed, beginning at Advent. This arithmetical rule is usable from 1969 to 1999. For example: the year 1981 has as its last two digits 81. They are divisible by 3, with the result being 27, and no fraction. Thus a congregation using the lectionary, and wanting to read the scriptures concurrently with its neighbors, would begin to use the readings for year B at Advent 1981 and would conclude year B just before Advent 1982. Year C would immediately follow and would be followed by Year A.

444

Advent

A four-week period in which the church joyfully remembers the coming of Christ and eagerly looks forward to his coming again. Beginning with the Sunday nearest November 30, the season is observed for the four Sundays prior to Christmas.

Sunday or Festival	*Year*	*First Lesson*	*Second Lesson*	*Gospel*
1st Sunday in Advent	A	Isa. 2:1–5	Rom. 13:11–14	Matt. 24:36–44
	B	Isa. 63:16 to 64:4	1 Cor. 1:3–9	Mark 13:32–37
	C	Jer. 33:14–16	1 Thess. 5:1–6	Luke 21:25–36
2d Sunday in Advent	A	Isa. 11:1–10	Rom. 15:4–9	Matt. 3:1–12
	B	Isa. 40:1–5, 9–11	2 Peter 3:8–14	Mark 1:1–8
	C	Isa. 9:2, 6–7	Phil. 1:3–11	Luke 3:1–6
3d Sunday in Advent	A	Isa. 35:1–6, 10	James 5:7–10	Matt. 11:2–11
	B	Isa. 61:1–4, 8–11	1 Thess. 5:16–24	John 1:6–8, 19–28
	C	Zeph. 3:14–18	Phil. 4:4–9	Luke 3:10–18
4th Sunday in Advent	A	Isa. 7:10–15	Rom. 1:1–7	Matt. 1:18–25
	B	2 Sam. 7:8–16	Rom. 16:25–27	Luke 1:26–38
	C	Micah 5:1–4	Heb. 10:5–10	Luke 1:39–47

Sunday or Festival	*Year*	*First Lesson*	*Second Lesson*	*Gospel*
Christmas Eve	A	Isa. 62:1–4	Col. 1:15–20	Luke 2:1–14
	B	Isa. 52:7–10	Heb. 1:1–9	John 1:1–14
	C	Zech. 2:10–13	Phil. 4:4–7	Luke 2:15–20

445

Christmastide

The festival of the birth of Christ, the celebration of the incarnation. A twelve-day period from December 25 to January 5, which may include either one or two Sundays after Christmas.

Sunday or Festival	*Year*	*First Lesson*	*Second Lesson*	*Gospel*
Christmas Day	A	Isa. 9:2, 6–7	Titus 2:11–15	Luke 2:1–14
	B	Isa. 62:6–12	Col. 1:15–20	Matt. 1:18–25
	C	Isa. 52:6–10	Eph. 1:3–10	John 1:1–14
1st Sunday	A	Eccl. 3:1–9, 14–17	Col. 3:12–17	Matt. 2:13–15, 19–23
After Christmas	B	Jer. 31:10–13	Heb. 2:10–18	Luke 2:25–35
	C	Isa. 45:18–22	Rom. 11:33 to 12:2	Luke 2:41–52
2d Sunday	A	Prov. 8:22–31	Eph. 1:15–23	John 1:1–5, 9–14
After Christmas	B	Isa. 60:1–5	Rev. 21:22 to 22:2	Luke 2:21–24
	C	Job 28:20–28	1 Cor. 1:18–25	Luke 2:36–40

446

Epiphany

A season marking the revelation of God's gift of himself to all men. Beginning with the day of Epiphany (January 6), this season continues until Ash Wednesday, and can include from four to nine Sundays.

Sunday or Festival	*Year*	*First Lesson*	*Second Lesson*	*Gospel*
Epiphany		Isa. 60:1–6	Eph. 3:1–6	Matt. 2:1–12
1st Sunday After Epiphany	A	Isa. 42:1–7	Acts 10:34–43	Matt. 3:13–17
	B	Isa. 61:1–4	Acts 11:4–18	Mark 1:4–11
	C	Gen. 1:1–5	Eph. 2:11–18	Luke 3:15–17, 21–22
		(or the readings for the day of Epiphany, if observed on Sunday)		

Sunday	*Year*	*First Lesson*	*Second Lesson*	*Gospel*
2d Sunday After Epiphany	A	Isa. 49:3–6	1 Cor. 1:1–9	John 1:29–34
	B	1 Sam. 3:1–10	1 Cor. 6:12–20	John 1:35–42
	C	Isa. 62:2–5	1 Cor. 12:4–11	John 2:1–12
3d Sunday After Epiphany	A	Isa. 9:1–4	1 Cor. 1:10–17	Matt. 4:12–23
	B	Jonah 3:1–5, 10	1 Cor. 7:29–31	Mark 1:14–22
	C	Neh. 8:1–3, 5–6, 8–10	1 Cor. 12:12–30	Luke 4:14–21
4th Sunday After Epiphany	A	Zeph. 2:3; 3:11–13	1 Cor. 1:26–31	Matt. 5:1–12
	B	Deut. 18:15–22	1 Cor. 7:32–35	Mark 1:21–28
	C	Jer. 1:4–10	1 Cor. 13:1–13	Luke 4:22–30
5th Sunday After Epiphany	A	Isa. 58:7–10	1 Cor. 2:1–5	Matt. 5:13–16
	B	Job 7:1–7	1 Cor. 9:16–19, 22–23	Mark 1:29–39
	C	Isa. 6:1–8	1 Cor. 15:1–11	Luke 5:1–11
6th Sunday After Epiphany	A	Deut. 30:15–20	1 Cor. 2:6–10	Matt. 5:27–37
	B	Lev. 13:1–2, 44–46	1 Cor. 10:31 to 11:1	Mark 1:40–45
	C	Jer. 17:5–8	1 Cor. 15:12–20	Luke 6:17–26
7th Sunday After Epiphany	A	Lev. 19:1–2, 17–18	1 Cor. 3:16–23	Matt. 5:38–48
	B	Isa. 43:18–25	2 Cor. 1:18–22	Mark 2:1–12
	C	1 Sam. 26:6–12	1 Cor. 15:42–50	Luke 6:27–36
8th Sunday After Epiphany	A	Isa. 49:14–18	1 Cor. 4:1–5	Matt. 6:24–34
	B	Hos. 2:14–20	2 Cor. 3:17 to 4:2	Mark 2:18–22
	C	Job 23:1–7	1 Cor. 15:54–58	Luke 6:39–45
9th Sunday After Epiphany		Use readings listed for 27th Sunday after Pentecost.		

447

Lent

A period of forty weekdays and six Sundays, beginning on Ash Wednesday and culminating in Holy Week. In joy and sorrow during this season, the church proclaims, remembers, and responds to the atoning death of Christ.

Sunday or Day	*Year*	*First Lesson*	*Second Lesson*	*Gospel*
Ash Wednesday	A	Joel 2:12–18	2 Cor. 5:20 to 6:2	Matt. 6:1–6, 16–18
	B	Isa. 58:3–12	James 1:12–18	Mark 2:15–20
	C	Zech. 7:4–10	1 Cor. 9:19–27	Luke 5:29–35

Sunday or Festival	*Year*	*First Lesson*	*Second Lesson*	*Gospel*
1st Sunday in Lent	A	Gen. 2:7–9; 3:1–7	Rom. 5:12–19	Matt. 4:1–11
	B	Gen. 9:8–15	1 Peter 3:18–22	Mark 1:12–15
	C	Deut. 26:5–11	Rom. 10:8–13	Luke 4:1–13
2d Sunday in Lent	A	Gen. 12:1–7	2 Tim. 1:8–14	Matt. 17:1–9
	B	Gen. 22:1–2, 9–13	Rom. 8:31–39	Mark 9:1–9
	C	Gen. 15:5–12, 17–18	Phil. 3:17 to 4:1	Luke 9:28b–36
3d Sunday in Lent	A	Ex. 24:12–18	Rom. 5:1–5	John 4:5–15, 19–26
	B	Ex. 20:1–3, 7–8, 12–17	1 Cor. 1:22–25	John 2:13–25
	C	Ex. 3:1–8, 13–15	1 Cor. 10:1–12	Luke 13:1–9
4th Sunday in Lent	A	2 Sam. 5:1–5	Eph. 5:8–14	John 9:1–11
	B	2 Chron. 36:14–21	Eph. 2:1–10	John 3:14–21
	C	Josh. 5:9–12	2 Cor. 5:16–21	Luke 15:11–32
5th Sunday in Lent	A	Ezek. 37:11–14	Rom. 8:6–11	John 11:1–4, 17, 34–44
	B	Jer. 31:31–34	Heb. 5:7–10	John 12:20–33
	C	Isa. 43:16–21	Phil. 3:8–14	Luke 22:14–30
Palm (Passion) Sunday	A	Isa. 50:4–7	Phil. 2:5–11	Matt. 21:1–11
	B	Zech. 9:9–12	Heb. 12:1–6	Mark 11:1–11
	C	Isa. 59:14–20	1 Tim. 1:12–17	Luke 19:28–40

448

Holy Week

The week prior to Easter, during which the church gratefully commemorates the passion and death of Jesus Christ.

Day of Holy Week	*Year*	*First Lesson*	*Second Lesson*	*Gospel*
Monday		Isa. 50:4–10	Heb. 9:11–15	Luke 19:41–48
Tuesday		Isa. 42:1–9	1 Tim. 6:11–16	John 12:37–50
Wednesday		Isa. 52:13 to 53:12	Rom. 5:6–11	Luke 22:1–16
Maundy Thursday	A	Ex. 12:1–8, 11–14	1 Cor. 11:23–32	John 13:1–15
	B	Deut. 16:1–8	Rev. 1:4–8	Matt. 26:17–30
	C	Num. 9:1–3, 11–12	1 Cor. 5:6–8	Mark 14:12–26

Day of Holy Week	*Year*	*First Lesson*	*Second Lesson*	*Gospel*
Good Friday	A	Isa. 52:13 to 53:12	Heb. 4:14–16; 5:7–9	John 19:17–30
	B	Lam. 1:7–12	Heb. 10:4–18	Luke 23:33–46
	C	Hos. 6:1–6	Rev. 5:6–14	Matt. 27:31–50

449

Eastertide

A fifty-day period of seven Sundays, beginning with Easter, the festival of Christ's resurrection. Ascension Day, forty days after Easter, is celebrated to affirm that Jesus Christ is Lord of all times and places.

Sunday or Festival	*Year*	*First Lesson*	*Second Lesson*	*Gospel*
Easter	A	Acts 10:34–43	Col. 3:1–11	John 20:1–9
	B	Isa. 25:6–9	1 Peter 1:3–9	Mark 16:1–8
	C	Ex. 15:1–11	1 Cor. 15:20–26	Luke 24:13–35
2d Sunday in Eastertide	A	Acts 2:42–47	1 Peter 1:3–9	John 20:19–31
	B	Acts 4:32–35	1 John 5:1–6	Matt. 28:11–20
	C	Acts 5:12–16	Rev. 1:9–13, 17–19	John 21:1–14
3d Sunday in Eastertide	A	Acts 2:22–28	1 Peter 1:17–21	Luke 24:13–35
	B	Acts 3:13–15, 17–19	1 John 2:1–6	Luke 24:36–49
	C	Acts 5:27–32	Rev. 5:11–14	John 21:15–19
4th Sunday in Eastertide	A	Acts 2:36–41	1 Peter 2:19–25	John 10:1–10
	B	Acts 4:8–12	1 John 3:1–3	John 10:11–18
	C	Acts 13:44–52	Rev. 7:9–17	John 10:22–30
5th Sunday in Eastertide	A	Acts 6:1–7	1 Peter 2:4–10	John 14:1–12
	B	Acts 9:26–31	1 John 3:18–24	John 15:1–8
	C	Acts 14:19–28	Rev. 21:1–5	John 13:31–35
6th Sunday in Eastertide	A	Acts 8:4–8, 14–17	1 Peter 3:13–18	John 14:15–21
	B	Acts 10:34–48	1 John 4:1–7	John 15:9–17
	C	Acts 15:1–2, 22–29	Rev. 21:10–14, 22–23	John 14:23–29
Ascension Day		Acts 1:1–11	Eph. 1:16–23	Luke 24:44–53
7th Sunday in Eastertide	A	Acts 1:12–14	1 Peter 4:12–19	John 17:1–11
	B	Acts 1:15–17, 21–26	1 John 4:11–16	John 17:11–19
	C	Acts 7:55–60	Rev. 22:12–14, 16–17, 20	John 17:20–26
		(or the readings for Ascension Day, if observed on Sunday)		

450 Pentecost

The festival commemorating the gift of the Holy Spirit to the church, and an extended season for reflecting on how God's people live under the guidance of his Spirit. The season extends from the seventh Sunday after Easter to the beginning of Advent.

Sunday	*Year*	*First Lesson*	*Second Lesson*	*Gospel*
Pentecost (Whitsunday)	A	1 Cor. 12:4–13	Acts 2:1–13	John 14:15–26
	B	Joel 2:28–32	Acts 2:1–13	John 16:5–15
	C	Isa. 65:17–25	Acts 2:1–13	John 14:25–31
1st Sunday After Pentecost (Trinity Sunday)	A	Ezek. 37:1–4	2 Cor. 13:5–13	Matt. 28:16–20
	B	Isa. 6:1–8	Rom. 8:12–17	John 3:1–8
	C	Prov. 8:22–31	1 Peter 1:1–9	John 20:19–23
2d Sunday After Pentecost	A	Deut. 11:18–21	Rom. 3:21–28	Matt. 7:21–29
	B	Deut. 5:12–15	2 Cor. 4:6–11	Mark 2:23 to 3:6
	C	1 Kings 8:41–43	Gal. 1:1–10	Luke 7:1–10
3d Sunday After Pentecost	A	Hos. 6:1–6	Rom. 4:13–25	Matt. 9:9–13
	B	Gen. 3:9–15	2 Cor. 4:13 to 5:1	Mark 3:20–35
	C	1 Kings 17:17–24	Gal. 1:11–19	Luke 7:11–17
4th Sunday After Pentecost	A	Ex. 19:2–6	Rom. 5:6–11	Matt. 9:36 to 10:8
	B	Ezek. 17:22–24	2 Cor. 5:6–10	Mark 4:26–34
	C	2 Sam. 12:1–7a	Gal. 2:15–21	Luke 7:36–50
5th Sunday After Pentecost	A	Jer. 20:10–13	Rom. 5:12–15	Matt. 10:26–33
	B	Job 38:1–11	2 Cor. 5:16–21	Mark 4:35–41
	C	Zech. 12:7–10	Gal. 3:23–29	Luke 9:18–24
6th Sunday After Pentecost	A	2 Kings 4:8–16	Rom. 6:1–11	Matt. 10:37–42
	B	Gen. 4:3–10	2 Cor. 8:7–15	Mark 5:21–43
	C	1 Kings 19:15–21	Gal. 5:1, 13–18	Luke 9:51–62
7th Sunday After Pentecost	A	Zech. 9:9–13	Rom. 8:6–11	Matt. 11:25–30
	B	Ezek. 2:1–5	2 Cor. 12:7–10	Mark 6:1–6
	C	Isa. 66:10–14	Gal. 6:11–18	Luke 10:1–9
8th Sunday After Pentecost	A	Isa. 55:10–13	Rom. 8:12–17	Matt. 13:1–17
	B	Amos 7:12–17	Eph. 1:3–10	Mark 6:7–13
	C	Deut. 30:9–14	Col. 1:15–20	Luke 10:25–37
9th Sunday After Pentecost	A	2 Sam. 7:18–22	Rom. 8:18–25	Matt. 13:24–35
	B	Jer. 23:1–6	Eph. 2:11–18	Mark 6:30–34
	C	Gen. 18:1–11	Col. 1:24–28	Luke 10:38–42
10th Sunday After Pentecost	A	1 Kings 3:5–12	Rom. 8:26–30	Matt. 13:44–52
	B	2 Kings 4:42–44	Eph. 4:1–6, 11–16	John 6:1–15
	C	Gen. 18:20–33	Col. 2:8–15	Luke 11:1–13
11th Sunday After Pentecost	A	Isa. 55:1–3	Rom. 8:31–39	Matt. 14:13–21
	B	Ex. 16:2–4, 12–15	Eph. 4:17–24	John 6:24–35
	C	Eccl. 2:18–23	Col. 3:1–11	Luke 12:13–21

Sunday	*Year*	*First Lesson*	*Second Lesson*	*Gospel*
12th Sunday After Pentecost	A	1 Kings 19:9–16	Rom. 9:1–5	Matt. 14:22–33
	B	1 Kings 19:4–8	Eph. 4:30 to 5:2	John 6:41–51
	C	2 Kings 17:33–40	Heb. 11:1–3, 8–12	Luke 12:35–40
13th Sunday After Pentecost	A	Isa. 56:1–7	Rom. 11:13–16, 29–32	Matt. 15:21–28
	B	Prov. 9:1–6	Eph. 5:15–20	John 6:51–59
	C	Jer. 38:1b–13	Heb. 12:1–6	Luke 12:49–53
14th Sunday After Pentecost	A	Isa. 22:19–23	Rom. 11:33–36	Matt. 16:13–20
	B	Josh. 24:14–18	Eph. 5:21–33	John 6:60–69
	C	Isa. 66:18–23	Heb. 12:7–13	Luke 13:22–30
15th Sunday After Pentecost	A	Jer. 20:7–9	Rom. 12:1–7	Matt. 16:21–28
	B	Deut. 4:1–8	James 1:19–25	Mark 7:1–8, 14–15, 21–23
	C	Prov. 22:1–9	Heb. 12:18–24	Luke 14:1, 7–14
16th Sunday After Pentecost	A	Ezek. 33:7–9	Rom. 13:8–10	Matt. 18:15–20
	B	Isa. 35:4–7	James 2:1–5	Mark 7:31–37
	C	Prov. 9:8–12	Philemon 8–17	Luke 14:25–33
17th Sunday After Pentecost	A	Gen. 4:13–16	Rom. 14:5–9	Matt. 18:21–35
	B	Isa. 50:4–9	James 2:14–18	Mark 8:27–35
	C	Ex. 32:7–14	1 Tim. 1:12–17	Luke 15:1–32
18th Sunday After Pentecost	A	Isa. 55:6–11	Phil. 1:21–27	Matt. 20:1–16
	B	Jer. 11:18–20	James 3:13 to 4:3	Mark 9:30–37
	C	Amos 8:4–8	1 Tim. 2:1–8	Luke 16:1–13
19th Sunday After Pentecost	A	Ezek. 18:25–29	Phil. 2:1–11	Matt. 21:28–32
	B	Num. 11:24–30	James 5:1–6	Mark 9:38–48
	C	Amos 6:1, 4–7	1 Tim. 6:11–16	Luke 16:19–31
20th Sunday After Pentecost	A	Isa. 5:1–7	Phil. 4:4–9	Matt. 21:33–43
	B	Gen. 2:18–24	Heb. 2:9–13	Mark 10:2–16
	C	Hab. 1:1–3; 2:1–4	2 Tim. 1:3–12	Luke 17:5–10
21st Sunday After Pentecost	A	Isa. 25:6–9	Phil. 4:12–20	Matt. 22:1–14
	B	Prov. 3:13–18	Heb. 4:12–16	Mark 10:17–27
	C	2 Kings 5:9–17	2 Tim. 2:8–13	Luke 17:11–19
22d Sunday After Pentecost	A	Isa. 45:1–6	1 Thess. 1:1–5	Matt. 22:15–22
	B	Isa. 53:10–12	Heb. 5:1–10	Mark 10:35–45
	C	Ex. 17:8–13	2 Tim. 3:14 to 4:2	Luke 18:1–8
23d Sunday After Pentecost	A	Ex. 22:21–27	1 Thess. 1:2–10	Matt. 22:34–40
	B	Jer. 31:7–9	Heb. 5:1–6	Mark 10:46–52
	C	Deut. 10:16–22	2 Tim. 4:6–8, 16–18	Luke 18:9–14
24th Sunday After Pentecost	A	Mal. 2:1–10	1 Thess. 2:7–13	Matt. 23:1–12
	B	Deut. 6:1–9	Heb. 7:23–28	Mark 12:28–34
	C	Ex. 34:5–9	2 Thess. 1:11 to 2:2	Luke 19:1–10

Sunday	*Year*	*First Lesson*	*Second Lesson*	*Gospel*
25th Sunday After Pentecost	A	S. of Sol. 3:1–5	1 Thess. 4:13–18	Matt. 25:1–13
	B	1 Kings 17:8–16	Heb. 9:24–28	Mark 12:38–44
	C	1 Chron. 29:10–13	2 Thess. 2:16 to 3:5	Luke 20:27–38
26th Sunday After Pentecost	A	Prov. 31:10–13, 19–20, 30–31	1 Thess. 5:1–6	Matt. 25:14–30
	B	Dan. 12:1–4	Heb. 10:11–18	Mark 13:24–32
	C	Mal. 3:16 to 4:2	2 Thess. 3:6–13	Luke 21:5–19
27th Sunday After Pentecost	A	Ezek. 34:11–17	1 Cor. 15:20–28	Matt. 25:31–46
	B	Dan. 7:13–14	Rev. 1:4–8	John 18:33–37
	C	2 Sam. 5:1–4	Col. 1:11–20	Luke 23:35–43
28th Sunday After Pentecost		Use readings listed for 8th Sunday after Epiphany.		

451

Special Days

It is also fitting that congregations celebrate such other days as recall the heritage of the reformed church, proclaim its mission, and forward its work; and such days as recognize the civic responsibilities of the people.

Special Day	*Year*	*First Lesson*	*Second Lesson*	*Gospel*
New Year's Eve or Day	A	Deut. 8:1–10	Rev. 21:1–7	Matt. 25:31–46
	B	Eccl. 3:1–13	Col. 2:1–7	Matt. 9:14–17
	C	Isa. 49:1–10	Eph. 3:1–10	Luke 14:16–24
Christian Unity	A	Isa. 11:1–9	Eph. 4:1–16	John 15:1–8
	B	Isa. 35:3–10	1 Cor. 3:1–11	Matt. 28:16–20
	C	Isa. 55:1–5	Rev. 5:11–14	John 17:1–11
World Communion	A	Isa. 49:18–23	Rev. 3:17–22	John 10:11–18
	B	Isa. 25:6–9	Rev. 7:9–17	Luke 24:13–35
	C	1 Chron. 16:23–34	Acts 2:42–47	Matt. 8:5–13
Reformation Sunday	A	Hab. 2:1–4	Rom. 3:21–28	John 8:31–36
	B	Gen. 12:1–4	2 Cor. 5:16–21	Matt. 21:17–22
	C	Ex. 33:12–17	Heb. 11:1–10	Luke 18:9–14
Thanksgiving Day	A	Isa. 61:10–11	1 Tim. 2:1–8	Luke 12:22–31
	B	Deut. 26:1–11	Gal. 6:6–10	Luke 17:11–19
	C	Deut. 8:6–17	2 Cor. 9:6–15	John 6:24–35
Day of civic or national significance	A	Deut. 28:1–9	Rom. 13:1–8	Luke 1:68–79
	B	Isa. 26:1–8	1 Thess. 5:12–23	Mark 12:13–17
	C	Dan. 9:3–10	1 Peter 2:11–17	Luke 20:21–26

ACKNOWLEDGMENTS

The following hymns and service music are covered by the publisher's copyright of the hymnal: 32 (harmonization), 51, 64 (musical setting), 75 (musical arrangement), 78 (harmonization), 93 (harmonization), 98 (tune), 110 (musical adaptation), 119 (harmonization), 138 (tune), 149 (words), 153 (words), 158 (English translation), 168 (words), 175 (words), 176 (tune), 217 (tune and music arrangement), 226 (harmonization), 230 (harmonization), 235 (musical setting), 240, 248 (musical setting), 251 (English translation and tune), 269 (musical setting), 283, 291 (musical setting), 314 (tune), 315 (tune), 316, 317, 318 (tune), 319 (tune), 320 (tune), 321, 322 (tune), 323, 324, 325 (tune), 326 (tune), 327 (tune), 328, 329 (tune), 335 (tune), 349 (tune), 354 (tune), 359, 360 (tune), 361 (tune), 362 (tune), 363 (tune), 384 (tune).

1 Music from *The English Hymnal.* Used by permission of Oxford University Press.

3 Words from the *Lutheran Service Book and Hymnal.* Used by permission of the Commission on the Liturgy and Hymnal.

4 Words used by permission of G. Schirmer, Inc.

8 Words and music used by permission of Richard D. Wetzel.

11 Words copyright © 1930 by H. W. Gray Co., Inc. Copyright renewed © 1958. Copyright assigned to Belwin-Mills Publishing Corp. Used by permission.

12 Words copyright © 1958 by the United Church Press.

13 Words reprinted by permission of Charles Scribner's Sons from *The Poems of Henry van Dyke.*

14 Words from *The Yattendon Hymnal* (edited by Robert Bridges and H. Ellis Wooldridge) by permission of Oxford University Press. Music from *The Cowley Carol Book* by G. R. Woodward and C. Wood. Used by permission of A. M. Mowbray & Co., Ltd., Oxford.

25 Words from *Songs of Praise.* Used by permission of Oxford University Press.

27 Words and music from *The Oxford Book of Carols.* Used by permission of Oxford University Press.

29 Words used by permission of David Higham Associates, Ltd. Music from *The Revised Church Hymnary.* Used by permission of Oxford University Press.

30 Words copyright by J. Curwen & Sons. Used by permission of G. Schirmer, Inc. Music from *The English Hymnal.* Used by permission of Oxford University Press.

31 Words copyright © 1966 by Galliard Ltd. All Rights Reserved. Used by permission of Galaxy Music Corp., N.Y., sole U.S. agent. Music used by permission of the composer, the Reverend Canon C. V. Taylor.

32 Words reprinted from *Thoughts for Everyday Living* by Maltbie D. Babcock.

33 Words reprinted from *Thoughts for Everyday Living* by Maltbie D. Babcock.

35 Arrangement used by permission of F. E. Röntgen.

36 Words used by permission of Mrs. Dorothy M. W. Bean. Music from *The English Hymnal.* Used by permission of Oxford University Press.

38 Music from *Three Hymn Tunes* by Calvin Hampton, copyright 1973 by Concordia Publishing House. Altered and used by permission.

40 "Lord, I Adore Thee," © copyright 1956 by Zondervan Music Publishers. All rights reserved. Used by permission.

44 Words and music copyright © 1969 by the United Church Press.

45 Words copyright by author. Used by permission. Music used by permission of Industrial Christian Fellowship.

47 Words copyright © 1966 by Curtis Beach. Used by permission.

50 Words from *The Yattendon Hymnal* (edited by Robert Bridges and H. Ellis Wooldridge) by permission of Oxford University Press.

52 Words used by permission of the author.

53 Words from *Sermons and Hymns.* Used by permission of the publishers, A. R. Mowbray & Co., Ltd.

54 Words used by permission of Eden Publishing House.

57 Music from *Enlarged Songs of Praise.* Used by permission of Oxford University Press.
59 Words from *Enlarged Songs of Praise.* Used by permission of Oxford University Press.
60 Words copyright by author. Used by permission. Music copyright 1969 by Erik Routley. Used by permission.
63 Words reprinted by permission of A. D. Peters and Company.
64 Words and music from *Sing a Tune.* Used by permission of Cooperative Recreation Service.
67 Words used by permission of the estate of William Merrill. Music used by permission of The Church Pension Fund.
69 Music from *Enlarged Songs of Praise.* Used by permission of Oxford University Press.
70 Words and music copyright Galaxy Music Corporation. Used by permission.
71 Words and music from *A New Song 3.* Copyright © 1971 by the United Church Press.
74 Tune copyright and reprinted here by permission of Mr. Noah Kirby, successor to the late Dr. John Ireland.
75 Words copyright 1967 by Willard F. Jabusch, St. Mary of the Lake Seminary, Mundelein, Ill. Used by permission.
77 Words and music from the *Lutheran Service Book and Hymnal.* Used by permission of the Commission on the Liturgy and Hymnal.
80 Music used by permission of the composer, H. Hugh Bancroft.
81 Translation used by permission of Jay Macpherson.
82 Music from *Hymnal for Colleges and Schools.* Used by permission of Yale University Press.
86 Words used by permission of Harper & Row, Publishers.
90 Words from *The New Church Hymnal.* Copyright 1937, copyright renewed 1965, Fleming H. Revell Company.
92 Words used by permission of the Proprietors of Hymns Ancient and Modern.
97 Words used by permission of Bethany Press.
98 Words © 1961 by Richard Wilbur. From his volume *Advice to a Prophet and Other Poems* by permission of Harcourt Brace Jovanovich, Inc. and Faber & Faber Ltd.
101 Copyright © 1919 by Stainer & Bell, Ltd. All Rights Reserved. Used by permission of Galaxy Music Corp., N.Y., sole U.S. agent.
102 Music used by permission of Oxford University Press.
103 Words used by permission of the Christian Conference of Asia.
104 Harmonization used by permission of Novello & Co., Ltd.
105 Adaptation used by permission of Mrs. John W. Work, Sr.
107 Music and words for stanza 1 used by permission of E. C. Schirmer Music Co. Words for stanza 2 copyright 1972 by The Westminster Press; from *The Worshipbook—Services and Hymns;* used by permission.
108 Words and music copyright 1924 by Gustav Holst. Reprinted by permission of the publishers, J. Curwen & Sons, Ltd., London.
110 Words from *A New Song 3.* Copyright © 1971 by the United Church Press.
113 Words used by permission of Eden Publishing House.
114 Words from the *Lutheran Service Book and Hymnal.* Used by permission of the Commission on the Liturgy and Hymnal.
115 Music from *The Cowley Carol Book* by G. R. Woodward and C. Wood. Used by permission of A. R. Mowbray & Co., Ltd., Oxford.
116 Words and music copyright © 1961 by Galliard Ltd. All Rights Reserved. Used by permission of Galaxy Music Corp., N.Y., sole U.S. agent.
120 Words and music from *A New Song 3.* Copyright © 1971 by the United Church Press.
121 Words used by permission of The Church Pension Fund.
122 Words and music from *A New Song 3.* Copyright © 1971 by the United Church Press.
124 Music copyright 1941 by Belwin-Mills Publishing Corp. Copyright renewed 1969. Used by permission.
125 Music from *Enlarged Songs of Praise.* Used by permission of Oxford University Press.
128 Words from *The Yattendon Hymnal* (edited by Robert Bridges and H. Ellis Wooldridge) by permission of Oxford University Press.
132 Words used by permission of the United States Trust Company, executor of the estate of Mrs. Howard Chandler Robbins.

133 Words used by permission of The Church Pension Fund. Music from *The Cowley Carol Book* by G. R. Woodward and C. Wood. Used by permission of A. R. Mowbray & Co., Ltd., Oxford.
138 Words used by permission of the author.
139 Words used with the permission of the World Student Christian Federation.
141 Words from the *Lutheran Service Book and Hymnal.* Used by permission of the Commission on the Liturgy and Hymnal.
143 Words from *Enlarged Songs of Praise.* Used by permission of Oxford University Press.
145 Words from *Enlarged Songs of Praise.* Used by permission of Oxford University Press. Music used by permission of League of Nations Union.
147 Music from *The English Hymnal.* Used by permission of Oxford University Press.
148 Words and music from *A New Song 3.* Copyright © 1971 by the United Church Press.
153 Music copyright © 1974 by Stanley Tagg. Used by permission.
155 Words by James Quinn, S.J., from *Hymns for All Seasons.* Used by permission of Geoffrey Chapman, Publishers. Music used by permission of the composer.
159 Words from *Enlarged Songs of Praise.* Used by permission of Oxford University Press.
160 Words used by permission of the author.
161 Words used by permission of the author, copyright owner.
162 Words used by permission of the author.
163 Words from *Monday Morning,* Apr. 28, 1958. Used by permission of the author. Music from *The Revised Church Hymnary.* Used by permission of Oxford University Press.
164 Words used by permission of Theo Oxenham.
166 Words used by permission of The Church Pension Fund.
167 Words from *The Yattendon Hymnal* (edited by Robert Bridges and H. Ellis Wooldridge) by permission of Oxford University Press. Music by permission of Novello & Co., Inc.
171 Words from *Ten Stewardship Hymns,* copyright 1961 by the Hymn Society of America; used by permission. Music from *The English Hymnal.* Used by permission of Oxford University Press.
172 Music used by permission of the Oxford University Press.
174 Words used by permission of the author. Music used by permission of Breitkopf and Haertel. Arrangement copyright 1933 by Presbyterian Board of Christian Education, renewed 1961; used by permission.
175 Music used by permission of the United Reformed Church in England and Wales.
176 Words from *Thirteen Marriage and Family Life Hymns,* copyright 1961 by the Hymn Society of America; used by permission.
177 Words from *The Unutterable Beauty* by G. A. Studdert Kennedy. Used by permission of the publisher, Hodder & Stoughton Ltd. Music used by permission of The Church Pension Fund.
178 Words from *The English Hymnal.* Used by permission of the Oxford University Press. Music used by permission of The Church Pension Fund.
179 Music used by permission of the Abbot of Downside.
180 Words and music used by permission of Scottish Churches' Council, Dunblane, Scotland.
181 Words copyright © 1959, United Church Board for World Ministries. Used by permission.
182 Words used by permission of Oxford University Press. Music from *Enlarged Songs of Praise.* Used by permission of Oxford University Press.
183 Words copyright 1966 by K. L. Cober. Used by permission of Judson Press.
184 Words and music copyright © 1965 by Galliard Ltd. All Rights Reserved. Used by permission of Galaxy Music Corp., N.Y., sole U.S. agent.
185 Music copyright 1918 by H. W. Gray Co. Copyright © renewed 1946 by H. W. Gray Co. Used by permission.
187 Words used by permission of Oxford University Press.
188 Words used by permission of Harper & Row, Publishers. Music used by permission of Novello & Co., Inc.
189 Words used by permission of Harper & Row, Publishers. Music used by permission of The Church Pension Fund.

191 Words used by permission of Roger W. Holmes.
192 Music used by permission of the Abbot of Downside.
193 Words from *Five New Hymns on the City,* copyright 1954 by the Hymn Society of America; used by permission. Harmony from *The Revised Church Hymnary.* Used by permission of Oxford University Press.
195 Music used by permission of Oxford University Press.
198 Words used by permission of Elinor F. Downs. Music © by Mrs. Dilys Webb, c/o Mechanical-Copyright Protection Society Limited, and reproduced by permission of the legal representatives of the composer who reserve all rights therein.
200 Harmony used by permission of William France.
201 Words and music by Jim Strathdee, in response to a Christmas poem by Howard Thurman. Copyright © 1969 by Jim Strathdee.
202 Words copyright 1929 by the Hymn Society of America; used by permission. Music from *Enlarged Songs of Praise.* Used by permission of Oxford University Press.
203 Music copyright 1918 by H. W. Gray Co., copyright renewed 1946. Used by permission of Belwin-Mills Music Co.
204 Words copyright © 1973 by James H. Hargett. Used by permission. Music used by permission of Gwenlyn Evans, Ltd.
205 Words used by permission of Gordon Hitchcock.
207 Words copyright © 1969 by the United Church Press.
208 Words used by permission of the author.
209 Words and music copyright © 1969 by the United Church Press.
211 Music used by permission of The Church Pension Fund.
213 Words and music from *A New Song 3.* Copyright © 1971 by the United Church Press.
214 Words used by permission of Robert F. Jefferys, Jr. Music copyright © 1959 by Abingdon Press. Used by permission.
215 Words from *Enlarged Songs of Praise.* Used by permission of Oxford University Press. Music copyright © 1964 by Belwin-Mills Publishing Corp.
216 Harmony used by permission of The Church Pension Fund.
217 Words copyright 1972 by The Westminster Press; from *The Worshipbook–Services and Hymns;* used by permission.
218 Words from *Enlarged Songs of Praise.* Used by permission of Oxford University Press. Music copyright © 1957 by H. W. Gray Co., Inc. Copyright assigned to Belwin-Mills Publishing Corp. Used by permission. Adaptation of tune by Jet Turner, copyright © 1967 by The Bethany Press, St. Louis, Mo. Used by permission.
219 Music from *Hymnal for Colleges and Schools.* Used by permission of Yale University Press.
221 From the *Worship Supplement,* copyright 1969 by Concordia Publishing House. Used by permission.
224 Music arrangement copyright by Galaxy Music Corp. Used by permission.
226 Words and music from *Songs of All Time.* Used by permission of Cooperative Recreation Service.
227 Words used by permission of Abingdon Press.
229 Words from *Eleven Ecumenical Hymns,* copyright 1954 by the Hymn Society of America; used by permission.
230 Words used by permission of The Church Pension Fund. Music copyright © Zann Music, Inc. Sole Selling Agent: Edward B. Marks Corporation. Used by permission.
236 Music from *Hymnal for Colleges and Schools.* Used by permission of Yale University Press.
237 Music used by courtesy of the Psalms and Hymns Trust.
241 Music used by courtesy of the Psalms and Hymns Trust.
246 Music from *Enlarged Songs of Praise.* Used by permission of Oxford University Press.
248 Words and music used by permission of Cooperative Recreation Service.
249 Music used by permission of Oxford University Press.
251 Words translated and paraphrased by Ford Lewis Battles from Dietrich Bonhoeffer, *Ich Habe Dieses Volk Geliebt,* with the permission of Chr. Kaiser Verlag München.
252 Music used by permission of Gwenlyn Evans, Ltd.
255 Words used by permission of American Peace Society. Music used by permission of Novello & Co., Ltd.
257 Words and arrangement of music copyright 1964 by The Youth Depart-

ment of The American Lutheran Church; from *Songs for Today;* used by permission. Harmonization from *Risk,* Vol. II, No. 3 (1966) published by the World Council of Churches; used by permission.

258 Music used by permission of Edith M. Work.

259 Words copyright © 1968 by Galliard Ltd. All Rights Reserved. Used by permission of Galaxy Music Corp., N.Y., sole U.S. agent. Music used by permission of The Church Pension Fund.

260 Words used by permission of R. B. Y. Scott.

261 Words from *The Incendiary Fellowship* by Elton Trueblood. Copyright © 1967 by David Elton Trueblood. Reprinted by permission of Harper & Row, Publishers, Inc. Music used by permission of Walton Music Corp.

264 Words from *Church Music,* 70. 1, edited by Carl Schalk, copyright 1970 by Concordia Publishing House. Used by permission.

268 Words and music used by permission of Eden Publishing House, St. Louis, Mo.

271 Harmony from *The Revised Church Hymnary.* Used by permission of Oxford University Press.

276 Music © by Mrs. Dilys Webb, c/o Mechanical-Copyright Protection Society Limited, and reproduced by permission of the legal representatives of the composer who reserve all rights therein.

278 Music used by permission of Oxford University Press.

282 Music from *The Revised Church Hymnary.* Used by permission of Oxford University Press.

288 Words from "A Prayer," *The Poem Book of the Gael,* selected and edited by Eleanor Hull. Used by permission of the Editor's Literary Estate and Chatto & Windus, Ltd. Harmony from *The Revised Church Hymnary.* Used by permission of Oxford University Press.

290 Words and music from *Upper Room Hymns,* published by Abingdon Press.

296 Music from *The English Hymnal.* Used by permission of Oxford University Press.

298 Words used by permission of Morehouse-Barlow Co., Inc., New York.

302 Words from the *Lutheran Service Book and Hymnal.* Used by permission of the Commission on the Liturgy and Hymnal.

303 From *The Cambridge Hymnal.* Copyright © 1967 by The Syndics of the Cambridge University Press. Used by permission.

306 Music from *Enlarged Songs of Praise.* Used by permission of Oxford University Press.

332 Music copyright 1956 by W. L. Jenkins; altered from *Service Music for the Adult Choir;* used by permission of The Westminster Press.

333 From *The American Lutheran Hymnal* © 1930, 1958, Augsburg Publishing House, Minneapolis, Minn.

340 Reprinted from *Hymnal for Colleges and Schools,* ed. E. Harold Geer. Copyright © 1956 by Yale University Press. Used by permission.

345 Music from *Songs of Praise for Boys and Girls.* Used by permission of Oxford University Press.

347 Music copyright © 1958 by the United Church Press.

348 Music copyright © 1960 by Belwin-Mills Publishing Corp. Used by permission.

350 Music from *Edric Connor Collection of West Indian Spirituals and Folk Tunes.* Copyright 1945 by Boosey & Hawkes Company Ltd; renewed 1973. Reprinted with permission.

356 "Through North and South" from *Enlarged Songs of Praise.* Used by permission of Oxford University Press.

357 Music from *The English Hymnal.* Used by permission of Oxford University Press.

358 Used by permission of Christian Conference of Asia.

365 From *Hymns and Responses for the Church Year* by Vincent Persichetti, © 1956 Elkan-Vogel, Inc., used by permission.

366 Arrangement reprinted from *We Praise Thee* by Healey Willan by permission of Concordia Publishing House.

368 Used by permission of Cooperative Recreation Service.

378 From *Hymns and Responses for the Church Year* by Vincent Persichetti, © 1956 Elkan-Vogel, Inc., used by permission.

379 From *Hymns and Responses for the Church Year* by Vincent Persichetti, © 1956 Elkan-Vogel, Inc., used by permission.

391 From *God Is Here—Let's Celebrate* by Leslie F. Brandt, copyright 1969 by

Concordia Publishing House. Used by permission.
394 From *The Covenant of Peace: A Liberation Prayer Book,* compiled by John Pairman Brown and Richard L. York, copyright © 1971 by the Free Church of Berkeley, published by Morehouse-Barlow Co., 14 E. 41st St., New York, N.Y. 10017, and used by permission of the publisher.
397 From *Good Lord, Where Are You?* by Leslie F. Brandt, copyright 1967 by Concordia Publishing House. Used by permission.
406 From *The Covenant of Peace: A Liberation Prayer Book,* compiled by John Pairman Brown and Richard L. York, copyright © 1971 by the Free Church of Berkeley, published by Morehouse-Barlow Co., 14 E. 41st St., New York, N.Y. 10017, and used by permission of the publisher.
410 From *God Is Here—Let's Celebrate* by Leslie F. Brandt, copyright 1969 by Concordia Publishing House. Used by permission.
413 From *Good Lord, Where Are You?* by Leslie F. Brandt, copyright 1967 by Concordia Publishing House. Used by permission.
415 From *Good Lord, Where Are You?* by Leslie F. Brandt, copyright 1967 by Concordia Publishing House. Used by permission.
419 From *Good Lord, Where Are You?* by Leslie F. Brandt, copyright 1967 by Concordia Publishing House. Used by permission.
423 From *The New English Bible.* Copyright © The Delegates of the Oxford University Press and the Syndics of the Cambridge University Press 1961, 1970. Reprinted by permission.
424 From *The New English Bible.* Copyright © The Delegates of the Oxford University Press and the Syndics of the Cambridge University Press 1961, 1970. Reprinted by permission.
426 From *The New English Bible.* Copyright © The Delegates of the Oxford University Press and the Syndics of the Cambridge University Press 1961, 1970. Reprinted by permission.
434 Excerpt from the *New American Bible* © 1970 used herein by permission of the Confraternity of Christian Doctrine, copyright owner.
437 Used by permission of Elinor Fosdick Downs.

453
INDEX OF AUTHORS, TRANSLATORS, AND SOURCES

454
INDEX OF COMPOSERS, ARRANGERS, AND SOURCES

455

METRICAL INDEX

456

ALPHABETICAL INDEX OF TUNES

457

LIST OF SCRIPTURE PASSAGES RELATED TO THE HYMNS

Genesis

1:1–2	O Splendor of God's glory 14
1:1, 3, 20	Eternal Father, strong to save (st. 3) 273
4:1–16	Am I my brother's keeper 180
31:42	The God of Abraham 6

Exodus

3:6	The God of Abraham 6
13:21–22	Lead on, O King eternal 231
17:1–6	Glorious things of thee 304
23:16	As men of old 171

Numbers

9:15	Glorious things of thee 304

Deuteronomy

1:21	He who would valiant be 178
33:27	What a fellowship 290

Joshua

3:17	Guide me, O thou great 276
24:15	Once to every man and nation 252

Ruth

1:16	Once to every man and nation 252

2 Samuel

22:7–20	God moves in a mysterious way 39

1 Kings

19:1–13	Dear Lord and Father of mankind (st. 6) 236

Job

28:23–28	God moves in a mysterious way 39
37:23	God moves in a mysterious way 39
38:10–11	Eternal Father, strong to save (st. 1) 273
38:22–23	God moves in a mysterious way 39

Psalms

8	O how glorious 35
18:1–2	A mighty fortress 263, 264
19:2	All beautiful the march (st. 3) 36
19:4–6	Jesus shall reign 312
19:14	Let the words of my mouth 344
	May the words of our mouths 347
20:5	Rejoice, ye pure in heart 156
23	My shepherd will supply 279
	The Lord's my shepherd 278
24:1	God of concrete 31
24:7–10	All glory, laud, and honor 123
	Lift up your heads 76
	The King of glory 75
29:10–11	O God of love 262
30:5	Lift thy head, O Zion 268
33:4–5	There's a wideness in God's mercy 272
45	O Morning Star, how fair 112
45:3–4	Come, thou almighty King (st. 2) 15
46	A mighty fortress 263, 264
46:9	O God of love 262
50:10–12	This is my Father's world 32, 33
51	Have mercy upon me, O Lord (MISERERE MEI DEUS) 377
	O for a thousand tongues 305
55:22	If thou but suffer God 29
65:5–13	I sing the mighty power 51
65:9–13	O beautiful for spacious skies 68
66:1–2	From all that dwell 1
67	God of grace and God of glory 198
67:6–7	Come, ye thankful people 42
72	Hail to the Lord's anointed 88
72:8, 12, 15, 19	Jesus shall reign 312
77:19	God moves in a mysterious way 39
78:52–54	O God, beneath thy guiding hand 10
87:1–3	Glorious things of thee 304
89:1	I will sing of the mercies 51
89:8–9	Eternal Father, strong to save 273
90	Our God, our help 9
90:1	We come unto our fathers' God 165
91	The man who once has found 270
91:4–5	All praise to thee, my God 238
95	O come, let us sing (VENITE) 370
98	Joy to the world 313
100	All people that on earth 2
	Before Jehovah's aweful throne 37
	Before the Lord Jehovah's throne 38
	O be joyful 12
	O be joyful (JUBILATE DEO) 371
103	O my soul, bless God 7
	Praise, my soul 23
	Praise to the Lord 25
103:19–22	Ye servants of God, 196
104	O worship the King 17
104:24–30	This is my Father's world 32, 33
105:1–3	Rejoice, ye pure in heart 156
107:23–32	Eternal Father, strong to save 273
113:3–6	The day thou gavest 49
117	From all that dwell 1
118:22	Christ, thou art the sure 157
118:24	This is the day 331
118:25–26	All glory, laud, and honor 123

121	Unto the hills around 294
	Unto the hills I lift 293
130	Out of the depths (DE PROFUNDIS) 376
134:2	Come, bless the Lord 332
136	Let us with a gladsome mind 41
137	By the Babylonian rivers 257
139:11–12	Abide with me 284
147:1	Rejoice, ye pure in heart 156
148	All creatures of our God 30
	Let the whole creation cry 308
	Men and children everywhere 11
	Praise the Lord from highest heav'n 8
	Praise the Lord, ye heav'ns 22
150	Praise God from whom 358
	Praise to the Lord 25
	Praise the Lord, his glories 26
Ecclesiastes	
2:11, 18	Turn back, O man 63
Isaiah	
2:12	O Day of God, draw nigh 260
6:3	Holy, holy, holy Lord 18
	Holy, holy, holy (SANCTUS) 319, 326, 362–365
7:14	O come, O come, Emmanuel 86
9:27	Break forth, O beauteous 107
11:9	God is working his purpose 57
21:11–12	Watchman, tell us of the night 85
33:20–21	Glorious things of thee 304
40:1–8	Comfort, comfort ye my people 55, 56
40:3–5	On Jordan's bank 84
40:3–11	There's a voice in the wilderness 80
40:11	O, rise and shine 299
40:23	Father eternal, Ruler 145
40:25–26	God of our fathers 254
43:1–2	How firm a foundation 266
45:5–8	God the omnipotent 256
52:7	Come, thou long-expected 78, 79
52:8	Sleepers, wake 81
	Watchman, tell us of the night 85
53:3–5	O sacred head, now wounded 127
	Ah, holy Jesus 128
54:7–8	God moves in a mysterious way 39
61:1–2	Hark, the glad sound 82
	Come, thou long-expected 78, 79
61:1–4	I am the light of the world 201
62:3	All hail the power 310, 311
64:8	Have thine own way, Lord 170
Jeremiah	
8:22	There is a balm in Gilead 235
Lamentations	
1:12	Alone thou goest forth 121
3	Good is the Lord 240
Ezekiel	
34:16	Judge Eternal, throned 58
Daniel	
2:22	God moves in a mysterious way 39
3:29–34	Blessed art thou, O Lord 373

10:11	The Lord's my shepherd 278
12:12–15	Ride on, ride on 124
13:7	God moves in a mysterious way 39
14:6	Thou art the way 109
15:13	Crown him with many crowns (st. 4) 309
15:13–17	What a friend we have 289
15:26–27	O Spirit of the living God 150
17:23	Lord, bless our homes 163
19:2	O sacred head, now wounded 127
Acts	
1:8	Come down, O Love divine 147
2:2–4	O Spirit of the living God 150
4:12	At the name of Jesus 69
	I greet thee who my sure 144
10:37	On Jordan's bank 84
26:22	Great God, we sing 20
Romans	
6:4	The day of resurrection 136
8:2	Jesus, I live to thee 225
8:4	Lord, bless our homes 163
8:14–17	In Christ there is no East 164
8:15–16	Our Father, by whose name 166
8:18–21	From the slave pens 52
8:18–25	Creation's Lord, we give thee 46
	Father eternal, Ruler 145
8:26–27	Come down, O Love divine 147
	Come, Holy Ghost, our souls 146
	Creator Spirit, come to us 148
8:28	God moves in a mysterious way 39
9:20–21	Have thine own way, Lord 170
10:3–4	Where restless crowds 193
10:14–15	Lord, we thank thee 160
11:17–21	The church of Christ is one 153
11:25–28	O Zion, haste 206
11:33–35	God moves in a mysterious way 39
	There's a wideness in God's mercy 272
13:12–13	Hark! a thrilling voice 77
14:8	Jesus, I live to thee 225
15:13	Hope of the world 229
16:17	O God of earth and altar 187
16:25–26	God of the prophets 62
1 Corinthians	
1:18	When I survey the wondrous cross 129
3:16	An ancient dwelling 158
6:19–20	An ancient dwelling 158
11:23–26	Here, O my Lord 219, 220
11:27–28	Let us break bread together 210
15:10	Amazing grace 233
15:20, 42	Alleluia! hearts to heaven 134
15:51–54	Alleluia! the strife is o'er 131
16:13	We are living 203
2 Corinthians	
4:1–2	We are living 203
4:3–7	O grant us light 48
4:4	Lighten the darkness 287
4:6	Let there be light 255
	O Splendor of God's glory (st. 1) 14

4:7–18	Strong Son of God 16
4:15	We praise thee, O God 3
5:1, 8	An ancient dwelling 158
5:6–11	Strong Son of God 16
5:14–15	Make me a captive, Lord 172, 173
5:17	The church's one foundation 152
6:16	An ancient dwelling 158
9:10–12	Come, ye thankful people 42
11:2	The church's one foundation 152

Galatians

3:7–9	The God of Abraham 6
3:28	In Christ there is no East 104
5:13	O Master, let me walk 186
5:25–26	Father eternal, Ruler 145
	Lord, bless our homes 163
	Spirit of God, descend 277
6:2	Am I my brother's keeper 180
	When I needed a neighbor 184
6:14	In the cross of Christ 239
	When I survey the wondrous cross 129

Ephesians

1:9–11	God is working his purpose 57
1:19–23	Holy God, we praise thy name 302
2:8	Amazing grace 233
2:13–17	Lord, we thank thee 160
2:19–21	Christ, thou art the sure 157
2:19–22	Not alone for mighty empire 67
2:19–23	The church's one foundation 152
3:14–15	Our Father, by whose name 166
4:4–7	We believe in one true God 5
4:31–32; 5:1–2	O brother man 179
6:10–12	A mighty fortress 263, 264
6:10–18	Soldiers of Christ, arise 169

Philippians

1:27	The church of Christ is one 153
2:4	Lord, bless our homes 163
2:5–7	Every star shall sing 116
2:5–11	All praise to thee, for thou 70
	At the name of Jesus 69
2:9–10	All hail the power 310, 311
3:7–8	When I survey the wondrous cross 129
3:8	God of the prophets 62
4:4	Rejoice, the Lord is king! 142
4:8–9	Not alone for mighty empire 67

Colossians

1:9–12	God of grace and God of glory 198
1:15–20	Of the Father's love begotten 72
2:6–7	A Christian must by faith 168
3:11	In Christ there is no East 164
3:16	Let thy word abide 349

1 Timothy

1:17	Immortal, invisible 21
6:12	Faith of our fathers 286
6:17	All my hope on God 167

TOPICAL INDEX

(Asterisks indicate ecumenical hymns.)

ALPHABETICAL INDEX OF FIRST LINES AND TITLES OF SERVICE MUSIC

(Asterisks indicate ecumenical hymns.)